Preface

THIS BOOK BEGAN with an initiative led by the Rennie Center for Education Research and Policy and funded by the Bill & Melinda Gates Foundation. The Rennie Center sought to examine the progress made under the decade-plus tenure of outgoing Boston school superintendent Thomas Payzant, and to extract lessons that would inform the future leadership of the Boston Public Schools. In the course of our local work, we quickly recognized that with so many other urban school leaders struggling to successfully implement instructionally focused, systemwide reform, Boston had important lessons to offer to districts throughout the nation. For that reason, we conceived of this book as a source of history, research findings, perspective, and inspiration.

The Rennie Center was both privileged and proud to lead this initiative. An independent nonprofit organization, the Rennie Center's mission is to conduct research, initiate policy conversations, and lead field work to develop a public agenda that informs and promotes significant improvement of public education for all children. Our work is motivated by a vision of an education system that creates the opportunity to educate every child to be successful in life, citizenship, employment, and lifelong learning.

We would like to express our gratitude to the many individuals who helped create this book. First and foremost, we gratefully acknowledge the generous sponsorship of the Bill & Melinda Gates Foundation. Not only did the foundation's financial support make this project possible, but the gentle guidance of Gates Foundation staffers Sheri Ranis and Adam Tucker made our work better.

We also appreciate general support received from the Noyce Foundation, the Nellie Mae Education Foundation, and the Irene B. and George A. Davis Foundation.

We feel fortunate to have worked with the book's researchers and authors, who produced exceptionally high-quality work on a tight timeline.

We would like to offer special thanks to Susan Kenyon, managing editor of this project, who served as our liaison to chapter authors. Susan worked tirelessly to ensure the success of this book.

We thank the many employees of the Boston Public Schools who provided access to invaluable data and background information.

We recognize and thank our partners at the Harvard Education Publishing Group for their support and guidance in publishing this text, especially our publisher, Douglas Clayton, and his colleague, Dody Riggs.

As we developed this book, we benefited from the insights and expertise of an esteemed group of stakeholders of the Boston Public Schools, including representatives of the Boston Teachers Union, the Boston School Committee, policy leaders, business and education activists, and community leaders.

We are also very grateful to our Rennie Center team, especially Jill Norton and Colleen Heffernan, who supplied key support and coordination throughout this complex project.

Finally, we especially want to extend our gratitude to Thomas Payzant for his extraordinary work on behalf of public education in Boston, as well as his openness to the in-depth analysis and critique of his work required for this project. His remarkable legacy will benefit the Boston Public Schools for years to come. Through this project, we hope that his efforts will continue to provide valuable lessons for others engaged in this vital and complex work throughout the nation.

S. PAUL REVILLE, *President*

CELINE COGGINS, *Research Director*

Rennie Center for Education Research and Policy

A Decade of Urban School Reform

Persistence and Progress in the Boston Public Schools

A Decade of Urban School Reform

Persistence and Progress in the Boston Public Schools

Edited by

S. PAUL REVILLE

with

CELINE COGGINS

HARVARD EDUCATION PRESS
8 STORY STREET
CAMBRIDGE, MA 02138

Library of Congress Control Number 2006939813

Paperback ISBN 978-1-891792-37-3
Library Edition ISBN 978-1-891792-38-0

Published by Harvard Education Press,
an imprint of the Harvard Education Publishing Group

Harvard Education Press
8 Story Street
Cambridge, MA 02138

Cover Design: Alyssa Morris

The typefaces used in this book are Bembo and Frutiger.

Table of Contents

INTRODUCTION

Setting the Stage

S. PAUL REVILLE

THE "PAYZANT ERA" in the Boston Public Schools is now officially over. Boston native Thomas Payzant took office as Boston's superintendent on October 1, 1995, and retired, nearly eleven years later, on June 30, 2006. Because of Payzant's lengthy tenure and his celebrated reputation as a thoughtful, determined, strategic school leader, his departure generated a great deal of interest and a healthy period of reflection for Boston and the national education reform community.

Studies were conducted. Reports were written. Many meetings were convened to discuss the results and implications of Payzant's decade-plus of work in Boston. Animating this healthy flurry of activity was a focus on the future and a central set of questions and concerns:

> What had been accomplished in the Payzant era? What had not been accomplished? What work remained to be done?
>
> Which strategies had been effective in improving student learning? Which strategies should be continued? Which ones should be modified or eliminated? Which new strategies should be added?
>
> What is the agenda for a new leader? What kind of leader is best suited to advance that agenda?

The Rennie Center for Education Research and Policy, an independent policy "think tank" in Cambridge, Massachusetts, was invited to enter this conversation by the Bill & Melinda Gates Foundation early in 2006. The Gates Foundation provided the Rennie Center with funds to commission a set of research papers on key strategies in the Payzant era and to convene a major Boston leadership conference in June of 2006 aimed at providing the community with an opportunity to engage deeply in considering the findings and recommendations of the research papers. The papers, the deliberations of the meeting, some additional research and background information, and the report, entitled "Strong Foundation, Evolving Challenges: A Case Study to Support Leadership Transition in the Boston Public Schools," by the Aspen Institute Education and Society Program and the Annenberg Institute for School Reform, constitute the body of this book, which has been designed to help guide and support the work of urban school reform leaders in Boston and across the country.

WHY THE BOSTON PUBLIC SCHOOL SYSTEM IS OF INTEREST

It is rare that an urban community retains a superintendent for eleven school years. In fact, the average tenure of superintendents in the nation's largest school systems is less than three years.[1] Payzant's lengthy tenure has attracted national interest, as did the fact that he was the first new superintendent selected after Boston became one of the nation's first cities to institute mayoral control over the school system. Mayoral control substantially increases the mayor's role in leading the school system, typically giving the mayor the responsibility for appointing the school board. School leaders and analysts everywhere saw in Payzant a highly respected, mature, low-ego, high-reform schools chief who had a research-based "theory of action" aimed at improving instruction in order to increase learning. He translated this theory into a set of comprehensive strategies, implemented the strategies across the system, and with minor modifications persistently stuck with these strategies over the course of his tenure.[2] In addition, Superintendent Payzant received strong and consistent support throughout his tenure from the mayor (who also has had a lengthy tenure in office), the Boston school committee, the business community, local and national foundations, a variety of partnership and intermediary organizations, the state, and the media. He had a reasonably cooperative relationship with the Boston Teachers Union, and he also enjoyed fairly consistent growth in his budget. He had the financial resources needed to support his ambitious educational improvement agenda. Add to these factors Boston's turbulent school history, the sheer volume of national and local foundation resources that were invested in supporting Payzant's work, his unusual partnerships with a variety of intermediary organizations and universities, Boston's general reputation as a hotbed of school reform, and you have what amounts to an intensely watched national case study in urban school leadership.

The implicit underlying question of the case is: *Could a strong, well-supported, long-term school leader with financial resources and a robust instructional improvement strategy actually bring about significant educational improvement in an urban school district?* This book is devoted to exploring various aspects of the complex answer to this question. The short answer is "yes, but . . ." Payzant's leadership and his strategies made a huge difference, but in eleven years, not surprisingly, he did not get the job done if the summit of job achievement is defined as building a school system that works effectively to educate every child to a high standard of learning. Of course, no one else in any other city has scaled that summit either.

Progress was made in improving educational performance and in building the capacity of the system to improve in the future. However, no miracles happened. Boston has persistent achievement gaps and a long way to go before all students attain academic proficiency. There are lessons to be learned from Boston's unique experience and pitfalls to be avoided. There are also unanswered questions and major challenges ahead. We hope that this book will help future leaders chart the course from here to the summit.

THE BOOK

This book consists of ten chapters. The introduction sets the stage. The Aspen/Annenberg paper then presents a broad overview. At the heart of the book, there are six chapters commissioned for the Boston conference held in June 2006. These papers focus on a set of important topics tied to Payzant's *Focus on Children* strategies that the Rennie Center determined would be vital to consider, since our central concern was the strengths and weaknesses of strategies implemented during Payzant's tenure.

After meeting with an advisory group convened for the purpose of providing feedback on our plans for the conference, the Rennie Center determined that there were several topics that needed additional attention. Some of those will be treated subsequently in this introductory chapter. One (Weiss) has been added in the form of an additional chapter on family and community engagement. Another (Portz) concerns the school governance changes and their impact on the leadership and support for change in the school system. In the final chapter, Tom Payzant has the last word in reflecting on his own experience and leadership.

CROSS-CUTTING THEMES AND TOPICS

Race and Class

Perhaps the most commonly mentioned but least specified issue for the Boston Public Schools centers on matters of race and class. Throughout the course of our work on the Boston Public Schools, the Rennie Center encountered, in public forums and private conversations, intense feelings about matters of race and, to a somewhat lesser extent, ethnicity and class in the Boston Public School system. It is fair to say that we found a veritable reservoir of pent-up feeling on these subjects.

Thirty years after the painfully divisive events associated with busing and school desegregation in Boston, nerves are still raw on matters of race and class. The city still suffers from a reputation as a difficult place for people of color. Trust is commonly lacking. Some of this feeling is attached to very specific grievances, such as the persistent achievement gap between black and white students; the high percentage of white students enrolled in the city's exam schools; or perceived racial injustices in hiring, promotion, and/or leadership development practices. Some of the feeling is more broadly expressed as concern that "minorities," now, statistically, the overwhelming majority of children in the school system, receive inferior or biased treatment or, at least, are the victims of persistent misunderstanding due to cultural insensitivities of the predominantly white leadership and faculty of the school system. For example, we heard many complaints about the failure of the school system to involve and include parents of color in meaningful engagement in shaping the policies and practices of the school system.

Critics of the system's performance on matters of race and class frequently state that the system needs "to deal" with these issues.[3] What this actually means is sometimes ambiguous, taking the form of a general challenge. However, a number of advocates are explicit, citing, for example, the need for "courageous conversations" framed in the context of instructional approaches that might be crafted to address the special learning needs of low-income and minority students. Inside and outside of the school system we found an urgent desire for the next generation of leaders to place issues of race and class squarely on the agenda and to develop strategies (such as the active development of "cultural competence") for paying attention to these issues and taking constructive action to address problems. Many advocates felt that cultural competency, defined as an understanding of and fluency in cultures beyond one's own, is an essential qualification for Boston teachers.

The question of diversity in leadership itself was also an issue for some. We heard complaints of an informal power structure in the Payzant administration that was perceived as favoring white males over black females. Some interviewees described this as an "A team, B team" phenomenon. Others noted a general scarcity of Latinos and black males in important leadership positions. Clearly, there are some tensions and challenges in building a strong, diverse team of system administrators.

We found widespread acceptance of the fact that for the foreseeable future Boston's teachers will be predominantly white, and we also found that advocates for children of color did not see this as an insurmountable barrier. To be sure, they argue for continued affirmative actions designed to develop a teaching force that more nearly resembles the student body. At the same time, they insist that much could be accomplished if the district would work harder at instilling greater cultural sensitivity in existing staff through the use of high-quality professional development designed to increase the cultural competency of BPS staff. They feel that the system's attention to these matters has been minimal and woefully insufficient, thereby contributing to countless misunderstandings between teachers and students, with the resulting educational fallout.

Finally, some advocates made a subtle but strategically important point about the concept of equity as it unfolded in the Payzant administration. Even though this view was critical of leadership over the past decade, we found no one who questioned the superintendent's general commitment to equity. However, in the view of some critics, the system's approach to equity over the past eleven years has been overly focused on making all schools good schools for all children. This "good faith" approach embodies an across-the-board commitment to excellence for all by making all schools high-performing schools. There is a belief in equality underlying this concept of equity. In this view, if all schools could be made to be equally good, then the problem would be solved. Some advocates for historically underserved populations argue that equality in schools will not be enough to overcome historical achievement gaps. They see a commitment to equity as entailing a willingness to supply intensive, differential educational strategies to those who need the most help in order to become academically proficient.

Issues of race and class in the Boston Public Schools run deep and involve complex feelings and solutions. Many leaders choose to avoid direct engagement on these matters, preferring a less risky, more indirect approach to addressing equity challenges. Our experience suggests that the next leaders of the Boston Public Schools will have a much greater chance of long-term success if they choose to confront these issues directly, beginning with explicit, honest conversations focused on matters of teaching and learning, followed by the implementation of a set of strategies designed to give each and every student the quality and quantity of instruction he or she needs to be successful. This approach, coupled with attention to professional development in cultural competency and a commitment to developing a diverse leadership team, will go a long way toward setting the stage for improved academic achievement by those children currently experiencing the greatest difficulty in the school system.

Mayoral Control

Boston's new system of mayoral control of education played an important role in the Payzant administration. However, it is difficult to generalize about the new governance structure since Payzant has been, incredibly, the only superintendent to take office since the school system came under mayoral control in 1992. (The subject of mayoral control is treated at greater length in the governance chapter, by John Portz.) Suffice it to say that mayoral control was instrumental in the stability of and support for Payzant's leadership throughout his tenure. For those who advocated for mayoral control in the early 1990s, the Payzant era was the fulfillment of their ideals. Mayoral control brought an end to the damaging divisions between City Hall and Court Street (the central administration office of the Boston Public Schools) that had had such a disastrous effect on the tenure of so many previous superintendents who, however well-intentioned and talented, lacked sufficient support to launch ambitious reforms in Boston. The new structure of mayoral control over education created the opportunity for two talented leaders to work collaboratively, ensuring vital unity and support and a powerful, city-school partnership that was essential to stabilizing the district and allowing a strong, reform-minded superintendent to thrive.

Payzant worked well with Mayor Menino, who was a strong education advocate. The mayor was, in many respects, an ideal partner for Payzant. He avoided interference and micromanagement in the district, while nevertheless becoming visibly and actively engaged, handling the external politics and showing the city that education was a top priority. Payzant, on the other hand, was more than willing to have the mayor take the public spotlight on school matters, while he guided strategy and attended to operational details of reforming the school system. Countless observers reiterate that Payzant needed and received the mayor's support to chart and sustain the demanding school improvement strategies he implemented. Some suggest that Payzant would not have lasted any longer than his predecessors had he not had the mayor's support. At a minimum, most observers agree that the Payzant-Menino partnership was vital to the success of the school system during this period, essential for the stability of leadership and school improvement strategy and helpful in extending the tenures of both the mayor and the superintendent.

Teachers Union/Labor-Management Relations

Urban school systems frequently suffer from the consequences of highly adversarial relationships between district managers and the powerful teachers' unions. A challenging result of those relationships is often a highly rigid teachers' contract that constricts education reform. Boston certainly has its own history of very challenging issues and sharp confrontations between the Boston Teachers Union (BTU) and the school committee, the superintendent and district managers. However, Boston's more recent history, dating back to at least the late 1980s, is characterized by a spirit of fairly open communication and some exceptional collaboration and innovation on key subjects ranging from collective bargaining itself to the joint creation (in 1994) of an internal network of semi-autonomous schools, the Pilot Schools.

Upon arriving in 1995, Superintendent Payzant inherited a union-management environment that had more promise than problems. Payzant seemed determined to build positive relationships with the BTU. He met regularly with long-term president Edward Doherty. By all accounts, the Doherty-Payzant relationship was cordial, open, and allowed for the freedom to disagree. Unlike relations in some previous administrations, there was no open hostility, "blind-siding," or manipulations of the press. Payzant was a good communicator not only with union leadership, but he also met regularly with the BTU's building representatives and sought to respond to their questions and concerns.

BTU leaders, to their credit, took the "high road" with the Payzant administration as well. They met, communicated, engaged in tough negotiations, agreed to disagree when needed, but kept respectful channels of discussion open. During the Payzant era, there was no shortage of tough issues on which there were significant disagreements between the BTU and the BPS. Among them: streamlining human resource systems; changing policies on seniority, transfers, and teacher/school assignments; school-based management and Pilot School expansion; high school reform and the break up of comprehensive schools into "small schools"; the use of instructional coaches in the schools; a wide array of new accountability mechanisms; and the usual issues surrounding compensation and benefits (especially health care).

While the disputes on these issues varied in intensity and duration, none of them derailed the generally favorable and collaborative union-management relations that allowed Payzant greater freedom of movement in implementing his reform agenda.

The new superintendent will inherit this positive atmosphere, but it would be naïve to assume an absence of significant challenges. Contract negotiations are currently underway and both sides report an arduous and frustrating process. The outcomes and consequences of this process are uncertain. Union observers see many challenges at the school level, where they view leadership as uneven, often rigid, and overly driven by "top-down" accountability mandates. They worry about low teacher morale, high teacher attrition, and insufficient recruitment of minority teachers. They want a system that allows for greater professional discretion by teachers. They yearn for a superintendent who will be more of a cheerleader for the system, its staff, and their accomplishments.

Administrators, on the other hand, see a number of contract-related issues that are impediments to accelerating reform and improvement. As managers, they naturally want more prerogatives with respect to matters involving teacher assignment and interventions in "underperforming" schools. They see the system facing significant performance challenges as a result of state accountability mandates, charter school competition, and middle-class flight from the city. They seek the flexibility to modify standard procedures to deal with extraordinary circumstances in which they must act or be acted upon by outside authorities.

Although both the BTU and the BPS are uncertain about the future, alternately seeing both promise and problems, the good news is that both are firmly committed to maintaining the kind of collaborative relationship that in the past has yielded innovative solutions to tough problems.

Alignment with Massachusetts State Policy

One of the least mentioned but historically most striking changes for the Boston Public Schools in the late twentieth and early twenty-first century was the district's integration into the state of Massachusetts's education system. Historically, Boston was an entity unto itself in the context of the Commonwealth of

Massachusetts. This meant that in matters of statute and enforcement, state policymakers and officials commonly made exceptions to the normal rules for Boston. Since the Boston school system had several times the enrollment of the next nearest district (it is still more than double the size of the next largest district), and since it was located in the state capital, Boston's exceptional status, while sometimes resented, was seldom challenged. With its large legislative delegation and even larger political power in the statehouse on Beacon Hill, the city of Boston had always been a "special case" in the matter of Massachusetts education policy. The busing crisis in the 1970s, so unlike events that transpired in other communities, served to underline Boston's unique circumstances and special status. Indeed, even today, Boston is the only community in the state to have its school system under mayoral control.

The Boston exception applied not only to matters of policy but to matters of practice as well. Boston seldom actively participated in the various statewide "communities of practice" (e.g., associations and education advocacy groups) because Boston educators tended, understandably, to see their needs and challenges as fundamentally different from those of their counterparts in smaller communities.

Although Boston is still an "exceptional" school district, its special, exceptional status in Massachusetts changed dramatically in the mid-1990s. Two major factors were responsible for this change: Massachusetts's landmark Education Reform Act of 1993 (MERA) was enacted and Tom Payzant assumed office.

Even the state's comprehensive reform act contained some minor exceptions for Boston. But much more importantly, the act delivered major new financial resources, especially to urban districts, including Boston, in exchange for mandates requiring all districts to become part of a statewide accountability system featuring standards, assessments, and real accountability. Standards-based reform in Massachusetts obligated Boston's schools and students to be subject to the same standards and expectations applied to all other schools in the Commonwealth.

Two years after the implementation of this sweeping law, Tom Payzant, an assistant secretary of education in the Clinton Administration, became school superintendent. His educational principles were right in line with MERA. He believed in high standards for all, regular measurement of progress, and real accountability. He not only aligned himself with the work of the Massachusetts Department of Education in implementing these complex reforms, but notably, he stood out as a leader on controversial but critical issues. For example, he was an outspoken advocate for maintaining the high graduation standards and graduation stakes attached to the MCAS (Massachusetts Comprehensive Assessment System) despite the opposition of many educators and groups and notwithstanding the fact that those stakes would hit hardest in communities like Boston. Payzant argued powerfully that the stakes were necessary to drive improvement and that students were owed not a diploma for seat time but a diploma that actually stood for the kind of real skill and knowledge that would make them successful in higher education and employment. His view prevailed and the standard was maintained.

Boston under Payzant's leadership emerged as a potent influence on state education policy. If Boston was no longer going to be exempted or treated differently on matters of policy, then the district had a major interest in seeing that its concerns were reflected in new state policy. Boston chose to help shape the potent mechanisms of accountability that would be part of the new era of accountability in Massachusetts. The Payzant administration, with the support of Mayor Menino, made activism at the state level a priority.

Partnerships and Foundations

Payzant was a believer in partnerships; however, he focused his partnership agenda on his core strategies for improving academic performance. He understood the value of partnerships not only in executing reform work, but in gaining external political leverage to promote change within the system. He and his administration invited many organizations to discuss system strategy but, over the years, he narrowed the partnership strategy to work closely with a select number of educational improvement organizations in the city. Payzant granted a few of these agencies and their leaders unprecedented access to senior management circles in his administration. These alliances formed powerful school reform teams, but they also sometimes created resentments from agencies without similar access or from senior administrators who felt their prerogatives were curtailed as a result of collaboration with external partners.

The Boston Plan for Excellence (BPE) was the most visible of the external partners. This well funded, local education foundation is headed by Ellen Guiney, who had formerly worked closely with Payzant when she had been Senator Edward Kennedy's chief education advisor in Washington and Payzant had been a deputy secretary of education in the Clinton administration. Their relationship, in combination with BPE's high-profile, well-respected board of directors and BPE's access to substantial funding for district initiatives, contributed to Guiney's gaining insider, cabinet-level status at the Court Street headquarters of the school district. BPE, for example, was the key entity in assuring that the Annenberg Challenge grant (some $35 million, in the first five years alone, from a variety of sources) came to Boston. With the Annenberg funding, BPE served as a critical operating partner in implementing the district's central whole-school improvement strategy. More recently, BPE collaboratively operates with the district an ambitious new district-based, preservice teacher training program called the "Boston Teacher Residency." Eventually, this program plans to prepare over a third of the new teachers hired by the school system. BPE's role in the Payzant administration was so significant that some critics accused BPE of being the "shadow administration" of BPS. Despite resentments, BPE clearly played a central contributing role in the successes of the Payzant era.

Other intermediary organizations, like the Boston Private Industry Council, Jobs for the Future, and the Center for Collaborative Education, all played very important roles in the reform work of the district under Payzant. Neil Sullivan, the executive director of the Private Industry Council, headed up his agency's stewardship of the renowned Boston Compact (an alliance of business, higher education, and the school system), focused on dropouts, out-of-school youth, and college persistence issues, while leading various efforts, including the summer youth jobs program, linking the education system to workforce development in the city. Sullivan had insider status as well, and was a key advisor to the administration.

Jobs for the Future played an important role in high school reform in Boston. The Center for Collaborative Education not only participated in high school reform, but it played a leadership role in the development of Boston's pathbreaking Pilot School initiative, in which the union and the BPS agreed to develop a network of schools that were relieved from certain contract provision and central office mandates.

The unprecedented partnership role played by these agencies clearly broadened and strengthened reform efforts in Boston, while also generating criticism from a number of advocacy, parent, and community-based agencies that felt excluded or at least less included in the key strategic decisions of the school system. In spite of the fact that Payzant did create the position of deputy superintendent for community and parent engagement, worked with the Efficacy Institute to launch a community-based "Campaign for Proficiency" in one area of the city, and met regularly with advocacy groups like Voices for Children and the Boston Parent Organizing Network, he was still often viewed as more interested in the academic improvement agenda than in community engagement.

Boston is renowned for being a center of higher education, and it is also home to the Boston Higher Education Partnership (BHEP), a long-standing collaborative that brings the city's colleges and universities to the table to assist the school system with student scholarships, research, professional development activities, and other programs. Payzant was actively engaged, through BHEP and on an individual basis, with many higher education institutions throughout his tenure.

Foundations, national and local, were key partners with the Payzant administration as well. The Annenberg Challenge was the largest initiative and it stimulated a wide range of matching local contributions. Also providing support were high-profile national funding organizations, including the Bill & Melinda Gates Foundation, Carnegie Corporation, The Broad Foundation, and the Noyce Foundation. Locally, a host of Boston foundations and corporations, led by the Bank of Boston and the Boston Foundation, provided critical financial and political support to the superintendent's agenda.[4]

The reform-oriented funds generated from private sources alone substantially topped $100 million in the Payzant era. This highly leveraged support enabled the school system to take risks and initiatives that would otherwise have been impossible. It also focused national attention on Payzant's reform agenda and generated a steady flow of experts and technical support that followed the funding in an effort to assure its success.

This powerful combination of financial resources, technical support, and high-quality partnerships became an important ingredient in Payzant's success.

Central Office Reform

When asked about the reform agenda for the future, many Bostonians will acknowledge past progress but point to a continuing need for reforming the operations of the Boston Public Schools central office (Court Street). While not treated in this book at length, it is worth noting that central office reform was an important aspect of the reform work of the Payzant administration.

Central office reforms were designed to address two major problems and lots of issues related to collaboration, communication, efficiency, and effectiveness. The two major problems in Boston's central office were commonly identified issues in many urban districts. The first: a modus operandi at Court Street in which business was done in a way that favored the bureaucracy's needs over those of the schools, and in which school needs were addressed unevenly, based on status and relationships of the particular principal. The second problem addressed by reformers was that of communication and collaboration between the various operating "silos" of the central office. The "left hand" often did not know what the "right hand" was doing, and the two "hands" sometimes sent conflicting signals to the field.

Some of the reform strategies were very specific interventions, like the acquisition of major new data technology to streamline the operations of a previously inefficient human resources office. Other strategies involved the creation of working groups and leadership teams, like the Resources Action Team, designed to be permanent, school-focused, cross-departmental forums for the improvement of services to the field. Outside partners, like BPE, the Barr and Broad Foundations, and the Dell Corporation, were often involved in these efforts. Central office leaders initiated innovative tactics like a consumer survey of principals' attitudes toward the central office, shadowing opportunities for central office staff to follow a principal for a day and a principal-focused open house at Court Street.

The orientation of the central office has clearly shifted to a service mentality, with the needs of schools of paramount importance. Favoritism has been dramatically reduced. At the same time, many of the chapters of this book point to continuing challenges and opportunities for improving the effectiveness of the central office.

THE FUTURE

The Rennie Center's Boston initiative was entitled "A Decade of Boston School Reform: Reflections and Aspirations." We chose this title deliberately to deemphasize the focus on Payzant as a leader, even though obviously his leadership was central to the story. However, we wanted to focus on reform strategies, reflecting on the strengths and weaknesses of the work to date and particularly calling attention to the challenges of the future. In the course of the process, we raised questions about the nature of the quest for educational excellence and equity. For example,

> There are other questions and challenges that must be acknowledged in this work. For one thing, the "theory of action" under study here—the idea that the improvement of improved teaching will yield increased learning—may be too simplistic and too tightly focused. Factors like students' family stability, health, motivation, attendance, mobility, and discipline have a profound effect on the potential success of teaching.
>
> One issue is whether, as Richard Rothstein has argued, improved schooling alone is enough to empower a high proportion of low-income youngsters to overcome the injuries of poverty.[5] The question is whether schools, even optimally led and operated, can create equal opportunity in a society widely divided by inequality. Yes, schools can do that for some, even many. But whether one looks at the proficiency rate for Boston students, the dropout rates, or the college persistence rates, the data are alarming. The bottom line is that large numbers of students are leaving school unprepared for the challenges of the future.
>
> The fact that noneducational factors play a huge role in potential student success does not excuse school failure, exempt school systems from accountability, or diminish the kind of ambitious reform that Payzant has personified. But it does put those reforms and the institution of schooling into perspective and cries out for a comprehensive, intergovernmental, child-focused, renewed war on poverty.[6]

To his credit, Payzant was always willing, albeit grudgingly, to acknowledge the wide-ranging, nonschool factors influencing educational outcomes, but he firmly insisted that not only can good schools make a huge difference in children's lives and learning, but that educators and leaders like himself should be held accountable for making schools better, and for increasing student learning while making efficient use of the enormous resources the public invests in school systems.[7]

Finally, the Rennie Center concluded its executive summary of the conference by acknowledging the unquestioned successes of the Payzant era, while pointing to the central challenges for Boston's next team of leaders:

> Payzant's legacy is one of effective reform initiatives that have left the district well prepared for the next phase of districtwide improvement. With the cultural and structural foundations put in place by Payzant, the next superintendent has the platform to initiate a more aggressive agenda. Evidence from this project suggests that the incoming administration

should concentrate its reform efforts on (1) continuing effective strategies like instructional workshops, more efficient hiring practices, and high school improvement, while deepening these efforts and accelerating the pace; (2) insisting on equity by making sure that instructional reforms penetrate all schools, and that teachers, resources, and curriculum match the challenges present in each school; and (3) intensifying the focus on instructional improvements and results, especially for students of color, English-language learners, and students with disabilities. Boston's sustained leadership and consistent progress leave the district poised to see breakthrough progress, but only if it accelerates and intensifies its work in these key areas and stays focused on success for all students.

Thomas Payzant concluded his tenure in the Boston Public Schools with a national reputation for effective districtwide reform and unmistakable indications of progress during his reign. As the dawn of the next era of Boston education reform approaches, the Rennie Center's research and deliberations emphasize that there is much left to be done to capitalize on the good work that Payzant initiated, to ensure that reform is equitably implemented, and to accelerate reform progress to a relentlessly ambitious pace so that Boston's school improvement strategies truly and quickly benefit all students.[8]

A CONCLUDING NOTE

Since we completed our research for this book, there have been several positive developments for the Boston Public Schools. One development is that after four years of being selected as a semifinalist, Boston was finally chosen, in September 2006, as the recipient of that year's Broad Prize in Urban Education. The $1 million Broad Prize is an annual award that honors large urban school districts that demonstrate the greatest overall performance and improvement in student achievement while reducing achievement gaps for poor and minority students. This fitting and prestigious recognition came, serendipitously, as the perfect capstone to Tom Payzant's Boston tenure. The Broad Prize was a tribute not only to the achievements of the men, women, and students of the Boston Public Schools, but to the leadership provided by Payzant.

Finally, we must say that even though our work has not been about Thomas Payzant as a leader, per se, this book is inevitably infused with commentary about his leadership and legacy. We conclude by acknowledging his extraordinary talent as a leader; his unstinting commitment to children, teaching, and learning; and his unusual capacity, as illustrated in his chapter of this book, to reflect with equanimity not only on his performance, but also on the running commentary about his work, here and elsewhere, by those of us who never had to do that work. Boston was fortunate to have had such a leader.[9]

CHAPTER I

Strong Foundation, Evolving Challenges

A Case Study to Support Leadership Transition in the Boston Public Schools

THE ASPEN INSTITUTE
EDUCATION AND SOCIETY PROGRAM
ANNENBERG INSTITUTE FOR SCHOOL REFORM
AT BROWN UNIVERSITY

TEN YEARS AGO, Thomas W. Payzant became superintendent of the Boston Public Schools and launched a reform program based on the idea that focusing on instruction, particularly in literacy and mathematics, would improve learning for all students. This case study examines the extent of instructional improvement a decade later, and the complementary efforts that the district has made to improve the abilities of teachers, principals, and the central office to improve instruction continuously. It also identifies some of the challenges now facing the Boston Public Schools.

The purpose of the study is to inform the leadership transition that will occur as Payzant's superintendency comes to a close in June 2006. While the superintendent's departure is a landmark event in itself, it is likely to be accompanied by the departure of several key central office staff, and it coincides with the expected retirement of a greater-than-usual number of Boston teachers. Thus, the study is designed to inform not just a superintendent search, but a broader transition in leadership of the Boston Public Schools.

Through its programs for urban superintendents, the Aspen Institute is acutely aware of how many city school systems will be experiencing transitions similar to the one in Boston. Boston hosted Aspen's biannual urban superintendents meeting in December 2005, and Superintendent Payzant agreed that a study examining Boston's experience would be informative for the group. Aspen joined with the Annenberg Institute for School Reform to undertake the study. Aspen and Annenberg fielded a team of researchers to conduct the research and interviews on which the case is based. The research design was coconstructed by the Aspen-Annenberg team and a team from the Boston school district and its partners. (See appendix 1A for a list of the members of the case-study team.)

The research was conducted from September through November 2005 (see appendix 1B for details on the study process and research methods). The process consisted of an extensive document review, a review of data on student outcomes, and interviews or focus groups with ninety-eight individuals: students, educators, central office administrators, and community leaders. While this set of respondents is not a representative sample of the Boston community, it does typify a set of key roles within the district, its partners, and the community. The resulting interviews generated a remarkably consistent set of observations about what has been accomplished, what is underway that should be preserved, and what are the challenges Boston's next leadership team must address. A major purpose of this case study is to share these observations.

The case has one additional and crucial purpose: to spark and support a conversation about how the city—its educators, families, and communities—searches for and identifies new leadership, engages that leadership in building on what has been accomplished, and formulates the remaining challenges that new leadership needs to address.

This report is not the final nor the only word on this important subject. Several local groups are also developing documents that will inform numerous discussions about leadership transition in the Boston schools. We hope that the accumulated body of evidence and recommendations will enable the city to proceed confidently into the next stage of its education reform.

CONTEXT: THE CITY AND ITS SCHOOLS

In recent years, the city of Boston has, by many indicators, benefited from a cultural, economic, and civic resurgence. Boston's economy boomed in the late 1990s, bringing historically low rates of crime, unemployment, and office vacancy. While Massachusetts and its flagship city are still recovering from the more difficult financial climate post-September 11, 2001, Boston remains vital. Wages in the city are well above the average among urban areas—though, correspondingly, so are housing prices, which are fourth highest in the country. The city is home to thirty-five colleges and universities and dozens of museums, and the region boasts one of the highest rates of educational attainment in the nation. The "Big Dig," the largest civil-works project in the history of the United States, is near completion, opening the way for improved travel in and out of the city and developing over three hundred acres of parks and open space. *Forbes* magazine reported in 2004 that Boston offered the best public education of any big city in the United States.[1]

Governance

Mayor Thomas Menino has led the city since 1993 and was reelected to a fourth term in November 2005. From the beginning, education reform has been at or near the top of his agenda, assisted in part by a 1992 referendum that dissolved the elected school board and replaced it with a school committee appointed by the mayor. The stars aligned in 1995, the first opportunity for the appointed school committee to hire a superintendent. Thomas Payzant took the reins of a school system in turmoil after frequent leadership turnover: he was the third superintendent in five years. Previously, he had led several large-city school systems and served as assistant secretary for elementary and secondary education in the Clinton administration. Payzant has enjoyed strong and consistent backing from the school committee and the mayor throughout his tenure in Boston.

A year after the school committee referendum, the Massachusetts Education Reform Act was signed into law. It led to the Massachusetts Comprehensive Assessment System (MCAS), a standards-based performance-measurement system for all students, schools, and districts in the commonwealth. MCAS testing associated with the statewide standards and curriculum frameworks began in 1998. In a comparison of the rigor of state assessment systems published in the summer 2005 issue of *Education Next*, Massachusetts was one of only five states to receive an overall grade of A, meaning it is among the most rigorous.[2] The Education Reform Act also led to the development of charter schools, public schools unaffiliated with a local school board and free from collective-bargaining agreements. The first Massachusetts charter schools opened their doors in 1995. Currently, more than four thousand Boston children attend charter schools.

The Boston Public Schools

The Boston Public Schools (BPS) comprises 145 schools (see appendix 1C). Seventeen of these schools are Pilot Schools, which, through an agreement with the Boston Teachers Union, operate with greater autonomy in scheduling, hiring, curriculum, and budgeting than the other schools in the district. There are also more than a dozen charter schools in Boston, including two Horace Mann Charter Schools, which operate independently from the district (as do all the charters), but are approved by the local school committee and the local collective bargaining unit.

The district enrolls over 58,000 students from a city population that is increasingly diverse. In 2000, more than one-quarter of Bostonians were foreign born, the highest rate since 1940, and today more than a third of Boston's residents speak a language other than English in their homes. The BPS student population is significantly more diverse than the standard breakdown (see appendix 1C) would suggest, including sizable groups of Dominican, Cape Verdean, Haitian, Chinese, Vietnamese, and South and Central American immigrants. Seventy-four percent of BPS students qualify for free or reduced-price meals. (For additional details on the BPS system, see appendix 1C.)

Boston's desegregation lawsuit, which began in 1972, has left a long and troubled legacy in the system. Concluding that the Boston Public Schools had intentionally avoided reducing segregation, Judge Arthur Garrity imposed mandatory busing, resulting in an ugly and violent response in predominantly poor, white neighborhoods. The proportion of white students attending Boston's public schools decreased sharply; even today, more than half of white students in Boston choose to attend private or parochial schools. Boston schools are actually now *more* racially isolated than they were when the desegregation lawsuit was first filed. There are also large discrepancies between the race/ethnicity of the teaching force and of the student body: 61 percent of the district's 4,500 teachers are white. Under Payzant, however, the proportion of administrators of color has grown dramatically: currently, 62 percent of school administrators are people of color.

The history of school desegregation in Boston has made school choice and school assignment critical issues for the district and the community. Boston's elementary and middle schools are separated into three geographic zones (high schools are citywide); students and families select their top choices and are assigned based on their zone of residence, their choices, and availability. From 1974 until 1999, racial balance was also a factor in school assignment. However, under threat of an unfavorable legal ruling, the school committee voted in 1999 to end race-based school assignments. The resultant plan set aside one-half of a school's available seats for students living in that school's "walk zone," with the remaining seats open to anyone in the school's geographic zone (north, west, or east).

The elimination of racial consideration in school assignment most affected Boston's three "exam" schools—high schools that require students to take and score well on an entrance test to attend. There is tremendous competition to get into the exam schools, and they are perceived as the best schools in the city, particularly Boston Latin, the nation's oldest public school. Only the exam score and GPA are considered in assigning students to Boston Latin, Latin Academy, and O'Bryant High School of Mathematics and Science. Compared with white enrollment in BPS as a whole (14%), both Boston Latin and Latin Academy are disproportionately white: Boston Latin's enrollment is over 53 percent white; Latin Academy is 39 percent white.

Public Funding

Massachusetts's and Boston's commitment to education reform in the 1990s brought an influx of financial resources to BPS. Overall, per pupil spending increased from \$6,587 in 1994 to \$11,795 in 2004, an average annual increase significantly higher than the statewide average. Thirty-five percent of the total city budget is directed to BPS.[3] Still, the district faced serious financial crises in fiscal years 2003 and 2004. Decreases in expected revenues, especially state aid and grants, coupled with increases in fixed costs related to salaries, benefits, new schools, and mandates, led to cuts of \$85 million over two years. The cuts included a 10 percent budget reduction in all schools, reductions of 20 percent or more in central office and support-service budgets, and school closings. The district is still recovering from this crisis, and, on average, school funding remains 6 percent below the level the district believes it should be.

PARTNERS

Private investment, key partnerships, community groups, and the teachers union have each had an impact on the reform effort in BPS.

Private Investment

Between 1995 and 2005, private foundations and other donors invested nearly $100 million in the city schools. For example, Carnegie Corporation of New York and the Bill & Melinda Gates Foundation have provided multiyear grants totaling over $21 million to focus on improving high school education in the city. Additionally, over the last decade the Annenberg Foundation has made two grants totaling $20 million that stimulated millions more in private dollars. These investments enabled the development of the Collaborative Coaching and Learning program and the implementation of the district's instructional model, Readers and Writers Workshop. (For more on these two elements, see the Reform in BPS section of this chapter, and chapter 5 by Barbara Neufeld.)

Massachusetts 2020, an organization focusing on expanding afterschool and summer learning opportunities for children across the state, in 2004 helped to launch Boston's After School and Beyond initiative, which became the largest public-private partnership dedicated to children in Boston's history. Built on a strong foundation laid by both Mayor Menino in the "2:00-to-6:00" initiative and the Boston Afterschool for All Partnership, this effort seeks to expand afterschool availability for low-income children, increase resources available for afterschool programs, and support research and data on out-of-school time and activities.

Local Partners

The Boston Plan for Excellence (BPE) has played a significant role in the district's reform efforts. BPE researched and codesigned key aspects of the reform, including the whole-school improvement planning model, collaborative coaching and learning, and readers and writers workshop. It also helped sustain the reform investment—both financial and political—of national funding organizations and the city's elites.

Other local organizations, such as the Boston Foundation, the Center for Collaborative Education, Jobs for the Future, and the Boston Private Industry Council (PIC), have also made it possible to build and sustain both structural and instructional reforms. For example, since 1982, the Boston PIC has convened the Boston Compact, an agreement among the city's elites to commit their resources and support to reach key educational goals. Signers of the current

Compact—made in 2000 and focused on meeting high standards, developing career and college opportunities, and developing principals and teachers—include the mayor, the school committee chair, the president and CEO of the Federal Reserve Bank of Boston, the board chair of the Boston Plan for Excellence (who is also chair emeritus of the Bank of America), the former Boston Teachers Union president, college presidents, and the chairs of the Boston Human Services Coalition and the Boston Cultural Partnership. Over the years, the Compact has had a role in the development of the Boston Plan for Excellence, Pilot Schools, and Mayor Menino's "2:00-to-6:00" afterschool initiative, among others.

Community

Lively and engaged community partners have also contributed much to the city's education reform efforts. The Boston Parent Organizing Network (BPON), with thirty-six member organizations, began as a citywide family- and community-engagement initiative launched by a diverse constituency of parents, activists, and community members "to support and advocate for the improvement of Boston Public Schools." BPON successfully advocated for the new position of deputy superintendent for family and community engagement and the reorganization of the BPS Family Resource Centers.

The Citywide Parents Council, Inc., Massachusetts Advocates for Children, the Black Ministerial Alliance of Greater Boston, Mass English Plus, and other groups have also worked relentlessly as voices for children and parents, particularly those without access to equal educational opportunities.

The Boston Teachers Union

The Boston Teachers Union (BTU) is a powerful force in the city. The BTU represents over 8,000 members, about 4,500 of whom are teachers working in the school system. In the past fifteen years, agreements to develop Pilot Schools, to limit some seniority-transfer provisions, and to build many of the components of whole-school improvement and collaborative coaching and learning into the contract have given the school district more flexibility in hiring and developing school staffs. The current contract, signed in 2003, expires in August 2006. Both Payzant and BTU's leader, Richard Stutman, hope to come to agreement before the superintendent departs. One potential sticking point is the BTU's current position on Pilot Schools: Stutman has pushed for compensation for teachers working longer hours and more days in those schools.

REFORM IN BPS: A THEORY OF ACTION

In 1996, under Payzant's leadership, the Boston Public Schools adopted *Focus on Children*, a five-year education reform plan. The goal, as Payzant explained it, was not to create a few more good schools; the idea was to improve the entire district, so that *all* schools would be good schools. An extension of the plan, *Focus on Children II*, was adopted in 2001. (For a timeline of major events in BPS related to the reform efforts, see appendix 1D.) To reach that goal, the reform focuses on five elements that collectively represent a theory of action for district change:

- Setting clear *expectations for what students should learn* in all major subjects. To accomplish this, Boston adopted citywide learning standards, one of the first large cities to do so.
- Establishing a *curriculum* that gives students and teachers access to rigorous content. In place of the plethora of materials in use throughout the district, Boston adopted a single mathematics program to be used in all schools for each grade level and a handful of reading programs from which schools could choose.
- Creating *expectations about instructional practices* through a pedagogical approach based on the Readers and Writers Workshop model but applicable to all subject areas, that encourages teachers to enable students to read, write, talk, and explore topics with teachers and their peers.
- Providing extensive *support for teachers* through a coherent professional development strategy designed to help them improve their instructional practice. As one element of this strategy, the district developed, in partnership with the Boston Plan for Excellence, a professional development approach to help teachers implement the workshop model effectively. Known as collaborative coaching and learning, the approach provides in-school, in-classroom support from coaches skilled in content areas, along with time for teachers to collaborate with one another and the coaches to analyze student data, observe model lessons, try out the model lessons, and reflect on their practices together.
- Developing and using *assessments* that serve two purposes: formative (ongoing review through the school year of the progress students are making) and summative (end-of-year assessments that can be used for accountability purposes).

In addition, the theory of action suggested that high-quality school leadership was vital to school success. To that end, the district enhanced the supervision of principals and headmasters, established a program to prepare new school leaders, and provided more professional development for school leaders.

FINDINGS

Our review of the data and our face-to-face interviews with a wide range of Boston residents yielded a rich story of an urban school district that has accomplished much and faces a number of challenges. Of course, the same could be said about many school districts. But Boston's challenges are different from those of many other districts, in large part because of its stability. Boston's ten-year effort to focus on instructional improvement has had some positive effects on classroom practices and outcomes; the challenge now is to build on the solid foundation and ensure that all children in all schools are served well. Some of these challenges might have been anticipated from the outset, but many grew out of the construction and implementation of the new system.

In some respects, one of the most remarkable aspects of Boston's situation is the fact that it is in that situation at all. The rapid turnover of leadership in urban districts—and the concomitant turnover in district agendas—are well known. Few large cities have pursued an educational reform path for a decade. That Boston is considering how to move reform to a *second* decade is highly unusual, and it speaks well to its leaders' vision and to the strong support for that vision in the community.

In this section we highlight some of the major findings—both accomplishments and challenges—from our review. We look first at accomplishments in four areas: student achievement, instructional capacity, culture/climate, and district supports.

Accomplishments

Over the past ten years, the Boston Public Schools has accomplished much and has much to be proud of. Although they acknowledged that the district still has much it can improve, central office administrators, principals/headmasters, teachers, and parents all spoke very positively about the district and what it has done. They believe the district is headed in the right direction.

Perhaps the most impressive accomplishment is the success of Superintendent Payzant and district leaders in laying out a compelling vision of a whole system of successful schools and implementing it in a sustained way. Keeping all eyes on the prize has helped ensure widespread ownership of the district's reforms.

Districtwide gains in achievement have attracted the attention of national funders, who have shown their support for the district's accomplishments by investing some $96 million over the past ten years.

Student Achievement

BPS has made strides in raising academic achievement, particularly among low-performing and minority students and particularly at the elementary level. (See appendices 1E and 1F for graphs of MCAS achievement overall and by subgroups.) For example, in fourth grade, the percentage of black students passing the state's English language arts test—that is, showing at least a "partial understanding of subject matter"—rose from 56 percent in 1998 to 71 percent in 2005, while the proportion of Hispanic fourth graders passing the test rose from 56 percent to 66 percent over the same period. These gains were not linear, however. Passing scores rose sharply from 1998 to 2001, then leveled off between 2001 and 2003. Scores rose again in 2004, but in 2005 there was another slight drop-off in scores that was consistent across most subgroups. Still, every subgroup is performing much better than it was in 1998.

The results in mathematics have been even more dramatic. The percentage of black fourth graders passing the state test rose from 35 percent to 60 percent between 1998 and 2005, and the percentage of Hispanic fourth graders passing the test increased from 41 percent to 65 percent. Unlike other districts in which improvements in elementary school have not been matched by gains in upper grades, Boston has seen achievement rise in middle and high school as well. Among tenth graders, for example, the proportion of black students passing the state mathematics test increased more than fourfold, from 15 percent to 62 percent from 1998 to 2005, while the proportion of Hispanic tenth graders passing the test jumped from 13 percent to 65 percent during that period. White and Asian passing rates, just above 50 percent in 1998, rose to 85 percent and 95 percent, respectively, in 2005. The white and Asian passing rates have been fairly steady since 2001, while the black and Hispanic passing rates have risen each year, except for 2005.

Boston's achievement results are also reflected on national tests. In the 2005 Trial Urban District Assessment conducted by the National Assessment of Educational Progress (NAEP), Boston fourth and eighth graders performed as well or better than their counterparts in other large central cities in both reading and mathematics. Average scale scores in reading and mathematics for black eighth graders were significantly higher in Boston than for black students in other large central cities.

Other measures of achievement also show improvements. More of Boston's high school graduates attended postsecondary education or training: a study conducted for the Boston Private Industry Council found that 74 percent of the class of 2003 was enrolled in education or training, the highest enrollment rate in the eighteen years in which the follow-up study of graduates has been conducted. Anecdotal evidence from our interviews also suggests improvements in student achievement. Middle and high school teachers told us that they believed that their students were more prepared than previous students.

Instructional Capacity

Our interviews with educators in the central office and the schools have convinced us that the achievement gains described above did not come about by accident. The district has made a concerted effort to build instructional capacity and improve the ability of teachers and school leaders to teach effectively; these efforts have taken root and borne fruit.

Focus on Children, Boston's education reform plan, focuses at its heart on instruction, and teaching and learning are the central issues throughout the district. Teachers, coaches, principals, and central office administrators all view instruction and learning as their primary responsibility—this is not the case in other districts. The BPS district has sought to build instructional capacity by addressing four areas: curriculum, instruction, professional development, and educator quality.

Educators interviewed cited the district's common curricula and pedagogical approaches in literacy and mathematics as a significant step.[4] The previous practice, in which each school essentially chose its own curriculum, resulted in what one interviewee called "Greek city-states" that produced wide variations in quality. By contrast, the common curriculum has helped create coherence and promote equity by helping to make it crystal clear that all children can and should be learning to the same standards, no matter where they happen to attend school.

And although teachers and parents have some concerns about the curriculum the district is using (see, for example, Coherence and Alignment), many we spoke with support the new curriculum programs. In mathematics, for example, elementary teachers praise the Investigations program, saying it provides good opportunities for open-ended problem solving that enables children to understand mathematics and see the connections to the real world. A study by the state office of Educational Quality and Accountability (EQA) confirms that there was a great effort at the elementary level to implement Investigations.

In addition to establishing a common curriculum, Boston took the unusual step of introducing a pedagogical model and providing support to help teachers implement and use it. The workshop model is now nearly ubiquitous in Boston classrooms, according to the EQA report, and our interviews suggest that teachers find it praiseworthy, particularly for English language arts, where teachers say the workshop model has increased rigor in reading and writing instruction.

The district took to heart the idea of reciprocal accountability: if teachers are responsible for improving student achievement, then the district is responsible for providing teachers with the support they need to improve student learning. In putting in place the instructional strategy, Boston made a considerable investment in professional development to enable teachers to learn and use the curriculum and pedagogical approach effectively in all subjects.

The district used a 1999 Boston Plan for Excellence audit of its professional development offerings to provide more focus and coherence in professional development.[5] Boston also invested heavily in school-based coaches, which teachers and principals—after some initial skepticism—now say they enthusiastically support. Teachers also told us that they consider coaching an opportunity for them to learn, which they greatly appreciate, and that they are thrilled that schools have provided them time to work on issues of practice in a sustained manner. Coaching also offers a first step toward differentiated career ladders for teachers.

The creation of instructional leadership teams in each school has strengthened school leadership by enabling principals/headmasters to distribute leadership responsibilities appropriately; and the teams, along with the institutionalization of coaching, have created new roles for classroom teachers. The recent turnover in school leadership, and the efforts by the district to strengthen the capacity of the new leaders, will help ensure stability during the transition in district leadership.

To bolster its commitment to strengthening instructional capacity, Boston and its partners have taken steps to develop a strong corps of teachers and school leaders. Despite concerns from area colleges and universities with teacher preparation programs, the district established the Boston Teacher Residency program to create an alternative route to certification for teaching in Boston. Likewise, the district created a School Leadership Institute to prepare school leaders at a time when district leaders believed that universities were not producing the leaders they needed. This program has produced a number of minority principals/headmasters.

Culture and Climate

Boston's accomplishments in improving the culture and the climate of the district have been remarkable. To a degree rare in large school systems, teachers, school leaders, and central office administrators are focused on teaching and learning. Teachers talk knowledgeably about their students' learning; principals talk capably about instruction; and central office administrators, through initiatives like REACT (Resource Action Team), are framing more of their decisions in terms of the likely effects on schools' ability to deliver quality instruction to all children. Moreover, educators at all levels tend to use the same language when talking about instruction. This atmosphere is far different from that of the days before the reform effort, when the focus was unclear and the language was far from coherent.

Like the improvements in achievement, these positive changes reflect the district's efforts to focus on instruction and to support this focus with a coherent set of policies and practices. The common curriculum has created a common vocabulary for teachers and administrators that facilitates discussions about learning. Focused professional development and coaching provide opportunities for teachers and school leaders to address instructional issues. And the steady emphasis on achieving success at scale, not just in a few schools or programs, signaled to people throughout the district that the reform could not be waited out or avoided.

These consistent messages from the district, combined with the accountability for student performance the state of Massachusetts has implemented, have strengthened Boston teachers' and principals'/headmasters' sense of accountability for student learning. Increasing numbers of teachers and other school staff are clear about what and how to teach and about their role in improving student achievement. The stability in the district's agenda also supports this cultural shift. Teachers and school leaders appear to believe that *Focus on Children* is the work of the district, not "the flavor of the month."

The cultural shift affects the district's relationships with its partners and with the city as well. The clarity of the district's goals have facilitated partnerships because partners can more easily be aligned with a focused agenda. The stability of the city and district leadership has also played a role in this shift toward a consistent, long-term improvement strategy. The mayor and the school committee have consistently lined up in support of the district agenda and have helped maintain its staying power. Mayor Menino, who is about to become Boston's longest-serving mayor, has strongly backed the reforms and has appointed school committee members who share his enthusiasm for them. The epic battles that once characterized Boston School Committee meetings are no more.

District Supports

In addition to developing policies and practices to support classroom instruction and help change the classroom culture in the district, Boston has also made impressive strides in creating district-level infrastructure to support schools, educators, and students. This infrastructure will help ensure that the improvements last over time.

One important piece of the infrastructure we heard about repeatedly in interviews is the MyBPS system. MyBPS is a Web-based system, updated daily, for examining student data by classroom and by school. MyBPS includes such basic data as individual attendance, report grades, and schedule information, as well as MCAS scores by student and by item. Teachers and especially principals/headmasters strongly support this system; more important, they say they use it to analyze data and understand students' strengths and needs. This tool is helping turn the Boston Public Schools into a district where evidence-based practice is becoming a way of life.

Another important part of the infrastructure is the emerging portfolio of high schools and a broadened set of options for students, including exam schools, Pilot Schools, new small schools, and small learning communities within larger schools. Students and parents told us they like having more options, and data suggest that Pilot School achievement exceeds achievement in other district schools.[6]

Boston has also strengthened many of the operations of the district central office. Notably, the human resources office is considered much more efficient than it was in the past; as a result, schools no longer have to scramble to hire teachers after the start of school. In addition, the 1999 merger of the Special Education Department and the Student Support Services Team into a single Unified Services Team has been a positive development. The goal was to align support services for students with support for classroom teaching in order to reduce the number of referrals to special education and out-of-school placements for students with disabilities. The effort has produced results: private placements are much lower, and the proportion of BPS students enrolled in special education has decreased modestly, from 22 percent to 19 percent.

The district also improved the communication with principals/headmasters and the supervision of the school leaders. Payzant named principals/headmasters to the superintendent's leadership team, which meets twice a month and has begun to hold monthly breakfasts with principals in a school cluster, so school leaders have a better sense of district policies and district leaders have a better sense of school concerns. And Payzant's decision to replace the reporting system for principals/headmasters with a system in which they report directly to one of three deputy superintendents has resulted in better support for principals. Principals, particularly those in elementary schools, now say they have stronger supervision and know whom to call for resources and support.

Superintendent Payzant has also undertaken a number of steps to engage communities in district reforms. Many cited the creation of the position of deputy superintendent for family and community engagement as a welcome move. The High School Renewal Group—a diverse team formed as part of the efforts to improve high school education in the city—includes, among others, partner representatives from the Boston Plan for Excellence, Jobs for the Future, and the Center for Collaborative Education in decision-making roles. And the superintendent launched regular informal meetings with a group of community leaders to listen to their concerns.

CHALLENGES

Boston's accomplishments are impressive and deserve recognition. But like any district, Boston also faces challenges. In many respects, the district's challenges are qualitatively different from those most districts face because Boston has accomplished so much. Boston is not moving from "below basic" to "basic" in developing and sustaining reform; the district is trying to reach for "proficiency" or beyond for the full range of students.

The data suggest that the district, despite its progress so far, still has a way to go. Although the passing rates on state tests have gone up, "passing" is not "proficient," which the state defines as "solid understanding of challenging subject matter." While the state proficiency level is one of the highest in the nation, the proportion of Boston students who demonstrate that level of understanding is quite low. In fourth grade, for example, only 25 percent of students attained the proficient level or higher in English language arts in 2005, and only 21 percent reached those levels in mathematics. In middle and high school, the proficiency rates in both subjects are generally higher, but from 50 percent to 60 percent of students are still below proficiency. Achievement gaps are also substantial. In eighth-grade mathematics, half of all white students (and two-thirds of Asian students) reached the proficient level or above in 2004; only 13 percent of black students and 15 percent of Hispanic students reached that level.

The four-year graduation rate in Boston high schools remains very low. Only

42 percent of the class of 2001—and only 30 percent of Hispanics in that class—graduated on time, according to a study by Christopher Swanson of the Urban Institute.[7] However, many students remain in school for more than four years; the proportion of the class of 2001 that dropped out over five years was 23 percent. The Boston Private Industry Council's follow-up study of graduates warns that the high dropout rate might have contributed to the unusually high rate of college-going among the class of 2003: the proportion of students attending college would be higher if lower-performing students never even made it to graduation.

The good news is that the work thus far provides a foundation on which the district can build in the next phase of reform. And the culture of learning that the district has adopted can enable that work to go forward. Boston's reform will never be "done"; improvement is continual.

Equity

In interviews, parents expressed concerns about the uneven quality of Boston schools. They spoke frankly about going to extraordinary lengths to secure places in programs and schools they believe are good—such as advanced work classes in elementary schools, some of the Pilot Schools, and the exam high schools. The Educational Quality and Accountability (EQA) study provides evidence that such concerns might be valid: the study found "noticeably" higher-quality instruction in the advanced classes and found that, except in Pilot and exam schools, high school instruction was generally poor. Parents believe that Pilot and exam schools will provide opportunities for their children that they might not get in other schools. These beliefs produce a race for a limited number of coveted spaces, which in turn places a premium on knowledge of the options that are available, which is not always equitably shared.

The EQA study also found wide variations in instructional conditions in schools, including disparities in resources, expectations, equipment, programs, and staffing, as well as in rates of student and teacher absenteeism. These findings corroborate the stories students told us about overcrowded classrooms and inadequate facilities.

The perceptions about school quality also carry a racial undercurrent. Two of the three exam schools, for example, have disproportionately high white populations. Enrollment in the exam schools is coveted in the district, but it is unclear what combination of factors contributes to the perception of these schools' superiority. Are they truly superior, or is that just a perception produced by selectivity, history, traditional curriculum, or reputation? Given Boston's racial history, the high white-student population might also be a factor in that perception. In any event, whether or not the exam schools are actually superior, the prevalence of the "best and the rest" categorizing of schools may be discouraging to students in the other schools, who in some cases appear to have set lower sights for their academic future.

We also heard considerable concern over the quality of instruction for students with disabilities and English-language learners (ELL). Despite an attempt to integrate special education with regular education at the district level, many schools continue to separate the two, and special education teachers end up with fewer opportunities for professional development.[8] As one principal put it, special education teachers have "almost zero" content knowledge and expectations for students with disabilities remain low. Largely as a result, achievement for students with disabilities is low and the gaps between students in special education and those in regular education are widening.

In addition, the state initiative limiting native-language instruction for English-language learners has curtailed supports for a large population of students (more than nine thousand students, or one-sixth of the student body). And there is little understanding of how this policy change has affected outcomes for these students. Teachers feel a need for support to address these students' needs. Teachers said that in some cases, ELL students are being referred to special education in order to receive instructional attention. Another possible concern is the literacy requirements in the elementary mathematics curriculum: students who are learning English may be having difficulty learning mathematics because of language barriers, not mathematics barriers.

We also heard concerns over equity in the central office. Although Payzant has done much to broaden and diversify the leadership team—of the ten highest-ranking central office administrators, six are people of color—informants we spoke with inside and outside the central office continue to hold the perception that a few administrators who are predominantly white and male control access to most resources and decision making.

Coherence and Alignment

Under *Focus on Children*, BPS has taken a number of steps to bring coherence to the instructional program and supports for schools. But our interviews suggest that a lack of alignment still remains in several areas.

One such area is the mathematics curriculum. Teachers are enthusiastic about the elementary curriculum and, to a lesser extent, the middle school program, but they also expressed concerns that these programs place too great an emphasis on problem solving and not enough on basic skills. Although schools can supplement the standard curriculum with additional materials, there is little central guidance on supplementary materials, and the quality of such materials varies widely from school to school. Teachers also noted that there appears to be a lack of coherence in the mathematics program across grade levels. While the K–8 programs stress investigations and problem solving, the high school program places a fairly traditional emphasis on procedures. Teachers feared that students leaving middle school might get lost in the high school program.

We also heard concerns about a lack of alignment in instruction. High school teachers told us the workshop model is not as effective in mathematics as it is in English language arts. The district's professional development efforts, while highly praised, have also been uneven. Teachers reported that there were not enough math coaches. And they suggested that coaches and other professional development strategies did not do enough to help them differentiate instruction for all students, particularly those far behind.

We also found concerns about the ability of teachers to learn from one another across schools. High school teachers and headmasters did not appear to have had opportunities to visit other schools, particularly the Pilot Schools, which were supposed to be "greenhouses" that fostered knowledge about effective practice. One Pilot School headmaster told us that she has received hundreds of visits from outside the district, but none from the Boston Public Schools. We do not know whether this is attributable to a lack of interest or opportunity on the part of Boston educators; a limitation imposed by the teachers union, which has been skeptical of the Pilots from the outset; or some other reason. In any case, the lack of communication across schools inhibits learning.

At the same time, there appears to be a lack of communication across departments within the central office. Although Payzant has reorganized the office to strengthen supervision of principals, improve human resource supports, and streamline services for students, people told us that the office also remains "siloed," with little sharing of information from department to department. For example, elementary teachers talked about the lack of direction from central office about how to integrate math, literacy, and other subject-area curricula. They attributed this to a lack of collaboration at the district office. And principals described the confusing array of coaches—literacy coaches, math coaches, and language-acquisition coaches, among others—all managed by different central office departments.

Another issue related to coherence concerns the schools' links with community agencies, particularly afterschool programs. In some cases, simple logistical problems impede the coordination that might enable the afterschool programs to enhance student learning. For example, if the district and city could coordinate bus schedules, students would have an easier time getting from school to afterschool programs. Due in part to the prevalence of choice in the district, BPS already spends about one-eighth of its budget on transportation.

Partnerships and Community Involvement

District leaders have reached out to the city community and have won an impressive level of support for the reform effort. But from parents and community groups we also heard concerns about inclusiveness. There is a sense that the city's elites—the political leadership, the business community, and the universities—have greater access to decision-making authority than other groups. The district's close partnership with the Boston Plan for Excellence, which is tied to the city's elites, is an example that many people referred to; one called the organization "the shadow government." In part, the close tie to the elites reflects historical connections: the twenty-year-old Boston Compact was a collaboration between the schools, the universities, and the business community. But many city residents and grassroots groups feel left out. They feel they have opportunities to provide input but are not at the table when decisions are made.

The concerns over community involvement also point to another issue we heard repeatedly: the perception of top-down decision making by the district leadership. This concern arose in particular around issues of high school redesign and the creation of small schools and small learning communities. Superintendent Payzant gave schools the opportunity to develop their own restructuring plans (although they failed to do so). Nevertheless, principals/headmasters and community leaders believe that decisions about high school redesign are made centrally, with little input from the field. One headmaster reported that he did not find out that his school was being converted into small learning communities until he heard it at a meeting.

We also heard concerns that the district's collective bargaining agreement with the Boston Teachers Union may be impeding reforms. Although a recent contract loosened some rules over seniority and gave principals/headmasters greater authority to choose teachers compatible with their school's mission, there are other provisions that some believe are hindering the reform effort. For example, even though the district is breaking some large high schools into small learning communities that are expected to be largely autonomous, some of these buildings remain, under the union agreement, single bargaining units with a single union representative. This structure threatens to undercut the redesign. In addition, union rules on overtime have made it impossible for Boston to implement the kind of extended learning opportunities enjoyed by students in some Pilot Schools, which are exempt from some parts of the bargaining agreement.

Union opposition to expanding the number of Pilot Schools threatens the district's efforts to build a "portfolio of schools" with a variety of options for students and families. Mayor Menino has indicated that he would support lifting the statewide cap on charter schools if the union persists in blocking Pilot School applications; a confrontation is not desirable, but parents strongly support additional options. The challenge is to provide more options without affecting equity and further challenging "the rest" of the schools by leaving them with the least-motivated teachers, students, and families, exacerbating their disadvantages.

MOVING FORWARD

Our findings point to a system that has in place many elements of a strong reform structure. The challenge is not that of creating a wholly new reform agenda.

The challenge is identifying improvements that can accelerate progress toward higher levels of performance so that the Boston school system works for all students in all schools. Our findings point to three areas that the Boston education community should address as the system prepares for a transition in leadership.

Equity

Many of the issues we heard about from educators and community leaders alike center on race and class. These are common concerns in urban districts, but few communities tackle them head on. In Boston, as in other communities, race and class are part of the story in the varying quality of schools, as well as part of the concerns about the education of English-language learners and special education students. Left unaddressed, they make reform hard to sustain. In examining whether all students are served well, Boston might ask the following questions:

- What can be done to catalyze productive community-wide conversations about the issues of race and class in the city and their impact on the city schools? How might these conversations be focused on areas of inequity that were identified above, especially high schools, special education, central office leadership, and faculty racial imbalance? How might the results of such focused conversations, as well as inevitable ongoing concerns, both real and perceived, be factored into improvement efforts of the future?
- How can BPS ensure that all children, no matter where they attend school, have access to high-quality instruction? And how can the system and schools work to develop a "portfolio" of schools in which programs vary to meet the different needs of students, but expectations, outcomes, and rigor are consistent?
- How can BPS improve the quality of instruction for students with disabilities and English-language learners? What changes in teacher professional development, curricula, and pedagogical approach are needed to meet these students' needs?
- How can district leaders ensure that a broad range of the city's communities are involved in decisions about schooling?

Coherence and Alignment

Focus on Children is a well-thought-out strategy to improve teaching and learning at scale in a large urban school system. The plan has a number of critical components, and Superintendent Payzant made clear from the outset that all of them had to be addressed simultaneously in order to produce the results the city needed. At this point of administrative transition, it might be worthwhile for the district to take stock of the plan's implementation to determine whether all the elements fit together and whether the district and the schools are organized as effectively as they might be to carry it out. In doing so, the district might seek answers to the following questions:

- How can the district's curriculum and instructional approach be strengthened to provide schools with a coherent program that meets the needs of all students at all grade levels?
- How can the central office be organized to provide more efficient and effective service to schools? Can it be accomplished by making changes to the existing structure or does the organization need to be altered more significantly? In particular, in the area of human resources, how can the district take advantage of and build on existing flexibility in the teachers' contract to accelerate the hiring of high-quality teachers and principals as well as expand its efforts to "grow its own"?
- What is the right mix of central authority and school/educator autonomy? In what ways can central instructional guidance both accommodate and build on teacher expertise and knowledge? In particular, how can the district use the Pilot Schools to better understand and address tensions between central authority and school and educator autonomy?
- What data, in addition to standardized test scores, does the district need to collect in order to evaluate school quality? What data would provide information on conditions that would lead to improvement in learning down the road?

Partnerships and Community Involvement

District leaders have engaged a wide range of partners to support reform efforts. Continuing and expanding the reform will require even greater resources, which additional community partners might provide. In engaging a broader segment of the community, Boston leaders should consider:

- How can parents and grassroots community members and organizations be involved to a greater degree than they now are in school decision making? How might relationships with existing partners, which are strongest among the elite civic, cultural, and business communities, need to change to incorporate more voices?
- What can the district do to enlist partners who can expand learning opportunities available to students?
- How can the district help parents and community members make better-informed decisions about school quality, school options, and district programs?

IMPLICATIONS FOR THE TRANSITION IN LEADERSHIP

In discussions of the transitions facing the Boston Public Schools, much of the attention has focused on Superintendent Payzant. He has been a visible symbol of the reform, and he has had an extraordinarily long tenure. But as Boston moves to the next phase of reform, the community needs to think about how the next leadership team will go forward.

Because of the strong, community-wide support for the vision of *Focus on Children* and because of the success of the reform so far, Boston would do well to select leaders who also embrace the vision and who bring the skills necessary to carry it forward to the next level. Three top priorities for moving forward that emerged from our interviews were community engagement, instruction for English-language learners and students with disabilities, and central office redesign.

The new leaders might also reexamine the pace of reform. Although the district has made considerable progress, there are concerns that recent achievement scores have plateaued. Whether that is true or not, the goal of proficiency for all students will require faster gains in achievement. To accelerate improvement, the new administration will need to seek a balance between staying the course in key areas, like the workshop model of instruction, and taking strong and innovative action in others, like community engagement. The community conversations during the transition should focus on whether the community is ready for the bolder approaches that will be needed to produce more dramatic improvements.

Yet as they consider the next phase of reform, community members and the new leaders should be mindful of history—both the history of the previous decade and the longer history of education in Boston. The undercurrent of race is never far from the surface, and the new leaders would do well to remember that some members of the community feel that reform is often *done to* them. Fortunately, Boston has a great deal of experience and expertise that can be brought to bear in support of the next stage of reform. By embracing partners from the community and from the local and national reform-support community, Boston can expand on the past decade's work and serve all students well.

APPENDIX 1A

The Case Study Team

MANY PEOPLE CONTRIBUTED to the development of this case study. A four-member External Review Team with deep expertise in complex urban school system reform led the design, data collection, analysis, and writing of the case study:

- Anthony Bryk, Aspen Education Program advisor and professor at the Stanford University School of Education
- Deanna Burney, an independent consultant with experience as a teacher, principal, and central administrator
- Norm Fruchter, Director, Institute for Education and Social Policy at New York University
- Warren Simmons, Executive Director, Annenberg Institute for School Reform

The work of the External Review Team and research staff was coordinated and organized by:

- Judy Wurtzel, Aspen Institute
- Ellen Foley, Annenberg Institute
- Dennie Palmer Wolf, Annenberg Institute, working closely with
- Greg Baker, superintendent-in-training working in Boston Public Schools

Baker served as the point person in the district for gathering documents, scheduling interviews and focus groups, and advising on the case study. He also led a Liaison Team made up of Boston Public School employees and partners, who advised on the design of the case study and reviewed draft versions of this report. The Liaison Team included:

- Rachel Curtis, Assistant Superintendent, Boston Public Schools
- Maryellen Donahue, Director of Research and Evaluation, Boston Public Schools
- Ellen Guiney, Executive Director, Boston Plan for Excellence
- Elliot Stern, Principal, Edison Middle School
- Anand Vaishnav, Chief of Staff, Boston Public Schools
- Janet Williams, Deputy Superintendent, Boston Public Schools

In addition, the Rev. Gregory Groover of the Black Ministerial Alliance and John Mudd of Massachusetts Advocates for Children commented on a draft of the case prior to its publication.

The following Annenberg Institute staff members reviewed documents, researched key background information, recorded notes in interviews and focus groups, coded and analyzed data, and/or responded to drafts of the case:

- Frank Barnes
- Charley Cummings
- Pia Durkin
- Deborah King
- Michael Kubiak
- Tracie Potochnik
- Hal Smith
- Joanne Thompson
- Marla Ucelli

Anita Nester of the Annenberg Institute developed the Web-based briefing book that housed all the background on the case for use by the members of the case-study team. Robert Rothman of the Annenberg Institute was the primary author of the case study. Susan Fisher edited and formatted the final document, with Margaret Balch-Gonzalez and Mary Arkins; Haewon Kim designed the cover.

APPENDIX 1B

Methods: How the Study Was Conducted

THIS CASE focused on Boston's efforts to build an infrastructure to support instructional improvement, with attention to the policies, investments, and partnerships related to building this capacity, the evidence about the effects of these efforts, and identification of the challenges that are the most stubborn and urgent to address in the future.

It is a core belief of both the Annenberg Institute and the Aspen Institute that collaboration and partnership are integral aspects of education reform and of effective practice in supporting education reform. To that end, we utilized a tiered staffing plan that drew on core leaders and partners of the Boston Public Schools and a team of major external consultants, as well as Annenberg and Aspen staff. Appendix 1A describes the roles of all the people involved.

Developing the case involved three major steps:

- Review of existing information on reform implementation and reform outcomes
- Research design, data collection, and coding
- Analysis and writing

STEP 1

Review of Existing Information

In September and October 2005, with the help of the Liaison Team and the BPS Point Person, Annenberg Institute staff developed an electronic briefing book that included over fifty documents, among them descriptions of key BPS policies, research reports done by external organizations, and additional information gathered by Annenberg staff (contextual information about Boston, a reform timeline, budget summary, etc.). Documents were organized in the following areas: Boston Background, Essential Reading on Instructional Improvement, Student Achievement, and Building Human Resources.

All the documents were reviewed and summarized systematically by Annenberg staff and coded summaries were loaded into a qualitative data analysis program (N6). This database was then used to support the development of lists of informants and interview and focus-group protocols for Step 2.

STEP 2

Research Design, Data Collection, and Coding

Through consultation among the BPS Liaison Team, the BPS Point Person, the External Review Team, and Annenberg Institute and Aspen Institute staff, a list of key informants and key focus areas was developed. The BPS Point Person scheduled almost all the data-collection efforts, totaling twenty-nine interviews and fourteen focus groups, primarily conducted by the External Review Team over four days in mid- to late October 2005. Table A1 describes the characteristics of all ninety-eight people who served as informants. Individuals are not identified because they were promised confidentiality.

External Review Team members facilitated a large majority of the interviews and all of the focus groups; Annenberg and Aspen staff documented them using a semistructured protocol. All informants were asked to reflect on the accomplishments and challenges of the Payzant era and on the key issues to be addressed under a new superintendent. Additionally, individuals with knowledge in particular areas (special education or family/community partnerships, for example) were asked questions specific to their expertise. All the notes from the interviews and focus groups were coded and loaded into the N6 qualitative database, housed at the Annenberg Institute, for further coding and analysis.

TABLE A1

Characteristics of Focus Group and Interview Participants, Boston Case Study: October–November 2005

		Race/Ethnicity					Gender		Data-Collection Methods	
Participant	Total	White	Black	Latino	Asian	Not Recorded	Male	Female	Interview	Focus Group
Central Office Staff	16	9	5	1	1	0	7	9	16	0
Partners	7	7	0	0	0	0	4	3	7	0
Community Leaders	9	3	5	1	0	0	5	4	5	1
Principals	10	4	4	2	0	0	4	6	1	2
Instructional Leaders*	17	10	3	2	1	1	3	14	0	4
Teachers	13	11	2	0	0	0	3	10	0	3
Students	17	1	5	6	4	1	9	8	0	2
Parents	9	4	3	2	0	0	3	6	0	2
Total Number	98	49	27	14	6	2	38	60	29	14
Percentage of Total	100.0	50.0	27.6	14.3	6.1	3.1	38.8	61.2		

*Includes Instructional Coaches and Instructional Leadership Team Members

STEP 3

Analysis and Writing

By early November 2005, the N6 database included about ninety coded documents, including close to fifty document summaries and forty-three sets of field notes. Through debriefs with the External Review Team and Aspen and Annenberg staff working on the case, a set of topic areas was generated and a text search feature was used to create additional nodes of coded data in such areas as coaching, special education, and literacy. Annenberg and Aspen staff were assigned specific sections of the notes to read and analyze, generating an early set of findings that was reviewed by the External Review Team. Their comments, revisions, and queries led to another draft of the document. That draft was shared with the Liaison Team and with Superintendent Payzant. Their comments, which helped us identify factual problems and add nuance to the case, were incorporated into this version of the case study and shared at the Aspen Urban Superintendents Network.

NEXT STEPS

Annenberg Institute and Aspen Institute staff members will consult with the new BPS superintendent to strategize about how to use the case study to inform the leadership transition in Boston. Annenberg and Aspen staff will collaborate on how to utilize our experience in this work to support other districts undergoing leadership transition.

APPENDIX 1C

Facts and Figures: Boston Public Schools at a Glance

(Source: http://boston.k12.ma.us/bps/bpsglance.asp)

SCHOOLS AND STUDENTS

Number of schools in the BPS: 145

6 early learning centers (K–grade 1)
67 elementary schools (K–5)
11 elementary & middle schools (K–8)
18 middle schools (6–8)
1 middle & high school (6–12)
30 high schools (9–12)
3 "exam" schools (7–12)
6 special education schools (K–12)
3 alternative (at-risk) programs

Of these, 17 are Pilot Schools (2 early learning centers, 1 elementary, 4 K–8, 2 middle, 8 high) and 2 high schools are Horace Mann charter schools approved and funded by the BPS.

Enrollment: 58,600, including:

5,470 students in kindergarten
20,500 students in grades 1-5
12,640 students in grades 6-8
18,810 students in grades 9-12

Student Demographics:

45% Black
32% Hispanic
14% White
8% Asian
<1% American Indian

Free/Reduced-Price Meals

74% of BPS students are eligible to receive free meals in school (67% free, 7% eligible for reduced-price meals).

Students Who Don't Attend the BPS*

Of the 80,300 (est.) school-age children living in Boston, 21,050 (or 26%) do not attend Boston Public Schools. They are: 44% white, 42% black, 10% Hispanic, and 3% Asian. Of these students:

13,450 go to private & parochial schools
3,000 go to suburban schools through METCO
4,020 go to public charter schools
580 go to private special education schools

*BPS data as of 4/5/04.

HISTORY: FIRST IN THE U.S.

Boston Latin School: oldest public school, 1635
Mather: oldest public elementary school, 1639
BPS: oldest public school system, 1647
English High: oldest public high school, 1821

STAFF

The 2005–06 school budget (all funds) includes 8,814 staff positions (FTE), a decrease of 43 positions from FY05. Here is a comparison of budgeted positions:

FY06	FY05	Positions
4,733	4,769	teachers
612	630	administrators
488	483	support personnel
1,063	1,050	aides & monitors
357	354	secretaries & clerical staff
1,109	1,124	custodial/safety/technical
451	448	part-time & summer staff

Staff Demographics

Group	% Teachers	% Administrators
Black	26	43
White	61	38
Hispanic	9	16
Asian	5	4
Male	27	33
Female	73	67

LEADERSHIP

Superintendent (since 10/95)	Dr. Thomas W. Payzant
Deputy Supt. for Teaching & Learning	Christopher Coxon
Deputy Supt. for Clusters & School Leaders	Dr. Ingrid Carney Dr. Muriel Leonard Dr. Janet Williams

Deputy Superintendent for Family & Community Engagement	Karen Richardson
Chief Communications Officer	Christopher Horan
Chief Operating Officer	Michael Contompasis
Chief Information Officer	Kimberly Rice
Chief of Staff	Anand Vaishnav
Chief Financial Officer	John McDonough

SCHOOL COMMITTEE

The BPS is governed by a 7-member School Committee, appointed by the Mayor from among nominees recommended by a broad-based Nominating Committee. Members serve 4-year terms.

The appointed committee replaced a 13-member elected committee in January 1992, as the result of a November 1991 referendum. In a November 1996 referendum, voters chose to retain the appointed committee rather than return to the 13-member elected committee. Current members and term expiration dates are:

Dr. Elizabeth Reilinger, Chair	1/2/06
Marchelle Raynor, Vice-Chair	1/7/08
William Boyan	1/1/07
Michele Brooks	1/5/09
Helen M. Dájer	1/2/06
Alfreda Harris	1/1/07
Dr. Angel Amy Moreno	1/7/08

SCHOOL IMPROVEMENT: THE SIX ESSENTIALS

Focus on Children II is the BPS's 5-year school improvement plan that builds on the work of the previous 5-year plan. Its goal is to continue raising student achievement. It states that from SY02–06, instruction will be organized around these Six Essentials of Whole-School Improvement:

1. Use effective instructional practices and create a collaborative school climate to improve student learning.
2. Examine student work and data to drive instruction and professional development.
3. Invest in professional development to improve instruction.
4. Share leadership to sustain instructional improvement.
5. Focus resources to support instructional improvement and improved student learning.
6. Partner with families and the community to support student learning.

(For a complete description of the Six Essentials, see the Appendix, page 271.)

SPECIAL EDUCATION

About 11,760 students with disabilities (19% of total) are enrolled in special education programs, including:

5,160	students with mild to moderate disabilities
5,680	students with more severe disabilities who attend special BPS schools
530	students with severe disabilities who attend private and residential schools
390	students, ages 3–4, in Early Childhood programs

In addition, about 550 students enrolled in non-BPS schools receive some special education services in BPS schools.

ENGLISH-LANGUAGE LEARNING AND SUPPORT

About 9,800 students (17% of total) are "English-language learners" (ELL) or "limited English proficient" (LEP): English is not their first language, and they are not able to perform ordinary class work in English. All receive English-language support—some in formal programs and others in general education from highly qualified teachers of English. Approximate ELL enrollment by program, grades 1–12, is:

Program	Approx. No. of Students
Sheltered English Instruction	5,450
General Education with ELL support	3,870
Transitional Bilingual Education	190
Two-Way*	300

*Students whose first language is Spanish and whose first language is English learn together in both languages.

The five most common home languages of LEP students are:

Spanish	4,670
Haitian Creole	810
Cape Verdean Creole	540
Chinese	540
Vietnamese	430

BPS English-language learners come from 114 different countries!

CLASS SIZE

Under the contract (9/1/03–8/31/06) between the BPS and the Boston Teachers Union, the maximum numbers of students per teacher in regular education classes are:

K–2	Grade 3–5	Grades 6–8	Grades 9–12
22	25	28	31

The FY05 systemwide ratio of all students to all teachers is about 13 to 1.

SCHOOL CHOICE

Elementary and middle schools are organized in three geographic zones. Students are assigned to schools in their zone of residence, based on choice and availability of seats. All high schools are systemwide.

In 1999, the School Committee voted to drop race-based assignments, a policy that had been in place since 1974. The 1999 plan sets aside 50% of a school's seats for students living in the school's walk zone. Remaining seats are open to all applicants.

In 12/03, the committee and superintendent appointed a task force to seek input from the public on what families like about the current plan and what they would change. In fall 2004, based on the task force's recommendations, the committee voted to:

- maintain the current zone structure and allow students to apply for schools outside their zone of residence but within their walk zone;
- create more K–8 schools; and
- convene a work group on how to measure school quality.

STUDENT ACHIEVEMENT

Massachusetts Comprehensive Assessment System (MCAS)

On the 2004 statewide tests, the percentage of students who "passed" (performed at levels Needs Improvement, Proficient, and Advanced) and percentage change from 2003 were:

% Students Passing 2004 MCAS and % Change from 2003

Grade/Test		% BPS	% +/−	%State	% +/−
3	Read	82	+ 3	94	+ 1
4	ELA	77	+ 5	91	+ 1
4	Math	70	+ 8	86	+ 2
6	Math	47	− 2	75	+ 1
7	ELA	85	+ 1	93	N/C
8	Math	53	+ 6	71	+ 4
10	ELA	77	+ 7	90	+ 2
10	Math	74	+ 10	85	+ 6

SAT I

63% of the BPS Class of 2004 took the 2004 SAT I.

SAT I Results

Group	'03 Verbal	'04 Verbal	'03 Math	'04 Math
BPS	434	431	453	445
MA	516	518	522	523
US	507	508	519	518

Dropout Rates

% of students who dropped out in one year	% of starting 9th graders who dropped out over five years
SY02: 7.2	1997–2001: 23.1
SY03: 8.0	1998–2002: 22.5

AFTER HIGH SCHOOL

77% of the 3,516 graduates of the Class of 2002 responded to a survey for the Boston Private Industry Council on post-high school activity:

65% are in college or a training program (32% school only; 33% school and work)
27% are working only or in the military
6% are jobless but looking for work
2% are jobless and not looking for work

MONEY MATTERS: BUDGET, SALARIES, PER-PUPIL COSTS

FY06 General Fund: $712,413,221*

Program	Budget	% of total
Instruction	**$417,667,702**	**58.6**
Regular ed.	239,905,784	33.7
Special ed.	145,535,028	20.4
Bilingual ed./SEI	27,504,033	3.9
Career & tech. ed.	4,139,201	0.6
Adult ed.	325,908	0.0
Summer session	257,748	0.0
Support Services	**$294,745,519**	**41.4**
Employee benefits	96,382,562	13.5
Transportation	67,775,400	9.5
Physical plant	62,917,487	8.8
Student/school support services	46,621,278	6.5
General admin.	16,827,840	2.4
Safety	4,220,952	0.6

*Approved budget as of March 23, 2005. Does not include supplemental appropriations for collective bargaining agreements approved after that date.

FY06 External Funds (est.): $139,959,146

Includes formula grants (e.g. No Child Left Behind), reimbursement grants (National School Lunch, Impact Aid), and competitive grants (e.g., National Science Foundation).

FY06 Average Salaries

Title	Average Salary
Teachers (reg. ed.)[1]	$70,215
Elementary school principals[2]	$93,999
Middle school principals[2]	$96,684
High school headmasters[2]	$103,767
Central administrators	$104,605
Custodians	$40,475
Secretaries/clerical staff	$39,843
School police officer	$42,051
Nurses	$74,304
Substitute teachers per diem	$108

[1] $41,521 to $80,092

[2] Base salary; does not include career awards, degrees, or enrollment factors.

FY04 Spending per Pupil (city budget):

Regular ed.	Bilingual ed.	Mod. sped (.3)	Sub. sep. sped (.4)	Private sped (.5)
$7,610	$9,269	$13,212	$20,982	$61,937

The average FY04 per-pupil expenditure (PPE) is about $10,739. In FY03, the BPS's PPE was $10,057.

The state average was $8,273. Other district PPEs: Brockton, $8,641; Brookline, $10,578; Cambridge, $14,840; Milton, $7,850; Worcester, $7,962.

APPENDIX 1D

Timeline of Major Events in BPS: 1992–2005

THIS TIMELINE was constructed by Annenberg Institute staff members by combining data from existing timelines. Most of the information was drawn from two sources: a Boston Plan for Excellence "Timeline of Major Events" and a timeline used in presentations by Assistant Superintendent Rachel Curtis.

We also consulted with other members of the Boston Case Study Liaison Team. Thanks go to all of them.

Time	Event
January 1992	New, appointed Boston School Committee sworn in
June 1993	Massachusetts Education Reform Act signed into law; includes commitment to develop state standards and assessments
August 1995	Ellen Guiney becomes director of the Boston Plan for Excellence (BPE) and takes on focus of helping district adopt standards-based instruction
October 1995	Tom Payzant becomes superintendent of Boston Public Schools
June 1996	Payzant releases *Focus on Children*, a five-year strategy to raise achievement through standards-based reform
	BPE awards 21st Century School grants to 27 schools (later to be known as Cohort I)
August 1996	The "Six Essentials" are introduced to Cohort I schools
	Cohort I schools get one day per week "coach" to support implementation of the Six Essentials
September 1996	Citywide Learning Standards in English Language Arts introduced
	Comprehensive School Planning implemented by BPS
November 1996	Annenberg Foundation awards Boston $10 million Challenge grant

Time	Event
May 1997	$20-million match for Annenberg Foundation grant raised
	Payzant pledges that Annenberg funds will be used to incorporate all BPS schools into reform over time
September 1997	23 more schools begin the reform work (Cohort II)
	Literacy coaches introduced in Cohort I schools
	Citywide Learning Standards in Math introduced
	Comprehensive School Reform grant
November 1997	Boston School Committee approves the Six Essentials as the basis for reform in all BPS schools
April 1998	Resource Action Team convened involving BPS leaders in crossdepartmental effort to resolve issues that inhibit reform
May 1998	First administration of Massachusetts Comprehensive Assessment System (MCAS) in grades 4, 8, and 10
September 1998	Cohort III schools begin reform work, managed by new BPS office
	Citywide Learning Standards in Science introduced
	SMART goals-promotion policy developed
	Teacher supervision and evaluation training for school administrators begins
	In-depth Review (a school quality-type review of every school) begins
December 1998	State releases results of first MCAS test
August 1999	Payzant adds math as an instructional focus for BPS
September 1999	Formative assessments in reading and writing begin
	Cohort IV begins reform work, managed by BPS; all BPS schools are now engaged in reform work
	Preparation for Principalship supports begins
	Whole-School Change [later, "Improvement"] Planning begins
December 1999	Boston Plan for Excellence undertakes, with district approval, an audit of the professional development offerings; the district used the findings to increase focus and coherence in the programs

Time	Event
January 2000	Payzant unifies responsibility for professional development under one deputy superintendent in response to BPE report concluding that BPS PD was "highly fragmented" and "unfocused"
March 2000	Open hiring—giving schools more control over their staffs—is incorporated into negotiations with the teachers union, based on recommendations by the REACT Team/BPE; this proposal supported in later months by a large coalition of civic, social service, and religious groups
September 2000	Implementation of new math curricula (K–12)
	Math coaches introduced
	BPS coaching model defined
	Math formative assessments developed/implemented
	Reinventing Education grant from IBM—developed foundation for MyBPS assessment
October 2000	Teachers' contract settled, achieving more time for professional development, more flexibility in hiring, smaller class sizes, and 12% pay raises over three years
March 2001	Payzant reorganizes central office to work more directly with principals on Whole-School Improvement Planning (WSIP)
May 2001	Payzant names 26 Effective Practice schools, based on improved achievement and implementation of WSIP
August 2001	Second Annenberg Foundation grant ($10 million over five years), this one focused on improving professional development
September 2001	"Cohorts" eliminated
	Collaborative Coaching and Learning (CCL) and instruction based on Readers and Writers Workshop piloted in Effective Practice schools
	School Climate initiative begins
	Literacy professional development includes Lucy Calkins, Carl Anderson, and Randy Bomer
	Revision of Six Essentials
	Development of new Whole-School Improvement Planning rubric

Time	Event
October 2001	Carnegie Corporation awards Boston a Schools for a New Society grant ($8.1 million over five years) to reform the city's 12 comprehensive high schools
August 2002	Superintendent makes CCL and Readers and Writers Workshop a priority for the system
	MyBPS—an online system to give school easy access to student performance data—begins development
September 2002	CCL scaled up in literacy and math
	Increase in literacy coaching in all schools
	High schools get full-time literacy coach and small learning communities begin to be developed
November 2002	MyBPS assessment goes online
January 2003	Federal No Child Left Behind law takes effect
	Whole-School Improvement Planning realigned to NCLB
	In-depth review suspended
May 2003	Boston Teacher Residency program is funded by Strategic Grant Partners
July 2003	Gates Foundation awards BPS and its partners a grant ($13.6 million over four years) to create more small high schools
August 2003	Payzant priorities include workshop instruction, CCL, and WSIP
September 2003	27 Effective Practice schools named; six of the original schools dropped, seven added
December 2003	Effective Practice schools pilot new MCAS-aligned formative assessments
March 2004	Teachers' contract settled with language formalizing staff roles in WSIP, CCL, and workshop instruction
April 2004	Disaggregated data (by gender and race/ethnicity) added to MyBPS assessment
May 2004	Payzant's contract extended through June 2006
June 2005	Payzant moves responsibility for professional development to one new institute
September 2005	Data coaches hired to work with schools on understanding formative assessment results

APPENDIX 1E

Boston Public Schools

English Language Arts and Mathematics Achievement in Grades 4, 8, and 10 1998–2005

(Source: Massachusetts Department of Education website [section on MCAS])

Boston Public Schools: Grade 4 MCAS English/Language Arts Achievement 1998 to 2005

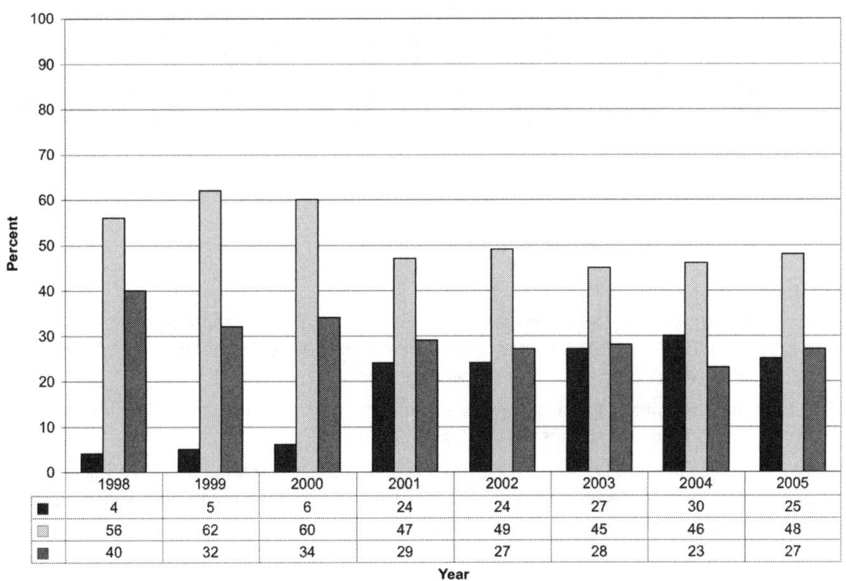

Grade 4 ELA:

- **Proficient or above:** Dramatic increase from 2000 to 2001, followed by two years of incremental increases (3 percentage points in 2002 and 2003), then dropping back to the 2001 level in 2005.
- **Needs Improvement:** Growth in that category in 1999 and 2000, followed by dramatic decrease in 2001 (13 points); has hovered between 45 and 49 percent from 2001 to 2005.
- **Warning:** Large decrease from 1998 to 1999 (8 percentage points), then sporadic small differences from 2000 to 2004; increase from 2004 to 2005 (from 23% to 27%).

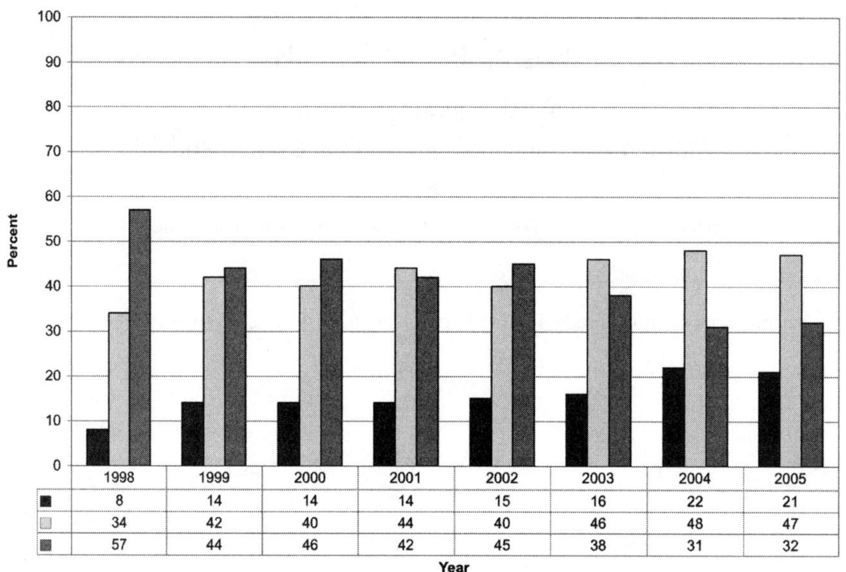

	1998	1999	2000	2001	2002	2003	2004	2005
■	8	14	14	14	15	16	22	21
□	34	42	40	44	40	46	48	47
▩	57	44	46	42	45	38	31	32

Grade 4 Math:

- ■ **Proficient or above:** Large increase from 1998 to 1999 (6 percentage points); basically steady from 1999 to 2003; another large increase in 2004 (6 percentage points) and basically maintained in 2005 (drop of 1 percentage point).
- □ **Needs Improvement:** Trend of increasing proportion of students scoring in this category from 1998 to 2005 (exceptions are 2000 and 2002).
- ▩ **Warning:** Overall trend of decreasing proportion of students scoring in this category (from 57% to 32%): large decreases from 2002 to 2004 (7 percentage points each year); basically maintained (1 percentage point higher in 2005 than 2004).

Boston Public Schools: Grade 8 MCAS English/Language Arts Achievement 1998 to 2005

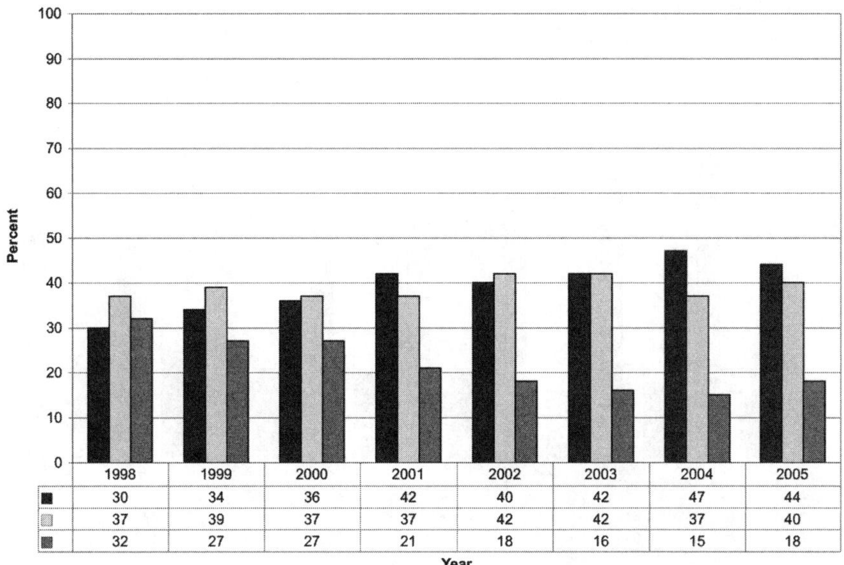

	1998	1999	2000	2001	2002	2003	2004	2005
■	30	34	36	42	40	42	47	44
▨	37	39	37	37	42	42	37	40
■	32	27	27	21	18	16	15	18

Grade 8 ELA:

- ■ **Proficient or above:** Steady but not large increases in proportion of students in this category from 1998 to 2000; large increase (6 percentage points) from 2000 to 2001; that increase basically maintained through 2005, with increase of 5 percentage points from 2003 to 2004 and slight drop back (3 percentage points) in 2005.
- ▨ **Needs Improvement:** The proportion of students in this category ranges from 37% to 42% from 1998 to 2005; no clear trend and no large increases or decreases.
- ■ **Warning:** Overall trend of steady decrease from 1998 to 2004; largest decrease from 2000 to 2001 with a drop of 6 percentage points; increase of 2 percentage points in 2005.

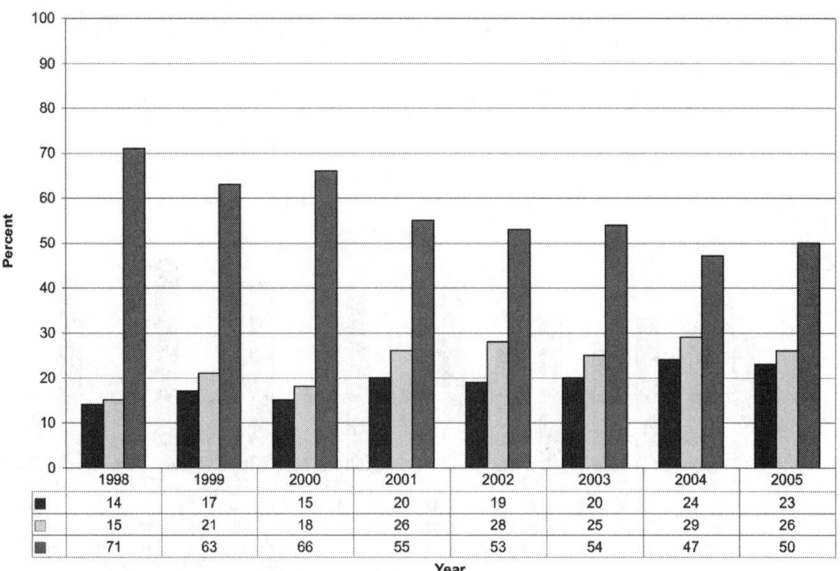

	1998	1999	2000	2001	2002	2003	2004	2005
■	14	17	15	20	19	20	24	23
░	15	21	18	26	28	25	29	26
■	71	63	66	55	53	54	47	50

Grade 8 Math:

- **Proficient or above:** No clear change from 1998 to 2000; increase of 5 percentage points from 2000 to 2001, maintained from 2001 to 2003; then another increase from 2003 to 2004 (4 percentage points); basically maintained (1 percentage point decrease) in 2005.
- **Needs Improvement:** Growth of students scoring in this category was sporadic between 1998 to 2000, then large increase from 2000 to 2001 (8 percentage points) that has been maintained, more or less, over the next 3 years.
- **Warning:** Overall steady trend of decreasing numbers of students in this category, with large decrease occurring from 1998 to 1999 (8 percentage points) and larger decrease from 2000 to 2001 (11 percentage points); since 2002, proportion hovers between 47% and 54%.

Boston Public Schools: Grade 10 MCAS English/Language Arts Achievement 1998 to 2005

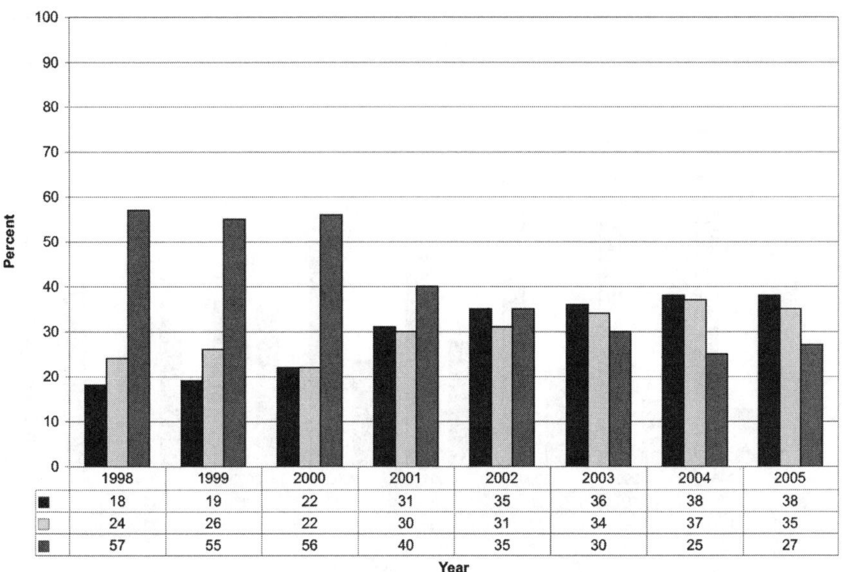

	1998	1999	2000	2001	2002	2003	2004	2005
■	18	19	22	31	35	36	38	38
▨	24	26	22	30	31	34	37	35
▩	57	55	56	40	35	30	25	27

Grade 10 ELA:

- ■ **Proficient or above:** Incremental improvement from 1998 to 2000; large increase from 2000 to 2001 (9 percentage points) and increase from 2001 to 2002 (4 percentage points); incremental progress since then.
- ▨ **Needs Improvement:** No clear trend from 1998 to 2000, but large increase from 2000 to 2001; incremental improvements in 2002 and 2003; slight drop-off in 2005 (2 percentage points).
- ▩ **Warning:** Steady and sometimes dramatic decreases of students scoring in this category, particularly from 2000 to 2001 (16 percentage points), followed by 5 percentage point decreases in 2002, 2003, and 2004; slight increase in 2005 (2 percentage points).

Boston Public Schools: Grade 10 MCAS Mathematics Achievement 1998 to 2005

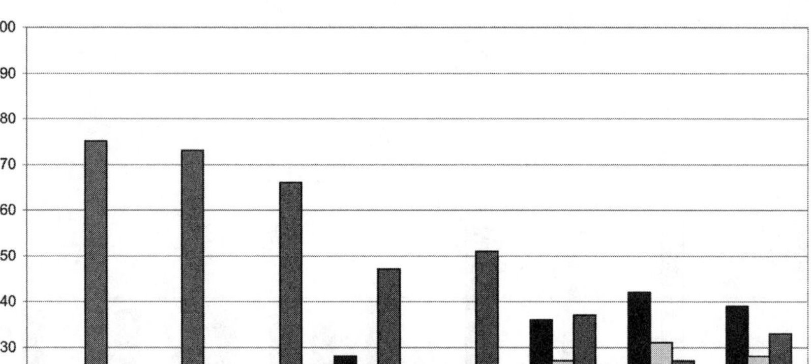

	1998	1999	2000	2001	2002	2003	2004	2005
■	13	15	22	28	24	36	42	39
▨	13	12	12	25	24	27	31	28
■	75	73	66	47	51	37	27	33

Year

Grade 10 Math:

- ■ **Proficient or above:** Fairly steady overall trend of improvement: incremental improvement from 1998 to 1999; increase of 7 percentage points from 1999 to 2000, followed by 6 point gain in 2001; 4 point drop-off in 2002, recovered with large increase in 2003 (12 percentage points), followed by 6 point gain in 2004; 3 point decrease in 2005.
- ▨ **Needs Improvement:** No real change from 1998 to 2000; dramatic increase from 2000 to 2001 (13 percentage points); basically steady in 2002 and incremental growth in 2003 and 2004, tailing off in 2005 (drop of 3 percentage points from 2004 to 2005).
- ■ **Warning:** Fairly steady trend of decreasing percentages of students in this category: no real change from 1998 to 1999, dramatic decreases in 2000 and 2001 (13 and 19 point drops respectively); 4 point increase in 2002, followed by dramatic drops in 2003 (14 points) and 2004 (10 points); 6 point growth between 2004 and 2005, but overall still 42 points lower than in 1998.

APPENDIX 1F

MCAS Performance by Race/Ethnicity, Grades 4, 7 & 8, and 10

MCAS Performance, Grade 4
Percent of Students Passing by Race/Ethnicity

English Language Arts

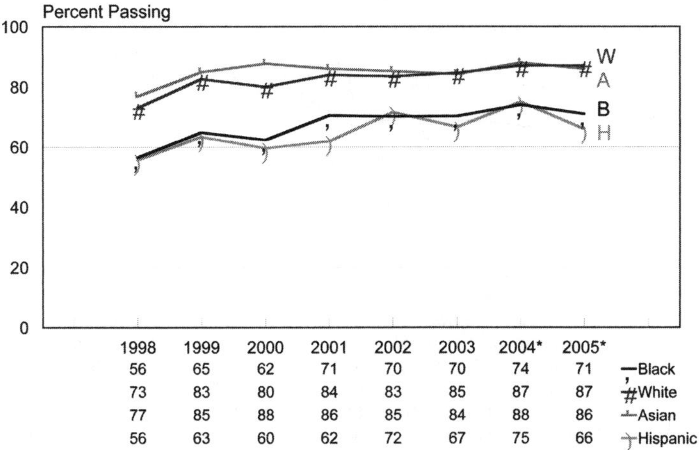

1998	1999	2000	2001	2002	2003	2004*	2005*	
56	65	62	71	70	70	74	71	Black
73	83	80	84	83	85	87	87	White
77	85	88	86	85	84	88	86	Asian
56	63	60	62	72	67	75	66	Hispanic

N & % of Native American Passing: 1998: 14 (74%) of 19; 1999: 17 (63%) of 27; 2002: 24 (80%) of 30; 2001: 18 (86%) of 21; 2002: 11 (69%) of 16; 2003: 15 (79%) of 19 2004*: 17 (74%) of 23; 2005*: 17 (71%) or 24.

Mathematics

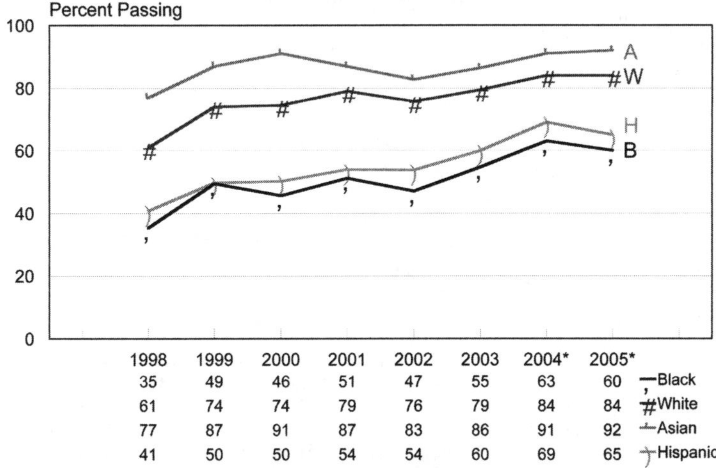

1998	1999	2000	2001	2002	2003	2004*	2005*	
35	49	46	51	47	55	63	60	Black
61	74	74	79	76	79	84	84	White
77	87	91	87	83	86	91	92	Asian
41	50	50	54	54	60	69	65	Hispanic

N & % of Native American Passing: 1998: 8 (42%) of 19; 1999: 12 (46%) of 26; 2000: 16 (53%) of 30; 2001: 17 (81%) of 21; 2002: 8 (50%) of 16; 2003: 14 (74%) of 19 2004*: 14 (61%) of 23; 2005*: 19 (80%) of 24.

Note: Grade 4 ELA test results prior to 2001 are not directly comparable with subsequent years because of changes in Performance Standards.

* SIMS file information (MCAS School and District Reports from Mass. DOE released on 9/20/04, 9/21/05)

MCAS Performance, Grades 7 & 8
Percent of Students Passing by Race/Ethnicity

English Language Arts (Grades 7 & 8)

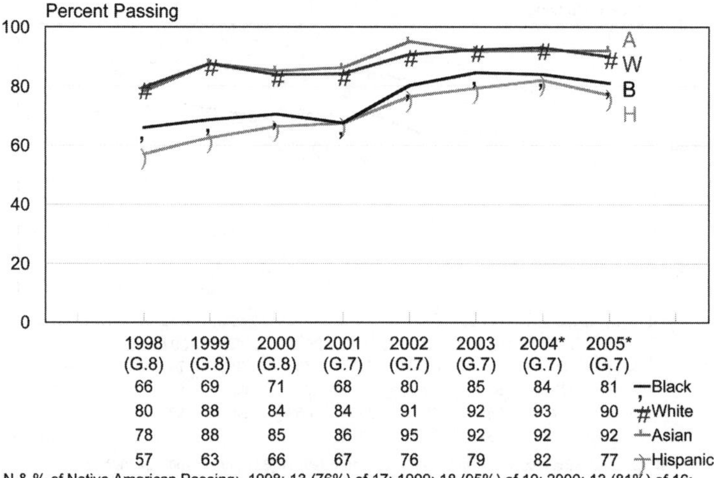

	1998 (G.8)	1999 (G.8)	2000 (G.8)	2001 (G.7)	2002 (G.7)	2003 (G.7)	2004* (G.7)	2005* (G.7)
Black	66	69	71	68	80	85	84	81
White	80	88	84	84	91	92	93	90
Asian	78	88	85	86	95	92	92	92
Hispanic	57	63	66	67	76	79	82	77

N & % of Native American Passing: 1998: 13 (76%) of 17; 1999: 18 (95%) of 19; 2000: 13 (81%) of 16; 2001: 13 (72%) of 18; 2002: 17 (77%) of 22; 2003: 17 (85%) of 20 2004*: 16 (100%) of 16; 2005*: fewer than 10 tested.

Mathematics (Grade 8)

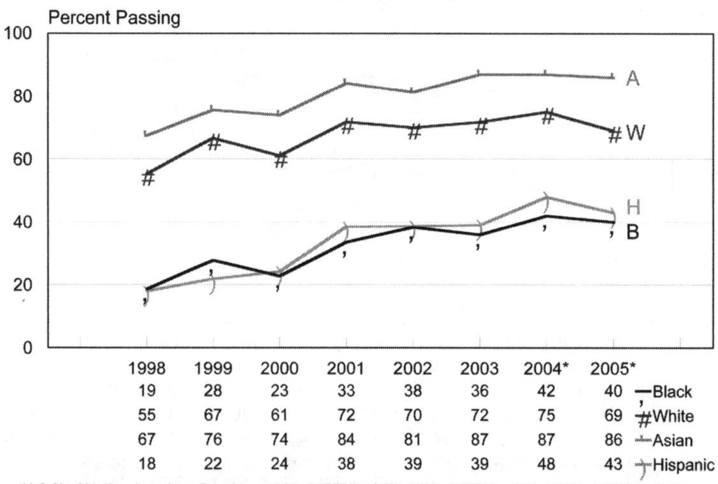

	1998	1999	2000	2001	2002	2003	2004*	2005*
Black	19	28	23	33	38	36	42	40
White	55	67	61	72	70	72	75	69
Asian	67	76	74	84	81	87	87	86
Hispanic	18	22	24	38	39	39	48	43

N & % of Native American Passing: 1998: 5 (29%) of 17; 1999: 6 (29%) of 21; 2000: 4 (25%) of 16; 2001: 10 (45%) of 22: 2002: 6 (35%) of 17; 2003: 8 (38%) of 21: 2004*: 8 (53%) of 15; 2005*: 12 (60%) of 20.

*SIMS file information (MCAS School and District Reports from Mass. DOE released on 9/20/04, 9/21/05)

MCAS Performance, Grade 10
Percent of Students Passing by Race/Ethnicity

English Language Arts

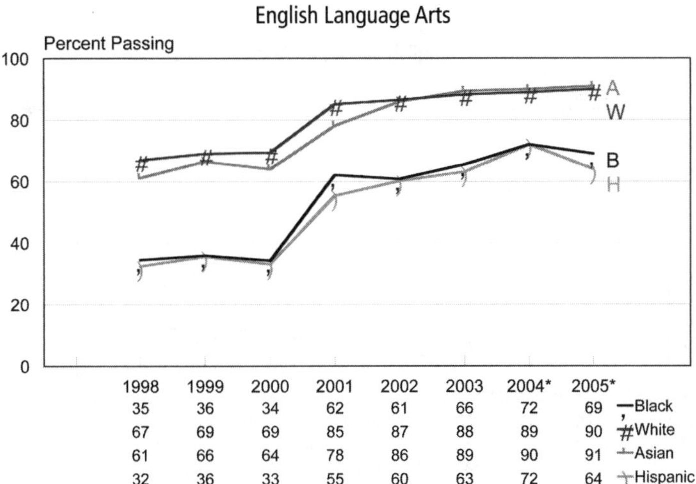

	1998	1999	2000	2001	2002	2003	2004*	2005*
Black	35	36	34	62	61	66	72	69
White	67	69	69	85	87	88	89	90
Asian	61	66	64	78	86	89	90	91
Hispanic	32	36	33	55	60	63	72	64

N & % of Native American Passing: 1998: 4 (40%) of 10; 1999: 2 (33%) of 6; 2001: 8 (89%) of 9; 2002: 7 (64%) of 11; 2003: 13 (87%) of 15; 2004*: frewer than 10 tested; 2005*: 15 (83%) of 18.

Mathematics

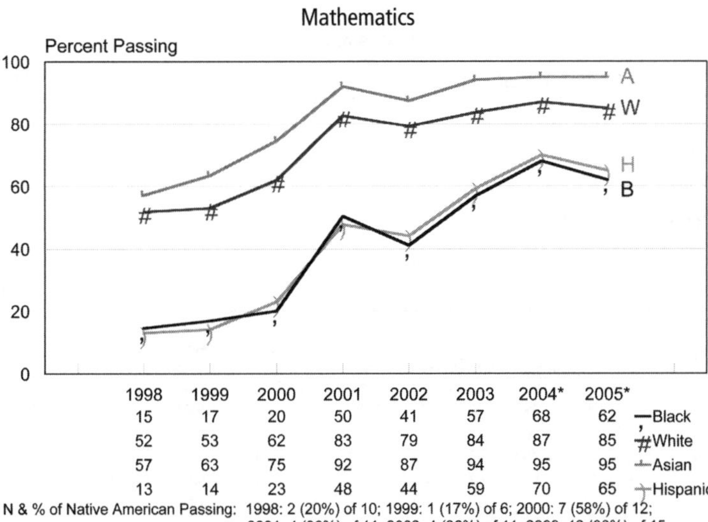

	1998	1999	2000	2001	2002	2003	2004*	2005*
Black	15	17	20	50	41	57	68	62
White	52	53	62	83	79	84	87	85
Asian	57	63	75	92	87	94	95	95
Hispanic	13	14	23	48	44	59	70	65

N & % of Native American Passing: 1998: 2 (20%) of 10; 1999: 1 (17%) of 6; 2000: 7 (58%) of 12; 2001: 4 (36%) of 11; 2002: 4 (36%) of 11; 2003: 12 (80%) of 15 2004*: 6 (55%) of 11; 2005*: 12 (67%) of 18.

* SIMS file information (MCAS School and District Reports from Mass. DOE released on 9/20/04, 9/21/05)

MCAS Performance, Grade 4
Percent of Students in Proficient and Advanced Levels by Race/Ethnicity

English Language Arts

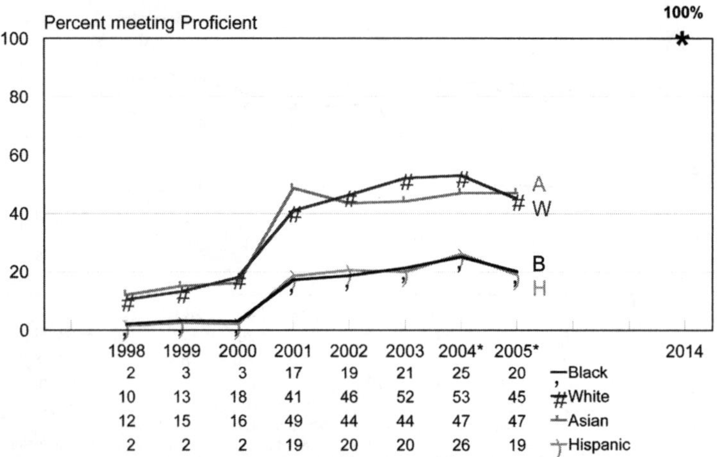

	1998	1999	2000	2001	2002	2003	2004*	2005*
Black	2	3	3	17	19	21	25	20
White	10	13	18	41	46	52	53	45
Asian	12	15	16	49	44	44	47	47
Hispanic	2	2	2	19	20	20	26	19

N & % of Native American in Proficient & Advanced Levels: 1998: 0 (0%) of 19; 1999: 2 (7%) of 27; 2000: 5 (17%) of 30; 2001: 11 (52%) of 21; 2002: 2 (13%) of 16; 2003: 7 (37%) of 19; 2004*: 8 (35%) of 23; 2005*: 7 (29%) of 24.

Mathematics

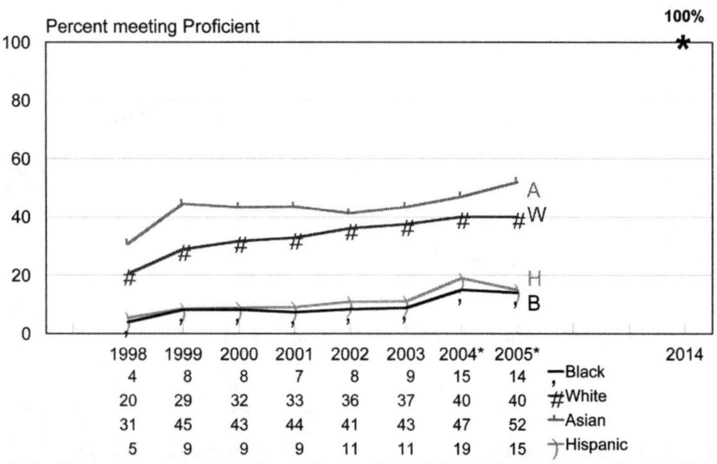

	1998	1999	2000	2001	2002	2003	2004*	2005*
Black	4	8	8	7	8	9	15	14
White	20	29	32	33	36	37	40	40
Asian	31	45	43	44	41	43	47	52
Hispanic	5	9	9	9	11	11	19	15

N & % of Native American in Proficient & Advanced Levels: 1998: 1 (5%) of 19; 1999: 2 (8%) of 26; 2000: 6 (20%) of 30; 2001: 3 (14%) of 21; 2002: 5 (31%) of 16; 2003: 2 (11%) of 19; 2004*: 3 (13%) of 23; 2005*: 4 (17%) of 24.

Note: Grade 4 ELA test results prior to 2001 are not directly comparable with subsequent years because of changes in Performance Standards.

*SIMS file information (MCAS School and District Reports from Mass. DOE released on 9/20/04, 9/21/05)

MCAS Performance, Grades 7 & 8 Percent of Students in Proficient and Advanced Levels by Race/Ethnicity

English Language Arts (Grades 7 & 8)

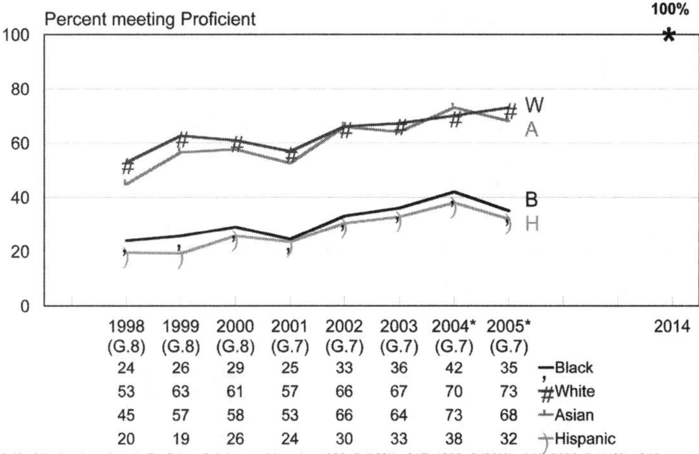

1998 (G.8)	1999 (G.8)	2000 (G.8)	2001 (G.7)	2002 (G.7)	2003 (G.7)	2004* (G.7)	2005* (G.7)		2014
24	26	29	25	33	36	42	35	Black	
53	63	61	57	66	67	70	73	White	
45	57	58	53	66	64	73	68	Asian	
20	19	26	24	30	33	38	32	Hispanic	

N & % of Native American in Proficient & Advanced Levels: 1998: 5 (29%) of 17; 1999: 6 (32%) of 19; 2000: 7 (44%) of 16; 2001: 3 (17%) of 18; 2002: 8 (36%) of 22; 2003: 11 (55%) of 20; 2004*: 13 (81%) of 16; 2005*: fewer than 10 tested.

Mathematics (Grade 8)

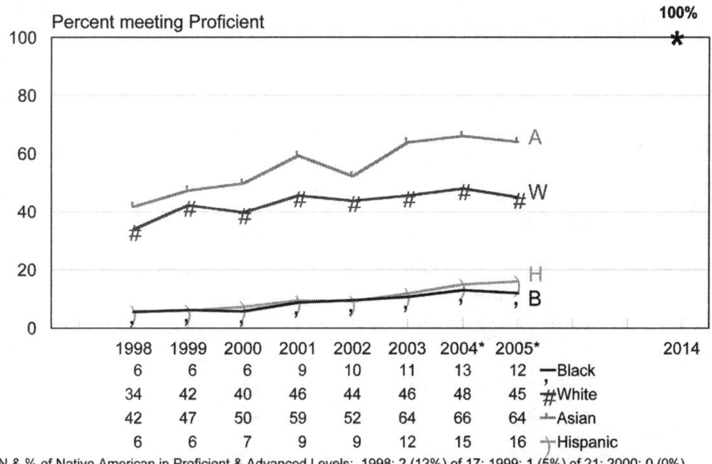

1998	1999	2000	2001	2002	2003	2004*	2005*		2014
6	6	6	9	10	11	13	12	Black	
34	42	40	46	44	46	48	45	White	
42	47	50	59	52	64	66	64	Asian	
6	6	7	9	9	12	15	16	Hispanic	

N & % of Native American in Proficient & Advanced Levels: 1998: 2 (12%) of 17; 1999: 1 (5%) of 21; 2000: 0 (0%) of 16; 2001: 5 (23%) of 22; 2002: 0 (0%) of 17; 2003: 2 (10%) of 21; 2004*: 5 (33%) of 15; 2005*: 4 (25%) of 20.

* SIMS file information (MCAS School and District Reports from Mass. DOE released on 9/20/04, 9/21/05)

MCAS Performance, Grade 10
Percent of Students in Proficient and Advanced Levels by Race/Ethnicity

English Language Arts

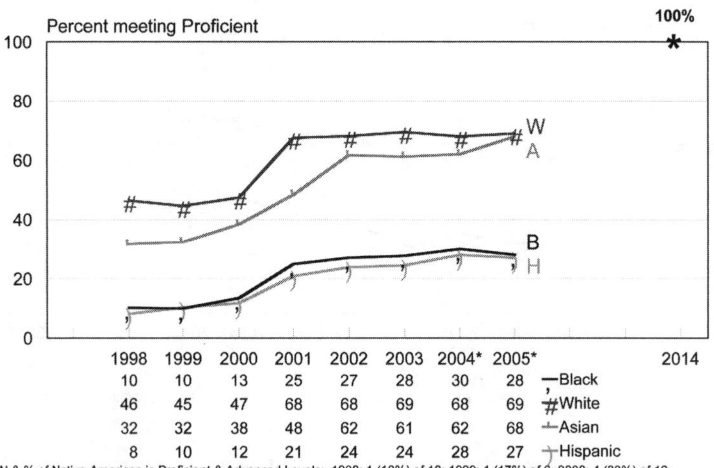

	1998	1999	2000	2001	2002	2003	2004*	2005*	2014
Black	10	10	13	25	27	28	30	28	
White	46	45	47	68	68	69	68	69	
Asian	32	32	38	48	62	61	62	68	
Hispanic	8	10	12	21	24	24	28	27	

N & % of Native American in Proficient & Advanced Levels: 1998: 1 (10%) of 10; 1999: 1 (17%) of 6; 2000: 4 (33%) of 12; 2001: 4 (44%) of 9; 2002: 1 (9%) of 11; 2003: 9 (60%) of 15; 2004*: fewer than 10 tested, 2005*: 9 (50%) of 18.

Mathematics

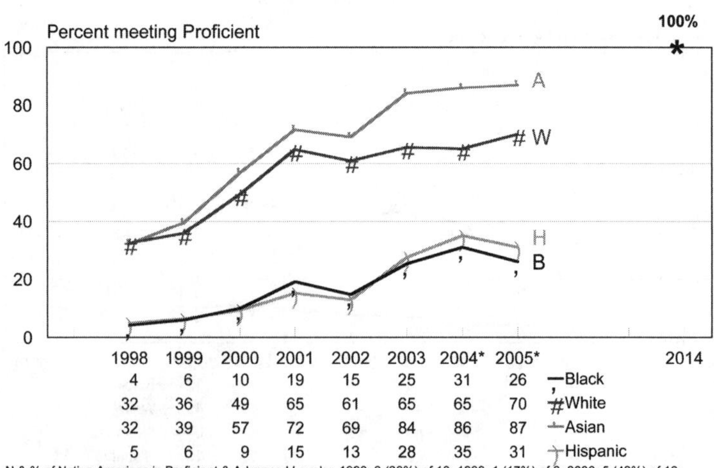

	1998	1999	2000	2001	2002	2003	2004*	2005*	2014
Black	4	6	10	19	15	25	31	26	
White	32	36	49	65	61	65	65	70	
Asian	32	39	57	72	69	84	86	87	
Hispanic	5	6	9	15	13	28	35	31	

N & % of Native American in Proficient & Advanced Levels: 1998: 2 (20%) of 10; 1999: 1 (17%) of 6; 2000: 5 (42%) of 12; 2001: 1 (9%) of 11; 2002: 0 (0%) of 11; 2003: 8 (53%) of 15; 2004*: 0 (0%) of 11, 2005*: 8 (45%) of 18.

*SIMS file information (MCAS School and District Reports from Mass. DOE released on 9/20/04, 9/21/05)

CHAPTER 11

Governance and the Boston Public Schools

JOHN H. PORTZ

SINCE 1995, the Boston Public Schools has enjoyed a level of stability in its governance that is nearly unique among urban school systems. During this eleven-year period, Thomas M. Menino served as mayor of the city and Thomas W. Payzant served as superintendent of the school department. In addition, only two different chairpersons sat at the helm of the Boston School Committee, and similarly, two different presidents guided the Boston Teachers Union. This continuity in leadership among key education actors stands in sharp contrast to the typical turnover and frequent turmoil in most urban school districts.

What has this stability and continuity meant for the Boston Public Schools? In part, the chapters in this book are responses to that question. The focus in this chapter is on the governance system itself. In 1992, Boston embarked upon a new governance arrangement in which the mayor appointed members of the school committee. This was a major break from the days of an elected school committee. Whereas previous mayors avoided the school system, now the mayor is at the center of political and fiscal accountability for public education. The story of how Boston arrived at this governance arrangement—and what it has meant for the school system—are the central concerns of this chapter.

GOVERNANCE AND PUBLIC SCHOOLS

The term "governance" refers to the authority structure by which major decisions are made and resources are allocated within a school system. As defined in a report by the Education Commission of the States, "governance arrangements establish the rules of the game, that is . . . who is responsible and accountable for what within the system."[1] A long-time observer of school politics noted that "governance is about control—who drives the educational bus."[2] Put differently, a recent study of school boards describes governing as "steering" the school district.[3] Governing involves the establishment of educational goals and policies that follow a vision and set of core beliefs about how academic achievement can be realized.

Historically, school boards have played a central role in governance. Typically elected, school board members represent the community as they oversee and guide the school district. In recent years, school boards have come under criticism for a host of reasons, including their frequent involvement in managerial aspects of school operations such as hiring principals, teachers, and other staff, as well as their ineffectiveness at improving overall educational outcomes.[4] To be certain, school boards do not act alone or unfettered. They operate within numerous rules and regulations established by state governments and, to a lesser extent, federal authorities. The superintendent also typically plays a role in school district governance, and professional associations, particularly the teachers union, might also have major governance responsibilities.

In recent years communities have been experimenting with other governance mechanisms. A market model, for example, is increasingly popular. Market governance uses the choices made by parents and students in the educational marketplace to drive the allocation of school resources, instead of relying upon traditional school bureaucracies and hierarchical systems like school boards. The school system is guided in setting goals and making policy by strategies that measure "customer satisfaction," such as school choice, charter schools, and vouchers.

In contrast, state departments of education in New Jersey and other states have moved back to bureaucratic decision making, assuming control of failing school districts. In some instances, this exercise of state authority is prompted by the financial failure of a school district that cannot balance its budget, but increasingly states are taking over in response to educational failures. In this form of governance, resource allocation is controlled by government bureaucrats.

In a more overt political strategy, mayors in a number of cities have become key actors through new powers, typically granted by state government, over school districts. Mayoral control can take different forms, but the most common involve appointment powers as well as fiscal controls. With respect to appointments, mayors are given authority to appoint school board members and, in some instances, the superintendent as well. With respect to fiscal controls, mayors are granted authority over the total funding support received by the school system. These appointment and budget powers move the mayor to center stage in the debates over school reform. In contrast to Progressive-era efforts to depoliticize school systems, mayoral control makes city hall a key actor in determining the allocation of resources in the school system.

Boston has chosen the strategy of mayoral influence and control. It is not alone. Mayors in New York City, Chicago, Washington, D.C., Cleveland, Philadelphia, Baltimore, and several other cities also are playing a major role in their respective school systems.[5] Mayoral involvement in governance is intended to align political and financial resources in the city in support of public education. In almost every instance, these are mayors in strong-mayor systems who exercise considerable authority over the allocation of resources within the city. Involvement in school policy brings the mayor into a system of "integrated governance" in which political and financial control is centralized to create a more rational and systematic allocation of educational resources.[6] Reaching this level of mayoral involvement, however, is not simple or without controversy, as we have seen in the Boston experience.

The "Stars" Are Aligned: The School Committee, Superintendent, and Mayor

The debate over school governance in Boston dominated school politics in the late 1980s and early 1990s.[7] Boston's thirteen-member elected school committee was at the center of the debate. It was widely criticized for political opportunism, policy fragmentation, and fiscal irresponsibility.[8] Battles over school closures were commonplace and racial divisions were prominent.

Claims of fiscal mismanagement were rooted in an institutional arrangement that clouded accountability. In particular, the school committee controlled the allocation of resources *within the school budget*, but the mayor and city council set the *total appropriation* for the school department. In this fiscally dependent arrangement, the school committee often decried city hall for providing inadequate financial resources to operate the school system, while city hall complained of having no control over the allocation of school monies. The school committee typically refused to make expenditure adjustments equal to those requested by city hall and would end the year in a deficit, requiring a last-minute appropriation from the mayor and city council.

Criticism was widespread of school governance generally and of the school committee in particular. The Boston Municipal Research Bureau, a business-supported government "watchdog" organization, had long advocated for greater clarity in governance roles by having the school committee focus on policy-making while the superintendent managed the school system.[9] During the late 1970s and mid-1980s, several legislative changes were made to clarify the relationships among the superintendent, school committee, and city hall, but problems persisted. The school committee received the focus of attention. A *Boston Globe* editorial described the school committee as "a disaster . . . [with] infighting, grandstanding, aspirations for higher political office, and incompetence . . . the system is floundering," and a mayoral commission declared that "frustration with school performance had reached an historic high" and that changes in governance were critical to the future of the system.[10] After reviewing the governance system for the schools, the study concluded: "Boston is unique. The buck does not appear to stop anywhere."[11]

The mayor's role was limited in this system. Boston's strong-mayor form of government granted the mayor extensive authority over the city side of local government, but a limited role in school policy. Administrative control of the schools resided with the superintendent and school committee and, as noted earlier, the allocation of funds within the school budget was outside the formal power of the mayor. Boston's mayors typically maintained an arm's-length distance from the public schools. Mayor Kevin White (1967–83) was a coalition builder who played a cautious role in desegregation debates and other discussions of school policy. Mayor Raymond Flynn (1984–93) also was hesitant during the early years of his tenure to become involved in school politics. As Flynn noted in remarks prepared for the business community, "public education is an area that can swallow up the most promising career and politicians are counseled at every step to 'stay away from the schools.'"[12]

Calls for a change in governance became increasingly widespread in the media and among many in the city, particularly in the business community.[13] Mayor Flynn also became more vocal in his criticisms and began to propose changes in governance. Among the governance proposals floated for consideration were elimination of the school committee along with direct appointment of the superintendent by the mayor and, as a less drastic alternative, a school committee composed of a mix of mayoral appointees and elected members.

The most popular governance proposal, particularly among state officials, was to replace the elected school committee with one appointed by the mayor. In April 1991, the city council approved, by a nine-to-four vote, a home-rule petition to the state to create a seven-member school committee appointed by the mayor. The two black members of the city council voted against the change, criticizing the loss of voting power for Boston's residents.[14] Debate continued, but the new committee structure received state approval, and Mayor Flynn, working from a list provided by a nominating committee, appointed seven individuals to begin terms in January 1992.

The shift to mayoral appointment marked a sharp break in school governance. Yet to be resolved, however, was how leadership within the school system would mesh with the new political control exercised by the mayor. More specifically, Superintendent Lois Harrison-Jones, Boston's second black superintendent who was hired in mid-1991 by the elected committee, now found herself working for the newly-appointed committee and, indirectly, for the mayor. The honeymoon was brief. Disagreements between the mayor and superintendent became increasingly public. The controversy subsided, at least temporarily, when Mayor Flynn resigned in mid-1993 to join the Clinton administration as ambassador to the Vatican. City council president Thomas Menino became acting mayor, then won the special election in November 1993.

With a new mayor in city hall, the relationship between the superintendent, school committee, and mayor was less volatile, but tensions continued. The superintendent pointed to the intervention of Boston politics into public education, while the mayor and others became increasingly critical of the superintendent's performance. In early 1995, Superintendent Harrison-Jones was informed that her contract, due to expire in July, would not be renewed. The school committee initiated a broad public search process. In July and August three finalists were interviewed and an offer was extended to Thomas Payzant, assistant secretary in the U.S. Department of Education and former superintendent in San Diego and Oklahoma City. Payzant accepted and became superintendent in September of 1995.

The key ingredients for school reform were now in place. As one school principal commented in an interview with the author, successful school reform requires that the mayor, superintendent, school committee, and school administrators be in accord, or as he put it, "all the planets have to be lined up." Since 1995, as noted earlier, the continuity in school governance has been striking. Payzant remained as superintendent for almost eleven years, retiring on June 30, 2006. He is the longest serving superintendent in the Boston schools since 1960. Thomas Menino, elected in 1993, continues as mayor, having won elections in 1997, 2001, and 2005. In 1997 he ran unopposed and won easily in the subsequent two elections. This continuity with the mayor and superintendent has provided a degree of stability in Boston that is rare among urban school systems.

Continuity also is the theme on the mayoral-appointed Boston School Committee as well as the Boston Teachers Union (BTU). For the school committee, the current chair, Elizabeth Reilinger, has served in that capacity for over seven years (since January 1998) and has been a committee member since January 1994. In more than a dozen years on the school committee, she has worked closely with both Payzant and Menino. For the Boston Teachers Union, Edward Doherty served as president of the union for twenty years, leaving the post in 2003. His replacement, Richard Stutman, is a long-time union member and teacher in the Boston school system.

This alignment of individuals has played an important role in fostering communication and cooperation around school improvement. To be certain, tensions sometimes develop, particularly during collective bargaining negotiations with the union, but familiarity among these key leaders plays a major role in sustaining broad support for the school system. Having worked together for a number of years, these leaders have developed adaptive styles that recognize the interests and proclivities of each. Mayor Menino and Superintendent Payzant, for example, have a working relationship that accommodates the political interests of the mayor while acknowledging the educational expertise of the superintendent.

This governance arrangement has received general support from Boston voters over the years. The clearest test of public approval came in November 1996, when a ballot question was put to the voters. Required by the state legislation that authorized the appointed committee, this ballot gave voters the choice of returning to a 13-member elected committee (a "yes" vote on the ballot) or keeping the seven-member appointed committee (a "no" vote). The appointed committee won the day, receiving 53 percent of the votes, compared to 23 percent for returning to an elected committee, and 23 percent blank votes. Said

Menino, "The message was clear throughout Boston that we should continue the progress we've made in the schools."[15]

Although the appointed committee won by a two-to-one margin among votes cast, it received less support within the minority community.[16] In two of Boston's twenty-two voting wards—minority areas in Roxbury and Dorchester—the appointed committee lost in the balloting. In general, in predominately black precincts, the average vote in favor of returning to an elected committee was 55 percent; in predominately white precincts the comparable vote was 28 percent. The African American community was considerably more inclined to support a return to an elected committee. Overall support in the city, however, remained strong for the appointed committee.

What has this new governance system meant for school politics and public education? In several areas the change is quite significant. As described below, Mayor Menino has raised the agenda status of education while the general nature of public discourse around education has shifted. Continuity in leadership has facilitated numerous reform efforts, and the mayor has supported an increase in financial resources for the schools. The school system has received national attention and praise.

MAYORAL SUPPORT

One of the most significant changes prompted by the new governance arrangement is strong mayoral support for public education in Boston. As noted earlier, under the elected-committee structure, mayors generally kept their distance from a school system over which they had little control. With the power to appoint committee members, however, this changed. This shift is evident in at least two ways: first, attention to the schools in the policy process, and second, financial support for the schools.

Setting the policy agenda is one of the most important sources of mayoral power. Particularly in strong-mayor cities, mayors have numerous opportunities to direct the course of public policy. Inaugural addresses, state-of-the-city speeches, budget messages, executive appointments, and public forums provide mayors with opportunities to shape the policy process. The Boston mayor's authority over school affairs has been accompanied by a significant elevation of public education on the policy agenda. Exemplifying this shift in attention are two excerpts from different annual state-of-the-city speeches. In early 1991, *prior* to the appointed committee, Mayor Flynn emphasized the traditional goals for Boston:

> The priorities in Boston are clear. Government has a job to do. We're going to keep providing the basic city services that you need and deserve, like maintaining the parks, picking up the trash, and having dedicated fire fighters and EMTs there when you need them . . . our number one priority is safe neighborhoods.[17]

Five years later, with an appointed committee in place and Payzant as superintendent, Mayor Menino outlined a distinctly different list of priorities in a state-of-the-city speech delivered at the Jeremiah Burke High School, which had just lost accreditation:

> Economic security. Good jobs. Safe streets. Quality of life. Public health. Those are the spokes of the wheel—but do you know what the HUB of that wheel is? Public education! . . . GOOD PUBLIC SCHOOLS ARE AT THE CENTER OF IT ALL![18]

In fact, Menino started that address with the statement:

> I want to be judged as your mayor by what happens now in the Boston public schools. . . . If I fail to bring about these specific reforms by the year 2001, then judge me harshly.

This shift in attention is captured by a content analysis of state-of-the-city speeches. During the last seven years of an elected committee, from 1985 through 1991, Mayor Flynn's state-of-the-city speeches devoted an average of only 3.7 percent of each speech to education.[19] In contrast, Mayors Flynn and Menino devoted an average of 28.4 percent of each speech to education during the first seven years of an appointed committee, from 1992 through 1998. Mayor Menino, in particular, used state-of-the-city speeches to highlight a range of reform efforts that included more computers in classrooms, expanded literacy programs, more extended-day programs, and other school improvement strategies. As one long-time observer of school politics notes, Mayor Menino became the school system's "biggest cheerleader."

The budget of the Boston Public Schools provides a second measure of the strength of the mayor's support for them. From the state and the city, the Boston Public Schools has received a growing piece of the city's fiscal pie, particularly in the mid- and late 1990s. The agenda status accorded to the schools translated into financial support. Although the recent economic and fiscal downturn has hit the schools as well as most other departments, the overall level of financial support remains significant.

Financial support for the schools is evident by a number of measures. As a percentage of general fund expenditures from the city, the school department's portion increased from the elected-committee to the appointed-committee years. During the last seven years of the elected-committee system, the school department averaged 31.6 percent of the city's general fund expenditures. During the first seven years of the appointed-committee system, this average increased to 35.9 percent, reaching a peak of 37.2 percent in fiscal year 2000.[20]

The total increase in school spending compared to spending for the police and fire departments reveals a similar trend. During the last seven years of the elected-committee system, general fund spending by the school department increased 49 percent, while general fund spending for police and fire increased 57 percent. In contrast, during the first seven years under the appointed-committee system, the increase in general fund spending for the school department actually exceeded police and fire: 55 percent compared to 52 percent.

This financial support for the school system during the 1990s is significant, although it should be noted that an increase in state school aid to Boston was a major contributor to the increase. The mayor was a major supporter of this increase in state aid, and Boston was a beneficiary. In addition, Boston has not been immune to cuts during hard times. In the early and mid-2000s, a downturn in the city's and state's economy led to level funding, at best, for the school system. With fixed costs continuing to increase, the school department reduced the workforce, including teacher layoffs, in order to balance the budget.

THE SCHOOL COMMITTEE AND THE COMMUNITY: A CHANGE IN PUBLIC DISCOURSE

Mayoral appointment and the new governance system have contributed to a change in the public discourse around school issues. Commented one business leader, "We have a mayor, a superintendent and a school committee singing from the same sheet of music."[21] Over the last eleven years, this accord, along with a state and national focus on school accountability and student achievement, has resulted in a shift in public discourse from conflict and sharp debate to a more consensual environment focused upon education issues.

This change in discourse is evident in how the school committee operates and relates to the public. Under an elected school committee, discussions concerning public education were often contentious and lengthy. Committee meetings were notable for their duration, averaging three hours in 1989 and 1990, and a divided committee was typical. In 1989 and 1990, 88 percent of committee votes included at least one dissenting member.[22] On occasion, a member would leave the meeting in disgust. Racial divisions were sometimes prominent in these debates. In 1990, for example, the four black members walked out in protest before the committee voted seven to one to fire Laval Wilson, the district's first black superintendent.

In an elected committee environment, interaction with the public was frequent and service oriented. In 1989 and 1990, the committee held ten public hearings on a range of topics. Outside of hearings, committee members frequently responded to complaints from parents. Each committee member received a $52,000 office allotment that was typically used to hire a staff person to receive phone calls from parents and other residents with complaints about school services. This constituent orientation provided a readily accessible avenue for citizen concerns and also prompted committee involvement in school operations.

Public interaction and discourse have changed significantly under an appointed committee. A more consensual dialogue has replaced contentious debate, racial divisions, and constituent services. In contrast to the long meetings and divided votes, the typical meeting of the appointed committee is shorter and less contentious. In 1994 and 1995, for example, committee meetings averaged 1 hour and 35 minutes, one-half as long as those under the elected committee, and the board voted unanimously on 98 percent of the votes during those two years.[23] A recent tabulation of committee votes found a similar pattern: all but one out of 121 nonprocedural votes in 2004 and 2005 were unanimous.[24]

With the appointed committee, public participation is less constituent-based and has generally declined. Appointed committee members lack the electoral incentives to seek parental input. For outreach, the appointed committee occasionally holds meetings in school buildings around the city and sponsors periodic public forums, but citizen participation is generally less than it was under the elected committee. In 1994 and 1995, for example, the appointed committee held five public hearings, compared to ten held by the elected committee in 1989 and 1990.

The consensual style of school committee meetings reflects the generally professional background of the members. Most appointed members have professional and/or administrative experiences that include higher education, business, and community organizations. Although the elected committee also included some individuals with such backgrounds, elected members by their nature were more attuned to the campaign trail of community meetings and voter forums and often sought to distinguish themselves for future electoral purposes.

The professionally oriented and consensual nature of the school committee has created an environment more compatible with business and institutional partners. The Boston Plan for Excellence and the Private Industry Council, in particular, work closely with the mayor and superintendent in shaping school reform. Both organizations supported the schools in the days of an elected committee, but mayoral accountability and an appointed school committee appeal to these partners as a rational way to exercise leadership in the otherwise fragmented world of public education.

The Boston Plan for Excellence shifted its focus in 1995 from scholarships and teacher minigrants to a much more involved role as a partner with the school system in designing and implementing school reform. The Boston Plan supported whole-school improvement throughout the district, and it focused considerable effort on developing and implementing a teacher coaching model known as Collaborative Coaching and Learning.[25] In the last few years, the Boston Plan also has been working with the Boston Private Industry Council and Jobs for the Future to support the school department's initiative to create smaller learning communities at the district high schools. To support these and other activities, the Boston Plan played a key role in raising more than $65 million between 1995 and 2004. This included two grants from the Annenberg Foundation as well as grants from the Carnegie Foundation, the Gates Foundation, and other donors.

The Private Industry Council hosts the Boston Compact, an agreement among city government, the public schools, business, labor, higher education, and community groups to support the Boston Public Schools. First signed in 1982, the Compact was reauthorized in 1989, 1994, and most recently in 2000. As Mayor Menino said at the last signing ceremony, "The only way we are going to meet the goals we share for our students . . . is if we all work together. Everyone here today recognizes that he or she is a stakeholder in education reform because our students are the future of this city."[26] The Compact focuses on three key goals: support for students to pass state-mandated tests; increase in student opportunities for college and career success; and recruitment and retention of new teachers and principals.

This change in public discourse has both critics and proponents. A common criticism is the lack of meaningful opportunities for discussion and debate of key policy decisions. As one longtime observer of the schools notes, there is very limited "space for discussion" of positions that conflict with those of the mayor, superintendent, and school committee. The close alignment among these three parties with respect to school issues has created an environment less receptive to criticism and challenges.[27]

The school committee meetings are commonly criticized for failing to truly debate issues and for making many decisions prior to public meetings, resulting in few dissenting votes. One community activist described the committee as a "rubber stamp," while a long-time educator questioned the committee for not "challenging" more of the proposals from the superintendent and mayor.[28] Increasingly, community activists and others are turning to the city council and its education committee as a venue to raise concerns and grievances.

Public critiques of the school system still exist, but they are difficult to sustain over time. Critical Friends, for example, was a citizen and community activist watchdog group formed at the time of Payzant's appointment. The group produced several reports critical of reform efforts, encouraging school leaders to make a "shift from rhetoric to radical action" in order to produce "significant, long-term and systemic" change.[29] Critical Friends faded as an organization by the end of the 1990s, although some of the key actors continued to observe and comment on the school system. With Payzant's departure imminent, several former members of Critical Friends were joined by others in the community to produce a report entitled, "Transforming the Boston Public Schools: A Roadmap for the New Superintendent." While recognizing some accomplishments over the past eleven years, the report focused on numerous shortfalls in the schools, concluding that the school system "urgently needed transformative change" if all students are to succeed.[30]

Proponents, however, point to the successes and accomplishments of the school system as well as the recognition received by Superintendent Payzant, the school committee, and Mayor Menino. As noted below and in other chapters in this volume, the school department has sustained a sharp focus on teaching and learning and overall test scores have risen during this period. The school committee, although less connected to the electorate, is seen by many as a more efficient and effective forum for discussions of educational policy. Even among many in the minority community, there is recognition that the appointed school committee has been relatively successful in focusing on educational matters. The committee, for example, approved successive districtwide improvement plans, citywide learning standards, and other reform initiatives.

The key education players in the governance system have received national attention. Mayor Menino is widely recognized among urban mayors as a leader in building and sustaining political support for public education. Superintendent Payzant has received numerous recognitions, including the 2004 Richard B. Green Award in Urban Excellence from the Council of Great City Schools and a 2005 Public Official of the Year award from *Governing* magazine. In 2004, the Boston School Committee received the first Award for Urban School Board Excellence from the National School Boards Association/Council of Urban Boards of Education. And finally, in 2006, the Boston Public Schools won the prestigious Broad Prize for Urban Education. As a finalist in the previous four years, the school system has been recognized consistently by a panel of educators and civic leaders as a leader among urban school districts in the effort to improve student achievement.

SCHOOL DEPARTMENT: A FOCUS ON TEACHING AND LEARNING

A common criticism of school systems, particularly urban school systems, is the frequent turnover of leaders and change in reform policies that then result in little, if any, improvement in the system. Rick Hess refers to "policy churn" and the constant "spinning of wheels" as the norm in urban education.[31] Boston is not immune to this charge, but in general, with the support of its governance structure, it has sustained a focus on reform that is unusual among urban school systems.

Superintendent Payzant launched a number of major reforms within the school system. In 1996 the superintendent proposed and the school committee adopted *Focus on Children* as a five-year reform plan for the schools.[32] Whole-school change is the guiding educational philosophy of this reform plan. With an emphasis on instructional improvement, the plan highlights Six Essentials of Whole-School Improvement: literacy and mathematics instruction, applying student work and data, professional development, replicating best practices, aligning resources with an instructional focus, and community engagement (see Appendix, page 271, for a complete description of the Six Essentials). Support for this reform effort came from the business community and an Annenberg grant. In 2001, the school committee adopted *Focus on Children II* as the next five-year plan to continue whole-school improvement within the system. Although some criticize these plans as vague, two successive and complementary five-year plans as a framework for reform is quite unusual in urban school systems.

A number of other reform initiatives have been put in place in recent years, some of which have been prompted by the Massachusetts Education Reform Act of 1993. The school department, for example, adopted citywide learning standards that are aligned with state standards. Along with these standards and the extension of whole-school change, a major focus is on improving literacy and mathematical skills. A rigorous promotion policy was adopted, and at the high school level, a number of schools are being restructured into smaller learning communities to support closer teacher-student interaction and better learning opportunities.

School reforms are present in a number of other areas as well. Since 1998, for example, all five-year-olds are guaranteed a full day of kindergarten. The school committee negotiated a class-size reduction plan with the teachers union, and a technology initiative increased dramatically the number of computers in the classroom. To expand school options, the school committee and Boston Teachers Union agreed to establish Pilot Schools within the district that operate with greater flexibility from school department regulations and union work rules. And to increase accountability, the school department put in place an extensive review system that includes an in-depth analysis with site visits at all schools. In addition, beyond reforms within school buildings, the superintendent sits as a member of the mayor's cabinet and works with other city departments to provide services that benefit school-age children.

The result of all this work has been some improvements in student academic achievement, although the record is mixed. As noted elsewhere in this volume, the school department can point to student test score gains over the last ten years. However, such gains are overshadowed by the challenge that remains to bring students to proficiency levels, as required by federal legislation. For example, based upon the 2005 state-mandated Massachusetts Comprehensive Assessment System (MCAS) tests, only 39 percent of tenth grade students scored at the proficiency or higher level in math, and only 38 percent performed similarly on the English language arts test. Over half of Boston's tenth-grade students are either failing or in need of improvement on these tests. The achievement gap also is a major concern. On the 2005 tenth-grade MCAS math test, for example, 87 percent of Asian and 70 percent of white students scored proficient or higher, while only 26 percent of black and 31 percent of Hispanic students scored at that higher level.

CONCLUSION

Important changes in political institutions—like school boards—are rarely neutral. They reshape political and policy processes, often shifting advantages and disadvantages among different groups and interests. So also, Boston's move to a new governance structure for public education has altered the city's political and policy world. Boston is fourteen years into this experiment. The public appears to accept the system, although a current of dissent persists. This governance system is praised for the continuity in leadership, attention, and resources it has brought to public education, but it also has raised concerns over the changing nature of school politics, policy debate, and citizen participation.

Placing the mayor at the center of school politics has raised the visibility of public education, and it has linked city hall and the school department in a cooperative manner not seen under the elected committee structure. Mayor Menino's frequent references to education in his state-of-the-city speeches are indicative of this trend. The substantial financial resources provided to the schools also highlight significant city support. Along with this support and visibility has come a more consensual style of decision making in which the mayor plays a key role. As the mayor stated in a speech for the Education Writers Association, "In a nutshell, when it comes to school change—the mayor must be like the hub in a wheel—you have got to be in the center to keep things rolling."[33]

Importantly, the mayor is part of a stable leadership structure that is rare among big city school systems. Mayor Menino and Superintendent Payzant have been educational partners for eleven years, and the Boston Teachers Union and the school committee have had very stable leadership. It is possible that this continuity could be achieved under an elected committee structure, but less likely given the dynamics of the electoral process. This period of stable leadership matches what Richard Wallace, a highly-acclaimed superintendent in Pittsburgh in the 1980s, noted as the necessary period to bring about significant change in an urban school system.[34]

This governance structure and the leadership continuity that has resulted are powerful *enabling factors* in support of school reform. They create a platform for coherent, consistent, and focused reform efforts that can be sustained over a period of years. This is a major accomplishment in any policy system, particularly in an urban educational arena. For the Boston schools, the last eleven years of Tom Payzant's superintendency have been marked by considerable progress. The school district and its governance leaders have been recognized by national organizations for their accomplishments. Even a recent report that is quite critical of the school system acknowledges that the Payzant years have provided a "solid platform for change."[35]

Enabling reform efforts, however, does not guarantee success. Are the correct policies chosen? Are they successfully implemented? For Boston, success as measured by student achievement remains elusive. Although progress has been made, most students in the Boston schools are still performing below the proficient standard on the MCAS, achievement gaps by race and student status continue, and the high school dropout rate remains high. The "stars" are aligned. Reform policies and practices are in place. But major challenges remain.

Can Boston's educational governance system help the school district to meet these challenges? The system certainly has strengths, but there are limitations as well. For one, as some have noted, there tends to be limited or circumscribed debate around educational policies. Critiques do not always reach decision makers in a consistent and coherent manner. Indeed, a tightly-aligned governance structure often is not conducive to debate and the weighing of alternatives. As the authors of one study of Boston note, "maybe there is too much stability, and perhaps the stars are *too* aligned," a situation that thereby reduces the pressure for reassessment and alternative reform strategies.[36] Furthermore, with an elected mayor at the center of this governance system, criticisms can become politically charged instead of remaining focused on educational policies. In Boston's governance system, the virtue of a sustained focus on chosen reform policies can come at the cost of close and systematic scrutiny of those very policies and practices. Building both a sustained focus and systematic scrutiny into a governance system is an important and challenging step.

Boston's governance system also is dependent upon the interests and personalities of key individuals, particularly the mayor and superintendent. In fact, good chemistry between these two is critical to the success of this system. However, a mayor's goals and aspirations can dominate educational policymaking. As one long-time observer of school politics describes the current structure, "it all depends on who the mayor is." Mayor Menino has been very supportive of public education, but a future mayor may be less inclined that way. Also, a mayor could turn the schools into a political "commodity" for patronage and other political purposes.[37] Mayor Menino has not pursued this path, but it could happen under a different mayor.

The superintendent's personality and professional orientation also is very important. Superintendent Payzant is generally recognized as an educator who preferred an incremental approach to school reform. The next superintendent might follow a similar path, or perhaps this person will take a very different approach. Given the important role of the superintendent in this governance system, the school system faces a potentially major shift in policies and practices. Some observers of the schools argue that such a major change is indeed needed. It does, however, represent an important part of the governance structure and pose a major challenge for future school reform efforts.

To be certain, the challenges of urban school reform—and the possibilities for success in Boston—are compounded by the social and economic conditions typical of most cities, including Boston. Over 70 percent of Boston Public School students are eligible for free and reduced-price lunch, a general indicator of poverty. Resources to support learning outside the school (at home and in the community) are often limited. Racial divisions in the classroom and in the community add another dimension to the school challenge.

Confronting these challenges along with the departure of Superintendent Payzant, Boston's school governance structure faces an important test. The mayor and new superintendent, whoever is chosen, along with the school committee and Boston Teachers Union, must work together to take school reform to the next level of student achievement. By many accounts, the pace and intensity of reform must intensify and deepen if a proficient level of student achievement is to be the norm. Boston's governance structure with the mayor in a prominent position places this challenge in the political arena. In contrast to the progressive-era legacy of removing schools from politics, a system of mayoral appointment places the schools in the larger political arena of the city. There are trade-offs with such a strategy, but in an era of generally tight fiscal constraints, as exists in most large cities, winning a share of resources requires competing in the political process. In this regard, casting one's lot with the mayor may be the most viable governance strategy for improving urban education. Boston has taken this step and will now see if a change among the key governance actors yields positive results on the path of school reform.

CHAPTER III

Leadership Development at the Boston Public Schools: 1995–2006

KAREN L. MAPP
JENNIFER M. SUESSE

IN HIS ARTICLE, "Building a New Structure for School Leadership," Richard Elmore argues that the demands of standards-based accountability have changed the educational landscape such that "school leaders are being asked to take on responsibilities they are largely unequipped to assume."[1] In response, schools and districts need to dramatically change the way that leadership is defined, developed, and practiced. Establishing new means for leadership development is a challenge not unique to public education. Corporations, nonprofits, and other public bureaucracies also face shifting leadership demands created by globalization, rapid change, and emerging technologies. Rather than accept the heroic leadership paradigm that implies leadership is a collection of inherent individual traits, Elmore challenges educators to look to a more distributive leadership paradigm in which leadership is learned and earned from experience in guiding and directing the instructional improvement process. Elmore states that for public schools to survive, "leaders will [need to] look very different from the way they presently look, both in who leads and in what these leaders do."[2]

Educational organizations at all levels—school districts, institutions of higher education, foundations, and other community stakeholders—are wrestling with the important challenge of defining and cultivating the leadership talent that is needed to improve education for all students. From The Broad Foundation's residencies in urban education to Harvard University's Public Education Leadership Project (PELP) and beyond, a variety of models for leadership development are emerging. Through the exploration and analysis of the leadership development process enacted by the Boston Public Schools during the eleven-year tenure of Superintendent Thomas Payzant, this chapter seeks to provide a portrait of one district's attempt to meet this emerging leadership development challenge. Even the definition of this task itself remains vague, so we begin the chapter by providing a conceptual framework of leadership development through which we then evaluate the district's progress. We feel that the work of Linda Hill, although created for the corporate sector, provides a provocative framework for viewing the development of leaders.[3] Hill identifies three components—technical, managerial, and personal skills—that must be addressed from both an individual and systems perspective. Using Hill's framework, we share our findings and recommendations regarding educational leadership development in the Boston Public Schools. While these findings and recommendations are specific to Boston, we believe they could be useful to all districts grappling with the demands of standards-based reform. Boston's historical and ongoing leadership development efforts may also be useful to foundations and institutions of higher education that seek to identify, cultivate, and sustain leadership in the education sector.

This chapter is focused on the development of leaders at three key management levels:

- Principals[4]
- Middle managers (both central and school level)
- Senior staff (deputy superintendents)

Given the time frame for our analysis, we chose to focus on these three positions because of their strategic influence on the instructional work at the schools. Our inquiry was shaped by the following guiding questions:

- What was the status of leadership development when Payzant joined the district in 1995?
- What has the district achieved in the area of leadership development?
- Where has the district struggled in terms of leadership development?
- How might the district move forward in the area of leadership development?

Our data collection strategy included interviews with key district stakeholders and a review of relevant reports and documents.[5]

Following our definition of leadership development, which informed this research, we provide an analysis of leadership development in the Boston Public Schools over the past ten years. The chapter closes with recommendations tailored to Boston district leadership, but applicable to any similarly situated district attempting to develop new leaders for public schools.

DEFINITION OF LEADERSHIP DEVELOPMENT

In order to analyze leadership development at the Boston Public Schools, we sought an existing leadership model with which to anchor and organize our research findings. We felt that the model of leadership development described by Hill in *Becoming a Manager* was best suited to this task because her definition provides a clear, concise framework for understanding what skills and compe-

FIGURE 1

Three Components of Leadership Development

Technical	Managerial	Personal
• Knowing what good instruction is • Understanding curriculum and pedagogy • Grasp of developmental psychology • Ability to offer differentiated instruction • Operational and financial skills	• Working with people (both individuals and teams) • Knowing how to motivate others • Capacity to manage complexity *and* change • Ability to see the enterprise as a whole, including internal and external interdependencies	• Capacity to cope with stress and emotion • Self-knowledge • Balancing strengths and weaknesses • Transformation of identity

Adapted from Linda A. Hill, *Becoming a Manager: How New Leaders Master the Challenges of Leadership*, 2nd ed. (Boston: Harvard Business School Press, 2003).

tencies school districts need as they develop leaders for the demanding, changing environment Elmore describes. We have modified Hill's definition of leadership development to reflect the specific needs of instructional leadership in a large school district. This adapted definition of leadership development rests on two fundamental assumptions, which Elmore and Hill share. First, we assume that leadership can be learned and developed. Second, we assume that leadership must be distributed across all levels of the organization. We believe that the ability to motivate and inspire excellent instruction and student achievement is everyone's job, and is no longer the province of "heroic leaders."

There are three basic components to the model: technical, managerial, and personal skills (see figure 1).

Technical Skills

"Technical skill involves specialized knowledge, analytical ability within that specialty, and facility in the use of tools and techniques of that specific discipline."[6] For instructional leadership, technical skills include, for example, knowing what good instruction is, understanding curriculum and pedagogy (e.g., the mechanics of collaborative coaching and leadership and writer's workshop), a working grasp of developmental psychology, the ability to offer (or at least recognize) differentiated instruction, and operational and financial skills.

Managerial Skills

Managerial skills are both human and conceptual: they are about working with people and having the ability to see the enterprise as a whole, including recognizing internal and external interdependencies. School leaders must be able to work with people as individuals and as teams and know how to motivate others. Leaders need the capacity to manage not only complexity but also change. These managerial skills require confronting myths we have about management as a locus of power, and understanding that the managerial job is often about creating the context for subordinates' success, rather than seeking individual glory.

Personal Skills

Personal skills include the capacity to cope with stress and emotion, as well as the self-knowledge necessary to lead a group. Regarding the importance of personal learning, Hill argues, "adopting the attitudes and a psychological perspective consistent with their new role . . . is the heart of the process of becoming a manager."[7] Yet, personal skills are often the least recognized aspect of leadership development. Hill's research shows that the transition to a management role involves a transformation of one's identity. No longer a specialist or individual contributor, leaders must learn new ways of understanding their role and what success means. Their new role involves setting the agenda for their group, orchestrating projects, acting as a generalist, and building networks. This new work can be stressful, and thus leaders must develop a deep self-knowledge and the ability to balance their personal strengths and weaknesses.

Individuals develop technical, managerial, and personal skills through experience and training. Experiential learning is a powerful way to develop leadership talent, and Hill provides a helpful diagram and concept of developmentally appropriate "stretch assignments" to explain how the process can take place within large, complex organizations (see figure 2).

The Concept of Stretch Assignments

A stretch assignment provides emerging leaders with an opportunity to work on issues or projects that are highly relevant and visible to their organization. Stretch assignments usually have considerable positional power, offering individuals the opportunity to develop expertise critical to the overall mission of the district. By accepting a stretch assignment, an individual has a chance to take on an important task, learn new things, meet new people, demonstrate success, build credibility, and accrue future rewards, such as other desirable assignments, salary increases, or promotions. Because they are important and visible, stretch assignments can be risky, but they carry great rewards.

In order to maximize the effectiveness of stretch assignments in building leadership capacity, organizations must identify emerging leaders and evaluate their performance on an ongoing basis. Evaluation can include both an assessment of strengths and weaknesses as well as the delivery of developmental feedback. Evaluating individual performance on key assignments allows district leadership to identify individuals who are ready for additional challenges, and these stretch assignments in turn enable emerging leaders to identify and ex-

FIGURE 2

Stretch Assignments

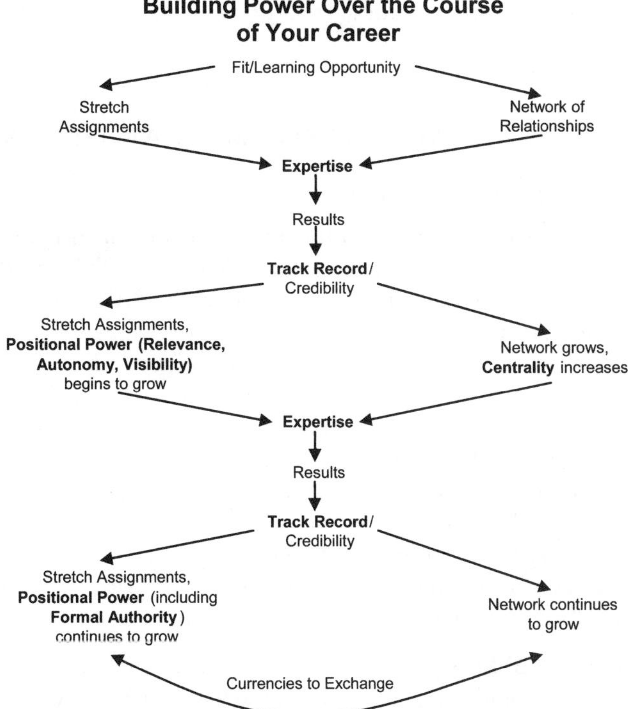

Source: Linda A. Hill, *Becoming a Manager: How New Managers Master the Challenges of Leadership*, 2nd ed. (Boston: Harvard Business School Press, 2003).

perience firsthand the organizational issues that need attention. This last point is critical for a twenty-first century school district. Hill notes, "With autonomy comes the latitude to develop and demonstrate initiative and to innovate—in short, to lead and shape the direction in which the organization (or specific unit), will head. These particular talents are especially important in contemporary organizations, which are constantly confronted with the need to adapt to new environmental contingencies."[8]

Identifying key stretch assignments and linking them to clearly established systems for evaluation, promotion, and advancement can help to insure that all staff have access to development. Further articulating the rationale and performance criteria for specific stretch assignments and promotions helps personnel understand what type of leadership talents are desired within the organization. As Hill's diagram indicates, these stretch assignments are not "add-ons," but rather the actual work of the organization. By completing them, individuals build skills and relationships needed to succeed within the organization. The assignments are experiential, systematic, and integrated into the work of the district. This approach demonstrates that the process of developing leaders is not just about establishing technical expertise, but also includes the work of developing a learning organization.

ANALYSIS OF LEADERSHIP DEVELOPMENT AT BPS: 1995–2006

BPS in 1995—What Payzant Inherited

When Tom Payzant came to the Boston Public Schools in August 1995, the district was organized by level—elementary, middle, and high—and the central office served an administrative function (see appendix 3A for 1995 organization chart). The district had little clarity around expectations for student learning. No learning standards or district-wide curriculum had been established, and there was wide variation across the district in terms of the level of teaching and learning occurring at each school. Most of the variation was dependent on the strength of the leadership at each site. The Center for Leadership Development (CLD) was established the year before in response to a contract agreement between the Boston Public Schools and the Boston Teachers Union. The CLD's primary focus was professional development (PD) for teachers.

Principal positions were filled following a traditional pattern in which individuals waited "in the queue" for promotion. Payzant described this pattern:

> The culture [in BPS] was similar to what at that time existed in many big cities, or I would say many school districts, that there was a career pathway—so you taught, you might have been a guidance counselor and then an assistant principal, and then you got in a queue, and your turn would come. And so it was more the expectation that if you paid your dues at these other levels and were patient to a point, then you would get tapped.

According to several interviewees, this traditional pattern of ascension to the principalship exacerbated the dynamic of principals being honored for their skills as operations managers but not necessarily for competencies needed for instructional leadership.

Leadership development of standing principals and headmasters and school and central office middle managers was informal and almost entirely dependent on individual initiative, other peer networks, and entrepreneurial spirit. Each school level was managed by a level superintendent. Level superintendents coordinated monthly meetings with principals, but these meetings were primarily informational and/or focused on operations issues. The superintendent and central office staff would occasionally attend level meetings to share information about particular operational- or systems-related initiatives or challenges; however, interviewees stated that principals felt disconnected from top-level leadership. Some principals, sensing the emerging focus on standards-based reform, began to seek out PD opportunities at local universities that focused on instructional leadership and also began to coordinate curriculum and instruction PD for their teachers.

The BPS culture in 1995 did not always support this individual pursuit of leadership development. These "go-getters" were sometimes perceived as individuals "out for themselves." Former Deputy Superintendent Janice Jackson stated, "There wasn't a sense of shared learning, nor was there a learning focus for the adults or for the children."[9]

ACCOMPLISHMENTS: EMERGENCE OF A NEW PHILOSOPHY OF LEADERSHIP DEVELOPMENT AND IMPLEMENTATION

Our review of data from interviews and relevant documents revealed that, during the tenure of Tom Payzant, a new leadership development philosophy emerged and was implemented. This philosophy was comprised of six components:

1. Begin with a focus on instruction.
2. Establish an organizational and reporting structure that supports leadership development at the level of the principalship.
3. Hire talented staff.
4. Engage external partners.
5. Offer district-coordinated programs and events for professional development.
6. Create space for individual leadership development efforts.

At the core of this philosophy were Payzant's beliefs about the key elements of whole-system improvement: a focus on the quality of instruction in the classroom and a focus on the quality of school leadership.

1. Begin with a Focus on Instruction: The Development of Citywide Learning Standards and Focus on Children

> This district has made a concerted effort to build instructional capacity and improve the ability of teachers and school leaders to teach effectively; these efforts have taken root and borne fruit. (Aspen Institute/Annenberg Report, see chapter 1 in this volume)

Without question, the legacy of Tom Payzant's superintendency in Boston will be the laser-like focus on improved instruction. Soon after his arrival in 1995, Payzant began to lay out a standards-based framework for the district. This framework emphasized (1) establishing clear expectations for learning; (2) identifying curriculum to give students and teachers access to the content and knowledge necessary to help students reach the standards; and (3) developing appropriate assessments to track students' progress. Payzant's strategy was to spread reform across *all* schools in the district instead of creating small pockets of good schools sprinkled throughout the district.

Within the first year, Payzant led the district in creating a five-year education reform plan, *Focus on Children,* and developing the Boston Citywide Learning Standards. This new systemic focus on high-quality instruction demanded a new type of school leader—one who knew a great deal about teaching and learning and could lead the instructional reform work at the school. This context provided the scaffolding for all future leadership development initiatives in the district. Leadership development initiatives that followed after *Focus on Children* were designed to increase the capacity of principals to understand the type of content and pedagogical skill required to provide high-quality teaching and learning for all BPS students.

2. Work to Establish Organizational and Reporting Structures that Support Leadership Development at the Principal Level

To signal his intent to focus on the development of school leaders, Payzant made two significant changes in his first year to improve the support and accountability process for principals.

The cluster system

In July of 1996, Payzant changed the organizational structure for schools from an elementary, middle, and high school-level system to a K–12 vertical structure with geographical clusters (see appendix 3B for a chart of the proposed reorganization). The intention was to create a system that would improve communication between the central office and school leaders. In an attempt to separate support from accountability functions and to foster open dialogue, clusters were led by a cluster leader who remained a standing principal with no supervisory authority over principals. Payzant selected ten cluster leaders and aimed, through his choices, for a balance of elementary, middle, and high school principals as well as a racially diverse group of school leaders. Likewise, six "team leaders" were appointed to head the central office support functions of teaching and learning, operations, finance and budget, parent support services, student support services, and human resources.

To foster better direct communication between school leaders and the superintendent, cluster leaders were made members of a senior leadership team that met once a month with Payzant and other top level administrators. Payzant stated:

> [The Clusters were] part of this very intentional strategy of getting much closer to what was going on in schools and with school leaders. So the idea was a very simple one. You create clusters of schools based on geographical proximity, only to make it easier for a cluster leader who was

> an active principal to meet with his or her cluster and convene them once a month. Then the cluster leaders became members of my leadership team, which gave me the direct engagement with principals and headmasters at the leadership team along with key central office folks.

Interviewees stated that the cluster system, particularly the nonsupervisory aspect of the system design, fostered leadership development by creating more open dialog among principals and allowing for coaching, mentoring, and support relationships to develop between cluster leaders and school leaders. They added that communication between principals and the superintendent improved because cluster leaders could voice principals' concerns directly to the superintendent. Interviewees noted that the effectiveness of the cluster structure and the PD coordinated by cluster leaders was highly dependent on the philosophy, skills, and competencies of individual cluster leaders.

Changes in the reporting structure

The second shift affecting the development of school leaders was a radical change in the reporting structure. Aided by the Massachusetts Education Reform Act of 1993, which removed principals from the collective bargaining unit, Payzant made the decision to have all principals report to him and Janice Jackson, whom he hired as deputy superintendent in January of 1996. Payzant acknowledges that this decision was organizationally unsound, but symbolically important. This new structure allowed Payzant and Jackson to be, according to Payzant, "close to where the work was happening, at the school level."

Over the course of eighteen months, Payzant and Jackson visited schools, spent time in classrooms with teachers and school leaders to observe instructional practice, and provided school leaders with feedback and support. They developed criteria to aid in their evaluation of school leaders, and the visits to schools created an opportunity to identify principals with strong instructional leadership skills and potential. The school visits also allowed Payzant and Jackson to identify principals and headmasters who were not establishing themselves as strong instructional leaders. At the end of the 1995–96 school year, Payzant reassigned six principals to other roles within BPS, a move contested by community leaders and parents. The district stood firm in its decision.[10]

Upon Janice Jackson's departure from BPS in 1998, Payzant created a new senior leadership structure, appointing three triad deputy superintendents to supervise the clusters and a deputy superintendent for teaching and learning to oversee the curriculum and support central office operations (see appendix 3C for the 2005-06 organization chart). Although triad deputies were responsible for various aspects of principal leadership development, each deputy received only a limited budget to coordinate development activities. Payzant retained supervisory oversight of a small number of schools.

3. Hire Talented Staff

Another component of the district's emergent leadership philosophy was to hire talented staff. Payzant was clear in his desire to hire highly competent staff both at the school level and within central office. His philosophy for his top central office staff was to hire talented people and then let them flourish without much interference or supervision. He explained, "I decided to put all of my focus on the schools because that's where the work was."

Payzant also assembled a staff of both insiders and outsiders to the system. This approach to leadership selection shaped the consistent balance of insiders and outsiders on the BPS senior leadership team. Interviewees did state that this desire for balance was not always clearly articulated during the search process for top-level leadership team members.

4. Engage External Partners

BPS also sought to engage the support of external partners. We highlight four major players who contributed to the leadership development work of the district by providing targeted technical assistance and/or training. In some instances, these partners served as a hiring pool for central office middle managers and senior level staff.

The Boston Plan for Excellence (BPE)[11]

In 1984, Boston's corporate community established the BPE, a foundation with the goal of providing resource support to improve the quality of education in the BPS.[12] In 1995, BPE changed its funding strategy to support more systemic and sustainable "whole school reform" strategies for BPS. Under the leadership of a new executive director, Ellen Guiney, and with advice and feedback from successful local educators and nationally recognized reform strategists, BPE, in partnership with BPS, developed the "21st Century Schools" project. With a budget of $5 million over four years, the 21st Century project focused on supporting twenty-seven schools in an effort to examine and fundamentally transform "their organization, their use of time and resources, and most importantly, their instruction."[13] An important criterion for selection was the presence at the school of a leader with demonstrated management skills and instructional leadership potential.

The 21st Century Schools model was replicated three times from 1995–97, creating four cohorts of schools engaged in the work of whole-school improvement. BPE required that school leaders create instructional teams and smaller instructional leadership teams as vehicles for change at the schools. Principals were encouraged to network across cohorts to share best practices and provide each other with constructive criticism.

Several other initiatives resulted from the collaboration between BPE and BPS:

Participation in The Institute for Learning

Sensing that the management of change portion of the whole-school reform work was a challenge for school leaders, BPE and BPS contracted with the Institute for Learning in Pittsburgh, Pennsylvania, to provide an intensive leadership development opportunity for a small team of 21st Century principals and central office staff.

The Boston team attended one full week of training every three to four months. In an attempt to spread the learning across the district, the BPS Center for Leadership Development (CLD) was charged with organizing parallel institutes in Boston. Interviewees stated that the scale-up strategy was unrealistic and constituted a "watered down version" of the Institute program. Nonetheless, an important outcome of involvement in the Institute, for school leaders and the district, was the eventual systemic adoption of "walkthroughs" and "accountable talk" as strategies to improve teaching and learning in the classroom.

Adoption of the Six Essentials

The concept of key "Essentials" was introduced by BPE in 1996 (see Appendix, page 271). The Essentials have evolved during Payzant's tenure from seven to six and were regarded as the "action steps" to operationalize the work of *Focus on Children.* The Essentials were designed to prompt principals and teachers to examine their instructional practices together and "take collective responsibility for individual student learning."[14] The Six Essentials form the conceptual framework for much of the current professional and leadership development in the district.

Creation of the Resource Action Team (REACT)

BPE was concerned that central office staff were not shifting their roles to support the focus on instruction at the schools. In 1998, in collaboration with BPS staff, REACT was formed to identify central office policy and practice obstacles to reform. BPE, district, and middle-level staff formed a cross-functional team to explore and tackle various themes seen as challenges to reform. REACT gave these individuals an opportunity to act across departments and organizations to solve district challenges.

Urban Superintendents Program (USP)

In 1990, the Harvard Graduate School of Education established the USP in response to the nation's call for educational leadership. During Payzant's tenure, BPS had a strong relationship with the USP program and relied heavily on its development of educational leaders. Payzant mentored six USP interns, one while he was superintendent in San Diego and five while in Boston. He offered positions in the BPS administration to three of the interns for whom he was a mentor.[15]

Broad Residency Program

The Broad Residency in Urban Education is a two-year management training program sponsored by The Broad Foundation. The Broad Residency places top graduate students from business, law, and public policy in managerial positions in the central operations of urban school districts. These aspiring leaders report directly to senior management and lead major projects such as opening new schools, district budgeting processes, and improving the management of human resources.[16] BPS began participating in the program in 2003 and has hosted four Broad Residents. Two residents have been hired by the district in key mid-level central office management positions. The district began hosting three additional Residents in July 2006.

Public Education Leadership Project (PELP)

Over the past three years, BPS participated in PELP, a joint initiative of Harvard's Business School and Graduate School of Education. A team from BPS joined with leadership teams from eight other urban districts to address issues facing those charged with leading districtwide academic improvement. PELP faculty led annual weeklong institutes and conducted research aimed at developing a set of powerful managerial ideas to enable effective district leadership. In recent years, the Boston team identified several areas in need of attention, such as the dynamic among members of the senior leadership team and implementation of the high school renewal effort.

5. Offer District-Coordinated Programs and Events for Professional Development

As a result of the new focus on instructional leadership and accountability, BPS experienced a remarkable turnover of school leadership. The district, therefore, targeted much of its leadership development strategy at hiring new leaders for schools.

The Boston School Leadership Institute (SLI)

Dismayed by the quality of leadership candidates coming from traditional sources such as higher education and other certification programs, the district elected to create its own pipeline to the principalship. The Boston SLI, established in 2002, is arguably the district's most prominent leadership development initiative and is a nationally recognized model of new principal leadership development. Each of the programs within the SLI has a unique purpose and set of goals related to increasing leadership knowledge and skill within the BPS. Education Matters, in their 2004 evaluation, summarized the four components of the program:[17]

> #### *Boston Principal Fellows (BPF)*
>
> The purpose of the BPF is to prepare the next generation of school leaders for the BPS. This intensive twelve-month program provides Fel-

lows with relevant course work coupled with a residency placement with a successful Boston principal as a setting to apply their learning. The curriculum is centered on Boston's Six Essentials of Whole-School Improvement and the dimensions of effective school leadership. The program focuses on ensuring that new principals deeply understand the district's focus on instruction and how to organize a school around student learning. Participants receive a full-time salary during their fellowship in return for a three-year commitment to BPS after completing the program. Graduating Fellows can receive a master's degree or certificate of advanced graduate studies. The Boston Principal Fellowship distinguishes Boston as one of the few school systems in the country to have a district-based principal certification program that has been recognized nationally as a promising model for principal preparation. Ten to twelve fellowships are awarded annually.

Between July 2003 and June 2006, twenty-eight Fellows completed the program. Of the twenty-eight, seventeen (59%) were placed in principals positions, and six (21%) are currently serving as assistant principals. The remaining Fellows await placement.

New Principal Support System (NPSS)

NPSS seeks to support twenty-five first- and second-year principals in becoming strong school leaders. NPSS aspires to create a customized system of support and a learning community for principals in their first two years in the position. The program includes mentoring by successful principals, monthly seminars, and school-based consultations to address the challenges faced by novice principals.

Exploring the Principalship (EPP)

The EPP program introduces thirty-five to forty educators with leadership potential and deep knowledge of instruction to the principalship. In particular, it tries to engage those who might not have considered becoming a principal.

Program for Non-Principal Administrators (NPA)

As a result of a report issued in June of 2005 revealing the dearth of leadership opportunities for "nonprincipal leaders and administrators," the BPS applied for a grant from the U.S. Department of Education Office of Innovation and Improvement (OII) to develop an additional phase of the SLI initiative with similar curriculum.[18,19] The NPA was designed to build a PD infrastructure for school-based nonprincipal administrators. The goals of this initiative were (1) to educate teachers about the role of nonprincipal administrators and recruit them into these roles; (2) to provide a two-year system of support for new, nonprincipal administrators that ensures their success; (3) to provide PD that supports all nonprincipal administrators to build the skills needed to work in school administration and facilitate instructional improvement; (4) to create job-alike networks that facilitate sharing of best practices across the system; and (5) to provide nonprincipal administrators who aspire to the principalship with the skills and experiences required for them to be competitive candidates for the principalship.

Other district leadership development programs and initiatives

Monthly Senior Leadership Team (SLT) meetings

The BPS SLT consists of the cluster leaders, senior level management staff, triad deputies, and the superintendent. The SLT meets once a month during the school year to share information, participate in PD activities, and identify and discuss areas of concern.

Principal meetings and Summer Institute

BPS central office staff coordinate three half-day trainings during the school year for principals and a three-day principals retreat in August. The responsibility for this coordination has shifted throughout the years. In the early years of Payzant's tenure, responsibility for the principals meetings (held once a month until 2002) was a collaborative effort between the deputy superintendent and the CLD office. In 2002, BPS planned to hire a staff person to coordinate PD for principals, but the position was never filled as a result of severe budget cuts. In recent years, coordination of the three school-year principals meetings has been shared by members of the SLT.

6. Create Space for Individual Leadership Development Efforts

One of the hallmarks of Payzant's approach to leadership development was his willingness to create space for individual leadership development efforts. As Payzant said, "I tend to hire at the top level. I hire good people and then let them go. I don't hover over them." Thus, individuals in leadership roles with the knowledge and skills to create leadership development activities within their departments or clusters were encouraged to do so. For example, when she was deputy superintendent, Janice Jackson hired a consulting firm specializing in leadership development to provide coaching for team leaders at the central office. When Jackson left the district, this work did not continue. Payzant neither encouraged nor discouraged these efforts, but let senior staff make their own decisions about what leadership development activities were appropriate.

CHALLENGES AND LIMITATIONS TO THE DISTRICT'S APPROACH

Although the leadership development approach described above yielded considerable progress for BPS, especially around the instructional core, its limitations created some significant challenges to the development of strong leadership in the district. In the course of our research at BPS, we identified five main challenges, each tied to our understanding of the current leadership development philosophy at the district. We discuss these shortcomings as they pertain to BPS, but we anticipate that other urban districts across the country may experience similar challenges. These include:

1. The district's current approach to leadership development addresses the "what," but not the "how," of instructional reform
2. The conversion of the central office to support the improvement of classroom instruction is incomplete
3. Identifying and developing internal leadership talent is assumed to be separate from the "work" of the district
4. The core systems and attitudes necessary to support comprehensive and deliberate leadership development are limited in the district
5. Limited capacity exists to address the managerial and personal aspects of leadership development at scale

The following analysis will discuss how these challenges and limitations have resulted from the district's philosophy and practices surrounding leadership development.

1. The District's Current Approach to Leadership Development Addresses the "What," but Not the "How," of Instructional Reform

The district's intense, largely singular focus on the "what"—the technical components of the work of instructional reform—proved problematic. As described earlier, BPS reform strategy included several elements that the administration believed were essential for improving student achievement.[20] These included establishing citywide learning standards, improving the quality of instruction in BPS classrooms, and improving the quality of school-level leadership. District professional development efforts sought to develop technical skills across the workforce, especially for classroom teachers and principals. Our research suggests that these components were well developed and widely understood, not only across the district but also across the nation, as BPS was recognized for its focus on teaching and learning.

In contrast to the strategic and systematic investments made by the district and by external partners in improving the instructional capacity of the principals and teaching staff, investments in developing leadership roles and talents were less organized and more varied. We found that the district's core belief that reform starts with instruction was never accompanied by a complementary, districtwide approach toward leadership development. This lack of consistency across the district encouraged experimentation with new ideas, and the various clusters and triads developed different approaches and standards for leadership and leadership development. Of course variation is not, in and of itself, problematic; but the system lacked any mechanisms for integrating or sharing these efforts across the district or even with the administrative team.

District leadership did a good job of establishing commitment for improved academic achievement and articulating "what" instructional reform would entail. However, we found that they were less clear about "how" it would unfold. BPS paid much more attention to enhancing the technical knowledge of school leaders—specifics about what good instruction entailed—than to the managerial and personal skills required to manage and promote change, create effective teams, and shift and cultivate school cultures and climates to support excellent teaching and learning. Our interviews revealed a lack of agreement about which managerial and personal leadership practices were most important for improving student achievement. This resulted in inconsistent decision-making and communication across the system about the theory of implementation and hindered the district's ability to foster young leaders.

We discovered that the leadership team did not share the same core values and beliefs about how the systemwide improvement should be achieved or what leadership skills should be developed. Without a shared understanding of *how* instructional reform would unfold, implementation varied tremendously across schools and triads. District leadership worked to communicate the mechanics of classroom-based reform, but struggled to achieve, in Payzant's words, "fidelity of implementation."

Our research confirmed that district leaders believed ongoing leadership development was necessary for the district's continued improvement. They identified many areas of need, including the need for more capacity to communicate the district's mission statement, to establish school cultures with high expectations, and to unleash talent within a teaching staff. Such consensus is a useful and necessary precursor to developing school and central office staff leadership talent *at scale* in order to realize the instructional improvement goals of *Focus on Children*. Nevertheless, we found no evidence that district leadership had a comprehensive plan for developing leadership talent among school and central office staff. Given the revolutionary changes in the demands of school and district leadership described earlier, this represents a worrisome gap.

Our conclusion is that although BPS did a yeoman's job of focusing the organization on developing standards and improving instruction as key levers for change, the district falls short of demonstrating a comprehensive, systemic, deliberate, and continuous leadership development strategy.

2. The Conversion of the Central Office to Support the Improvement of Classroom Instruction Is Incomplete

The district's second limitation is the incomplete conversion of the whole institution to support instruction. Payzant and his team reorganized the district to support school leaders and classroom instruction by focusing on principals and technical issues. They did not, however, fully address the concurrent need to establish an instructional focus for the rest of the organization, especially the central office. Interviewees stated that this presents a major structural barrier for the district in its ongoing efforts to implement comprehensive leadership development activities.

A huge structural reorganization was needed to transform a system that had historically been organized by levels (and prior to desegregation mandates, by neighborhoods) into a comprehensive, K–12 model of public education with a consistent curriculum and instructional focus. In our analysis, Boston sought to adopt this model without an adequate strategy for supporting the transformation across the entire district. Some of this failure stemmed from the district's choice to focus its efforts on establishing an instructional focus for school leadership. Leadership development efforts in the district sought to address how line staff could work to become instructional leaders, and early on, the district invested heavily in working to convert the role of school leaders to focus on instruction rather than operations or site management. While this choice was important, we found no significant corresponding training or discussion of the new role of central office staff as they moved to convert from a control organization to one focused on supporting instruction.

Without a complementary plan for redesigning central office roles or departments to support instruction and articulate how the various pieces of the organization would fit together and support each other, the preexisting disconnect between central office and schools persisted. Existing departments remained organized in silos, preventing the development of meaningful collaboration between even the most senior leaders. Without information-sharing across departments or the opportunity to work on cross-functional teams, senior leaders and middle managers lacked the opportunities to integrate their efforts or identify significant areas for collaboration and improvement. The persistent silo mentality of functional departments (HR, finance, research, teaching, and learning) at the central office presented a barrier to lateral learning and the kind of cross-functional and collaborative projects that would support systemwide thinking and leadership skills in midlevel managers.

We heard of isolated instances where individuals sought out opportunities to work with their peers across existing silos, but these were anomalies. Instead, the organizational structure encouraged isolation. Some departments worked to establish supportive relationships with school sites, but their efforts were uncoordinated and not well understood or integrated with others across the system. Overall, the structural response added more layers to address emerging problems, but has not yet responded to the core challenges of establishing opportunities for collaboration or cross-functional leadership development.

The one major attempt to reconnect the central office and the schools was the triad and cluster structures. Clusters were intended to address the schools' needs for smaller work groups, and triads were intended to foster integration.

There was not, however, a clear understanding across the organization about how these different structures were meant to function collectively. Some felt that the cluster structure had potential, while others were frustrated with its functioning. Tim Knowles, former deputy for teaching and learning, stated:

> The cluster did not become the powerful mechanism for developing leaders, as was envisioned. There was an ongoing narrative about how the cluster structure needed to change—more time for clusters to coach and mentor; the need for clearer expectations and more support to help cluster leaders learn how to do the work; the need to provide cluster leaders with supervisory authority so they could demand changes of principals, not negotiate it; and finally, the problem with cluster meetings morphing into the minidistricts—becoming extensions of compliance-oriented offices downtown—not the locus for adult development. We made modifications along the way, but the cluster model did not evolve into a central office vehicle for principal development. School leaders had to find that elsewhere.

The district's strategic choice to separate line accountability from the support function added complexity to these issues. For example, the triad deputies, who each supervise a large number of schools, do not have clear, well-defined relationships to the support functions of the central organization (e.g., office of teaching and learning, research, professional development). If a deputy identifies an urgent need at a school site, for example, he or she does not have the authority to quickly assign resources or delegate support staff. Instead, the deputy must negotiate with department leadership to ensure response. Department leaders field requests from all three deputies and often weigh trade-offs independently from one another. This absence of structural clarity creates uncertainty about decision-making authority and perpetuates problems with accountability, especially in the area of leadership development. Without an articulated, comprehensive plan for leadership development across the system, or mechanisms for coordination across triads, each deputy is left to make her own decisions about what leadership development activities are necessary within her triad. Limited funds and the challenge of negotiating with other departments for training or support staff present barriers to the deputies' ability to achieve effective and systematic implementation of these activities. Some deputies have paid for PD for their triad and cluster leaders out of their own personal funds.

In our analysis, the unfinished transformation from a level organization to a comprehensive K–12 system, coupled with a central office that is not designed to support instruction, yield serious implementation issues. Given the lack of clarity regarding the rationale for the existing structure, it is difficult to see how some jobs are connected to the instructional core or to each other. Without structures or incentives in place for figuring this out on an individual or departmental basis, the structure discourages sharing or meaningful, systematic collaboration. Interviewees described ways in which the district differentiated leadership development activities among individual schools, clusters, and triads without any corresponding mechanisms for unifying or integrating the leadership development needs with the goals of the larger system.

3. Identifying and Developing Internal Leadership Talent Is Assumed to Be Separate from the "Work" of the District

The third limitation facing the BPS is that it has paid insufficient attention to identifying and developing internal leadership talent across the district. BPS culture encourages the perception that leadership development is an individual concern, separate from the work of the organization. Indeed, many of the leadership development experiences cited in interviews were associated with external programs. While these relationships with external partners are important, we saw less evidence of a progression and promotion system within the district, and worry that many of the external programs are not integrated into the regular functioning of the district. We heard few stories of internally motivated stretch assignments, promotions, or mentoring.

Our evaluation of the formal and informal arrangements, reporting structures, and working relationships across the district revealed great interest in developing leadership, without adequate formal or informal structural support for these efforts. Most of those we interviewed were unable to identify any stretch assignments within the district. Even after explaining the concept (as this language was unfamiliar at BPS), interviewees were unable to identify a set of assignments that had the qualities of building credibility, competence, visibility, and relevance for emerging leaders. We heard some discussion of technical skill development, but few examples of managerial or personal skill development. The SLI was a notable exception to these findings. It provided a limited number of individuals with significant stretch assignments. SLI was an important step toward establishing a systematic approach to leadership development, but its activities were insufficient to support the entire organization.

Leadership at all levels of the organization pointed to the dearth of ongoing, internal professional leadership development opportunities for standing principals and senior leadership. Over the past decade, investment in principal professional development has decreased and the responsibility for principal professional development has been passed around. Interviews revealed that central administrators had few and inconsistent opportunities for leadership development. One deputy observed:

> There isn't much effort to develop our current principals' leadership skills, and the leadership development that I do see violates what we know about best practices for adult learning. It is often scheduled at the end of the day and does not address key issues like building school cultures, developing school missions, and offering inspirational instructional leadership.

> Senior leadership lacks the training in effective staff development that we need to offer stronger programs.

Even in the domain of technical leadership development, where the district focused most of its leadership development energies, BPS exhibited a tendency to assume that all staff had a similar capacity and failed to design implementation strategies that would accommodate differences in leadership capacity or beliefs. For example, when reflecting on the implementation of literacy learning standards across the city, Tom Payzant recalled that he misjudged the school leaders' capacity. He said:

> In retrospect, we underestimated the disparity in capacity at our school sites to make informed choices about a new literacy curriculum. At the time, we decided to offer schools a choice of three or four options that fit within our balanced literacy framework. Many of the other decisions around instructional reform at that point had been top-down and fast track, and I wanted to get the right balance between bottom-up and top-down. School leaders at our first cohort of schools mostly had the capacity to select an appropriate program, but, what we underestimated—or certainly I did and nobody pushed back because people were worried about taking on too much too fast—was that there was wide disparity in capacity across the schools in the second, third, and fourth cohorts to make informed choices for their sites.

This willingness of BPS leadership to assume capacity among its staff is honorable, but problematic. It also shows that the district neglected to plan for teaching staff *how* to implement instructional reform and did not seek to create meaningful structures for lateral learning while new programs were being launched.

Our research also revealed that little, if any, leadership development work is being done with middle managers. Opportunities for assistant principals have also been few and far between, until the Program for Non-Principal Administrators was launched this year. The consensus seemed to be that the focus on developing school and site leadership drew attention away from the rest of the system. This is of particular concern, as midlevel individuals often represent the "next generation" of senior leadership in an organization.

Our findings indicate that much of the leadership development task for BPS has been informally delegated to external partners. For example, several of the leadership team staff over the past eleven years have come from the Harvard USP program. These individuals have benefited from stretch assignments associated with the program. We also heard about the challenging and important work that principals who participated in the early Institute for Learning programs undertook. Finally, there are a number of current Broad Residents who are benefiting from required mentoring and stretch assignments.

While outsourcing leadership development to external organizations is one valid strategy, we found no mechanism for linking these programs to internal activities or promotion cycles. We also found that no one had responsibility for integration or oversight of external program participation. Indeed, most individuals who participated in these programs did so at their own expense and initiative, without any district support. Thus, some individuals had opportunities for leadership development but others did not. The lack of an overarching strategy for leadership development, combined with structures that discouraged collaboration and collective development, reinforced the belief that leadership development is separate from the work of the organization and also made it challenging for individuals to incorporate their new leadership skills into the organization.

4. The Core Systems and Attitudes Necessary to Support Comprehensive and Deliberate Leadership Development Are Limited in the District

Although the district exhibited a consistent effort to offer district-coordinated programs and events for professional development, with the notable exception of the SLI, these PD offerings were not integrated or coordinated. We found that BPS lacks the systems and attitudes necessary to ensure comprehensive and deliberate leadership development across the organization. The district's systems for and attitudes around promotion and evaluation were particularly revealing.

We found no evidence of systematic succession planning or evaluation that would provide a cadre of senior leadership with the necessary portfolio of experiences to prepare them for organizational leadership. Without the benefit of a comprehensive organizational strategy, structure, and culture to support the district's leadership development efforts, the procedures used to manage leadership development for principals, middle managers, and senior staff at BPS are idiosyncratic or invisible. This feeds into personnel uncertainty about who is excelling, who is eligible for promotion, and whose job is on the line.

Without a clear path for the development of internal candidates for top leadership positions, including the superintendency, district leaders are unable to respond to vacancies. They lack the systems and culture for developing or evaluating internal candidates for existing or anticipated openings. For example, even though in 2004 Payzant announced his intention to retire in 2006, no transparent process for developing a list of internal candidates or for grooming his successor was established.

This hands-off attitude toward career progression and evaluation was evident throughout the system. Our research suggested that district leadership assumed that hiring alone would provide organizational capacity for reform and that there was no need to invest in developing human or personal attributes. We found that BPS did focus on hiring good candidates, but did not establish mechanisms for moving people from one assignment to another or developing them for future positions. Without a system of stretch assignments or career ladders, the system perpetuates a one-person, one-job culture.

The rationale for job progression or succession within the district was not well understood. More typical than moving people across assignments is having them stay in one position for decades. Also, multiple people mentioned that rather than addressing this weak system of promotion, the district practice was to promote people by putting them in "acting" positions and then eventually giving them a permanent role.

Without a clear and transparent rationale for career progression or set of clearly defined stretch assignments, district managers have no natural incentive for offering their subordinates meaningful evaluation of their accomplishments and feedback about their strengths and weaknesses. While the BPS has an evaluation system for management in place, we found that it was not enforced or taken seriously by most leaders. Most interviewees said that the evaluation system was "underutilized" or "not used systematically," especially at the central office. Interviewees stated that evaluation is perceived negatively by most BPS staff because it is used punitively, not formatively, in most cases. Evaluation at BPS seems to be used most often to identify weaknesses when "you want to get someone out," rather than in a thorough or developmental way.

Serious evaluation of the district's leadership talent could help BPS identify leading candidates for increasing responsibility, which in turn would provide a pipeline of future leadership. Again, we found one excellent example of these systems at work in the SLI. This activity provides a limited number of individuals with opportunities for promotion (as well as significant stretch assignments while they are involved with the faculty) and meaningful evaluation. It also offers participants the opportunity to develop their managerial and emotional capacity, although these skills are not emphasized by the organization overall. We felt that the SLI was an important step toward establishing a system for leadership development. However, it is only a small step toward a districtwide approach to systematic career progression and evaluation.

5. Limited Capacity Exists to Address the Managerial and Personal Aspects of Leadership Development at Scale

While BPS leadership seemed willing to create space for individual leadership development efforts, we believe this is precisely because they perceive leadership development to be an individual concern. For the last decade, professional development opportunities of all kinds seem to have shifted constantly across the organization and have been influenced heavily by individual managers and supervisors. We found that "who the manager is" and his or her belief system about leadership development determines the kind of leadership development subordinates receive. Different beliefs about leadership and the district's theory of implementation amplify variation across departments, triads, and clusters, and contribute to the uneven fidelity of implementation and varied quality of leadership across the district.

Modeling behavior is one way to learn about an organization's leadership, and we found that leadership does not model behaviors evenly. Senior leaders hold different beliefs about the evaluation process, mechanisms for accountability, and means of establishing participatory decision making. This variation results in confusion about organizational priorities and values, and also contributes to the uneven fidelity of implementation that the district struggles to overcome. Even at lower levels of the organization, where coaches do much of the training, we found evidence that the array of coaching beliefs is confusing and not coordinated. This presents a serious limitation to the district's capacity for leadership development.

Furthermore, some members of the leadership team feel that there is an uneven distribution of trust and credibility among senior leaders (i.e., some people's opinions matter more than others), which creates an oppositional culture. Observers from both inside and outside the district are discouraged by the unhealthy patterns of communication at the senior leadership level. Thus, without a commitment to establishing shared beliefs about the leadership and direction of the district, and with limited collaboration at the senior level, it is difficult to establish a district approach to leadership development.

These issues of trust and credibility are even more complicated when the impact of race on leadership development at BPS is considered. Opinions on this issue vary widely, and we found deep disagreements about the role of race in the district. Some feel it is a primary driver when it comes to particular hires and offers real opportunity to minority candidates, while others feel that leaders of color occupy too many positions of powerlessness. Several interviewees described an "A team and B team" mentality that some said is a key factor in determining the formal and informal resources one can access and the opportunities available to develop oneself and one's team.

Given that the district is seeking to narrow the achievement gap between white and Asian and black and Hispanic students, we also spoke with leaders about how they are working to develop their own competencies in working with students and adults from different races, classes, and cultures. Some felt that they were not getting enough support in this difficult area, especially in how to facilitate discussions focused on race, class, and culture. Tim Knowles recalled that during his tenure at the district this was an issue:

> I know in the last several years there has been substantial energy and time devoted to understanding the achievement gap. But the early conversations about the intersection of race and schooling felt academic. Without being explicit about how one's own race, class, and culture impact practice, difficult discussions have a way of feeling antiseptic—focused outside not within—not influencing the quality of instruction and leadership.

The feeling that the district takes an "academic" approach to personnel learning and development was consistent across our conversations with leaders at

BPS. Overall, leaders told stories of how leadership development was perceived as separate from the work. The organization does not have a culture of "sharing struggles" or transferring best practices. In short, it is not set up as a learning organization. Professional development of all types is seen as an add-on, except with some classroom teachers, for whom coaching and development has become part of the work itself. Although some leaders believe that mentoring is part of their job, this is not a shared belief or practice. Rather, it is an individual decision. Ingrid Carney, a new deputy, observed that she was "surprised to discover that principals are given a hard time about being out of their schools for professional development." The culture does not seem to encourage leaders to learn from experts and other sites as part of their PD, but rather wants leaders to stay put.

Overall, these attitudes have created a culture that engenders distrust, encourages the hoarding of rare stretch assignments, and generates an unhealthy dynamic of race and power. This lack of commitment to establishing system-wide ownership also yields a full-time-equivalent (FTE) mentality. Rather than seeking to develop leaders wherever they are discovered, district leaders seek to get FTE allocations and fill them with the best available candidates.

It is our conclusion that the district needs to adopt a new way of thinking about how it will develop the leadership knowledge, skills, behaviors, attitudes, and experience it needs, especially regarding the managerial and emotional/personal. As director of Human Resources Barbara McGann observed, "this is where it's at. Our job is to inspire someone to believe that they can do anything. It is a very personal task." Deputy Superintendent Janet Williams added, the "area of ongoing support and coaching is our greatest need. For us to be effective, we require a significant transformation to occur as our leaders internalize the new priorities."

RECOMMENDATIONS

The BPS's improved instructional capacity and continued community support demonstrate the district's ability to make meaningful change. The momentum gained and lessons learned provide BPS and those observing its progress with a valuable opportunity: to reflect upon ten years of effort and thoughtfully plan for the future. Our research indicates that one critical component of the district's plan moving forward must be to develop leadership at all levels so as to sustain the progress already made and continue improvement system wide. While every district must take into consideration its own unique cultural, political, and historical context, it is safe to say that Boston, and any other urban district undertaking a leadership development initiative, must be sure to have certain components in place. To that end, we offer the following recommendations regarding *who* the plan must include, *what* it must encompass, and *how* it should be implemented:

1. A comprehensive leadership development plan must be deliberate and incorporate staff at all levels of the system.
2. The leadership development plan must build capacity in multiple domains, including technical, managerial, and personal leadership skills.
3. The plan must embed learning opportunities such as role-shift and stretch assignments in the "day-to-day work" of its developing leaders.

1. A Comprehensive Leadership Development Plan Must Be Deliberate and Incorporate Staff at All Levels of the System

Nurturing the leadership talent necessary to carry out the work of instructional improvement requires an explicit plan for leadership development that includes both line and support staff. This plan must be systemic, consistent, deliberate, and comprehensive. It must complement the instructional reform strategy. Such a plan demands shifting the structure and culture of the central office in order to align, integrate, and connect the departments with the schools. To be successful, an organization must reach agreement about its priorities, its theory of change, and its way of thinking about leadership. In the BPS, this means completing its conversion from a system organized by levels (elementary, middle, high) to a K–12 educational system, and resolving the structural challenges that prevent internal accountability and transparent decision making. Working to create an integrated system is a leadership development opportunity for up-and-coming leaders in the organization.

2. The Leadership Development Plan Must Build Capacity in Multiple Domains, Including Technical, Managerial, and Personal Leadership Skills

A reform initiative on the scale that BPS has undertaken requires increased overall capacity for leadership development, with a special focus on developing managerial and personal leadership skills across the organization. Leadership development involves facilitated, developmentally-appropriate activities.[21] Ongoing technical skill development is important, but managerial topics must also be added to the leadership development agenda. For example, in the BPS, development for administrators should focus not just on interpretation of data, but on priority-setting and action planning. Providing principals with the opportunity to discuss how they can use data to develop strategies for change would not only increase leadership capacity, but also directly affect the district's stated goals of lowering the achievement gap, addressing English-language learners, special education students, and improving instruction for all learners.

A more deliberate approach to internal development should also include opportunities for peer learning and mentoring. A school district attempting to improve instruction must do so at all levels. In Boston, the central office has received minimal attention to date. This is problematic. The district must provide professional development opportunities aimed at coordinating instructional support. Ideally, these opportunities can spring from the day-to-day work and challenges of the district, since leadership development need not, and in fact, should not, be separate from the regular work of the organization. In Boston and presumably in most traditional urban districts, this transition will involve a significant change of mindset, which can be considered a leadership development activity in its own right.

Continued development of consistent standards for supervision and support of principals, managers, and teachers is also essential. Leadership development should focus on developing internal capacity to think and work across silos. In Boston, we heard that principals need continued development in mobilizing change, establishing organizational alignment, creating school cultures with high expectations, and coaching, mentoring, and evaluating their teaching staff. As one former administrator summarized, "We must continually develop principals' capacity for managing teachers and getting them to move from one place to the next." Related to this is the need to develop everyone's capacity to work with district stakeholders, including union relationships, and to increase capacity for parent, family, and community engagement, especially in the area of supporting immigrant parents. These are knotty issues, and creative thinking about how to support instruction will be needed. All of these can help the district address issues of fidelity of implementation.

In the personal domain, our BPS research indicated that people want to have more focused conversations about the role of race in leadership development. The call is not just for academic conversations, but for personalized discussions about such topics as, "How does my race affect how I do the work?" In addition, Linda Hill's research calls for the district to develop leaders' capacity to cope with stress and emotion, build networks of developmental relationships, establish trust and credibility, and coach and mentor others. Drawing on these capacities will enable educators and administrators to begin articulating common core values.

3. The Plan Must Embed Learning Opportunities Such As Role-Shift and Stretch Assignments in the "Day-to-Day Work" of Its Developing Leaders

The sustainability of strong leadership and school improvement hinges on a district's development of systems and attitudes that enable succession planning, role-shift and stretch assignments, and meaningful evaluation. These should be transparent, clearly articulated processes so that people know they are being groomed and developed; this goes hand in hand with a deliberate strategy for leadership development. An example of this kind of process can be seen in the Long Beach Unified School District, where principals and other administrators are rotated from assignment to assignment approximately every five years, and senior leadership deliberately grooms successors.[22]

BPS has outgrown its early focus on finding talented leaders. Now they must reorganize internal systems and expectations to address leadership development that entails job-embedded and differentiated support. In his book *High Flyers*, developmental scholar Morgan McCall details how, with the right mindset, leadership development can be incorporated into the *everyday* work of an organization.[23] McCall writes about moving from a "survival of the fittest" attitude to one in which the organization seeks to "develop the fittest."

McCall argues that organizations can identify the strategic challenges that leaders must face and then identify the types of experiences that would help them meet those challenges. The goal of "developing the fittest" is to "help people succeed." Given that the reality of school leadership is constantly changing, we feel that this developmental approach has strong application within school districts. There are few individuals who already know how to establish school systems where all children excel, thus we cannot expect to hire talented individuals who already know how to do the work. Rather, our school districts must be organized to develop this talent as greater understanding of the task emerges.

CONCLUSION

School systems nationwide are grappling with the need to cultivate leadership talent. To realize the goal of high-quality instruction and improved outcomes for students, districts must provide opportunities and experiences to enhance the leadership skills and knowledge of *all* stakeholders in their schools. Change of the magnitude recommended here is no small undertaking. However, in Boston it is crucial in order to sustain the instructional improvements already accomplished in the district and to support continuous improvement going forward.

At the end of our interview with Tim Knowles, former BPS deputy superintendent, we asked what advice he would offer to the district administration. We feel his response can be helpful not only to Boston but to all districts facing the challenges of standards based accountability and districtwide reform:

> I encourage the leadership team in Boston to have the willingness to look hard and make ambitious changes to help the district become more nimble. Tom came in and has been heroic in his focus on teaching and learning. Now, the work is to distribute authority in a deep way to enable continued improvement.

APPENDIX 3A

Boston Public Schools Organization Charts, September 11, 1995

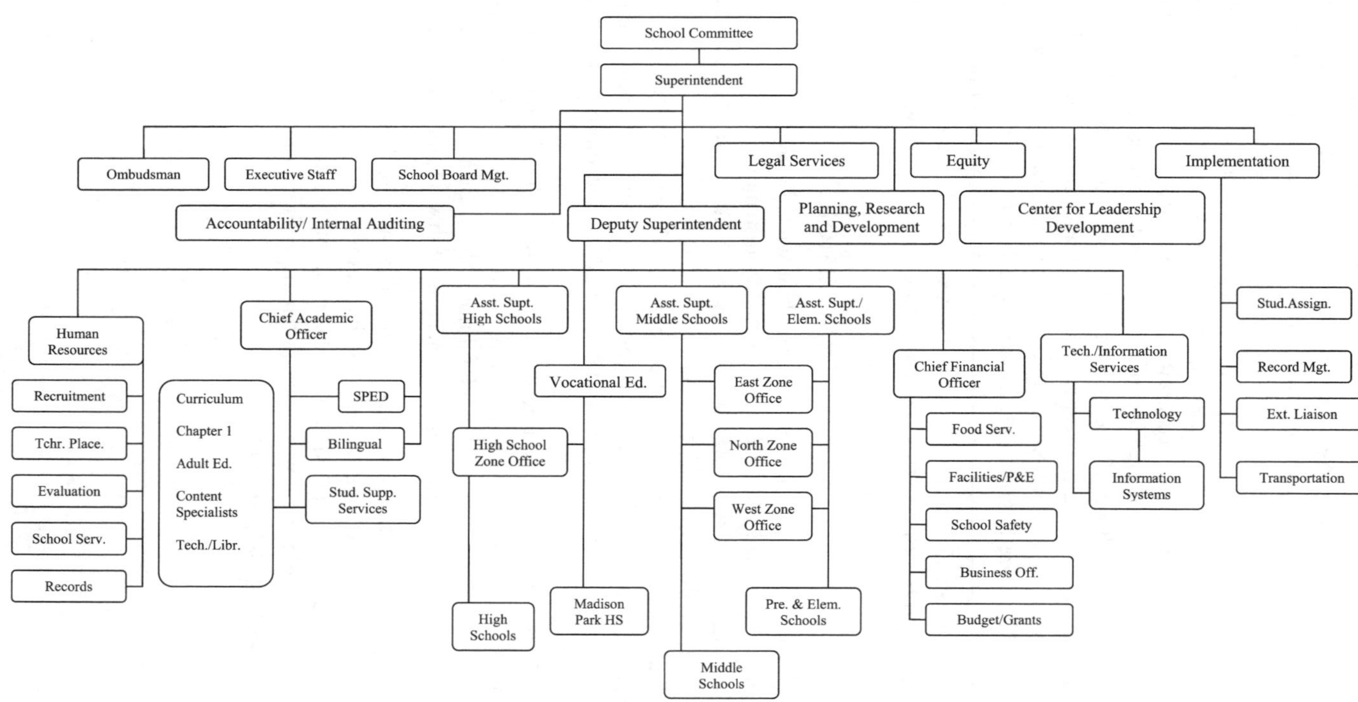

APPENDIX 3B

Administrative Reorganization Chart, February 14, 1996

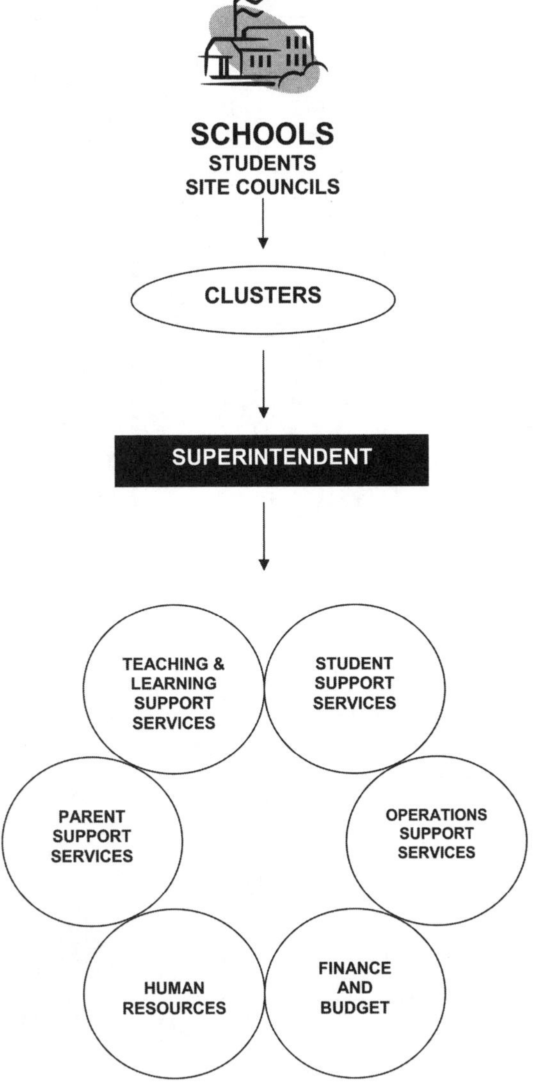

APPENDIX 3C

Boston Public Schools, Administrative Organization 2005–2006

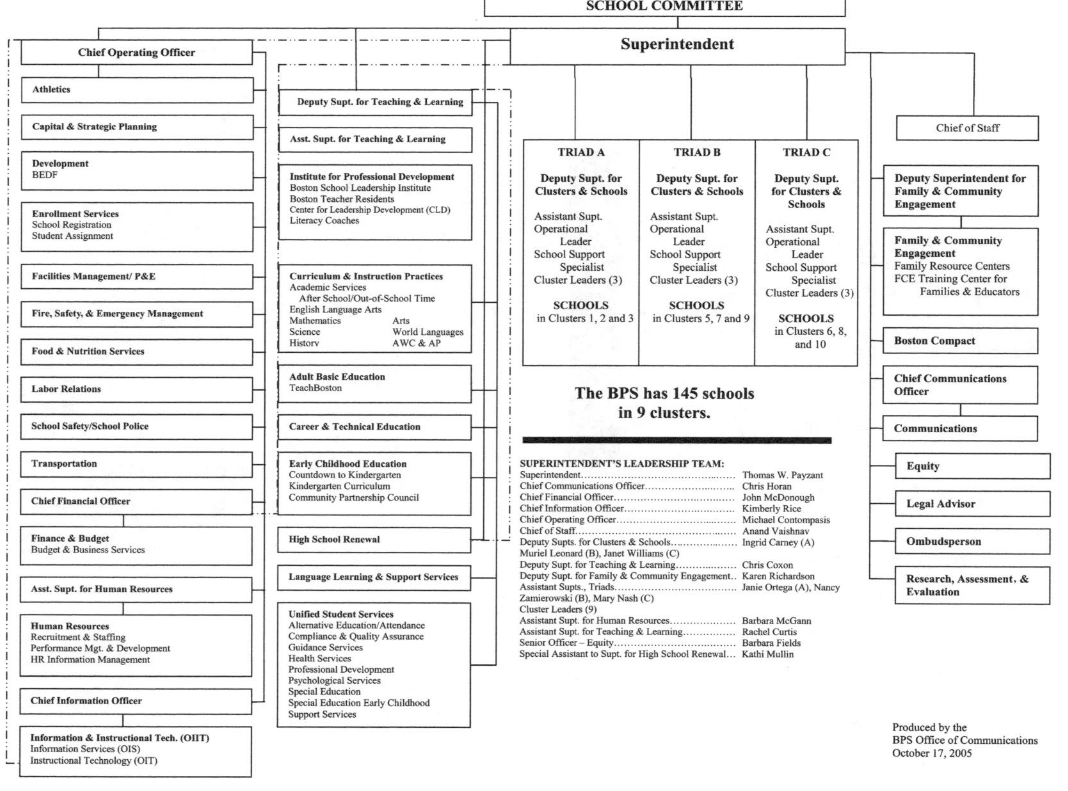

APPENDIX 3D

Boston Principal Fellowship Dimensions of Principal Leadership

1. Understanding and Managing Self
1.1 Integrity
1.2 Emotional self-control
1.3 Personal growth and reflection on practice
1.4 Time management
1.5 Self-awareness

2. Resilience
2.1 Constructive reaction to disappointment; willingness to admit error
2.2 Constructive response to disagreement and dissent
2.3 Strategy and stamina
2.4 Renewal

Essential 1: Use effective instructional practices and create a collaborative school climate to improve student learning

3. School Culture and Climate
3.1 Core beliefs and values
3.2 Communication
3.3 Physical environment
3.4 Boundaries for behavior
3.5 Systems, structures, rituals, and routines
3.6 Collegial, reflective environment

4. Learning and Teaching
4.1 Child and adult learning
4.2 Academic standards and student performance requirements
4.3 Learning needs of all students
4.4 Cultural competency
4.5 Achievement gap
4.6 Research on standards, curriculum, instruction, and assessment

5. Supervision and Evaluation
5.1 Clear performance expectations
5.2 Supervision
5.3 Formal evaluation
5.4 Difficult decisions

Essential 2: Examine student work and data to drive instruction and professional development

6. Data
6.1 Multiple data sources
6.2 Communication of data
6.3 Data-based decision making

Essential 3: Invest in professional development to improve instruction

7. Professional Development
7.1 Faculty strengths and needs
7.2 Collaboration
7.3 Participation in learning community
7.4 Assessment of effectiveness

Essential 4: Share leadership to sustain instructional improvement

8. Shared Leadership
8.1 Decision-making structures and processes
8.2 Different points of view
8.3 Delegation
8.4 Leadership development

Essential 5: Focus resources to support instructional improvement and improved student learning

9. Resources
9.1 Budget, staff, and time
9.2 Resource-allocation decisions
9.3 Corporate and community resources

Essential 6: Partner with families and community to support student learning.

10. Family and Community Engagement
10.1 Communication with families and community
10.2 Needs and assets
10.3 Connection to student learning

CHAPTER IV

Building a Human Resource System in the Boston Public Schools

SUSAN MOORE JOHNSON
MORGAEN L. DONALDSON

TEACHERS ARE, without question, the most important school-level factor affecting students' learning. A skilled and committed teacher makes an enormous difference in what students know and can do, while having a series of ineffective teachers can have a devastating effect on a student's progress.[1]

Recent public attention to teacher quality reflects the consensus about the importance of teachers in promoting student learning. The No Child Left Behind Act required that by June 2006 all public school teachers must be "highly qualified." Such teachers must have a bachelor's degree, a teaching license, and a passing score on the state teachers exam. However, these credentials are only a first step in ensuring effective teachers for all students in large, urban districts such as Boston. Like many of its counterparts, the Boston Public Schools (BPS) serves large numbers of students from low-income and minority communities who often need special education services or transitional support while learning English. It is not enough for a teacher to know her subject. She must also know how to teach that subject effectively to students with a range of abilities and from many backgrounds. She must care deeply about her work and collaborate with fellow teachers to ensure that all students in her school do well. Ultimately, the success of Boston Public Schools and other large, urban districts is dependent on a skilled and stable teaching force.

A Brief History

Beginning in the late 1990s, the BPS, like many other school districts, recognized that it would need to hire large numbers of new teachers by 2010. Based on estimates that half the nation's teachers would retire between 2000 and 2010, analysts projected a national need for 2.2 million new teachers. Mirroring these broader trends, BPS expected to replace approximately 3,500 teachers—

more than half its workforce—within the decade.[2] Having hired relatively few new teachers since 1980, the district was not prepared for such demands. District administrators also realized that successful recruitment and hiring provided no guarantee of a stable teaching force, since many teachers stay in the classroom for only a short time. Nationally, one-third of novice teachers leave within three years and one-half leave within five.[3] Many administrators and researchers think turnover rates are even higher in large, urban districts. In fact, by 2005, close to half of Boston's new recruits were leaving within three years.[4] Thus, the challenge of retaining effective teachers soon became as important as recruiting or hiring them.

Like most urban districts, BPS was not well organized for either recruitment or retention, and there was no simple recipe for becoming so. Personnel offices that were isolated, bureaucratic, and paper-bound suddenly had to operate in a labor market that called for integrated services, flexibility, and the rapid information and response that only technology could provide. For an organization so dependent on human capital, the BPS had shockingly little accurate data about its teachers—how many were employed, whether they were licensed, how much experience they had, how long they stayed, or why they left. The available data were stored in "separate and redundant" databases maintained by different departments.[5] Also, district officials could not unilaterally change human resources (HR) practices because many employment procedures had been negotiated with the Boston Teachers Union (BTU). For example, seniority-based provisions in the contract required that the district handle current teachers' transfer requests before opening jobs to outside candidates. That process, coupled with bureaucratic delay and late approval of state and municipal budgets, often meant that new teachers could not be hired until late August, a situation common in other large, urban districts as well.[6] As a result, newly hired recruits were often unready for their assignment, unfamiliar with the BPS curriculum, and unprepared for the challenges of teaching effectively in an urban setting. The district's day-long orientation program for new teachers was too brief to address all the new teachers' questions about their students, their curriculum, or their school.

It is no surprise, then, that large numbers of Boston's newly hired teachers were leaving their schools through what national research has called the "revolving door" of turnover.[7] Not only would Boston have to develop an ambitious program for hiring and assigning well-qualified teachers to each school, it would also have to build a deliberate and systemic approach to support them in their work.

Superintendent Tom Payzant recognized these problems in the late 1990s and set out to build a "21st-century HR organization" in the BPS.[8] Internal and external reports commissioned by Payzant detailed the district's human resources challenges. However, at that time there was insufficient funding to update technology, and early efforts to reform HR policy and practice moved slowly.

In 2004 the pace of change accelerated. Payzant hired Barbara McGann, former commander of naval recruiting, to head and strengthen HR. A grant from a private foundation supported improvements. McGann began to define and steadily implement a coherent and integrated human resource initiative informed by best practice nationally. Although still understaffed, underfunded, and insufficiently integrated, this initiative offers promise that the BPS will build a skilled, strong, and stable teaching force to serve all students.

We examine here the changes that the BPS has instituted in its HR policies and practices with regard to teachers. We document the considerable progress that has been made in practices such as recruitment and hiring, and we identify areas such as teacher assignment and induction that still require focused attention. We conclude with recommendations for how the BPS approach to human resources could be further strengthened and coordinated in order to attract and retain the best possible teachers for Boston's students. Lessons learned in Boston have meaning for those seeking to improve HR policy and practice in other large, urban districts.

FINDING AND RECRUITING NEW TEACHERS

Labor markets for teachers are remarkably local. They differ between and even within regions in response to factors such as funding for education, housing patterns, and birth and immigration patterns, which create the level of demand for teachers. As a result, some regions and even school districts within the same region will report shortages, while others must lay off staff. Nonetheless, across the nation, a large cohort of veteran teachers who started their careers in the late 1960s and early 1970s have begun to retire, creating an increasing demand for new teachers. Importantly, even districts with a surplus of teachers overall regularly report an ongoing need for qualified staff in math, science, special education, and foreign languages. In most school districts, minority and male teachers continue to be in short supply.

Some school districts, particularly those in rural areas, suffer from being far removed from the source of university programs that prepare teachers. However, the BPS has the distinct advantage of being located at the center of a large higher education community that includes thirty-six undergraduate and graduate institutions that prepare teachers.[9] Broadly speaking, teacher supply should not be a concern for the BPS. However, district officials report recurrent and persistent vacancies in math, science, and special education. Moreover, even when all positions are filled, the teaching force falls short of providing the uniformly high-quality staff that all students deserve. Some positions are filled with teachers working under emergency licenses, and teacher race and gender are also issues. By far the largest proportion of BPS teaching applicants are white and female, while the student body is 51 percent male and includes 86 percent students of color (see figure 1).[10]

FIGURE 1

BPS Student and Teacher Composition by Race, 2005–06

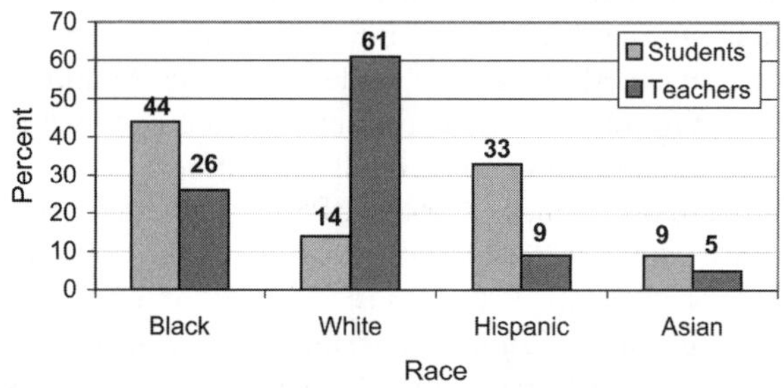

In addition, new recruits who are well-schooled in their subject and how to teach it still may be unprepared to teach in an urban context, which calls on them to build productive relationships with students and families across boundaries of race, ethnicity, and social class. Finally, prospective teachers may be unfamiliar with the curriculum the district uses as it moves to a more consistent approach to instruction. Thus, analyzing the district's demand for teachers requires close attention to variation across the fields of shortage, to the demographic match between teachers and students, and to candidates' readiness to teach urban students and the district's curriculum.

Recruitment of Licensed Teachers

Until recently, BPS was known as a system that prospective teachers found difficult to navigate, especially if they were unfamiliar with the schools and district.[11] There was no sustained recruitment effort, and candidates seeking to work in the city rather than the suburbs often gave up before finding a job in Boston. Staff in the personnel office had become accustomed to processing a surplus of candidates and relying on principals to find their own teachers. The personnel office offered perfunctory interviews and accumulated piles of candidates' applications, rarely forwarding them to principals or informing the prospective teachers of their fate in the process. Until recently, job openings were irregularly and inconveniently posted. Sometimes this was a deliberate strategy used by principals who wanted to have a free hand in hiring their own teachers. This obscure, incomprehensible hiring process, often driven by informal politics, discouraged candidates who lacked an insider's knowledge of Boston's schools and how to get a principal's attention. Each year when the district had to fill large numbers of vacancies by late August, most eager and viable candidates had given up and taken jobs in other cities or the suburbs.

In 2001, HR director Ray Shurtleff began to address some of these problems by using funding from an outside source to open an attractive walk-in recruitment office on the first floor of the district office on Court Street. Equipped with computers and staffed with helpful assistants, this office provided information about job openings and for the first time allowed candidates to apply online. Despite the obvious progress that the new office signaled, recruitment efforts were modest, information about job openings remained incomplete, and the process of application was disjointed, with poor links to the principals who ultimately would select candidates.

Since 2001, the BPS has invested substantial resources in improving the recruitment process. Two full-time recruiters actively pursue candidates by advertising widely on websites and by visiting institutions such as historically black colleges and universities to encourage candidates who might not otherwise consider teaching in Boston. Meanwhile, prospective teachers with an interest in the system can find current information about openings on the BPS website and apply online. In July 2005, HR launched a Web-based recruitment and hiring system that eliminated all paper applications and reduced the possibility that candidates would be lost in the bureaucratic shuffle. The website includes a handbook with straightforward explanations about how the hiring process works, what candidates seeking positions should do to find a job, and what communication and assistance they can expect from HR. Partly in response to this far more transparent process and an increased number of positions posted for hiring, applications by licensed candidates have increased, even in special education, a field in which the BPS has long experienced shortages.

Online applications now allow school officials to screen prospective teachers' credentials and assess their "disposition to teach" using the Gallup assessment, TeacherInsight™. Principals can then use these data along with information about race and gender to decide which candidates to interview. Meanwhile, candidates can track the progress of their application online. HR staff promote the process of matching candidates with schools by holding three job fairs for prescreened candidates and principals who seek new teachers. Principals can conduct interviews and make job offers on the spot or arrange for follow-up interviews at their schools. Thus, within a relatively short time, the BPS has moved from having a largely passive, paper-based, and sluggish recruitment process to offering one that is increasingly informative, timely, welcoming, and interactive.

Growing Their Own

The BPS has also increased the supply of promising candidates by creating an in-district program to prepare new teachers for its schools. Payzant decided in 2002 that the district could not rely entirely on the available supply of teachers, so he envisioned and established the Boston Teacher Residency Program (BTR). Developed by Jesse Solomon, this twelve-month program focuses on recruiting and preparing cohorts of "community-engaged" candidates with a deep knowledge and understanding of Boston.[12] The program actively seeks both individuals of color and candidates in the high-need fields of math, science, and special education. During the school year, BTR interns are assigned to one of ten host schools where they coteach with a mentor teacher, learning to use the BPS curriculum as they increase their instructional skills. In addition, they take coursework in both pedagogy and content.

Starting with 12 interns the first year (2003–04), the program grew to 50 in 2005–06, with a goal of eventually preparing 120 teachers each year, approximately one-third of Boston's new hires. The efforts of a half-time BTR recruiter, who searches for promising candidates throughout the city and beyond, yielded a 2005–06 cohort that included 50 percent individuals of color and 50 percent who were preparing to teach math or science at the secondary level. All participants became certified in both their subject area or grade level and in special education, thus increasing their instructional repertoire. Residents are paid $10,000 for their year of work and the program's $10,000 tuition is forgiven if they teach in BPS for three years after completing their training.

The BTR program is sponsored in collaboration with the University of Massachusetts Boston under a provision of the state board of education authorizing district-based teacher education programs. During the first two years, the program was funded by a grant from Strategic Grant Partners, who sought to support promising educational programs. Gradually, the BPS has assumed responsibility for BTR costs of $30,000 per candidate. By 2006–07, BPS funds should cover 60 percent of what it takes to run the program, clear evidence of Payzant's continued commitment to the initiative.

HIRING AND ASSIGNMENT

Recruiting new teachers is an important first step in building a strong and stable teaching force. However, a deep application pool is of little use unless teachers are hired and assigned in a timely way that ensures the best possible match between teacher, school, and assignment. BPS officials realized that ensuring teachers would be well prepared and matched to their classrooms would require a substantial change in operations. Not only would they need to upgrade their own administrative practices, but they would have to work with the BTU to revise the collective bargaining agreement.

In recent years, the BPS and BTU have worked to eliminate persistent delays in the hiring process. Boston, like many urban districts, has had a long and problematic history of hiring candidates late in August. A survey of new teachers in four states, including Massachusetts, revealed that only one-third of novice teachers had been hired more than a month before school started; one-third were hired during the month before school opened; and one-third were hired *after* the start of the school year.[13] BPS administrators do not know how many prospective teachers never completed the hiring process, but it seems certain that large numbers of very able candidates have been lost annually to other districts. Those who persisted in their hunt for a Boston teaching position typically encountered rushed hiring, with little exchange of information about the schools where they would teach or the special interests and qualifications they could contribute. Research shows that teaching candidates who have a good preview of their work setting are more satisfied as teachers, even when they work in challenging settings.[14] It is no surprise that candidates hired late in the summer rarely have such a preview. Therefore, investing in a timely, school-based hiring process has great potential payoff: good matches can be made between candidates and schools and new hires can prepare in advance for their students.

Many factors contribute to late hiring in large urban districts. The most often-blamed factor is seniority-based transfer provisions in teacher contracts that give tenured teachers priority for open positions and, in some districts, even allow them to bump junior teachers from their positions.[15] Many districts are required by contract to complete this transfer and assignment process before jobs are posted for external candidates. But a restrictive teachers contract is only one of many potential obstacles to timely hiring. Others include principals' delay—sometimes deliberate—in identifying open positions, unexpected June retirement announcements, delays caused by bureaucratic procedures in a human resources office, and stalled approval of state and municipal budgets. This array of potential challenges to timely hiring is daunting, but over time Boston has addressed each one.

Contract Changes

Since 1985, the BPS and the BTU have negotiated changes in the collective bargaining agreement that diminish the role of seniority (as measured by the length of employment in the district) in teacher assignment. In the 2000 contract negotiations, substantial advances were made, some of them championed by community and nonprofit organizations, including the Boston Plan for Excellence in the Public Schools (BPE) and the Boston Parent Organizing Network. At one time, a licensed teacher with sufficient qualifications could claim the job of any more junior colleague in the district; now seniority affects a teacher's assignment only through tenure, not through a measure of longevity. Principals also have gained a far greater say in the transfer of teachers into their schools. Currently, if two or more tenured teachers apply to transfer to an open position, a principal must accept one of them, though not necessarily the more senior. Otherwise, the principal can post the job and hire an outside candidate. Even first-year teachers cannot be displaced as long as they have a "letter of reasonable assurance" from their principal stating that they are very likely to be reemployed in the same position the next year. One by one, the disruptive effects of seniority-based assignment in Boston have been eliminated at the bargaining table.

What has not changed, however, is the district's ongoing legal obligation to its long-term teachers. Teacher tenure—called "professional status" in Massachusetts—is established and protected by state law, not the local teachers contract.

Because a school district must find a place for every teacher it has tenured, open positions are first filled with teachers to whom the district is bound, even if a principal would prefer to hire a new recruit. In Boston, all permanent teachers who lack a position because they are returning from leave or have been transferred involuntarily due to program cuts are matched with openings through a formally bargained process called the "excess pool." If three or more candidates from the excess pool apply for an open position, principals are required to accept one of these teachers. Principals may interview and rank the candidates, but HR decides which teacher is placed in the open position.[16]

Historically, BPS principals who believed that dismissing unsatisfactory tenured teachers was impossible chose instead to involuntarily transfer them to other schools or convinced them to enter the excess pool. This practice, informally called "the dance of the lemons," led to the repeated transfer of poor teachers from school to school. It also led to the concentration of underperforming teachers in a few schools. In the 2000 negotiations, teachers lost the right to enter the excess pool voluntarily and principals lost the right to move unsatisfactory teachers out of their schools and into the excess pool. Although some principals maneuver around these restrictions by eliminating the program in which an unsatisfactory teacher works, the excess pool appears increasingly to be composed of competent candidates for open positions—those returning from leave and those whose schools experienced true enrollment declines or program changes. However, until the district aggressively deals with unsatisfactory tenured teachers, jobs that might have been open to new candidates will be assigned to teachers, however weak, whom the district is obliged by the state's tenure law to employ.

Hiring, which is very centralized in some urban districts, has traditionally been decentralized in Boston. In the early 1980s, the BPS and BTU formalized this approach by establishing school-based hiring committees at each school site. In many schools today, these hiring committees actively participate in decisions made before summer break. In theory, school-based hiring would encourage a rich exchange of information and a good match between a candidate and a school's principal, teachers, and parents. However, school-based hiring committees are convened less often than they might be, sometimes because the principal wants to make his/her own hiring decisions and sometimes because a delayed timetable means that colleagues and parents are not readily available to meet with candidates in July and August.

Finally, the BPS and BTU agreed in October 2000 to compress the schedule for transfers and hiring. They set an ambitious timetable for the spring of 2001 that would allow HR to post all openings on March 1. This would enable BPS to complete its internal transfer and excess processes earlier and permit schools to hire external candidates three months before they had historically been hired.[17] Further, schools could hire external candidates beginning in March under any one of three conditions: (1) if no permanent teacher applied for a position during transfer or excess; (2) if 60 percent of the school faculty voted to open post the position to outside candidates; (3) if the position carried a stipend of at least $1,000. By posting positions earlier and opening up the hiring process, BPS might better compete with suburban districts for the most talented candidates in the pool. In the spring of 2001, the district made great progress, condensing the process from three months to four weeks, but in 2002 state delays in approving the budget again stalled progress.

However, the difficulties were not all external to the hiring process itself. In a 2002 report, the Boston Municipal Research Bureau concluded that "While progress was achieved, principals and headmasters did not take full advantage of provisions in the contract that enabled schools to interview and hire outside candidates much earlier in the process."[18] Clearly, reforming teacher assignment and hiring would require more than simply changing the contract.

Upgrades in HR

Early in her tenure, Barbara McGann sought to reform the Department of Human Resources. This was an important step because not only had the office been inaccessible to prospective teachers, it was virtually impenetrable to principals who had not nurtured relationships with the staff, whose approval they needed to move the hiring process along. The office included a number of separate subunits, or "silos," that divided HR staff by function—for example, recruitment, staff, and data-management—leaving the district dependent on one or two people to accomplish any particular task. Together, these subunits constituted a fragmented arrangement that frustrated principals, other district staff, and teachers.

In 2004, McGann removed the cubicles that physically divided people and tasks, and she began to eliminate the staff's specialized roles and to cross-train them in teams. She hired new, skilled administrators to speed up implementation of the redesign and created a two-person New Teacher Support Team to provide "red-carpet treatment" for candidates throughout the hiring process. Prospective teachers received a personal e-mail of welcome when they applied, were assisted in moving their paperwork through the City Hall employment bureaucracy, and, once hired, were invited to attend a welcome reception.

Bureaucracies are hard to dismantle, and seasoned staff are often slow to adopt new approaches. However, the concerted, coordinated efforts of McGann and her colleagues yielded notable, positive results. Delay in the budget approval process, which accounted for the postponement of hiring until August in 2002, ceased disrupting the process when the district began to take reasonable risks in making timely job offers rather than waiting for formal confirmation of resources through the budget process. In an important policy change, BPS officials decided that if budget cuts were imposed, the district would not meet them by reducing instructional positions. This action helped resolve an unnecessary and recurring source of teacher loss in the form of routine layoff notices. Each spring, large numbers of nontenured teachers received these notices, knowing that they probably would be reinstated when the budget passed. However, despite the assurances, every year many of these teachers found jobs elsewhere. These notices are no longer sent out, which has made BPS more successful in attracting and retaining teachers.

Supported by new administrative staff and technology, staffing decisions in early 2006 proceeded on schedule. In January, principals filed their staffing plans ("probable organization") and identified open positions. In keeping with an agreement negotiated in the 2000 contract, principals offered selected early-career teachers "letters of reasonable assurance" that secured their positions for the 2006–07 school year. Simultaneously, they granted permanent contracts to outstanding novices. In February, teachers seeking to change schools petitioned to fill open positions through the voluntary transfer process. Concurrently, principals could post for open hiring any position meeting the negotiated standards—approval by 60 percent of the faculty or having an additional stipend of at least $1,000. In late March, 130 teachers returning from leave or transferred because of program cuts were assigned to positions during the excess pool meetings, which used to be delayed until the close of school. McGann had filled virtually all teaching positions by the end of June.

By all accounts, hiring and assignment in the BPS have improved markedly as a result of changes in the BTU contract and improvements in HR organization and practices. Boston now can compete for talented teachers with other districts that hire early, rather than losing out and making do with a much smaller and arguably weaker pool of candidates in August. Because hiring can occur during the spring, candidates can visit a school in session, see the students, meet with prospective colleagues, and decide whether that school would provide a good match for their interests and skills. Prescreening by district HR staff ensures that candidates and principals will not encounter unexpected problems with licensing, and assistance by New Teacher Support staff personalizes the application process from the start. Candidates can be assured that principals will have access to their application, and they, themselves, can track the progress of their job search in Boston. The opportunities exist in the BPS today for timely, school-based hiring, but taking full advantage of those opportunities continues to be a challenge for those inside the system.

The Persistent Problem of Inequitable Assignment

Although HR and the teachers union have eliminated many factors that delayed transfers and hiring, there remains a persistent problem of uneven assignment. As in many large, urban districts, low-performing schools get less than their share of strong talent, and at present there is no systematic way to redress this imbalance. The current staffing and assignment process depends on principals being well-informed and taking initiative to post positions, attend job fairs, encourage candidates, and engage school-based committees in the hiring process. Those involved report that the principals who are the best prepared and most savvy in recruiting and hiring teachers often head schools that are already successful. These principals' initiative and understanding of hiring reinforces their schools' success. By contrast, principals who are unfamiliar or passive participants in the hiring process often head low-performing schools. Over time, these schools lose in the competition for new teachers, while their students (who are likely to be from low-income, high-minority communities) likely pay a serious, long-term price.

INDUCTION AND RETENTION OF NEW TEACHERS

There are many steps to ensuring that all Boston students have good teachers. Once it seemed that if the district could successfully recruit, hire, and assign new teachers to schools and classes, the challenge would be largely met. However, ongoing teacher turnover is a far greater problem than anyone anticipated. No longer can school officials assume that a new teacher will make a lifelong career in the classroom.

Turnover includes both attrition—leaving teaching for another line of work—and transfer—moving from one school or district to another. Policymakers and teacher educators are concerned with attrition, wanting to know whether their investment in teacher preparation is realized, while district officials want to know how long new teachers remain in their district and what it costs when they leave. Far less attention is focused on whether and why teachers transfer from school to school within a district. In either case, the students, principal, and staff of any school feel the loss of a skilled teacher, for in leaving, that teacher takes with her experience and knowledge about the school, its program, and its community that are not easily replaced. When teachers transfer repeatedly and in large numbers—as they tend to do from low-income, low-performing schools—those schools must spend an inordinate amount of time each year hiring and acclimating new staff.[19] Moreover, transfer patterns can lead to concentrations of more skilled teachers in some schools and less skilled teachers in others. Unfortunately, the schools that consistently lose teachers often already face enormous demands, which the principal and teachers must meet with diminished professional resources.

Retention Rates in the BPS

Administrators in HR have no data about patterns of teacher retention over time, although a recent analysis of the 2004–05 data by Birkeland and Curtis revealed a worrisome picture.[20] Early-career teachers who left the district during that school year included eighty-nine in their first year of teaching (19%), sixty-one in their second year (22%), and forty-four in their third year (15%). Based on these figures, the authors extrapolated an alarmingly high attrition rate of 47 percent during the first three years of teaching in the BPS.[21]

Even more troubling, perhaps, is the fact that BPS may be losing black, Hispanic, and Asian teachers at a higher rate than white teachers. During 2004–05, 22 percent of first-year minority teachers left the BPS, while 17 percent of white teachers did. Second-year teachers of color also left at higher rates (26% vs. 19%), as did third-year teachers of color (18% vs. 13%). Based on these data, Birkeland and Curtis estimate that the likelihood that BPS minority teachers will leave before their fourth year is 53 percent, while the comparable figure for white teachers is 42 percent. According to their analysis, black teachers are 16 percentage points more likely than white teachers to leave the district within three years. Given Boston's high proportion of minority students and its low proportion of minority teachers, it is especially important to understand the reasons for such attrition from the district. There is some evidence that teachers of color have more difficulty passing the state licensing examination (MTEL) than white teachers, even when they have met all other licensing requirements. This pattern of attrition may increase as the BPS complies with NCLB and dismisses teachers who do not qualify as "highly qualified" under the law.

A reverse trend can be observed for graduates of the BTR program, which has shown promising retention rates in its early years. Basic to this initiative is the idea that teachers who are committed and well prepared to teach in Boston will succeed in BPS classrooms and that this success, coupled with a financial incentive, will lead these teachers to choose to stay. So far, the logic that targeted selection, preparation, and incentives will promote higher teacher retention has held up, with 100 percent retention of the forty-three teachers prepared in BTR through 2005. However, it is difficult to judge what plays the largest role in these teachers' decision to stay in the district—their careful selection, their specific preparation for teaching in Boston schools, or the $3,333 in tuition forgiven for each year they teach in BPS. It will be important to track the number of BTR teachers who remain in BPS after three years, when their $10,000 tuition loan is fully forgiven.

The Costs of Turnover

Before discussing the reasons for high teacher turnover and what kinds of support might remedy it, we consider the financial and organizational costs that teacher attrition and transfer impose on districts and schools. Efforts to estimate such costs using models from the private sector, which typically calculate the expense as a percentage of salary earned, have yielded conservative, rough estimates of per-teacher costs ranging from $354.92 to $5,165.76.[22] Birkeland and Curtis collected detailed information about the costs to the BPS of recruiting, hiring, providing professional development, and processing the job terminations of new teachers who leave. They calculated replacement costs to be $10,547 for a first-year teacher, $18,617 for a second-year teacher, and $26,687 for a third-year teacher, with the annual increases largely due to the district's investment in professional development. These estimates do not include the added value that accrues with teaching experience, which research has shown increases teachers' effectiveness through at least their fifth year.[23] Birkeland and Curtis estimate that it cost the BPS $3.3 million in 2004–05 to replace the 194 first-year, second-year, and third-year teachers who left the district. And that figure does not reflect the incalculable organizational costs of turnover within each school. Given the high cost of turnover, it is essential to understand the reasons behind it and what can be done about them.

Why Teachers Leave or Move

Researchers have begun to analyze national data and better understand the reasons behind teacher turnover.[24] Low pay and low status relative to other professions lead some to decide that they cannot afford to teach, however much they love the work. A twenty-four-year-old teacher may be able to live on a beginning salary of $42,000, yet see no way to afford a mortgage in the Boston metropolitan area on the incremental raises that the salary scale promises. Also, a surprising number of new teachers—especially those who enter the classroom right after college—never intend to stay in teaching for long. Rather, they expect to make a two- or three-year commitment to public education before moving on to another line of work.[25] It is still unclear whether these "short-termers" have a fixed career plan or whether they might stay longer if they find their experience as teachers sufficiently rewarding. Other new teachers initially plan to stay in teaching longer, hoping that they will enjoy the work and make an important contribution to public education. However, given current turnover rates, it is clear that many of those potential "long-termers" are also leaving the classroom before they planned.

The BPS has little information about why teachers leave or transfer, since they have only recently begun to conduct regular exit interviews. Moreover, BPS has not solicited explanations from teachers who transfer voluntarily to different schools. These career choices by teachers clearly warrant attention, particularly with regard to the decisions of minority teachers and transfer patterns out of hard-to-staff schools. Without far better information, strategies for improving retention will be ill informed.

Surveys of new teachers by the BPE in 2003 offer insight into what novices seek. Researchers found that early-career teachers are more apt to "shorten their plans for staying in BPS" when they lack access to "immediate and practical support."[26] The supports that new teachers reported to be most valuable were:

- feedback on their teaching practices;
- help managing student behavior and creating effective classroom routines;
- help finding the appropriate curriculum and understanding how to use it;
- help planning lessons; and
- opportunities to observe other teachers' practices.

These teachers reported that they found colleagues to be their most important source of support and that in-classroom observation and assistance were their most valued forms of professional development. The novices sought early professional development in how to differentiate instruction for their various students, how to teach English-language learners, and how to implement the district's literacy model.[27]

These responses and priorities mirror what other researchers have learned about why teachers move to new schools or leave teaching. Nationwide, teachers report that they leave schools because of inadequate support from administrators, inconsistent handling of student discipline problems, and limited faculty input into schoolwide decisions.[28] In a longitudinal study of fifty new Massachusetts teachers, researchers found that approximately one-third of the respondents (17) had left public school teaching after four years, one-third (16) had changed schools, and one-third (17) were still in their original schools.[29] Although a few of those who left did so because they were dissatisfied with their pay and status, many more left because they lacked the supports needed to do good work. Some, who had planned to teach for only a few years, left even before they completed that stint. Others, who had expected to remain longer, decided to leave when they found they could not succeed with their students. In both cases, the new teachers reported that they had found insufficient support in their schools.

It is a complex matter to address the needs of these beginning teachers because it requires not only providing targeted orientation and assistance to individuals, but also reforming the schools in which they work. Fortunately, the changes needed to support new teachers are consistent with approaches that would reinforce best practices for all teachers and students. BPS has taken notable steps in this direction.

The Value of Mentors and Induction Programs

Many reformers believe that the best support for new teachers comes from individual mentors, experienced and expert colleagues working closely with novices as they learn to teach. There is evidence that sustained work alongside a well-trained mentor who has time dedicated to such an assignment is a positive form of induction.[30] However, the reality of mentoring routinely falls short of this ideal. Often school officials with limited resources assume that experienced teachers can undertake mentoring relationships with little or no preparation. Mentoring assignments seldom are aligned so that the mentor and new teacher share the same subject or grade. Furthermore, mentoring pairs are rarely allocated time for common planning or observation of one another in the classroom. The value of investing in a partial or inadequate mentoring program thus remains in question.

The BPS introduced mentoring for all new teachers through its Center for Leadership Development (CLD) in the mid-1990s. Lead teachers were appointed to serve as mentors under the joint BPS/BTU Career in Teaching Program; sometimes their teaching assignments matched those of their novice teachers, but often not. Over time, demands for new mentors grew while resources to train and pay them shrank and the CLD staff was reduced in size. Although there has been no systematic study of the program, most administrators and teachers report that it falls far short of what it might be, for all the reasons discussed above.

Mentors receive an additional stipend of 7 percent of their salary to mentor one novice and 14 percent to mentor two. The program, which costs $1.2 million for mentor stipends alone, has not been fully funded since 2001–02, and consequently, not all new teachers are assigned mentors and those who are rarely receive a full year of mentoring.[31] However, many contend that new teachers need more than an assigned mentor and that there are better ways to use these resources.

Researchers who surveyed teachers nationwide have found no relationship between a new teacher's having a mentor and reporting being satisfied with teaching.[32] There is growing evidence, however, that effective induction programs that incorporate more than mentoring have positive effects on new teachers' satisfaction and retention. Based on analysis of national data, Smith and Ingersoll report that new teachers with larger "bundles" of induction support are more likely to stay in teaching than those who receive fewer supports.[33] For example, new teachers who simultaneously experienced mentoring, collaboration, seminars, teacher networks, and a reduced course load were half as likely to leave teaching as those who received mentoring alone.

Meanwhile, a survey of new teachers in four states found they reported satisfaction with their work when they were regularly engaged with experienced colleagues.[34] There is evidence that good induction programs lead to better rates of retention and accelerate a new teacher's development, which is especially important when entrants expect to remain in teaching only a few years.[35] Experience with improved hiring and induction in Philadelphia suggest that targeted initiatives can yield improvements relatively quickly.[36]

Because new teachers focus with laser-like intensity on their schools and their students, rather than on the larger district, efforts to support their day-to-day work and ongoing development must be grounded in the schools.[37] Exemplary induction programs are not marginal to the rest of the school, but are embedded in day-to-day practice, with the school's experienced teachers assuming shared responsibility for new teachers' induction. Novices in such programs have time to meet with colleagues, to observe them at work, and to receive feedback about their teaching. They receive current, detailed information about the practices and procedures of their school, such as what is expected for a teacher on bus duty or how to prepare report cards. These teachers have access to the curriculum they are expected to teach, along with the professional development that will prepare them to teach it. They get good advice about how to build constructive relationships with parents and the community, how to interpret and respond to student test data, and how to meet the special needs of students within the school.

Current Supports in Boston

In their recent assessment of teacher induction in the BPS, Birkeland and Curtis conclude that the district provides some elements of exemplary programs, but "does not implement any of these elements to the full extent recommended by researchers and experts in the field."[38] Well-matched mentors are not available for all new teachers and the supports they do receive vary widely from school to school.

HR has recently instituted some promising new practices that can make an important difference to new teachers. The New Teacher Support Team sponsors a three-day New Teacher Institute in August, addressing topics such as classroom management, lesson planning, and BPS professional development offerings. In 2005 all new teachers participated in the same program, but there are plans to create more specialized sessions for subgroups of teachers, such as those planning to teach special education; mid-career entrants, who bring specialized experience with them; or BTR participants, who have already served one year as an intern in a BPS classroom. In the fall, HR sponsors two professional development courses, each spanning two Saturdays, on topics that new teachers have identified as important. The first focuses on classroom behavioral management, the second on how to differentiate instruction and build community within a class. The New Teacher Support staff also provide "customer service" for new teachers throughout the first few months, visiting approximately twenty schools, trouble-shooting problems such as inaccurate or late paychecks, and publishing a newsletter that includes information for new teachers about opportunities, supports, and obligations.

To provide more school-based support, HR staff prepared a handbook for principals containing suggestions for developing and tailoring a school-based induction program. It is not known how many principals are creating such programs, but research suggests that this approach has payoffs for students and other teachers as well.

One promising pilot project involves two experienced math teachers who have been trained as mentors at the New Teacher Center in Santa Cruz, California. These "new teacher developers," who serve as math coaches, were selected in 2005 by a joint BPS/BTU committee. Unlike BPS mentors, who assume their responsibilities on top of a full-time teaching load, these new teacher developers work full time in that role, each supporting twelve to thirteen first-year teachers. This federally-funded initiative, called the Impact Evaluation of Teacher Induction Program, is being studied by researchers from Mathematica Policy Research, who will focus both on the teachers served and the performance of their students over several years. BPS is considering expanding an amended version of this program to provide teacher developers for all novices.

Keeping the Best

Although the BPS should make it a high priority to improve retention, the district must simultaneously be selective about which teachers it retains. Principals have complete discretion in deciding whether to reemploy teachers in their first three years who have not been made permanent. However, by Massachusetts law, if a teacher meets all licensing requirements and works even one day after the third year of employment, the district has obligations to her as a tenured employee. A teacher can be dismissed for unsatisfactory performance at any time, but the task becomes much more exacting after year three. Thus, principals must not only focus on induction and retention of new teachers, but also carefully assess their performance. Tenure should not be awarded inadvertently by failing to observe and carefully assess new teachers during these trial years.

Under Superintendent Payzant, principals have been expected to conduct substantive and procedurally correct evaluations of nonpermanent teachers. Despite efforts to bolster evaluation, it continues to be an irregular process that some principals take very seriously and others do not. Until the district can assure that all principals conduct the required evaluations and provide assistance to teachers who need it, the ranks of BPS teachers will surely include individuals who should have left the classroom before receiving tenure.

The district recently has increased its attention to unsatisfactory teachers and dismissed five to ten tenured teachers per year, while counseling out approximately ten more.[39] Formal dismissal requires administrators to meet procedural requirements for classroom observations and written evaluations, and these requirements are set out in the teachers contract. When a principal misses an observation or deadline, the union has a legal duty to represent the teacher, whatever the substantive merits of the case. Unless administrators systematically evaluate their teachers, no union leaders can be expected to step in and "police their own."

There are many stories in the BPS and comparable urban districts about incompetent teachers whom no principal wants to accept even though their personnel file includes satisfactory ratings by other principals who never actually observed or assisted them. In years past, it was simply easier to give unsatisfactory teachers an acceptable rating and send them off to another school. Building a successful case to dismiss these individuals is challenging, given the legal standards of demonstrating just cause, but it can be done. It requires professional and legal support for HR administrators, who have recently begun to take on this responsibility.

Changing the Schools

Good school-based induction and selective tenure are essential to ensure that new BPS teachers will choose to remain in Boston classrooms and will be effective in their work. However, to focus all energy and resources on induction and evaluation would be to neglect other important aspects of new teachers' experience. New teachers, experienced teachers, and students all suffer when their school environment is disorganized or chaotic, teaching assignments fail to make the best use of teachers' skills, the daily schedule provides no time for shared planning among teachers, or perfunctory faculty meetings preclude meaningful discussion. There is some evidence that hard-to-staff schools remain hard to staff because they are not good places for any teachers to work or any students to learn. Each year they experience an influx of new teachers who arrive to fill the vacancies created when dissatisfied and disillusioned teachers leave for other schools, districts, or lines of work.

Many studies report that teachers regularly transfer from schools serving low-income students of color to schools in higher-income communities serving larger proportions of white students. However, there is also evidence that teacher retention is not a problem in high-performing schools that serve low-income students. Those schools are organized thoughtfully and purposefully to support good teaching and learning. They are orderly, assign teachers purposefully, use time well, provide in-class supports for novice teachers, sponsor ongoing professional development, and constantly engage the faculty in assessing and improving their work. The challenge of providing a strong and stable teaching staff in all schools extends well beyond offering a good induction program and appropriately evaluating new teachers.

CONCLUSIONS AND RECOMMENDATIONS

Under Superintendent Payzant's leadership, the BPS has taken major steps toward establishing a comprehensive HR system that will attract, prepare, support, and retain a strong and stable teaching force. In a relatively short time, there have been substantial improvements in HR's organization, policies, and practices. Changes in the teachers contract have accelerated the process of assignment and hiring. The BTR has developed a model district-based preparation program. Increasingly, departments within the system are coordinating their efforts to ensure effective staffing. Steady progress in each of these initiatives will continue to strengthen the district as accomplishments in one area positively affect others. Other large, urban districts have launched similar initiatives. For Boston and its counterparts, it is important to continue to work on individual initiatives while developing an overarching human resources system that links and integrates them.

There are several important areas that warrant particular attention and effort:

1. Retrieve, Collect, and Analyze Data

Without an effective system for collecting, retrieving, and analyzing data about teachers and their career choices, policies and practices necessarily will result from guesswork and chance. Complete, accurate, and longitudinal data make it possible to know where to direct resources, whether new initiatives work, or what problems of policy and practice should be addressed first. In addition, district officials must track patterns of retention by subgroup (including men, different racial and ethnic groups, and those who teach math, science, or special education). Identifying persistent problems, such as higher attrition rates among African American teachers, is the first step in addressing them.

It is also important to monitor staffing changes at both the district and school levels. Not only should district staff seek to understand what prompts teachers to leave the district by interviewing each individual who resigns, but they should also survey teachers who petition to transfer from one school to another within the district. Understanding the reasons behind such transfer patterns can inform efforts to improve the schools that teachers most often leave and seldom choose during the transfer process.

2. Establish School-Based Induction throughout the District

Boston's gains in staffing result from a purposeful effort to address the challenges that all urban districts face in the hiring and assignment process. Just as the challenges are similar across districts, so too is the need to sustain progress once it is made. For example, Boston's staffing gains must be protected by fully-funded induction programs that are school-based in design. Particular attention should be given to new teachers who are hired after the beginning of school and miss orientation because these individuals may be most in need of focused support. Consistent with Birkeland and Curtis's recommendations to build on the district's pilot project for full-time math coaches, BPS will appoint up to fifteen new teacher developers, screened and selected by a joint BPS/BTU committee, to perform responsibilities traditionally assigned to mentor teachers. Individuals chosen for these largely school-based positions will prepare for their work during more than twelve days of professional development scheduled over the course of the year. Each will be released from full-time classroom teaching to observe and advise fourteen new teachers weekly. Birkeland and Curtis recommend that the program eventually include second- and third-year teachers, in keeping with evidence that new teachers need support through at least their first three years in teaching.

3. Ensure that Principals Can Do the Job

This analysis demonstrates the crucial role that principals play in the staffing process. Whether a school has a principal who seizes the opportunity to recruit and hire first-rate teachers determines much about the quality and character of a school's staff. Whether a school's principal observes and evaluates teachers in a timely and careful way determines whether individual teachers get the support they need, whether tenure is awarded deliberately rather than accidentally, and whether unsatisfactory teachers are dismissed fairly and effectively. A principal is key in building a sense of purpose and responsibility among teachers, students, and their families. A principal can, quite simply, make or break a school. Given the generally high rate of turnover among principals in urban districts, it is essential that careful attention be given to their ongoing training and support.

4. Focus on the Challenges of Hard-to-Staff Schools

The most important HR challenge that the BPS and other urban districts face today is to staff each classroom of every low-performing, low-income school with an effective teacher. Otherwise, the achievement gap simply will not be closed. Some analysts recommend that districts equalize the distribution of high-quality teachers by limiting voluntary transfers and reassigning talented teachers from high-performing to low-performing schools. Others recommend using financial incentives to entice teachers to work in hard-to-staff schools. The difficulty with both approaches is that they focus on the teachers as commodities who bring skills and talents to the schools, but they do not address these schools' fundamental problem—that they are not places that support good teachers as they try to do good work. Rather, teachers' best efforts often are undermined by passive, erratic, or autocratic principals, inadequate resources, weak infrastructures, and poor relationships with the communities they serve. If these schools are to attract and retain rather than repel strong teachers, they must change in deep ways that extend far beyond the annual restocking of the faculty.

No school district has yet developed a reliable approach to stabilizing turnover and making low-performing schools places that attract the strongest and most dedicated teachers. However, it seems clear that such an approach would be multipronged. First and foremost, it would require seeing that every school has a first-rate principal—the kind of leader that parents would fight to keep at their child's school. Other components of a well-crafted approach might include financial incentives for teachers to work over time in special programs at these schools; opportunities and incentives for cohorts of expert teachers (including those with certification from the National Board for Professional Teaching Standards) to move to these schools; additional instructional resources for teaching students who struggle; extensive social and medical services for students and families; and school facilities that are safe, well stocked, and carefully maintained. In the end, these hard-to-staff schools must become places where committed teachers can reasonably hope to succeed.

5. Develop Professional Roles That Better Support a Career in Teaching

There is considerable evidence that new teachers today will not tolerate having the same job responsibilities throughout a thirty-five-year career. Rather, they look for differentiated roles that will allow them to develop new skills and extend their influence beyond their classroom. Creating the roles that constitute a complete career ladder is a complicated, costly, and controversial undertaking. However, it is possible for the district to explore ways to create differentiated roles for classroom teachers—roles that will keep them close to students and instruction, while extending the reach of their knowledge and influence within the school and district. Current roles for teachers as coaches, members of data analysis committees or instructional leadership teams, along with the new roles for BPS teacher developers, provide the opportunity to systematically define and develop positions that would establish a career continuum in teaching.

6. Move Ahead Together

Creating a comprehensive HR system requires collaboration among many individuals, departments, and institutions. There is no more important relationship than that of the district's central office and the local teachers union. If issues of teacher quality and student success are truly to be addressed, labor and management must work together and their constituents, both inside and outside the system, must endorse their collaboration. For example, the retirement of a large cohort of teachers and the repeated turnover of recently-hired teachers puts the BTU at a crossroads. Among the new generation of teachers, interest in traditional union values and confrontational tactics has fallen rapidly. When new teachers look to their union leaders these days, it is not only for higher salary, better benefits, and improved working conditions, but also for professional development. Teachers want a union of which they can be proud. They want their union leaders to defend a teacher's right to due process, but they do not want them to defend poor teaching. Few new teachers sympathize with industrial-style tactics, and they eschew public battles between labor and management that they believe make all educators look bad. If every school is to be well staffed over time—not for just a season—labor and management must do the hard work of changing rules, norms, and day-to-day practices. In the process, there will be small gains and losses for all parties, but in the end, students must win. Everyone has a stake in that outcome.

Just as the union and management must develop new ways of working, so too must the various departments in the central office, principals across the district, and individuals within a school. Learning to work effectively with the staff person across the hall or the principal across town may be as challenging as building a productive labor-management relationship. Despite considerable goodwill and progress over the past decade, divisions still exist in the BPS that delay progress and compromise accomplishments. Critical resources and energy are sometimes needlessly squandered as individuals and subunits seek to reinforce their own positions, practices, and privileges. The goal of ensuring that every student is taught by an effective teacher can be achieved only if those with a stake in the future of the BPS work together to support that goal. Building support for such a system should be a priority for the next superintendent.

CHAPTER V

Instructional Improvement in the Boston Public Schools

The Limits of Focus and Stability

BARBARA NEUFELD

OVER THE PAST TEN YEARS, the Boston Public Schools (BPS) has undergone a major transformation. Prior to the 1996–97 school year, educators in Boston would have been hard pressed to articulate a coherent, district-wide instructional strategy. In 2006, teachers and administrators, whether or not they agreed with the district's direction, would report that they work in a school district with a whole-school improvement agenda characterized by an explicit set of "Essentials" and specific curricular and instructional methods and supports. Boston educators would report that they are expected to use "workshop" as their primary approach to instruction in English language arts (ELA), and that "workshop-like" instruction should guide the improvement of teaching and learning in all content areas.[1]

Observers of urban school reform might find this success surprising. Many point out that multiple and endemic factors ordinarily prevent the development of the kind of focus reported in Boston. Superintendents are hired to make rapid, significant improvements, but their tenure is typically short due to corrosive local conditions that include contentious relationships with school boards, mayors, the business community, and local citizen advocacy groups. Too much is expected too quickly; superintendents depart; and new saviors take their turn.[2] This did not happen during Tom Payzant's tenure in Boston.

Indeed, the superintendent kept his job for over ten years. The school committee and the mayor never publicly stood in the way of the superintendent's approaches to changing and improving teaching and learning.[3] The civic community provided the district with considerable resources and expressed confidence in the superintendent's approach to reform.[4] The superintendent was able to hire knowledgeable central office administrators and appoint, over time, principals and headmasters of his own choosing.[5] Foundations poured close to

$100 million into the district, most of it to improve instruction. Universities and colleges provided expertise in numerous areas. And the district had a skillful, committed partner in Boston's local education foundation, the Boston Plan for Excellence (BPE). All of these factors, taken together, enabled Boston to establish a focused, consistent agenda for instructional improvement. This was a great feat for Boston, a city not known for congenial school and community relations.

Still, despite the favorable context and conditions and the considerable accomplishments, after more than ten years of sustained attention, there is only limited and spotty implementation of the district's instructional agenda across the schools. Under what could be described as the best of conditions, teaching has not yet been fully transformed. Student achievement has improved as measured by the standardized tests required by the state. However while that improvement represents real growth, it has not yet reached a level reflective of the literacy and math proficiency students need to succeed as adults. As Hubie Jones, a long-time advocate for improvement in the BPS, states:

> While we are heartened by the progress Boston has made in raising academic achievement during Superintendent Thomas Payzant's tenure, we are deeply troubled that the majority of Boston's students have not achieved proficiency in any of the subjects measured by the MCAS. A school and civic culture that celebrates the "needs improvement" result on the MCAS institutionalizes low expectations for student achievement.[6]

What might explain these mixed findings?

Historians of education might argue that the Boston story is the latest chapter in a long history of instructional stability. Analyses of instructional change over a century suggest that the forces of stability—school organization, purpose, traditional teaching practices—most often prevail over the forces of change.[7] From the perspective of institutional theory, Levin notes that it is not surprising that those who study charter schools and other alternatives to traditional public schools find "that almost all instructional 'innovations' reported by schools in their charters and reports are practices already found in many conventional public schools," and that "successful educational entrepreneurship must overcome a deeply-rooted institutional conservatism that is largely explained by modern institutional theory."[8] Others suggest that it is the practice of teaching itself that contributes mightily to the constancy of traditional practices. They remind us that it is extremely difficult to change teaching practice not only because of the conservative organizational structure and culture of schools and teaching, but also because changing instruction is about changing minds.[9] These analyses could lead to the gloomy conclusion that, try as we might, schools will be schools and traditional teaching will persist.

But there is another way to view the status of school improvement and teaching practice in Boston. There are conditions that foster the adoption of new practices. In his study of teaching practices between 1890 and 1980, Cuban concluded that where implementation strategies were well-thought out and well-supported with professional development, teachers adopted the progressive teaching strategies that developed out of Dewey's work, for example.[10] Cohen and Hill found that when instructional policies were linked to appropriate curriculum, assessment, and professional development, teachers were more likely to improve their practices.[11] And Jennings, in analyzing reading reform in Michigan, concluded that

> we must think of policy implementation as an exercise in teaching in the best sense. Policymakers' ideas may be a real improvement over current practices and policymakers may be better informed or more knowledgeable than practitioners about good and effective instruction. . . . But we need to recognize that the measure of a policy's worth is not knowing the better way or even knowing better ways to teach teachers the better way. *The worth of a policy is in what teachers learn from it* [italics in original]. This means we must attend more to teachers' learning than to policymakers' actions.[12]

When teachers learn, many can and will implement new instructional strategies.

These and related studies suggest that while the forces for instructional stability are mighty, it is possible to make significant changes. What does this imply for understanding the outcomes of ten years of instructional improvement efforts in Boston?

In adopting the Essentials and workshop instruction as policy, Boston was attempting to develop a new professional culture and a nontraditional approach to instruction in all of its schools. To succeed, it had to fundamentally change teachers' and administrators' minds about what good teaching included, and it had to teach them the new skills that went along with the new ideas. The BPS succeeded in putting in place many pieces of the desired instructional system. At the end of ten years, the district has laid a strong intellectual foundation for its whole-school improvement agenda. A small set of schools, most prominently the Effective Practice schools, demonstrate the feasibility and benefits of implementing the improvement agenda.[13] But most schools have not fundamentally changed; instruction is only superficially different in most of the district's elementary schools and hardly different in its high schools.

By looking at Boston through the lens of implementation as learning, it is possible to consider what Boston accomplished in the last ten years, what was missing from the effort, and most importantly, what next steps need to be taken to deepen and broaden the implementation and impact of the desired instructional changes. Other districts attempting to design instructional reforms might benefit from this analysis and glean lessons from the Boston experience. Perhaps hindsight will ensure that, going forward, instructional reforms will lead to a fuller realization of their desired outcomes. This chapter is organized with that goal in mind.

Organization of the Chapter

This chapter begins with a review of Boston's approach to whole-school improvement, an approach that began with BPE's 21st Century Schools initiative. It then describes the journey that took the district along a literacy-focused, standards-based improvement path that (a) started with the adoption of a set of literacy programs, (b) then moved to a nonprogrammatic instructional focus based on the tenets of workshop instruction, and (c) ultimately returned to a set of programs in an effort to better support schools with curriculum resources embedded in workshop instructional strategies. The journey is important because it demonstrates (a) the difficulty of designing a perfect ten-year plan at the outset, and (b) the need to learn from experience and make sensible revisions. The review concludes with a discussion of the district's approach to improving teaching and learning in mathematics.

The chapter then turns to coaching, the district's signature on-site professional development support. Boston has always recognized that the success of implementing improved teaching practices rests on teachers', principals', and headmasters' ability to learn about new strategies, learn how to use them, and see for themselves that they are effective. Coaching toward this goal has been integral to whole-school improvement since BPE began working with the first cohort of reforming schools, and it remains central to establishing and improving instruction in the BPS. The chapter ends with a discussion of Boston's instructional improvement accomplishments and considers the ways in which Boston's experience and crucial next steps might inform improvement efforts in other urban districts throughout the country.

BOSTON'S APPROACH TO WHOLE-SCHOOL IMPROVEMENT: FOCUS ON LITERACY

Boston's whole-school improvement agenda, designed collaboratively by the BPS and the Boston Plan for Excellence (BPE), has an underlying theory of action that begins with the hypothesis that improved instruction will improve student achievement. It postulates that the way to achieve improved instruction is to support teachers at their school sites as they learn in collaboration with one another. Collaborative learning would be facilitated by having teachers and principals engage in specific activities, called "Essentials," which when undertaken with skillful support would foster change in the social structure of each school.[14] In November 1997 the Boston School Committee adopted the Boston Public Schools Plan for Whole-School Change that outlines the Essentials.[15]

Since then, BPE has served as a research and development (R&D) arm of the district, dedicating itself to developing school improvement components and processes, pilot testing them in a sample of the district's schools, and developing additional supports with the potential to increase the district's instructional capacity. The district, for its part, then adopted what BPE had developed, making adaptations as it saw fit in light of its needs and resources in order to scale-up whole-school improvement to all of its schools. The partnership has been a unique, successful collaboration between the BPS and this local education fund.[16]

The first phase of the agenda was the advent of the 21st Century Schools program during the 1996–97 school year. The BPE worked with twenty-seven early learning centers, elementary, middle, and high schools that were competitively selected to be 21st Century Schools, the district's first of four cohorts of reforming schools. Using the Essentials as a guide, the BPE supported the educators in each of the schools to work together to develop common language, common practices, and common goals for their students. The Essentials required teachers and principals to focus initially on one content area and to research "best practices" in that area. Their research and adoption of "best practices" involved them in attending to the specific content to be taught and its alignment with state and district standards. Virtually all of the funding provided to schools was for professional development designed to increase schools' capacity to support implementation of the Essentials.

When BPE launched its 21st Century Schools program, the number one requirement, or Essential, was to "develop a vision and focus for the school's academic priorities."[17] The idea behind this Essential was to "mobilize collaboration across the school toward one instructional goal or approach." The instructional goal would "serve as an initial entry point for standards-based reform," the framework for teaching and learning that Tom Payzant brought to the BPS.[18] Each school's choice of an instructional goal had to be data-based and emerge from a review of student work and achievement data.

BPE provided 21st Century Schools with Whole-School Change (WSC) coaches to help them in coming to consensus about their instructional focus, investigating a variety of programmatic options, attending presentations, and visiting schools that were using different literacy models.[19] WSC coaches then helped their schools select a literacy model or develop their own home-grown approach.[20]

Acceptable models met the guidelines for "balanced literacy," a response to the long-standing "reading wars" that reflected disagreements within the research community about whether to stress phonics (the sound/symbol relationships) in beginning reading, or whether to begin teaching reading with a focus on "meaning," as exemplified by the "whole language" approach. The reading wars had not produced any definitive findings. Therefore, balanced literacy programs attempted to include both approaches in their reading models.[21]

The literacy programs available to the 21st Century Schools had additional research-based features such as lessons learned from Reading Recovery, a program developed to support struggling readers.[22] The programs also included tools teachers could use to identify and respond to individual student's learning needs, such as assessment strategies that provided data to use for developing next steps in instruction. Finally, the balanced literacy programs included attention to different ways in which reading instruction involved students: reading to students, reading with students, and reading by students.[23] Most schools decided to adopt research-based literacy programs; a few opted to develop home-grown programs.[24]

Cohort II schools began their work in the 1998–99 school year; Cohort III in the 1999–2000 school year; and Cohort IV in the 2000–01 school year.[25] Schools in these cohorts selected their literacy programs in the spring prior to beginning their cohort-related work.[26] Professional development began in the summer with implementation beginning at the start of the school year.[27]

The programs that elementary schools selected, for the most part, focused on literacy in grades K–2. As a result, teachers of grades 3 through 5 felt left out of the improvement effort. At the middle and high school level, where there were few options for externally-developed literacy programs, many teachers and administrators found themselves without clear ideas about how to develop or address their literacy focus. As a result, in the first few years of Boston's whole-school improvement agenda many upper elementary and middle school teachers did not actually begin learning new instructional strategies.

Other challenges were specific to high schools. First, high school English teachers did not generally think of themselves as reading teachers and were not convinced they wanted to become reading teachers. Second, it was clear that all content area teachers at the high school level would need to become reading teachers if they were going to help their students become skillful readers across content areas. Third, high schools were devoting much of their teachers' common planning time to the development of the high school restructuring plans required by the district. Attention to restructuring left scant time for discussions of literacy and literacy instruction.[28]

Early results at the elementary schools were encouraging. Teachers reported that the focus on literacy created a valuable, common sense of purpose among them that facilitated collegial communication. They also reported that the singular focus on literacy supported their Looking at Student Work (LASW) sessions that, in turn, supported their teaching.[29] Identifying and implementing an instructional focus seemed to be achieving the district's goal of mobilizing collaboration in the service of improving instruction. Data from the first few evaluation studies suggested that implementing a literacy program made it much easier for teachers to share a common focus on instruction.[30]

But there were growing concerns in the district about the wisdom of creating systemic, whole-school improvement with multiple, conceptually similar yet disparate instructional programs. Implementing externally developed programs was not developing the BPS's internal capacity to sustain instructional improvement in literacy. Nor was it necessarily keeping the district's focus on the citywide learning standards that the school committee had adopted.

Reframing the Approach: Systemwide Balanced Literacy and Workshop Instruction

At the beginning of the 2000–01 school year, in recognition of the need to create districtwide instructional coherence rather than school-based loyalty to specific programs, the superintendent subsumed the group of literacy programs under the rubric of "balanced literacy." This designation was meant to indicate the similarity of their features and the fact that the district was supporting balanced literacy rather than distinct programs as its systemic instructional approach. It was the first step in a process of reframing the district's approach to literacy instruction, indeed, to instruction in all content areas. The balanced literacy approach included the characteristics of most adopted programs: minilessons, independent reading, guided reading, conferences with students to assess their growing skill, and sharing in which students reported on what they had learned by using a reading skill. At the schools, this reframing made little difference. Teachers continued to implement the programs they had selected.[31]

At the beginning of the 2002–03 school year, the superintendent designated workshop as the district's instructional approach in literacy and in all curricular areas. Workshop instruction, presented to the district's principals and headmasters in their August 2002 back-to-school superintendent's memo, was described as a structured approach to instruction that included a minilesson, independent reading or writing, and sharing what was learned at the end of class.[32] Because workshop was tied neither to a specific program nor to the implementation of defined curricula or content, the superintendent concluded that all of the district's teachers could implement the workshop model of instruction regardless of the content they taught.

Many teachers and principals who had begun their whole-school improvement work in Cohort I or II, especially those selected to be Effective Practice Schools, could see the logic of the progression and the similarities in the approaches. Many had begun to use "workshop" as the term for their instructional approach.

This was not the case, however, for teachers in Cohorts III and IV who had more recently begun to learn to use their literacy programs. Nor was it the case for all of the district's principals and headmasters. Rather than seeing a logical progression, these educators construed the superintendent's memo as an example of the district going back on its promise to let schools select a literacy program, and were confused and somewhat dismayed by what they saw as a shift in the district's approach to literacy instruction.

To understand the status of the district's literacy initiatives when the superintendent announced the shift to workshop, three points are worth mentioning. First, at least half of the district's language arts teachers had not had an opportunity to learn what the district was trying to accomplish with the literacy programs before being asked to shift gears. They had had only one or two years to work with their literacy programs before being asked to drop them and use generic workshop strategies. Second, high school English teachers had not learned new instructional strategies and, therefore, had not significantly changed their instruction regardless of the cohort in which they were situated. And third, secondary school content teachers were suddenly thrust into an instructional reform about which they knew little.

A literacy reform that began by giving schools a set of tools, strategies, coach support, and permission to select a literacy reform was now a reform that directed them to use workshop. The fact that workshop was similar to what most schools had chosen did not matter. From the perspective of many teachers, principals, and headmasters, their decision-making authority had been removed and they were being asked to do something new. Nevertheless, four years later, BPS educators across grade levels and content areas can articulate the components of a workshop lesson and what each is designed to accomplish.

But while they can articulate the features of workshop, too often it is the superficial aspects of this instructional strategy that are being implemented: the minilessons, independent reading, conferences, and sharing. In too many classrooms, there are few coherent links among the components. Too many teachers still struggle to hold student conferences that enable students to reflect deeply on what they are reading and learning. The absence of well-developed curriculum and materials complicates the implementation of workshop instruction. So does the fact that some teachers and principals remain firm in their conviction that workshop is not an appropriate instructional strategy for their students. As a result, they do not use the strategies or they adapt them to look like more familiar, teacher-centered instruction.

While there are schools that are well on their way to using workshop strategies competently, high quality workshop instruction remains an elusive goal in many schools and classrooms. At the high school level, where changing instruction would pose the most challenges under the best of circumstances, weak implementation seems to be related to the time high schools had to spend restructuring themselves. Organizational restructuring, not instructional improvement, was the required focus of the district's high schools during most of the last ten years.

Overall, the limited implementation is related to (a) a weak understanding of workshop on the part of teachers, principals, and headmasters, (b) disagreement about the value of workshop among teachers, principals, headmasters, and many central office administrators, (c) insufficient attention to the heavy demands of this instructional approach on teachers, (d) insufficient principal leadership, and (e) inconsistent accountability for implementation at the district and school levels.

Curriculum Support for Workshop Instruction

The need to implement workshop strategies led district administrators, teachers, principals and headmasters to realize that, in focusing intently on workshop as pedagogy and eliminating literacy programs, they had left teachers without curriculum and materials to use within the workshop framework.[33] Although some teachers worked with their coaches to develop units of study, in general developing high-quality units and finding appropriate materials required specialized knowledge that most teachers did not have. Those teachers who had the requisite literacy backgrounds for this work reported that they did not have the time to create their entire literacy curriculum.[34] In response, the district began, once again, to adopt literacy programs.

First, the BPS in collaboration with BPE investigated whether Making Meaning™ could be integrated into workshop instruction as an appropriate reading comprehension curriculum for the district's elementary teachers. To test this idea, Making Meaning™ was implemented in a set of volunteer schools during the second half of the 2003–04 school year. The program was well-received and approximately thirty-five of the district's schools are currently using some of its components.

Federal funds available through the Reading First Initiative as well as other funds have enabled the district to provide schools with additional literacy programs that include the Trophies program for early literacy, America's Choice for some of the middle and high schools, and the Ramp Up component of America's Choice for schools that requested an intensive remediation approach to literacy for its students. Schools chose the program(s) they preferred and most teachers value the added structure and curricular materials that accompany them.[35] Schools' enthusiasm for the programs confirms the fact that workshop alone was making too many demands on teachers—demands that they could not meet.

The adoption of this new set of programs, then, can be seen as the next step in the advancement of standards-based, literacy-focused, workshop instruction in the BPS. But not everyone involved in the improvement of literacy sees it this way. There is disagreement within the district about the extent to which these programs support and build on workshop instruction or are a retreat. It is too soon to know what instruction will look like as a result of their implementation.

DEVELOPMENT OF THE FOCUS ON MATHEMATICS INSTRUCTION

In the fall of 2000, BPS added mathematics as its second curriculum initiative, with a plan that called for phasing in whole-district implementation over a three-year period. All schools were required to adopt the district's standards-based curriculum programs—Investigations in Number, Data, and Space for K–5; the Connected Math Program (CMP) for grades 6–8; and Math Connections for grades 9–12. The district supported implementation of the new programs with professional development institutes, seminars, and workshops for teachers and principals, along with in-school coach support.[36]

At the elementary level, schools identified Math Leadership Teams of three to six teachers who were the focus of initial professional development and coach support. All teachers became involved in the program in subsequent years but the emphasis on developing teacher leaders in math continued and strengthened. To this end, teachers partnered with coaches in teaching the Developing Mathematical Ideas (DMI) seminars and some now facilitate those seminars on their own. With the support of coaches, teachers learned to lead math team meetings, Looking at Student Work sessions, and unit study seminars that focused on student thinking in the context of specific units of study in mathematics. Some teachers developed their classrooms as learning sites in which others could observe implementation of the Investigations program. Teacher leaders have also partnered with parent leaders to provide workshops for parents.

The middle schools implemented CMP by adding one grade level per year in every school, starting with sixth grade in the 2000–01 school year. The district offered workshops prior to the teachers' first use of each unit, and a math coach was available to work with the seventh-grade teachers as well as with the sixth-grade math specialist. As part of the middle school plan, sixth-grade math specialists were expected to support their grade level peers' work. These math specialists were key to the middle school math plan's approach to developing school-based teacher leadership.

At the high school level, implementation proceeded in much the same manner as at the middle school; over three years the district introduced algebra, geometry, and advanced algebra materials. During these years, middle and high school teachers also had the opportunity to increase their mathematics content knowledge by enrolling in math courses offered by Northeastern University and Harvard University's Extension School.[37]

The underlying assumptions about instruction that informed the district's overall math plan were fundamentally the same as those that informed literacy instruction. However, there were significant differences:

- There was far less funding available for coaching in mathematics than in literacy. Therefore, schools had less on-site coach time to support implementation of the curriculum and associated pedagogy.
- The math plan was intentionally designed to create teacher leaders who could nurture and lead the improvement of teaching and learning in their schools.
- The instructional approach to teaching mathematics was embedded in the selected materials. Therefore, teachers were simultaneously learning the new curricular content and the new approach to teaching and learning. The separation that developed between literacy instruction and the literacy curriculum did not occur in mathematics.

Fundamentally, the initiative to improve mathematics in the BPS has remained constant since its inception.[38]

COACHING: SCHOOL-BASED SUPPORT FOR WHOLE-SCHOOL IMPROVEMENT

During the 1997–98 school year literacy coaches were provided to the 21st Century schools. These coaches, like their WSC coach counterparts, spent one day per week in schools helping with the implementation of the school's literacy program and supporting implementation of the Essentials. Literacy coaches, like their WSC counterparts, participated in ongoing professional development throughout each school year.[39] As the district moved from literacy programs to workshop and back to programs, coaches have been provided with relevant professional development either under the auspices of the Office of Curriculum and Instruction (C & I) or those of the instructional leader for literacy and coaching.

The math coach role, initiated at the start of the 2000–01 school year, included responsibilities at the school and district levels. For example, elementary math coaches worked with teachers to help them understand the new curriculum, its content, and how to use it with students.[40] Coaches helped teachers interpret and respond to students' mathematical thinking, given that students were now expected to explain their thinking as part of the learning process. And, finally, math coaches had a role in (a) developing districtwide math assessments that accompany the new curriculum, (b) serving as a conduit for information between the district and the schools with respect to school-based requirements, and (c) providing small-group, on-site professional development for teachers and for principals.

Collaborative Coaching and Learning (CCL) in Literacy

Although teachers and principals valued the literacy coaches' work, literacy coaches were frustrated by challenges that limited their impact on instruction. First, coaches did not think they could make a meaningful difference with the one-day-per-week, one-teacher-at-a-time coaching model. Put simply, they did not have enough time with teachers. Second, and related to this point, coaches often had to omit the debrief that followed a demonstration lesson or observation due to time constraints. This weakened their impact on teacher learning. Third, coaches who worked with teachers who had serious classroom management problems wondered whether this was a good use of their time. Fourth, coaches could work only with those teachers who wanted their help. This made it unlikely that improved instruction would develop schoolwide. These and other challenges left coaches, many principals, and BPE concerned that the coach role was too limited and would not lead to whole-school instructional improvement.

Therefore, BPE redesigned its literacy coaching model to better support the goals of whole-school improvement and to better align its approach to coaching with the district's newly defined coaching model that included: *classroom experience*—using the classroom as a laboratory for adult learning; *reflection and inquiry*—engaging in reflection and inquiry related to practice with the teacher; *feedback*—providing the teacher with feedback she can use to refine her instruction; and *theory and content knowledge*—helping the teacher to deepen her understanding of theory and knowledge of content.[41] The Collaborative

Coaching and Learning (CCL) model was designed to remedy the weaknesses of the initial coaching model.[42] CCL was pilot-tested by the Effective Practice schools with BPE providing technical support for first-year implementation. One year later, at the start of the 2002–03 school year, CCL was adopted as the literacy-focused coaching model for all Boston schools.

CCL has four components: inquiry, preconference, demonstration/observation lesson, and debrief. These are described in BPE's publication, *Straight Talk about CCL: A Guide for School Leaders.*[43] A CCL cycle should last for eight weeks and involve teachers in setting their own goals for classroom implementation of the strategies they are studying. During and after the cycle, the coach should help individual teachers implement the strategies that were the focus of the inquiry and were modeled in the demonstration lessons. CCL is now a significant feature of professional development in the district and a standard practice in the district's schools—primarily in literacy but, increasingly, across all content areas.

The quality and fidelity with which CCL is implemented in literacy, however, varies considerably across and within schools. Evaluation studies reveal that variations can be primarily attributed to school-based factors such as the extent to which schools have implemented the Essentials; principals' commitment to and understanding of workshop and the coaching model; and coaches' understanding of and agreement with the CCL model. These factors are exacerbated at the district's new small high schools and small learning communities. The fall 2005 Education Matters study found that schools and coaches were making adaptations to the model that were likely to weaken its effectiveness.[44] These changes included reducing the number of demonstration lessons to no more than three or four in an eight-week cycle and eliminating the one-on-one coaching that must be provided to individual teachers. CCL without one-on-one coaching is unlikely to lead to needed improvements in teaching. These variations and their causes lead to the conclusion that CCL in literacy is not yet a strong professional development tool in many of the district's schools.[45]

CCL in Mathematics

The senior program directors for mathematics and colleagues within C & I saw the benefits of CCL for literacy and adapted the model for mathematics. The resulting Collaborative Coaching and Learning in Mathematics (CCLM) model has three components: the *Previsit*, the *Classroom Observation Visit*, and the *Postvisit Discussion* that focuses on what all participants can learn about (a) the math content of the class, (b) the students' mathematical thinking, and (c) questions that arose among the participants from the interactions in the classroom.[46] Inquiry in math takes place during the previsit and is tied directly to the curriculum that is being implemented. By design, CCLM, like CCL, supports and nurtures the collaborative, instructionally-focused school culture that is a significant goal of whole-school improvement in the BPS. Like its

CCL counterpart, CCLM provides teachers, principals, and coaches with opportunities to learn from one another's practice. However, whereas CCL runs on eight-week cycles, a CCLM session is completed within one day.

Despite the fact that the district has adopted CCL and CCLM as its coaching models, there are differences of opinion about how best to use coaches so that teachers benefit maximally from their expertise. Some district-level and school-based educators prefer to have coaches work with the weakest teachers; others prefer to have coaches work with the strongest to develop their leadership capacity; still others expect the best result will come from working with all teachers. Everyone seems to agree that coaches must spend time in one-on-one coaching of individual teachers, an aspect of teacher support that does not occur regularly when schools implement CCL. It will require careful data collection and analysis to determine the relative benefits of these coaching approaches. Their differences, however, do not take away from the fact that the BPS now supports coaching as its primary teacher professional development tool.

The Selection, Allocation, and Supervision of Literacy and Math Coaches

From the outset, BPE and then BPS were responsible for the hiring, professional development, supervision, and evaluation of coaches. This made sense. First, coaches were hired to implement the *district's* instructional focus in literacy and mathematics. Second, the superintendent ultimately was accountable for the impact of the whole-school improvement effort. Therefore, it was the district that had to hold accountable the coaches as well as the principals/headmasters. Third, coaches needed the backing of the district in order to do their work. Coaches, on their own, lacked the positional authority to insist on faithful implementation of instructional practices and/or the coaching models.

In January 2006, the district altered this policy regarding the selection, allocation, and supervision of coaches. It determined that all schools would have half-time coaches in either literacy or math. As a result of the policy change, coaches would work in no more than two schools. This was particularly significant for math coaches, who had spent little time in individual schools in order to provide all schools with some coaching. Late in the winter of 2006 principals and headmasters were asked to select one half-time coach for either literacy or mathematics (but not both) for the 2006–07 school year.[47] Schools that were large and/or were designated as in "corrective action" by the state, for example, could be assigned additional coaching time or a second coach by the deputies. Schools with fewer than ten teachers might only have 0.2 full-time equivalent coaches because of their size. While it will take time to assess the overall impact of this policy change, it is immediately clear that a good number of schools will be without key instructional support in either literacy or math and some district flexibility with respect to the deployment of coaches will be gone. For example, approximately fifty elementary schools will be without a math coach in the 2006–07 school year.

The new policy also placed responsibility for the supervision and evaluation of coaches with principals and headmasters. Now, neither the senior program directors nor the instructional leader for literacy and coaching will have the capacity to respond to schools' requests for specific help because principals will make the decisions about how coaches spend their time. Under the former allocation policy, for example, the elementary math department was able to deploy coaches for targeted assistance. Math coaches who had expertise in special education or with the curricular programs used in Advanced Work Class (AWC) could provide assistance to the coach already assigned to a school. More specifically, in the case of AWC, where fifth-grade students use the middle school math curriculum in addition to Investigations, coaches with specialized knowledge would be assigned to help the elementary math coach work with the middle school program. This targeted support is not likely to be available under the new policy due to principals and headmasters having the authority to determine coaches' work. The new allocation and supervision policy thus appears to have reduced central office's capacity to be responsive to schools' needs.

Multiple challenges to the district's coaching models may lie ahead. There are considerable data pointing to the fact that some principals and headmasters do not share the district's high regard for CCL or CCLM. No one knows how they will use their supervisory authority to define the coaches' work. Evaluation studies have also repeatedly demonstrated that some principals, even if they value CCL and CCLM, lack the knowledge and skills with which to insure their effective implementation. The district has not yet demonstrated the capacity to provide such principals and headmasters with the knowledge and skill they need to implement the coaching models. Finally, the district acknowledges that the details of the new coaching policy must still be developed. These include, for example, "coaching and principal/headmaster professional development, job descriptions, overall management of coaches, system accountability, CCL support, a common vision and philosophy, and how schools without coaches in particular areas will be supported."[48]

ACCOMPLISHMENTS AND CHALLENGES

Under the leadership of Tom Payzant, first the BPS developed and sustained a whole-school improvement agenda based on a strong theory of action, an explicit set of Essentials, and specific instructional interventions and supports. This represented a dramatic break with past practice in Boston. Second, the district strove to establish collaborative, instructionally-focused cultures in its schools. To this end, teachers engaged in LASW sessions, CCL, and CCLM, for example. Third, the BPS established instructional coaching as a primary professional development tool with which to support the instructional focus. Fourth, the district provided curriculum supports in literacy while stressing the importance of maintaining workshop instructional strategies. Fifth, the superintendent succeeded in maintaining the support of the mayor, civic community, and the school committee. These are significant accomplishments. But they are not accompanied by the level of progress that Boston's children need and deserve. Student achievement, as noted at the beginning of the chapter, does not meet the *Proficient* standard that Boston's children must demonstrate if they are to leave high school academically well-prepared for their next steps as young men and women.

What has stood in the way of greater achievement? Ten years of implementation and evaluation research in Boston reveal that the quality of implementation of the superintendent's whole-school improvement agenda has not matched the quality of the foundation on which it rests.

In July 2000, the district was first alerted to the fact that many schools were either (a) struggling to implement the Essentials, or (b) were making little effort to implement them.[49] Recent studies of the implementation of CCL and the use of workshop in high schools, cited earlier, suggest that leadership for the district's instructional agenda is weak in many schools. The strong foundation and the focus on instruction were not turned into strong school-based practices despite the supports the district had in place.

Addressing the Challenges of Implementation: Recommendations

How might Boston address the quality of implementation? What can other urban districts learn from Boston's efforts? Again, we return to Jennings's conclusion that effective implementation depends on viewing policy implementation as a case of teaching and learning where we must "attend more to teachers' learning than to policymakers' actions."[50]

In exploring how to deepen implementation of instructional improvement in Boston and other districts, it would be worthwhile to expand Jennings's list of learners. Certainly many teachers have not yet learned to successfully implement the district's instructional strategies and they need additional opportunities to learn not only the skills associated with workshop but also the intellectual constructs on which this approach to instruction is based. In addition, however,

- principals and headmasters must be better schooled in the instructional programs their teachers are to implement and in the skills they need to help teachers with implementation;
- central office administrators must (a) improve their knowledge of the district's instructional strategies, (b) learn how to help principals and headmasters help their teachers implement them, and (c) have the time to work closely with principals and headmasters to insure high quality implementation;

- the superintendent must hold central office administrators, principals, and headmasters accountable for high-quality implementation of the district's instructional agenda in light of the supports for learning that it provides.

This is a recommendation for whole-district improvement, for whole-system learning. Studies of instructional improvement in San Diego demonstrate that school districts can organize to achieve this goal.[51] Boston must develop such a system if it expects to achieve high-quality implementation of and results from its whole-school improvement agenda in all of its schools. Meaningful change requires *both* a whole-district improvement agenda *and* a whole-school improvement agenda.

This is a "big ticket" recommendation. Implementing it would require changing the culture of central office, a task more daunting, perhaps, than changing the culture of schools. It is a task, however, that most urban districts must contemplate if they expect to improve achievement in all schools and for all students.

In the process of developing such an organization, there are a number of broad tasks that must be accomplished. In this chapter, the details of the tasks are specific to Boston. But other urban districts could readily adapt them to their own contexts.

1. Conduct School-Based Inquiries to Determine the Status of Implementation and the Factors Associated with Weak and Strong Implementation

Central office staff responsible for oversight and support of individual schools must monitor implementation and uncover root causes of variation in quality. In Boston, this means the deputies for schools and clusters need to inquire into the reasons for wide variation in the implementation of workshop, coaching, and the Essentials across the schools.[52] Then they must develop and implement school-specific sets of improvement interventions designed to increase high-quality implementation.

2. Organize Central Office and Develop Capacity of Central Office Staff to Supervise and Evaluate Principals Effectively

If central office staff are to support school-level leaders in implementing an instructional improvement strategy and its component programs, their task must be manageable and the organizational structure of central office must support their efforts. The absence of these conditions has proven problematic for Boston's deputies. First, the deputies are responsible for the quality of teaching and learning, K–12, in approximately fifty schools. This is too many schools. Deputies cannot pay sufficient attention to so many schools. Second, there is no organizational structure in which deputies can have collaborative, instructionally-focused discussions among themselves. There is no Looking at District Work group akin to the Looking at Student Work groups at the schools, but there could be. Deputies, in other words, have scant opportunity to learn from their colleagues, share what they learn, and seek new knowledge when necessary.

3. Develop Supports to Ensure that School Leaders Have the Knowledge and Skill to Implement the District's Whole-School Improvement Agenda

Any district attempting to undertake an instructional improvement initiative must look to principals as a key to success. Ten years of studies have led Education Matters to conclude repeatedly that principal and headmaster leadership is a major factor associated with the implementation of BPS's instructional agenda. In virtually every one of the reports cited in this chapter, the firm identifies leadership factors associated with variations in the quality of implementation. If workshop, literacy programs, math programs, and CCL/CCLM are to remain the routes to improved teaching and learning in Boston, then district leadership needs to fully understand the relationship between school leadership and level of implementation and develop interventions and supports that foster strong implementation.

4. Provide High Schools with the Resources They Need to Improve Teaching and Learning

Regardless of where they are located, urban high schools share distinct characteristics and challenges that differ fundamentally from those associated with lower and middle grade schools. Instructional improvement cannot be implemented on a one-size-fits-all basis. In Boston, the implementation process in high schools is further complicated by the fact that instructional improvement has not been central to high school renewal due to the district's emphasis on restructuring into smaller schools and learning communities. Now that the restructuring phase is complete, the districts and the schools must turn their attention to instruction. Those challenges are described here in reference to specific components of Boston's reform, but the overall message regarding capacity and "fit" is relevant to most urban high schools attempting change.[53]

Learning within content area

Due to size-related constraints on scheduling, same-content area teachers in each of Boston's small high schools or cross-grade SLCs rarely have common planning time in which to work together. As a result, CCL groups are often formed across content areas. Teachers in such CCL cycles learn workshop instructional strategies, but those strategies remain disconnected from the teaching of specific content. It is unlikely that content-free professional development at the high school level (or at other levels) will enable teachers to greatly enhance their teaching. In addition, BPS high schools no longer have subject-specific department chairs. This leaves many of them without in-house subject expertise and capacity to support teachers' development in their content areas.[54]

"Fit" of workshop in high schools

Additional challenges spring from the fact that high school teachers, for the most part, do not understand the instructional strategies associated with workshop and, as a result, cannot attempt them. And many teachers and some headmasters remain unconvinced that workshop will improve student learning. The district must consider these concerns, assess the status of instruction and instructional need in each of its high schools, develop strategies that can be implemented in the new, smaller high school structures, and ensure that teachers and headmasters are supported in learning the strategies and held accountable for using them.

5. Examine the District's Professional Development Model to Ensure That It Meets Teachers' and Students' Learning Needs

The need to tailor professional development carefully is by no means unique to Boston, but it is certainly crucial to maintaining the momentum Boston has gained. Ongoing concerns about BPS teachers' level of expertise with workshop-based instructional strategies indicate it is time to examine the district's primary professional development strategy, CCL and CCLM, and make adjustments where needed.

6. Consider the Impact of Selection, Allocation, and Supervision Policies Related to Coaching and Other Supports

Like professional development, sustaining and supporting instruction is central to any improvement strategy. In Boston, the new coach allocation policy (effective 2006–07) means that some schools will be without an instructional coach in either literacy or math. Yet it is unlikely that any of the district's schools is ready to sustain its instructional work without coach support. Therefore, the district is in danger of having its teachers and students lose ground. The district will have to ensure, for example, that principals and headmasters of these schools are able to keep their math teams functioning effectively and that teachers have opportunities to continue to develop their ability to implement the curriculum. The district will need to help schools implement CCL or CCLM or a substitute in the absence of a coach.

The district will also need to keep track of how principals and headmasters define coaches' work now that they hire, supervise, and evaluate them. Some principals and headmasters may define coach responsibilities and/or the organization of their work in ways that do not support implementation of workshop instruction and/or the CCL model of coaching. Coaches, for their part, will be in a weak position to argue with principals who are their supervisors, and they will no longer have central office administrators to intervene on their behalf. Without careful attention to this new organizational reality, central office may be in a weak position to strengthen coaching and, thereby, instructional improvement at the schools.

CONCLUSION

When Tom Payzant retired from the BPS on June 30, 2006, central office administrators, principals, headmasters, and teachers praised him even as they pondered the future of whole-school improvement in the district. Many worried about the future of workshop instruction in light of multiple new literacy program adoptions, coaching as high quality professional development for literacy and math in light of the district's new policy regarding selection, allocation, and supervision of coaches, and instructional improvement in the district's high schools.

Doubtless, a decade of focus and stability led to significant improvements that are worth lauding. But the impact of these improvements has yet to be seen in the achievement of the district's students. And the conditions that fostered stability seem fragile as Boston contemplates its future.

The district's interim superintendent, central office administrators, principals, headmasters, and teachers need to maintain momentum to improve teaching and learning. After all, regardless of changes in the administrative team over time, children will still arrive at school each morning and they and their families will expect teachers to be using the best practices available. Instructional improvement need not, indeed, must not be delayed by the transitions central office will undergo with a new administration. The foundation upon which to build is already in place. Now it is up to those responsible for the district's students to take responsibility for deepening and broadening the agenda's implementation and impact. The outcome of their efforts will determine whether the foundation established by Tom Payzant rests on deep or shallow roots.

APPENDIX 5A

Excerpt of Superintendent's Memo to Principals and Headmasters, August 2002

BY SEPTEMBER 2003, all Boston elementary school teachers, middle and high school English language arts teachers, native language teachers, and ESL teachers will have implemented Readers' Workshop in their classrooms, under the leadership of the principal-headmaster. Each school will have support from a full- or part-time Literacy Coach trained in workshop strategies and will receive additional reading and writing materials for workshop instruction.

Workshop instruction will begin to be used in all subjects, and the district will provide professional development for teachers on workshop instruction and how it can be adapted to science, social studies, and other subject areas. Much of Boston's curricula already supports workshop instruction: Investigations, Connected Math, Math Connections, History Alive, and the Foss, STC, Carolina Biological, and Cambridge Physics science kits.

Professional development in workshop instruction and support will be provided for all principals-headmasters, directors of instruction, program directors, and other instructional supervisors. By June 2003, all supervisors will have received sufficient training and support to effectively supervise the implementation of workshop instruction in all classrooms.

CHAPTER VI

Using Data to Inform Decision Making in Urban School Districts

Progress and New Challenges

RICHARD J. MURNANE
ELIZABETH A. CITY
KRISTAN SINGLETON[1]

ONE OF THE CHALLENGES every school district faces is to provide schools with the information and tools to educate children well. The challenge is particularly great in urban districts, which serve high concentrations of students living in poverty and students whose first language is not English. The life prospects for these students are critically influenced by the extent to which they master the skills needed to thrive in a rapidly changing society. Detailed understanding of the skills and knowledge that individual students have mastered is essential to making the best use of scarce instructional time. Having the tools to manage information on students' skills and to do so efficiently is essential to making use of that information.

From the beginning of Thomas Payzant's eleven-year tenure as superintendent of the Boston Public Schools (BPS), using student assessment results to inform decision making has been a part of the district's strategy to increase student achievement. Understanding the progress Boston has made and the challenges it still faces in developing a system of student assessments and tools to facilitate good decision making is relevant not only to improving education in Boston, but indeed education throughout the country.

The purpose of this chapter is three-fold. First, we provide a framework for thinking about the challenge of developing an assessment system that will promote student learning. Second, we describe key elements of the progress BPS has made in moving toward a comprehensive assessment system. Third, we describe critical issues that every district must face as it strives to provide schools with the information and tools needed to improve instruction.

All of the authors have worked with BPS on the issues discussed in this chapter. While on leave from Harvard for the 2001–02 school year, Richard Murnane worked with BPS leadership to conceptualize the data tools that became known as MyBPS Assessment and for the next three years facilitated monthly meetings of the BPS Data Governance Group that oversaw development of the tools. Kristan Singleton, while assistant director of the Boston Plan for Excellence (BPE), led the BPE team that worked with BPS to develop MyBPS Assessment and to train BPS educators in its use. Elizabeth City worked for BPS as a literacy coach and change coach and helped schools to learn from student assessment results and to improve English language arts instruction.

THE VALUE OF ASSESSMENT

There are at least four reasons why public school systems assess the skills of students on a regular basis. First, state and federal governments require them to do so as part of external accountability systems. Since 1998, all Massachusetts public schools have been required to administer English language arts (ELA) and/or mathematics examinations that are part of the Massachusetts Comprehensive Assessment System (MCAS) to virtually all students in particular grades. The 2001 federal No Child Left Behind legislation further increased testing requirements. Second, the school district leadership team needs information on student achievement in order to provide oversight of school performance. Third, schools need data on student academic performances in order to make a variety of decisions about student placements, including which students to invite to participate in advanced work classes, which students to send to mandatory summer school, and which students to retain in grade. Fourth, by providing information on students' mastery of particular skills, assessment results can help school faculties judge the effectiveness of their instruction and can help them in targeting future instruction.

One of many complications in designing a comprehensive student assessment system is that the characteristics of assessments that serve different purposes differ, as do procedures for administering them. This would not be a problem if there were no costs associated with administering tests to students; separate tests could be administered for each purpose, using the optimal administrative procedures for that use. Of course, there are costs to administering assessments, and the greatest of these is the loss of instructional time. The following is a discussion of some of the initiatives BPS has undertaken to provide decision makers with information about students' skills and knowledge. We make no attempt to be exhaustive or to retain a chronological order to the presentation. Instead, we attempt to develop themes relevant to BPS and other urban districts attempting to use data to inform decision making. We organize those themes around a framework of three key questions. We begin with the question of whether an assessment is part of a comprehensive system for determining whether students are mastering state learning standards. What role does the assessment play in this system? In other words, is it designed to be used formatively by teachers or to be used for accountability purposes by district or state officials? Are the administration procedures consistent with the assessment's use?

Informing Instruction through Assessment

Since 1998, the Boston Public Schools have been required to administer the MCAS ELA and mathematics tests to virtually all students in designated grades. Given that administering these mandatory tests consumes a considerable amount of instructional time, it makes sense to ask what information other assessments provide, over and above that provided by MCAS results. We begin to answer this question by summarizing briefly the strengths and limitations of the MCAS assessments for informing district oversight of schools, student placements, and instructional improvement.

MCAS

In important respects, the MCAS tests differ from those that BPS and other school districts in the state have historically administered to students:

- The ELA exam includes a five-paragraph essay to assess students' writing skills, and many of the questions on the mathematics exam require that students provide open-ended responses and explain their reasoning.
- The content of the tests becomes publicly available on the state department of education website shortly after the tests are administered to students.
- The distribution of scores for every public school in the state is made public and most local newspapers publish these results and provide commentary.
- Several months after the tests are administered, every school in the state receives a large set of computer printouts providing item-by-item score distributions for the students who have taken the MCAS tests in that school in the previous May, as well as the score distributions for all students in the state.

The MCAS tests carry substantial stakes. Beginning with the high school graduating class of 2003, Massachusetts students have had to pass both the tenth grade MCAS ELA and mathematics exams in order to receive a high school diploma. Under No Child Left Behind, students' MCAS scores must annually increase enough for the school to meet "Adequate Yearly Progress" requirements or the school will face sanctions that can ultimately include dissolution. Superintendent Payzant made clear that a key challenge for BPS schools was to improve MCAS scores and to do so in a way that actually improved the quality of education BPS students received. In a January 2001 memo to the Boston School Committee, he announced that learning from MCAS results would be an element of the strategy to accomplish this goal.[2]

The number of BPS schools that constructively use MCAS assessment results to diagnose their students' learning problems increases each year. However, as school faculties have devoted more attention to MCAS results, they have increasingly recognized the limitations of the MCAS testing program as a source of information for informing instructional improvements. Perhaps the greatest limitation is the significant time lag between the May testing date and the fall delivery date when schools receive the results—well after students have moved on to other teachers. Another limitation is the variability in the content covered on each spring's MCAS. Because any single administration of the MCAS covers only a relatively small portion of the topics in the Massachusetts Curriculum Frameworks, student results do not provide detailed information on the extent to which students have mastered particular skills.

Clearly, some properties of the MCAS limit its value as a tool to identify key student learning problems and limit its value to the central office as a means to evaluate which BPS schools are experiencing difficulty in teaching the curriculum effectively. This has led the BPS central office to examine whether other assessments already in use in BPS could fill the holes.

Benchmark assessments

One of Thomas Payzant's first initiatives after becoming superintendent of the Boston Public Schools in 1995 was to develop a comprehensive five-year plan for improving Boston's schools. Part of the plan was the establishment of citywide learning standards that would specify the mathematics and English language arts skills students at each grade level should master. The plan's approval by the Boston School Committee in July 1996 created the need to measure, on a regular basis, whether BPS students were indeed acquiring the critical skills described in the learning standards. In response to this need for data on student performance, the BPS Office of Curriculum and Instruction mandated that each BPS school administer a variety of skill assessments and send the results to the central office each year. Over the subsequent decade, the number of tests included in these benchmark assessments grew (see appendix 6A for examples).

The benchmark assessments have proved useful to BPS educators. For example, SAT-9 scores are used to determine which students should be offered places in advanced work classes and which should be required to attend summer school. Frequent administration of the developmental reading assessment (DRA) helps teachers to judge the progress students are making in mastering reading skills.

Still, both BPS teachers and central office officials have found that the original benchmark assessments do not meet all of their needs. For example, since the SAT-9 was designed for use throughout the country and is not closely aligned either with citywide or state learning standards, students' scores on this assessment are not very helpful in diagnosing the extent to which BPS students have mastered city and state learning standards. Nor are the results of great value to the central office leadership team in judging the extent to which students are mastering the content of particular courses, such as Algebra 1. These concerns were at least partially addressed by the initiatives described below.

Midyear and end-of-year course-specific exams

In the last ten years, BPS has adopted new math curriculum at every grade level. It has also invested heavily in professional development aimed at helping teachers learn to teach the new curriculum effectively. To provide BPS teachers, principals, and the central office with information about the extent to which BPS students are mastering the skills emphasized in the new math curricula, BPS developed a set of course-specific midyear and end-of-year mathematics examinations for middle and high school mathematics courses. Soon after came elementary grade math examinations. Recently, the BPS central office began the development of districtwide, course-specific examinations in other subject areas.

The literature on accountability supports the value of course-specific exams as a way to motivate students to do the hard work required to master important skills, and as a way for the central office to learn which teachers are having difficulty teaching critical skills.[3] In addition, BPS central office officials see the test results as providing important diagnostic information to teachers about topics they need to reteach or teach in a different way.

The laudable desire to use the results of the midyear and end-of-year exams for multiple purposes has led to tensions. To encourage all students to do their best on the course-specific examinations, the central office would like all teachers to give the exam scores considerable weight in calculating students' term grades. Some teachers see this as interfering with their prerogatives. Similarly, the central office wants all schools to administer the course-specific examinations on approximately the same date and with the same security provisions. These requirements are necessary to make comparisons of scores across classrooms and schools meaningful. However, to some teachers these requirements make the examinations another example of externally imposed mandates. This perception reduces educators' interest in using the test results to diagnose students' learning problems.

Another tension concerns the process of designing the course-specific examinations and making students' responses to the exam questions available to teachers to inform their professional development and planning. The exam designers are curriculum-area directors who want to put the exams into use as soon as possible with the requisite electronic mechanisms to support comparing student performance across schools. However, good testing practice dictates that the examinations meet appropriate psychometric standards before the results are made available electronically in a manner that permits comparisons. A tension between these competing objectives—a desire to put the examinations into use promptly and a desire to make sure that the examinations meet particular technical standards—has characterized the process of developing and implementing the course-specific examinations. While the conflict has proved frustrating, it has led to the development of a protocol for reviewing student work (including examination scores) that will be made available electronically to BPS teachers.

One important next step for the BPS leadership and any district attempting to use midyear and end-of-year exams will be to clarify the role of the assessments. This is crucial given that the requisite psychometric standards and administration procedures differ significantly depending upon whether the examinations are to be used for accountability purposes or as formative assessments by teachers.

FAST-R

Throughout Tom Payzant's tenure, the Boston Public Schools have worked closely with the Boston Plan for Excellence (BPE), the local education foundation. One of several roles that BPE has played is working with a group of schools known as Effective Practice (EP) schools to develop pilot school–improvement ideas. Beginning in SY2003–04, the EP schools began to grapple with the difficulties in using MCAS data and data from the district's benchmark assessments to plan instruction. For example, whereas the benchmark assessment data showing that an eighth-grade student scored a 950 on the Scholastic Reading Inventory (SRI) was not specific enough to tell a teacher how to modify instruction to respond to the student's learning needs, the student's seventh-grade MCAS data revealed the types of questions in the seventh-grade curriculum with which she struggled, but told her teacher little about her mastery of the eighth-grade curriculum. In addition, the district's workshop instruction model required yet another type of assessment to help teachers gauge students' skills as readers, writers, and thinkers. After studying the issue for several months, the EP principals recommended to BPE and BPS that a new set of MCAS-aligned assessments be created.

With support from the Noyce Foundation and later from the Hewlett Foundation, BPE organized the design and testing of a series of ELA formative assessments that focused on two critical reading skills: the ability to find evidence in a text and the ability to make inferences based on what was read. The resulting assessments have come to be known as the Formative Assessment of Student Thinking in Reading (FAST-R). Designed for third, fourth, seventh, and tenth grades, the assessments consist of either five or ten multiple choice questions about a reading passage drawn from a previously-administered MCAS ELA exam. Figure 1 provides an example of FAST-R questions.

Schools and teachers are free to use FAST-R in truly formative ways because students' scores do not count toward school accountability metrics or student grades and do not have to be administered under the same conditions across the district. Teams of teachers at each school decide whether, when, and

FIGURE 1

FAST-R **Formative Assessments of Student Thinking in Reading**

Name ____________________ "Jack London" • Journalistic Nonfiction

Date ____________________ Teacher/Class ____________________

Directions: On your answer sheet, fill in the circle for the correct answer.

1. **When did the earthquake take place?**
   A. 1990
   B. 1906
   C. 1896
   D. 2006

2. **According to the passage, how long did the actual earthquake last?**
   A. an hour
   B. three days and nights
   C. thirty seconds
   D. twelve hours

3. **Based on details in the passage, the greatest amount of damage was caused by:**
   A. the earthquake.
   B. the looting.
   C. the fire.
   D. the wind.

how they use FAST-R; the only requirements are that teachers work in teams and have a school plan for FAST-R's use.

Many school teams use FAST-R as a pretest prior to teaching a unit on a particular genre (e.g., poetry), and then schedule a follow-up FAST-R after completing the unit to see if their teaching is making a difference and to identify strategies they might need to teach next. Other teams devote their school-based cycles of professional development to studying and practicing teaching strategies that can address the student learning needs they saw in their FAST-R data. As a result of strong support from the BPS central office in scanning student answer sheets, schools receive their FAST-R results within a week after administration. Teachers consider this timeliness to be critically important.

One reason educators like FAST-R is that they receive on-site support in using it from former teachers who serve as data and implementation coaches. The support extends not only to administering the assessment and interpreting the results, but also to the difficult process of drawing lessons from the results about where to focus instructional improvements. Without coaching or other instructional leadership, FAST-R is more likely to be used as a form of sophisticated test preparation and not as a tool for engaging in reflective teaching practice.

On the horizon: Creating assessments from an electronic item bank

Strong demand for access to FAST-R suggests that formative assessments and logistical support for using them are emerging as an important part of how teachers would like to work with their students. As schools become more adept at implementing collaborative inquiry into the culture of teaching, it is likely that they will want and need assessments that gauge a wider range of students' skills and abilities. One approach to meeting these needs could be the continued development of forms of FAST-R. An alternative is to provide the tools needed to design assessments from an electronic item bank.

BPS has begun to make progress in increasing the supply of formative assessments available to schools. Under the leadership of the district's director of curriculum and instruction, a bank of test items has been created that will allow schools and the central office to create assessments that focus on the specific types of information that educators would like to learn about students. To properly implement this project, BPS will need to devote significant attention to providing appropriate assessment design resources. For example, merely providing schools with the tools to design assessments does not automatically mean that the resulting assessments will be useful. Providing coaching support to help educators design effective instruments and to make productive use of the results will be critical, just as it has been with FAST-R.

An important issue to contend with as the supply of formative assessments increases will be the types of items used to gauge students' abilities. The current trend is toward the design of quickly administered assessments that use multiple choice items. However, if one seeks to learn about students' skills in writing expository essays, it makes more sense to have students write essays than to ask them multiple-choice questions about the process. Of course, it takes particular skills and considerable time to judge the quality of student writing against the rubric provided by the state and to develop an understanding of why some students' writing is weak. BPS must ensure that the time crunch that besets all teachers does not lead to a narrowing of assessment methods.

KNOWLEDGE AND TOOLS

BPS has made enormous progress in providing schools with technical tools (e.g., the MCAS Tool Kit developed by the district assessment office) for learning from MCAS results. These tools are important because they save teachers and administrators large amounts of time, which is the scarcest resource in schools. Still, technical tools are not sufficient for schools to make constructive use of student assessment results. A culture change is also necessary, a change from a culture in which teachers work independently to a culture in which teachers work collaboratively to identify students' learning problems and to design and implement coherent strategies to ameliorate them. As we explain at the end of this section, creating a culture of shared responsibility for student learning in every school is proving more difficult to achieve than creating common facility with technical tools to examine student assessment results. We begin by describing some of the advances in technical tools.

MCAS Tool Kit

As schools began to use their MCAS results to plan instructional changes, it became clear that they would need guidance to ensure that high stakes testing data were not being used for purposes to which they were not well suited. For example, students' poor performance on a particular type of MCAS item does not mean that instruction should be focused in that area. Conversely, students' strong performance on another type of question does not necessarily mean that a teacher should not devote any of her instructional time to that content. To help schools implement responsible data-driven decision making, Maryellen Donahue, director of the BPS Office of Research, Assessment, and Evaluation, developed a protocol known as the MCAS Tool Kit for interpreting and analyzing student MCAS performance.

The MCAS Tool Kit was designed to provide school instructional leadership teams and data teams with an inquiry process for analyzing the data reports provided by the Massachusetts Department of Education (DOE). The Tool Kit encouraged teachers to think through a series of questions as they analyzed individual and group MCAS performance. For example:

- Was the relevant content covered during the course of the academic year?
- Did students use an incorrect or only partially correct problem-solving strategy?
- What primary and alternative teaching strategies could be used?

The MCAS Tool Kit provided a sound foundation for analyzing student data. However, it was time consuming to use, especially since the state-generated MCAS reports included the performance results for an entire grade within a school. To thoroughly analyze the data, school-level data teams needed to organize them into classes and into groups with particular characteristics. Doing this by hand was very time consuming. A few schools overcame this obstacle by inputting all of the data into an electronic spreadsheet program. However, the vast majority of schools lacked the resources for this work.

LIZA

In response to the problems of working with paper printouts, Albert Lau, who was at that time the director of the BPS Office of Information Systems, developed the Local Internet Zone for Administrators (LIZA). LIZA provided principals with school-based computer access to information on the school district's central data system pertaining to individual children in their schools. For example, a principal could access attendance information for individual children as well as their MCAS scores and scores on other tests, including the Stanford 9. LIZA also enabled school principals to download, to their own computers in Excel file format, test scores for groups of students in their schools.

Many school principals found the information on individual students available through LIZA to be helpful in preparing for conferences with parents. A few principals also took advantage of the capability to download test score information, which they could then examine using the Excel software. However, relatively few principals did this, in part because LIZA was somewhat cumbersome to use and in part because they lacked the time and/or skill to analyze test score data using Excel.

FAST Track

One of the consequences of mandating that BPS students complete benchmark assessments and later MCAS ELA and mathematics tests was a significant increase in the amount of available data on student achievement. Given the varying sources and types of student data, it was not uncommon for a school to have more than thirty pieces of data on each student. To fulfill central office requirements for data summaries, school principals needed to aggregate the data to grade and school levels and also present summaries for groups of students defined by race and special education status. This work was extremely time consuming.

In response to principals' requests for help in managing these data, BPE designed and implemented a Microsoft Access-based Formative Assessment Summary Tool (FAST Track). Using FAST Track, school teams could import student profile data files provided by the central office and MCAS data provided by the DOE. They could also enter data from benchmark assessments. FAST Track enabled school data teams to easily disaggregate scores by race, gender, free/reduced-price lunch status, and up to fifteen other school-defined student variables. By 2001–02, approximately one-third of BPS schools were using FAST Track.

Although FAST Track was a valuable tool to many school data teams, it had a critical shortcoming: FAST Track was not a "live" system that kept pace with the mobility of students within BPS. Consequently, a member of the school staff had to maintain the student profile data to keep it current. Further, the benchmark assessment data entered in FAST Track did not follow students as they moved among schools. As the school year progressed, if schools were not consistent with the data upkeep, they found that the students in their FAST Track database were not the students in their school, and that they had a good deal of missing data for students who had recently transferred to their school.

MyBPS Assessment

During the 2001–02 school year, Maryellen Donahue and Richard Murnane formed two working groups that met regularly to discuss ways the BPS central office could help schools learn from student assessment results. Out of these meetings came the idea for a BPS-BPE collaboration to develop a new set of tools. Early in the development process, the BPS leadership group decided to make the new tools a part of MyBPS, the Boston Public School District's intranet portal that provides teachers, administrators, principals, and staff with access to information and resources. For that reason, the new tools became known as MyBPS Assessment.

Over the next four years, teams from BPS and BPE worked together to develop and improve MyBPS Assessment, the main focus of which was to provide tools for efficient examination of patterns in MCAS data. Inevitably with such a new initiative, a great many questions arose. To answer these questions and push the work forward, a data governance group met monthly, reviewed progress reports, and debated thorny issues. One example of the many issues that arose concerned who would have access to data on student MCAS scores for all students in a school. Some school principals wanted access restricted to themselves. Others wanted to empower members of a large data team to examine patterns. Ultimately, the group decided to limit access to members of each school's data team with each school principal designating the membership of the team.

MyBPS Assessment was designed to lead teachers and data teams through a series of analyses that began with high-level summaries of student performance and then drilled down to finer levels of detail about student peformance. Figure 2 provides an illustration of the graph a teacher might receive in response to the question, "How did my students perform on the MCAS?"

Figure 3 provides an illustration of the graph a teacher might receive in response to the more detailed question, "How did my students perform on the MCAS multiple choice questions?" Using this summary, a school data team might focus its inquiries on the questions that seemed to pose the greatest difficulties

FIGURE 2

MCAS Performance-Level Summary (example high school in Boston)
Spring 2005 10th-Grade MCAS Mathematics Exam

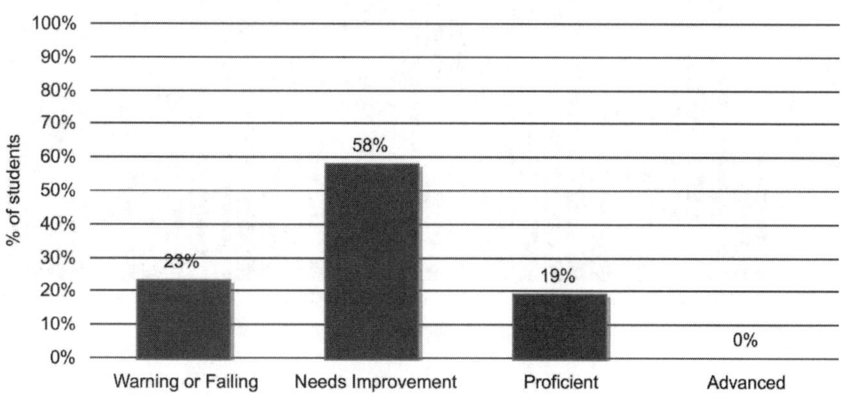

FIGURE 3

Summary of Student Performance on Multiple-Choice Questions
(example high school in Boston) Spring 2005 10th-Grade MCAS Mathematics Exam

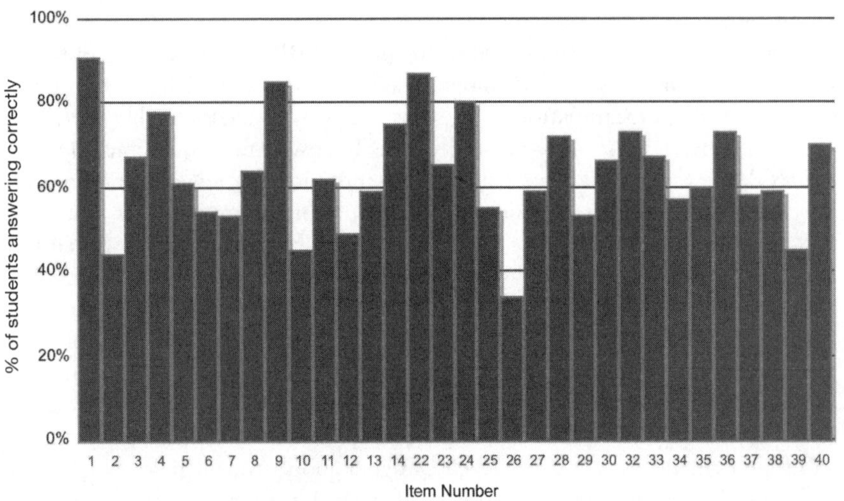

FIGURE 4

Summary of Student Performance on Multiple-Choice Questions
Compared to the District and State Performance
(example high school in Boston) Spring 2005 10th-Grade MCAS Mathematics Exam

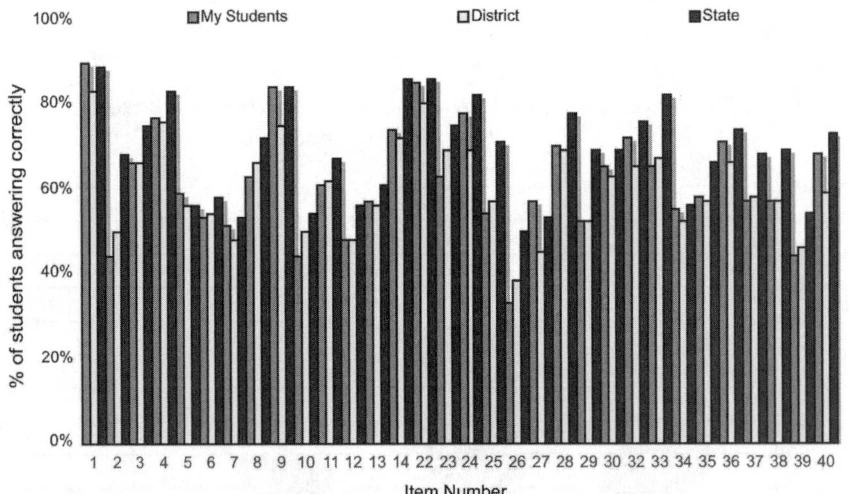

for students. Of course, examination of figure 3 would lead many teachers to ask, "How did children in other schools in the district and state perform on these same questions?" Figure 4 illustrates the type of graph the teacher could easily request to address this question. The MyBPS Assessment system also provides immediate access to a copy of the original test item, essential information for engaging in fruitful discussion of graphs like figure 3 and figure 4.

An important part of the implementation of the MyBPS Assessment system was training school-based educators in its use. The BPS Office of Research, Assessment, and Evaluation and BPE cooperatively developed and implemented a training program in which school principals and key members of school data teams learned a process for reviewing their data. They also received sets of materials aimed at helping them to replicate the training process with groups of teachers at their schools.

Including Data in Whole-School Improvement Plans

Beginning in 1996, the BPS central office required that every BPS school complete an annual Whole-School Improvement Plan (WSIP) in which it identified goals for the next year and described a plan for meeting these goals.[4] The WSIP grew out of BPS's Six Essentials, which have guided the district's reform efforts during Superintendent Payzant's tenure (see Appendix, page 271). From their inception, WSIPs were supposed to include data as the basis for identifying student needs and improvement goals. However, data did not appear in most plans until the deputy superintendents refused to accept plans without data in 2002. This central-office mandate created demand for tools that would help schools make sense of MCAS data more efficiently than they could with highlighters and state-generated score reports.

Having designed the MyBPS Assessment system for schools to conduct MCAS data analyses, BPS wanted to ensure that schools used the online tools to guide their improvement efforts. Pressure to do this also came from the Massachusetts DOE, which demanded that schools not making adequate yearly progress create WSIPs that contained evidence of data-driven instructional improvement strategies. The state DOE required that lagging schools conduct "root cause analyses" of student performance for grades within a school and also for major subgroups within the school (e.g., students by race, by primary language, and free/reduced-price lunch status). To meet these requirements, the MyBPS Assessment tool was enhanced to provide three features:

- Comparisons of a school's MCAS performance to the performance of the district and the performance of the state
- Side-by-side comparisons of student performance data disaggregated by race or gender
- The ability for schools to create ad hoc groupings of students for disaggregation of data

These enhancements made it easier for schools to obtain the MCAS data needed for inclusion in the WSIP. In most schools, instructional leadership teams (ILTs) took the lead in analyzing the MCAS data and creating the WSIP.

Most BPS schools can now use the tools in MyBPS Assessment to identify a problem, hypothesize causes of that problem, and generate proposed solutions to address those causes in the form of the WSIP. These are all steps forward. However, within each level (elementary, middle, high) and even across grade levels, WSIPs look strikingly similar: students struggle with inference and multi-step problems and open-response questions and vocabulary; students with disabilities and students who are English-language learners struggle more; and teachers struggle with teaching all of these things to all of their students. The similarity is in part because students and teachers across the district really do struggle with these skills, in part because schools are relying almost exclusively on the MCAS as the source of their information, and in part because the schools think that the district expects WSIPs that make these points. The district's expectations are signaled in model WSIPs that serve as examples for schools and in deputy superintendents' communication about what is acceptable for a WSIP. The similarity in WSIPs is also evident on the remedies side, where the solutions to these struggles are usually some form of professional development and better implementation of the district's instructional models in math and literacy.

Although all of these problems and solutions represent teaching and learning challenges, they are inauthentic in the sense that most schools know what they are going to write down in the WSIP before they even begin to look at their MCAS data. This affects the level of engagement in the improvement process, which in turn affects the level and quality of implementation of the improvement plan. Some schools embrace the WSIP process as a whole-school conversation about goals and ways to reach those goals, while at other schools, one or two people complete the WSIP. There is a core tension between standardization across the district (e.g., all WSIPs look and sound very similar) and letting schools really individualize their WSIPs.

Another issue is that the WSIP process is often approached as a two- or three-month exercise, rather than an ongoing process. The timeline that many schools use for engaging in the WSIP process is too short for schools to do all the steps of an effective improvement process, and usually what drops out is looking at multiple forms of data and examining instruction.

At this point, most schools know the fundamentals of identifying learning problems and have had enough years to work on basic implementation of the workshop and math models. Schools are ready to look at data sources in addition to MCAS, to think of new ways of framing problems, and to generate solutions that are more particular to the problem than saying that good implementation of workshop or Technical Education Research Centers (TERC) will solve the problem. The highest performing schools in BPS use the WSIP as a living document and use the WSIP process as a real opportunity for examining practice. These schools often have WSIPs that look a little different from other schools, which is evidence of their ownership and agency in the process. However, they are still the exceptions. The enormous growth in the way schools think about and plan for improvement over the last ten years means that schools are now poised to probe more deeply into data that support improvement.

Looking at Student Work (LASW)

Developing a culture of shared responsibility for student learning is a challenge in any school. The BPS experience with looking at student work provides an interesting case study of just how difficult this process of cultural change can be. As mentioned above, the second Essential of Whole-School Improvement in BPS is that all schools should "examine student work and data to drive instruction and professional development." Initially, the energy and resources for using data were aimed at the first part of that phrase—looking at student work. By 2001–02, all schools were supposed to have built "common planning time" into the schedule for teachers and were supposed to be using that time to examine student work, preferably in at least sixty-minute blocks. The theory behind the practice was that if teachers examined and discussed student work, they would reach some consistency in assessment (e.g., we all agree what a score of "4" means and what a "4" paper looks like on the rubric we are using), would have common standards, and would identify areas of student need. This discussion would then lead to instructional improvements in individual classrooms. In short, looking at student work was to provide a window into teachers' work.

Looking at student work (LASW) has provided an important first step in the shift from autonomous, closed-door teaching to collaborative, open discussions about teaching and learning that would eventually extend to peer classroom observations and the collaborative coaching and learning (CCL) model. However, several challenges arose as schools tackled LASW. First, there was not time in the schedule for it. Time as a barrier has two dimensions: (1) sheer quantity—there is never enough of it; and (2) scheduling so that the right people are able to talk with one another. In the early years of LASW, the primary challenge was the latter. Quantity would become an issue later, when there were more demands on limited professional development time. However, initially, most schools used almost all their professional development time for LASW. Even when schools became more adept at using their schedules to arrange common planning time, there were several questions related to deciding which teachers should meet with each other. At the secondary level, should teachers meet by grade-level or content area? When they met by grade-level, they discussed common students, but not common content. When they met by content, they were usually discussing different grade levels and different courses of the same general content (e.g., seventh-grade world history and eighth-grade U.S. history, or algebra and geometry). At the elementary level, small schools often had only one or two classes in each grade and thus clustered multiple grades together or clustered regular education, special education, and bilingual classes. At all levels, with these tradeoffs, teachers inevitably felt that the conversation might help with general alignment, but was not specific to their classroom.

A second challenge as schools began to look at student work was the realization that they did not know how to do it. A related challenge was that they did not necessarily want to do it. This is not surprising since many teachers saw LASW as reducing the time they could be spending fruitfully teaching their students. Moreover, doing LASW properly required new skills that took time to master and required that teachers interact with each other in new and potentially threatening ways.

Like other data practices, LASW has both a technical element—in this case, knowing how to select a piece of work and follow a protocol to discuss it—and an adaptive element—in this case, shifting from closed-door teaching to discussing teaching and learning openly with colleagues, grounded in actual evidence of learning or lack thereof from one's own classroom. Teachers were used to looking at student work behind their own closed doors and did not have practice discussing student work with colleagues.

BPE and the Annenberg Challenge dispatched "change coaches" to the first two cohorts of BPS schools undertaking reform (about half of BPS schools) to help them learn to look at student work and data. Big schools had their own change coaches and smaller schools shared them. Change coaches varied in their own expertise in looking at student work and data, and there was not an intensive, coordinated effort to raise the level of their expertise. Change coaches helped create the schedule, introduced protocols for looking at student work, and facilitated the LASW sessions—in short, they jump-started and sustained much of the LASW movement.

The practice of LASW was more ingrained in some schools than others, in part because some schools had been actively involved in the improvement process longer and had received change coach support longer. At the end of the 2001–02 school year, change coaches were eliminated from schools due both to shrinking district resources and a general sense that change coaches were not helping to move the improvement work in schools forward as far and as fast as hoped. The twin issues of schools being at different levels of progress and needing extensive, but differing expert support in order to use data well have persisted in BPS.

A third challenge that surfaced as schools looked at student work was that teachers in most schools did not change their teaching practices as a result of the LASW sessions. There were exceptions, and in some schools LASW became a powerful way to examine and improve practice. However, in most schools, teachers engaged in LASW because it was a district mandate, and then went back to their classrooms and continued teaching in the same ways as before the LASW session. This central challenge of translating looking at data into improved instruction continues today.

Joint BPS-HGSE Data Course

Another strategy for increasing BPS educators' skill and knowledge in using data emerged in a collaboration between BPS and the Harvard Graduate School of Education (HGSE). After a year of working with BPS on developing the MyBPS assessment system, HGSE professor Richard Murnane recognized that schools now needed help in using the tools to improve instruction in their schools. He invited ten BPS schools to bring teams to a course in the 2002–03 school year. HGSE graduate students were matched with BPS school teams and together they learned about the brand new MyBPS assessment tools as well as other tools for using data. Now taught by Kathryn Boudett, the course, titled A-306: Using Student Assessment Data to Improve Instruction: A Workshop, is completing its fourth year. Teams from more than thirty BPS schools have participated, with some schools participating for more than one year. Several lessons about what it takes to support schools in using data have emerged from the course.

The first lesson is that data analysis is a process, not an event. The course stretches over a full year, with more intensive work in the fall and follow-up work in the spring. Schools need lots of support to use data well, and they need that support over time. The second lesson is that using data is both a technical and an adaptive challenge, and the hard work is the adaptive part. This includes bringing about fundamental changes in daily work routines, attitudes, and values. While the course teaches technical skills, it focuses on helping school-based teams learn to engage their faculty colleagues in conversations about data that support improvement.

The third lesson is that there is enormous variation in capacity among schools. Even across a relatively small sample of eight to ten schools each year, there is wide variation in ability and commitment to analyzing data, having discussions about it across a range of teams, and making decisions based on data. Each school requires individualized support to respond to its particular context, needs, and knowledge and skill levels.

A fourth lesson is that going to scale is a challenge. The course only serves eight to ten schools per year and there is more need for support than the course can address. Currently, the course is being revised to provide more support to schools and to allow more BPS educators to participate.

The BPS central office has made important progress in providing schools with the tools and knowledge to make constructive use of student assessment results. Advances in the area of technical tools are most pronounced. BPS has also invested significant resources in the form of change coaches and instructional coaches to help schools develop a culture of collaboration and shared responsibility and greater capacity for improving instruction. Some schools have made great progress in this dimension. However, most have a long way to go. Having the right assessments and individuals who possess the knowledge and tools to make appropriate inferences from assessment data does not guarantee that decision makers will take constructive actions based on what they learn from analyzing that data. Clearly, analysis of assessment results must lead to decisions that improve the quality of children's education or it does not make sense to administer the assessment.

BETTER DECISIONS

Translating improvements in tools and assessments into improvements in teaching and learning has been the greatest challenge for BPS. The difficulties are of three kinds: knowing what to do next; accountability for action; and assessing improvement.

Knowing What to Do Next

As one BPS principal said to us, "We know that we have an achievement gap. If we knew what to do about it, we'd be doing it." For the last five years, the "solutions" have usually been to do a better job in implementing readers and writers workshops and in teaching the districtwide mathematics curricula. While sensible, the slow pace with which MCAS scores have improved and the number of schools not reaching the adequate yearly progress mark indicate these "solutions" are not enough.

Accountability for Action

In most schools, principals do not regularly monitor whether teachers are taking action as a result of examining data and making decisions. This pattern is also present at the district level. School supervisors make sure that schools turn in WSIP documents, but they do not systematically assure that all schools implement their WSIPs. The accountability mechanism defaults to MCAS scores. They are clearly important. However, they are too blunt a measuring instrument to provide guidance about whether teachers' daily instructional practices are changing and, if so, whether the changes are producing improvements in student learning.

Assessing Improvement

Much of BPS's focus in using data has been examining MCAS results to identify student learning problems. Although valuable, this work does not provide teachers with timely information about whether particular changes in instructional practices have resulted in fine-grained increases in students' skills and knowledge. Interest in FAST-R among BPS schools indicates a hunger for well-designed formative assessments. Providing these to BPS schools may be a necessary condition for stimulating improvements in instructional methods.

LOOKING AHEAD

The Boston Public Schools have made important progress in providing school-based educators with information and tools. However, BPS, like every other urban district, struggles with the immense challenge of continuously improving instruction. We conclude with some suggestions for next steps toward the goal of using data to guide instructional improvement.

Right Assessments

A comprehensive assessment system provides teachers and central office officials with the information they need to do their work more effectively. Building one is difficult because the technical standards of assessments that district officials will use for holding schools accountable are quite different from those of formative assessments that teachers will use to guide instructional improvements. Questions to ask about assessments currently in use include: What is each assessment used for? What would be lost if we eliminated some assessments? Do we need some assessments that we do not have—perhaps formative assessments? Given the uses of assessments, which should be mandatory with common administration procedures? The goal in addressing these questions should be to achieve clarity on the contributions of every assessment, the reasons the benefits of administering each exceed the costs, and how the assessments fit together to form a coherent system.

One possibility that districts might fruitfully explore is joining groups focused on producing course-specific examinations. For example, under the auspices of the American Diploma Project, educators from several states are developing end-of-course algebra examinations. Since test development is technically challenging and expensive, and since Algebra 1 and Algebra 2 should include the same basic content in Boston as in Houston, there may be important savings in joining groups that are developing course-specific examinations in common core subjects.

Many districts, including BPS, face two pressing needs in terms of assessments. The first is for more formative assessments that provide timely information to teachers on the extent to which their students have mastered skills they have recently been taught. The second is for assessments that measure growth in student skills. Measures of growth are important to retain morale among teachers who are doing a good job but are frustrated because they do not see this translated rapidly into improvements in scores on state accountability tests. Growth measures also can guide oversight of district schools by central office supervisors.

Knowledge and Tools

As schools become more skilled in using computer-based tools for analyzing student assessment results, the analysis capabilities they request grow. District leadership must consider whether to invest in making home-grown tools like

MyBPS Assessment more flexible, or whether to purchase data analysis software from an external vendor. An important consideration in evaluating the "make or buy" decision may be the inclusion of tools for the central office to improve oversight of schools. Currently, deputy superintendents in Boston have no flexible computer-based tools to compare student assessment results in the schools that they supervise.

Of course, providing district leadership teams with tools for evaluating the performance of schools will be a step forward only if team members have the skills to use the tools wisely. This will take considerable investment. There could be two related benefits of this investment. First, deputy superintendents could provide better guidance about the performance strengths and limitations of the schools they supervise, and second they would be modeling constructive, effective data use.

Better Decisions and Action

There is currently no urban school district in the United States where all students become proficient readers, writers, and problem solvers. Improving on this record will require both continued support to schools and consistent pressure for change. One source of support may be instructional coaches who understand not only how to make sense of student assessment results, but also how to engage school faculties in discussions of how to bring about instructional improvements. Constructive pressure for change will require central office supervisors who have good tools for comparing the performance of students in different schools and for assessing improvements in student performance for individual schools over time.

A persistent challenge for district central offices is how to support schools with enormous variation in capacity. Relevant questions include: What forms might this differentiated support take? Which assessments are mandatory and which are optional, and how does that vary across schools? How can the central office use assessments to identify which schools need what kinds of support?

We conclude where we started, by suggesting that analysis of student assessment results can play a critical role in improving instruction. As district leadership teams think about how to do this work better, it may be helpful to ask the questions that provide the organizing structure of this paper: Do we have the right assessments? Do our educators have the knowledge and tools they need? Is the work of looking at student data resulting in better decisions about how to improve instruction? The Boston experience over the last decade demonstrates that real progress can be made in providing school-based educators with the knowledge and tools to learn from student assessment results. The experience also demonstrates that each step forward reveals new challenges.

APPENDIX 6A

Boston Public Schools

Formative Assessment Program, 2005–06

Reading and Writing (Elementary Schools)

Grade	Fall	Winter	Spring
K0–1		▪ Pretend Reading Checklist ▪ Interactive Read Aloud Checklist ▪ Independent Writing Sample	▪ Pretend Reading Checklist ▪ Interactive Read Aloud Checklist ▪ Independent Writing Sample
K2	▪ Observation Survey: Letter Identification, Concepts about Print ▪ Independent Writing Sample	▪ Record of Oral Language, level 2, part 1 ▪ Observation Survey: Letter Identification, Hearing & Recording Sounds in Words ▪ Independent Writing Sample	▪ Record of Oral Language, level 2, part 2: students below 7 in winter ▪ Observation Survey: Letter Identification, Word Test, Concepts about Print, Writing Vocabulary, Hearing & Recording Sounds in Words ▪ Independent Writing Sample
1	▪ *Developmental Reading Assessment* (all students)* ▪ *Observation Survey 1-5* (students below level 4 or C) ▪ Writing: *Personal Narrative & Response to Literature-Oral Open Response Question)*	▪ *Running Record*: all students (+ DRA for students who scored below level 12 or G) ▪ *Observation Survey 1-5* (below level 6 or D) ▪ Writing: *Personal Narrative & Response to Literature-Written (Open Response Question)*	▪ *Running Record*: w/adequate comprehension and attention to fluency
2	▪ *Developmental Reading Assessment* (all students) ▪ Writing: *Description of Character, Scene, or Event & Response to Literature (Open Response Question)*	▪ *Running Record*: all students (+ DRA for students who scored below level 20 or K) ▪ Writing: *Description of Character, Scene, or Event & Response to Literature (Open Response Question)*	▪ *Running Record*: w/adequate comprehension and attention to fluency
3	▪ *Developmental Reading Assessment* (all students) ▪ Writing: *Personal Nonfiction*** & *Response to Literature (Open Response Question)*	▪ *Running Record*: all students (+ DRA for students who scored below level 30 or N) ▪ Writing: *Retelling & Response to Literature (Open Response Question)*	▪ *Running Record*: w/adequate comprehension and attention to fluency
4	▪ *Scholastic Reading Inventory* ▪ Writing: *Personal Narrative & Response to Literature (Open Response Question)*	▪ *SRI* (students who have not met grade-level proficiency benchmark: 750) ▪ *QRI or DRA 4-8* (students scoring below 600) ▪ Writing: *Personal Narrative & Response to Literature (Open Response Question)*	▪ *SRI*: students who have not met grade-level proficiency benchmark
5	▪ *Scholastic Reading Inventory* ▪ Writing: *Persuasive Essay w/Research & Response to Literature (Open Response Question)*	▪ *SRI* (students who have not met grade-level proficiency benchmark: 850) ▪ *QRI or DRA 4-8* (students scoring below 700) ▪ Writing: *Persuasive Essay & Response to Literature (Open Response Question)*	▪ *SRI*: students who have not met grade-level proficiency benchmark

* or Flynt-Cooter

** Students will write about a topic they know something about. Samples are available on the Elementary ELA MyBPS website.

Reading, Writing, English Language Arts, Science, History (Middle and High Schools)

	Fall	Midyear	End-of-Year
Reading	*Gr. 6–9:* Scholastic Reading Inventory*	*Gr. 6–9:* Scholastic Reading Inventory (students who have not met grade-level proficiency) *Gr. 6–11:* BPS Midyear ELA Assessment** (multiple choice + open response)	*Gr. 6–9:* Scholastic Reading Inventory (gr. 6, 9: all students; gr. 7, 8: students who have not met grade-level proficiency) *Gr. 6–11:* BPS End-of-Year ELA Assessment** (multiple choice + open response)
Writing	School or Centrally-Developed *Gr. 6–12:* Composition – Personal Narrative, Expository Writing, Persuasive Essay, or Literary Analysis	Centrally-Developed *Gr. 6–11:* BPS Midyear ELA Assessment** (composition)	Centrally-Developed *Gr. 6–11:* BPS End-of-Year ELA** Assessment (composition)
Science	Centrally-Developed *Gr. 6–8:* End-of-Unit Assessments (upon the completion of the 1st kit; will be at midyear for some teachers)	Centrally-Developed *High School:* BPS Midcourse Assessments – Physics, Biology, Chemistry	Centrally-Developed *Gr. 6–8:* End-of-Course Assessments *High School:* BPS End-of-Course Assessments – Physics, Biology, Chemistry
History		Centrally-Developed *Grade 6–8:* BPS Midcourse Assessments *High School:* BPS Midcourse Assessments – U.S. History 1, U. S. History 2, World History–1800 to Present	Centrally-Developed *Grade 6–8:* BPS End-of-Course Assessments *High School:* BPS End-of-Course Assessments – U.S. History 1, U. S. History 2, World History–1800 to Present

* *The Qualitative Reading Inventory or DRA 4-8* is administered to students reading significantly below the grade-level *minimum competency* benchmarks, as determined by the Scholastic Reading Inventory, in the fall, winter, and spring.

** The English Language Arts Mid- and End-of-Year assessments are comprehensive assessments of the ELA grade-level standards.

Mathematics (Middle and High Schools)

Grade	Fall	Winter	Spring
K2–5	• *Investigations* End-of-Unit Assessments	• BPS Midyear Math Assessment • *Investigations* End-of-Unit Assessments	• BPS End-of-Year Math Assessment • *Investigations* End-of-Unit Assessments
6–8	• BPS Math Tasks	• BPS Math Tasks • BPS Midyear Math Assessment	• BPS Math Tasks • BPS End-of-Year Math Assessment
9–12	• BPS Math Tasks	• BPS Math Tasks • BPS Midyear Math Assessment	• BPS Math Tasks • BPS End-of-Year Math Assessment

CHAPTER VII

On the Road to Reform

Building a System of Excellent and Equitable High Schools in Boston

ADRIA STEINBERG
LILI ALLEN

FOR TEN YEARS the country has looked to Boston for lessons on reforming high schools. Visitors have come seeking information on a wide range of fronts: school-to-career partnerships, small learning communities, and K–12 improvement strategies with teaching and learning at the center—all reforms implemented or expanded by the district's longtime superintendent, Thomas Payzant.

Today Boston is viewed as a pioneer in developing a "portfolio" approach to its high schools. Visitors see education complexes that represent conversions of large high schools into several small schools; free-standing small schools, including some with charter-like autonomy over budget, curriculum, schedule, and governance; large high schools divided administratively into small learning communities; large exam schools; and alternative high schools for over-age and under-credited youth.

Certainly Boston is not the only city to attempt to reinvent high schools. What sets Boston apart is the high-level, sustained commitment, led by Payzant, to making these reforms systemic and the successes to date. Over the past four years, every high school in Boston has either been converted into small schools or redesigned into ninth-through-twelfth-grade, semiautonomous, small learning communities. The teaching and administrative staff already in the buildings have been primarily responsible for carrying out these reforms. The changes are still in progress so final results are not in, but the reform efforts appear promising and there have been some clear successes. Student achievement, as measured by the state's tenth-grade test that all students must pass to graduate, is up significantly, and the achievement gap is smaller, though still too large.

Less visible to visitors are the many challenges inherent in moving away from a high school system in which family income and race are the best predictors of who graduates prepared for college. The Boston changes have involved grappling with knotty issues such as how school choice affects both equity and excellence, and how to guarantee that every student leaves high school prepared for postsecondary education and careers. The reforms also have highlighted the delicate balancing act between systemic and managed reform on the one hand, and maintaining flexibility for school-based decision making and problem solving on the other. Although every community must carry out its reform work within a particular political and social context, Boston's successes and challenges can be instructive for others engaged in similar efforts. This chapter tells the story of how the Boston Public Schools (BPS) has tried to realize its ambitious vision of creating an equitable system of excellent high schools.

The first section, which describes the origins of key strategies, policies, and reform partners that have guided high school renewal in Boston, focuses primarily on the progress made under the leadership of Superintendent Payzant, who recently retired after a highly regarded tenure. The second section provides a deeper look at the possibilities and challenges embodied in Boston's strategy of going "from large to small" with all of its high schools. The concluding section gleans lessons from Boston that may be useful to urban communities across the country seeking to improve their graduation rates and move all students to college-readiness and college matriculation.

THE EVOLUTION OF HIGH SCHOOL REFORM IN BOSTON

When Thomas Payzant arrived in Boston in 1994, he found a school system beset with many of the problems faced by beleaguered urban districts around the country: rapid superintendent turnover, buildings in disrepair, difficulty recruiting and retaining teachers because of slow and antiquated human resource processes, a highly politicized school board still dealing with the legacy of court-ordered desegregation, and an overall erosion of public confidence in public schools. A few schools stood out for their quality, but they were exceptions, "islands of excellence" amid overall disappointing levels of student performance. But the time was ripe for reform. Massachusetts policymakers were working out details of implementing the state's landmark Education Reform Act of 1993, which ushered in a new era of high academic standards and annual assessments, along with significant additional funding. Embracing standards-based reform and data-driven change, the new superintendent, in concert with Mayor Thomas Menino and his newly appointed school board, moved quickly to stabilize the situation and launch a period of steady improvement.

By the beginning of the new century, progress in many Boston elementary schools was evidenced by positive trends in student English and math achievement. However, the city's twelve comprehensive high schools lagged behind, for the most part. In 2001, when the class of 2003 became the first to take the new high-stakes Massachusetts Comprehensive Assessment System (MCAS) exam, only 40 percent reached the "needs improvement" standard that would allow them to graduate two years later.[1] Few Boston students not enrolled in BPS exam schools (which admit students on a competitive basis) were reaching the higher standard of "proficiency" that many experts considered a suitable proxy for readiness to succeed in college. Most disturbing, the achievement gap remained large among students of different races, ethnicities, income levels, and educational programs. Observations by district leaders and partners revealed striking symptoms of student disengagement and alienation: from the "hall-walkers" and frequent fire alarms that disrupted learning, to the many classrooms where students seemed bored, passive, or sometimes asleep.

The high school renewal agenda that has evolved over the past five years in Boston is a bold response to this set of challenges. The goal is to improve student and teacher performance by changing the very culture of the traditional "comprehensive high school" and its basic conditions for teaching and learning. Instead of huge schools with up to 1,400 students, many left to pass anonymously through the halls, Boston decided to create more intimate groupings of no more than 400 students, making it difficult for individuals to fly under the radar, so to speak. Research from a variety of studies indicated that while small schools are beneficial for all kinds of students, they can be especially valuable for those from low-income backgrounds, who make up the vast majority of Boston's eighteen thousand high school students.[2]

The Boston strategy has three major components: (1) engaging every student in a small, personalized, and rigorous learning environment in which they are known, respected, and prepared for college; (2) engaging every teacher in Collaborative Coaching and Learning (CCL), Boston's method for improving teaching quality by making the practice of teaching more public and more reflective; and (3) balancing a more directive approach by the district in regard to texts and core curriculum with opportunities for individual schools to design their own curriculum in order to more effectively engage their specific student population. The image promoted by Payzant is of a triangle in which strong relationships are at the apex, supported by a base defined at one end by rigorous and relevant curriculum and the other by engaging instruction.

Laying the Groundwork for High School Reform: The Boston Compact, Pilot Schools, and Whole-School Improvement (1982–97)

While the Boston high school reforms were groundbreaking in their systemwide scope, they did not spring suddenly from radical new ideas in secondary education. Rather, they represent a distillation of ideas and lessons culled from two decades of prior efforts to improve student achievement in Boston and other pioneering districts across the country. Two of these efforts themselves became national models: the Boston Compact and Boston's Pilot School framework.

Launched in 1982, the inaugural Boston Compact arranged for leaders of business, higher education, cultural, and human service organizations to make substantial commitments to providing scholarships and jobs for students and graduates in exchange for a unified commitment to measurable school improvement from the superintendent, the teachers union, the mayor's office, and the school committee. The business community helped develop a robust school-to-career initiative in the high schools, for the first time offering Boston students career pathways (small learning communities organized around career themes) and work-based learning opportunities such as internships. Some of the career themes introduced then today serve as the organizing principles for "pathway courses" and business partnerships in Boston's new small schools and small learning communities.

In 1994 Boston introduced in-district charter schools, called Pilot Schools, that had flexibility in budgeting, staffing, curriculum, scheduling, and governance. These schools were another important precursor to the high school reforms to come. Intended to help stem a potential loss of students to the state's new, independent charter schools, the then-unusual agreement between the district and the teachers union provided an opportunity to experiment with new program models that would be more attractive to students, parents, and teachers alike. Pilot Schools, with their personalized environment of smaller class sizes, extended day programs, and support services, quickly became "schools of choice" for parents most adept at negotiating Boston's controlled-choice system. Today Pilot Schools serve about 10 percent of the Boston Public Schools population, or 5,900 students, including the same mix of racial, ethnic, and economic backgrounds as other nonselective schools (though fewer Latino and limited English students). Ten of the city's thirty-five high schools are now Pilot Schools. Recent data show that they outperform other nonselective high schools on both engagement and performance measures.[3]

Payzant's first attempt to improve Boston's high schools came early in his tenure (in 1996) as part of a broader K–12 reform plan called *Focus on Children*. Intended to complement the 1993 Massachusetts Education Reform Act, its straightforward yet challenging mission was to prepare "all of our students to achieve at high levels." The focus was on whole-school instructional improvement for all grades within newly established citywide learning standards that were "rigorous, relevant, and teacher-driven."

As was true in other districts attempting similar reforms, it soon became clear that elementary schools were improving faster than secondary schools. This grew especially troubling as the class of 2003 moved into Boston's high schools, since these were the first students who would not get diplomas if they failed the state's high-stakes tenth-grade exam. School officials knew they had to intensify their focus on high schools with specific new strategies aimed at helping older students master more complex curriculum.

Early Attempts to Restructure High Schools: A Voluntary Approach, Then Intervention (1997–2001)

By the late 1990s, school leaders in Boston were coming to the realization that the deep-rooted culture of the comprehensive high school was defeating attempts to improve teaching and learning. It was difficult to achieve "whole-school reform" in big buildings with large student bodies and faculties, scheduled into forty-five-minute periods, and balkanized by the organizational complexity of different grade levels, subject matter departments, and, in some cases, career pathways. A joke going around at the time identified the problem: "We can't change the schedule; the schedule won't let us." Constantly shifting from teacher to teacher, it was easy for students to feel that no one knew them and no one cared, causing many to lose interest in schoolwork or drop out altogether. Teaching one hundred to one hundred fifty students each day and rubbing shoulders with hundreds more, faculty found it difficult to develop a collective sense of purpose or collaborate with colleagues to address key issues.

Meanwhile, success stories from several Pilot high schools and school-to-career schools, underscored by emerging research, suggested the strategy of establishing smaller, more personalized learning environments. In 1997, the district and the teachers union set up a joint High School Restructuring Task Force, which articulated ten key practices for all high schools. The most dramatic of these practices required each school to break into several "small learning communities." All were to provide varied instructional strategies, an extended array of supports, and closer collaborations with families, business, higher education, and community-based organizations. But each was free to choose among several options and timelines for doing so. With the goal of maximizing faculty engagement and ownership of reform, the superintendent decided to allow high schools to choose among several options and timelines for executing the changes.

By 2000 there was little evidence that this "voluntary" approach had resulted in real change, and Payzant decided to intervene. Using a formal joint management/union process first laid out in the 1989 teachers contract, Payzant convened district/union/community "intervention teams" that spurred turnarounds at three high schools that had particularly high dropout rates, low graduation rates, and few signs of improvement. With intensive support from the district and its partners, South Boston and Dorchester High Schools were to hire new headmasters and develop small learning communities. Boston High was to shut down altogether. Within two years, the South Boston and Dorchester reorganizations became the basis for their conversion to several smaller, autonomous schools sharing the original buildings. Under a new headmaster, Boston High opted to convert itself into a small Pilot School—the Boston Community Leadership Academy—rather than close.

A New Spotlight on High Schools: Outside Investment and Community Partners Accelerate Progress (2001–present)

Boston school leaders learned important lessons in the 1990s about the difficulties of making fundamental change in their sprawling high schools. As national interest and funding for high school improvement grew in the early years of the new decade, they were poised to take advantage of opportunities for significant outside assistance and set a bolder course for systemic reform. Between 2001 and 2003, the district received an infusion of over $21 million that would prove critical for helping Payzant finally start to realize his goals for Boston's secondary schools.

First, in 2001, Carnegie Corporation of New York selected Boston to participate in its "Schools for a New Society" initiative, a national effort to help urban districts improve high schools based on the principles of youth development and standards-based reform. Following a year to plan the changes, Boston was chosen as one of seven cities to receive a five-year grant of $8 million to implement the plan. As was often true in the past, the district would be working collaboratively with several community partners, led by the Boston Plan for Excellence, Boston's education foundation and close partner in instructional improvement efforts. Two years later, the Bill & Melinda Gates Foundation provided a $13.6 million grant for the development of small high schools embodying "rigor, relevance, and relationships." Jobs for the Future, a Boston-based national research and advocacy organization focused on creating educational and economic opportunity for underserved youth and adults, was the lead intermediary for this endeavor.

Buoyed by these substantial investments, Boston was able to create two new "engines" of reform to help both district and building leaders translate the blueprint for change into ground-level action. The district's new Office of High School Renewal (OHSR)—headed by the former director of the School-to-Career Office—serves an entrepreneurial function, helping to identify how central office functions can be carried out in ways that remove barriers and provide support to small schools and learning communities. Drawing on the expertise of former administrators and teachers from Pilot high schools and small learning communities, OHSR also provides direct assistance, helping principals and their leadership teams develop new organizational and instructional leadership skills.

Providing an outside perspective is the High School Renewal Work Group, which brings together the lead staff of the partner organizations that were most involved in earlier reform efforts: the Boston Plan for Excellence and Jobs for the Future, along with the Private Industry Council (a business-led intermediary organization that connects youth and adults to education and employment opportunities and staffs the Boston Compact) and the Center for Collaborative Education (a school development and reform organization that coordinates the Pilot Schools). Working with the Office of High School Renewal, this group has collaborated since 2001 to build on lessons from previous reform plans and bring evidence of progress, options, and policy recommendations to the superintendent and his leadership team.

The result over the past five years has been the transformation of virtually all of Boston's high schools. Once a system dominated by twelve comprehensive high schools, Boston now has thirty-five small high schools, five large schools organized into three or four semiautonomous small learning communities, and one vocational-technical school organized into theme-based academies. The five "education complexes" created in old comprehensive high school buildings house a total of fifteen autonomous small high schools, and another eleven small high schools have been created from scratch, several in the past few years. The only schools left untouched were the city's three exam schools—protected from the winds of change by the high levels of student performance on tests and their long histories, powerful alumni associations, and active parent bodies.

While Boston invested in creating new schools and converting old schools, the former strategy has been used sparingly because of the difficulty finding affordable facilities in the city's highly competitive real estate market. Nevertheless, although limited by space issues, the approach of starting up new schools has had its advantages. All but one of the start-ups have Pilot status and the autonomy to hire staff committed to a small-school approach and to the particular school mission.

The conversion strategy, by contrast, has presented numerous organizational and political challenges—perhaps exacerbated by Payzant's decision to take a "big bang" approach. The superintendent wanted to make fundamental changes while relying primarily on existing staff; only the headmasters would be new. So he closed down the "old school" and redistributed the faculty and students through a choice process into the new schools in the same building (unless they requested a transfer out). This approach contrasts to the gradual approach used in New York and some other cities that have grown new schools one grade at a time, with a mix of newly hired and veteran faculty, while slowly phasing out the old school. Payzant's "big bang" had the advantage of avoiding some of the festering hard feelings that can occur when new and old ways of doing business have to coexist. But it proved tricky to create new school cultures with faculties steeped in the traditions of the large comprehensive high school and without commensurately dramatic changes in district, contractual, and statutory policies and practices. For example, most conversion schools have opened with the same six-period day as in the former large schools. Changing the schedule to better suit workshop or project-based instructional approaches has been challenging, particularly because changes in schedule require a two-thirds faculty vote.

The speed of the district's conversions of South Boston and Dorchester intensified these problems because there was little faculty involvement in the planning. Learning from these experiences, the High School Renewal Work Group invited competitive proposals for new small schools in the next two conversions, Hyde Park and West Roxbury. Design teams included faculty, students, parents, and community partners and had extensive time to develop proposals. The new headmasters came on board six months before the schools opened, providing time to get to know teachers and students and to plan for a smooth beginning.

A similar process was then used to engage teachers and administrators in the design of small learning communities within the remaining nonselective high schools, but the process has been challenging for different reasons. These high schools intend to maintain their large-school identity while forging new bonds within small learning groups. While garnering the best of both worlds has an understandable appeal, it is proving difficult to put into practice. Without the defining moment of "big-bang" change in the launch of an entirely new school, there has been less opportunity for a fundamental rethinking of the usual ways of doing business. If job descriptions, schedules, and other elements of the fundamental architecture remain the same, the small learning communities could simply become another, perhaps competing, layer in an already complex organizational structure.

A New Graduation Policy: Setting the Stage for Continuing Reform

While asking individual schools to rethink every aspect of what they do, district leaders have been reexamining their own key policies in search of new ways to support the reforms. An important step forward has been a groundbreaking new graduation policy that aims to eliminate the entrenched problem of "multiple repeaters," the large number of students who lack the credits to advance with their class and later end up leaving school altogether due to a sense of futility, boredom, and frustration. Although the district's annual dropout rate is lower than that of many cities, the Massachusetts Department of Education estimates that Boston loses nearly a third of its students (32%) between ninth grade and graduation. This translates to 1,400 to 1,600 students dropping out each year.

The new policy calls for replacing grade-by-grade promotion requirements with a more transparent, credit-based system of moving toward graduation. The goal is to keep students moving forward in their stronger areas while providing help with others. The policy also creates an opening for curricular innovation in ways that could accelerate credit recovery and progress towards graduation, for example, allowing schools to create courses that award credit based on performance and competency, not just seat-time. All high schools are given the option of using either the district's curricula, setting up their own humanities courses (combining English language arts and history), or, more ambitiously, redesigning their full scope and sequence of courses.

THE POSSIBILITIES AND CHALLENGES OF GOING FROM LARGE TO SMALL

Restructuring Boston's high schools so far has taken nearly ten years, millions of dollars, and the committed effort of hundreds of people. But important work remains to be done. In each converted small school and small learning community, staff and students are still discovering how to take full advantage of their new environment. Much of the work of the district and its community partners over the past five years has been to identify how best to support teachers and administrators in this endeavor. This section explores both the possibilities and the challenges embodied in the strategy of going "from large to small" in Boston's high schools. In particular, it considers how far the schools have progressed toward their goal of improving each of the three key areas of relationships, instruction, and curriculum in their mission to raise student achievement.

Relationships: Personalizing the Experience of High School for Students and Teachers

A key aim of the plan to shrink Boston's high schools was to minimize the feelings of alienation that cause many students to lose interest in their schoolwork and teachers to lose their sense of purpose. Yet Boston leaders have discovered that reorganizing into smaller units comes with its own complications, upsetting the delicate balance of relationships within a school. As in a small town where everybody knows one another, it is harder to hide in a smaller school community. Students may want teachers to know and respect them, but they may not be entirely happy about the accountability that comes with teachers paying closer attention to their performance. Teachers can no longer shut their doors to what is happening in other classrooms or relate primarily to like-minded colleagues; the responsibilities of collaborative planning may unearth differences in values and philosophy that are difficult to resolve. Principals may find it difficult to manage such conflicts while also building a collective sense of mission, vision, and effort among the whole faculty.

In light of these dilemmas, Boston has used specific strategies to maximize the benefits of smallness. Primary among these is "capacity coaching" to help headmasters lead instructional, cultural, and organizational improvement. For example, some coaches have helped headmasters generate faculty support for key program changes. Others are helping to implement advisories—daily or weekly small-group meetings of students with a faculty member to ensure that every student has an adult who knows him/her well and is aware of academic progress and problems. Schools with the most success and the least faculty resistance toward advisories have had coaches help them establish simple classroom routines and develop concrete lesson plans on relevant subjects, such as college planning.

To ensure that students have a voice in what happens in their schools, a growing number of schools are welcoming Boston's youth development organizations: Youth on Board, Teen Empowerment, and the Boston Student Advisory Council. Having relied on these organizations to help design the small schools and small learning communities, many are now using them to help run community meetings to solicit student participation and to organize other forms of input into governance.

Schools also have made striking progress in increasing student access to adults outside of school. More students than ever before are participating in work-based learning opportunities such as internships, in part because many schools have themes such as engineering or health that lend themselves to business partnerships. Almost all high schools have significant partnership activity, offering employment, volunteers, technical assistance, and charitable contributions. Postsecondary partners continue to offer tutoring, as well as opportunities for faculty and students to participate in events on campus.

Instruction: Getting the Conditions Right for Ambitious Teaching and Learning

From his earliest days in Boston, Superintendent Payzant made high-quality instruction his signature issue. The district's high school reform efforts have further defined what this means at the secondary level: teachers are expected to make their practice more public, plan collaboratively with colleagues, and continually work to improve their ability to engage students in the deep exploration of content. Boston has tried a number of strategies to address these issues, but has met with mixed success so far.

A system-wide approach to increase teacher collaboration has not yet gained a strong foothold in the high schools. The goal of Collaborative Coaching and Learning (CCL) is to have every teacher participate every year in opportunities to see and discuss model lessons and try out new practices in the classroom with the support of a coach and group. The main focus in high schools is on increasing the value of "readers and writers workshop," an approach intended to make learning less "teacher directed," in which students read independently, write, and confer with peers. While every high school has implemented CCL to some extent, it has failed to become a central professional development strategy in many schools due to scheduling problems and uneven headmaster leadership. The district recently convened a coaching "work group" to try to achieve greater alignment and coherence in the teaching strategies promulgated by the various coaches. In addition, the BPS is making it easier for individual schools to determine how to use their coaching allocation.

Pilot high schools have successfully built teacher collaboration by engaging faculty in curriculum planning that is based on an analysis of the needs and interests of their students. Using the scheduling flexibility that comes with Pilot status, much of this work has occurred during afterschool hours. Pilot leaders report that this process has been a central contributor to their strong outcomes in both engagement and achievement measures.[4] However, in non–Pilot Schools, collaborative curriculum planning has been more challenging to schedule because of long-standing teacher expectations about the length of the school day and the contractual requirement that teachers be paid for additional work beyond the school day.

In some of the conversion small schools, faculty collaboration has also prompted changes in how time is organized for student learning. Several high school faculties have voted to institute longer class periods, and several schools also have begun to add instructional time by extending the school day. These approaches, combined with other cutting-edge strategies such as e-learning opportunities, are helping students catch up on skills needed for high school success and to recover credits quickly enough to progress toward an on-time graduation. This work is fragile at best, however, and reliant at this point on a combination of grant funds, teacher goodwill, and financial and volunteer support from partner organizations.

The knottiest instructional challenges have emerged in relation to two student populations requiring specialized instruction: special education students (19% of BPS total) and English-language learners (17% of total). Boston, like many cities, has hired a growing number of specialists to provide pull-out services for these students, while at the same time shrinking the proportion of regular education classroom teachers due to budget constraints. This means that despite the district's focus on "small" learning environments, average class size has not been reduced (except in Pilot Schools, which use their staffing and budget flexibility to lower class sizes).[5] At the same time, the composition of the "regular education" classroom includes a growing number of students with significant learning challenges. For example, a typical classroom of twenty-five students contains seven to ten special education students and five to seven students who live in households where English is not the spoken language. A related problem is that most separate and pull-out classes are taught by special education or bilingual instructors who may not have expertise in the subject matter that students are supposed to learn. A recent newspaper article noted that Boston segregates special education students in separate classes more than other districts in the state.[6]

The process of converting large schools into smaller units—and the related analysis of their demographics—also has uncovered the disproportionately high numbers of special education students in some schools. Over the past few years, efforts to distribute these students more evenly across the district has resulted in a smaller special education population in some high schools and a corresponding increase in others, in Pilot Schools in particular. Recently, headmasters of small schools have pushed for a policy that would minimize the number of different special education designations and programs within any one school in an effort to facilitate mainstreaming by allowing teachers to focus on inclusion strategies for a particular subgroup of students. Headmasters also have been asking for more help to build the capacity of their staffs to handle differentiated instruction, hoping to make "regular" classrooms productive learning environments for all students.

Boston is still responding to the enormity of the challenge created by the state-mandated end of bilingual education following the passage of ballot Question 2 in 2002. It has proven particularly difficult to get all regular education classroom teachers "up to speed" in English as a Second Language strategies, especially given the significant professional development still required for all teachers to practice workshop instruction.

Curriculum: Increasing Academic Challenge in Preparation for College Success

Boston's high school reform work has elevated concern about how prepared graduates are to succeed in college and careers. Very few students reach the proficiency level on the state's MCAS exam, considered by many to be a proxy for readiness for college. And only a small percentage take at least one Advanced Placement course, considered by many to be a primary measure of rigor in high schools.[7] With attention focused on better preparing students for their transition to high school—and for the tenth grade MCAS, which they must pass to graduate—high schools have struggled to find resources to invest in helping upper-grade students reach college-ready standards.

Over the past decade, Boston has increased the number of courses required for graduation and, in core subjects such as mathematics, has determined which courses are offered in what sequence and required the use of certain textbooks and professional development programs. While this more directive approach to curriculum has been instrumental in increasing consistency across district classrooms, it has become clear that it cannot, by itself, reach the ambitious goal of bringing all students, regardless of their entering skills, to college-ready standards.

In championing the new graduation policy, which allows schools to use the district's curriculum or design their own (or part of their own), Superintendent Payzant was seeking to balance mandates and management with innovation and creativity. Using the Pilot high schools as a model, fourteen small high schools recently indicated their intent to propose a school-based set and sequence of courses. One reason for this high level of interest in setting their own curricula is the desire among small-school faculty to incorporate the theme of the school more fully into its academic program and to make required core courses, which now take up most of the school day, more engaging for students and teachers alike. Schools have increasingly turned to Boston-area colleges and curriculum development organizations for help in designing and implementing curricula that will ignite student interest while also preparing them for the demands of college.

LESSONS LEARNED ON THE ROAD TO REFORM

Many school systems have set the goal of educating every student to a college preparatory level and many are trying to accomplish this ambitious agenda through developing an equitable system of high-quality high schools. Boston has gone further than most, instituting system-wide changes to create small, personalized learning environments for all high school students. The process is still underway, but much can be gleaned from Boston's experiences so far, the successes as well as the challenges. This chapter concludes by identifying four key lessons emerging from the work in Boston that can guide the next superintendent and inform national high school reform efforts.

1. The National Focus on Graduation and Dropout Rates Offers Communities an Opportunity to Expand High School Reform to Encompass a Dual Agenda of High Standards and High Graduation Rates

Many policymakers and educators have assumed that making progress in raising the value of a high school diploma means losing ground in ensuring that struggling youth stay in school and graduate. Boston's high school reform efforts—and especially the ninth-through-twelfth-grade vertical structure and the graduation policy—point to the kinds of policy and practice changes necessary to achieve a "dual agenda" of high standards and high graduation rates.[8]

A strong underlying theme of the Payzant era has been the drive to ensure that high schools both hold on to students and hold them to higher standards. Starting in 2001, concerns about student disengagement and the lack of holding and promotion power helped to fuel the push for high school reform in Boston. More recently, a well-timed, hard-hitting report from the Youth Transitions Task Force[9]—a partnership including community-based organizations and advocates, civic leaders, and high-level school department personnel—has helped to galvanize school committee and senior district leadership to take on the dropout issue more aggressively.

Building on a growing national research base[10] pointing to the value of an "early warning system" to reduce the number of dropouts, Boston is participating in a national "Dual Agenda" initiative funded by the Carnegie Corporation of New York to monitor "on track" indicators at the critical transition points of sixth and ninth grade. By flagging younger students who fail a core course, demonstrate poor attendance, or receive a disciplinary referral, schools will be able to identify—and intervene with—many of those likely to drop out later.

Boston is well set up to make use of such an early warning system: smaller learning units and personalization strategies such as advisories make early identification possible. Accountability through grades 9–12, with teachers in a small school or small learning community responsible for ensuring that their entering ninth graders graduate college-ready, makes intervention an early and ongoing collective faculty effort. The graduation policy allows schools to offer credit-recovery programs designed specifically by and for students inside that school. The district's alternative education schools provide opportunities for students who need a different, more flexible, and rigorous setting in which to complete high school. All of these policy innovations offer important lessons for other districts seeking to stem the dropout tide, and Boston's ability to capitalize on such policy supports over the next few years should prove instructive, as well.

2. Providing a Choice-Based Portfolio of Schools Requires Aggressive Steps to Address Equity and Excellence Challenges

Students and families in Boston are now able to choose the kind of high school they would like to attend from a portfolio of options broader than any in the country: small schools in large complexes, small learning communities within a large school, stand-alone small schools, or Pilot Schools, all with a range of thematic academic foci; even alternative schools where former dropouts can work toward a diploma. At the same time, Boston has been striving to ensure that every student across the system has access to an excellent high school and that every school can organize resources effectively to educate all its students.[11] Boston's challenges in reaching this goal can prove instructive for other communities attempting similar efforts.

For example, a critical underpinning of a portfolio system is that families understand their full range of options. The first step in ensuring this is to provide clear communications materials in multiple languages. However, Boston has learned that more aggressive efforts are needed. Boston reformers have concluded that a partnership between the school district, community-based organizations, and parent organizers could result in a range of parent-friendly information sessions and school visits that help parents make a more informed choice.

A related challenge is the lack of comprehensive data on school performance available to families and students assessing their options. As in many districts across the country, individual school-level data on the BPS website provides only "snapshot" information on student achievement, such as the percentage of students passing state exams each year. This does not allow comparison of a school's effectiveness in helping all students—including those entering with lower skill levels—to stay engaged and reach high standards. Families and students need a data system that illustrates which schools are having the most success with various groups of students (broken down by age and credits, as well as demography). Boston is in the process of developing such a data system.

Boston's experience offering a choice-based portfolio also illustrates that there can be unintended consequences of a school's success that need to be addressed. Schools that "get it right" for struggling students have become exceptionally popular, resulting in more competition for few slots, and fewer openings for the least advantaged families, who tend to be least informed of the options. Fenway High School, once a school for the least engaged students, was "discovered" by academically avid students and their parents who were seeking a personalized learning environment. The school quickly learned that it had to take concrete steps to ensure continued access for struggling students. By holding aside seats for various populations of students (e.g., over-age and behind in skills, court-involved, students with disabilities, referrals from community agencies working with troubled youth), the school now serves students who range from formerly adjudicated to formerly private school–educated youth. Other schools have adopted different approaches, some instead continuing to accept students by lottery, preferring to ensure equity by *not* managing the process. For this approach to work, it will be critical for less empowered parents to learn about the school and how it has helped children like their own.

Perhaps the biggest challenge facing Boston regarding choice and equity is how to ensure a high-quality education for special education students and English-language learners. Of particular concern is where to educate them and how to support the diverse range of student needs in the "new regular education classroom." The district's commitment to ensuring equitable access to a wide range of options for substantially separate special education students has meant that many schools, even small ones, offer multiple program types, which can make it harder for a faculty to practice inclusion. For example, mainstreaming behaviorally challenged students requires different strategies and skills from mainstreaming cognitively challenged students. Any district with a portfolio of different types of schools will have to consider the difficult trade-offs between offering all students all options and ensuring that the options available to specific populations are well-designed to meet their needs. While the latter could mean fewer choices available to families, the choices more likely would be among stronger programming models, with increasingly effective inclusion.

3. High School Change Requires Both Internal and External Change Agents

One of the main reasons Boston was able to move quickly to restructure its high school system was the presence of an internal "engine" of reform, the Office of High School Renewal, led by a longtime administrator with a history as an innovator and implementer within the BPS and with a direct reporting line to the superintendent. The High School Renewal Work Group, comprised of the Office of High School Renewal and a set of external partner organizations, all with track records of collaborating with the district, has further fueled Boston's reform efforts.[12] This group has met on a monthly basis with the superintendent and members of his leadership team to examine evidence of progress, consider modifications, and even formulate new policies. Powered by these two "engines"—one internal and one external—the BPS has been able to draw quickly on research and ideas from around the country, adapt these to the local context (while learning quickly from initial missteps), and put new strategies into practice in the schools.

However, to ensure the success and sustainability of reform, it has become clear that the district and the organizations with which it partners must make a far more robust attempt to engage the community in their work. Parents and other community members can play a critical role in both supporting reforms that are working and demanding further changes that are likely to have a bigger impact. Boston has a deputy superintendent for community and parent engagement, but this office is viewed as lacking the independence to prod the district on challenging issues, especially those related to racial equity and equal access. While the external partner organizations have a history of collaboration with the district, they do not represent the BPS students' communities. Past efforts to engage the community in high school reform have met with limited success, in large part because they came from these same, previously-empowered partner organizations. Just recently, these organizations have moved to a strategy of offering funding for a coalition of community organizations and advocates to lead the community engagement work, and the High School Renewal Work Group will now expand to include a community organization—Freedom House—with legitimacy in Boston's neighborhoods.

It also has become evident in Boston that the long-term success of high school reform requires fundamental changes in the way the district's central office does business. High school leaders cannot go it alone. They need certain policies and conditions in place to enable them to make changes in their schools, as well as support in developing their capacity to execute the changes. Increasingly, in Boston and across the country, school leaders are asking for a more service delivery-oriented relationship with the central office—one that offers them support based on the specific needs and strengths of students and staff in their buildings. In Boston, this type of support is often offered through an "inside-outside" strategy of district staff and partner organizations, such as the approach used by the BPS Budget Office and the Center for Collaborative Education in working out the budgeting flexibility of the Pilot Schools. The fundamental challenge for Boston and other communities is to reorient the entire central office toward a service delivery approach. New York City has taken a radical approach in the recent decision to dramatically expand its "Autonomy Zone" to a much larger number of "Empowerment Schools" that have the freedom to determine which services to purchase from the central office.

Some urban districts have recognized that the goal of college-readiness for all cannot be met without a fundamental rethinking of how specific central office departments operate, nor without a greater degree of collaboration among high school reformers, central office leaders, and district and state policymakers.[13] Boston has created a vehicle through its High School Renewal Work Group for such collaboration to occur. Still, the challenge remains of how best to ensure both autonomy and protection of internal change agents as they prod the district to change how it does business.

4. To Answer the Question "Is It Working?" High School Reform Leaders Need a Benchmarking and Performance Measurement System That Captures the Complexity of Systemic Change

As the Boston story demonstrates, high school reform requires simultaneous action at many levels—not just in the schools, but also at the central office and on the part of partners and stakeholders in the community. The complexity of reform makes it challenging to answer the simple question that must be asked: "Is it working?"

During the period of the reforms of the Payzant era, the overall trend of achievement test data has been positive, indicating that far more students are passing the state's high-stakes tenth-grade exam and showing some signs of reduction in the achievement gap. Although such news is encouraging, it does not provide the kind of detailed information that reform leaders need to be effective. Thus, over the last four years, the BPS and its reform partners have invested in multiple forms of documentation and evaluation in an effort to analyze which efforts have been successful and where additional energy or resources might be required. These include classroom observations and teacher and student surveys, as well as formal and informal interviews and focus groups with teachers, students, and headmasters conducted by a variety of people, including outside researchers, the BPS and its partners, and some students.

The complexity—and sometimes contradictory nature—of the findings from these evaluative efforts offer an important lesson in the challenges of evaluating systemic reforms. For example, while one evaluation found more use of "progressive pedagogies" such as individual reading, discussion groups, and peer review of written work, another found little use of readers and writers workshop—which includes largely the same type of teaching methods. Because assessments have taken place at different times in the unfolding of reform and represent, in many cases, people's views in the first or second year of implementing changes, the data across assessments and from different schools has not always been consistent regarding the depth and breadth of changes in teaching and learning, and a clear synthesis of their meaning has been elusive. In many cases, results may reflect reactions to the change process itself. At such moments of transition, it is not unusual to find people mourning and romanticizing the way things were done before and finding fault with the new way of doing business.

Boston and other districts trying to develop more sophisticated evaluation mechanisms may want to explore a benchmarking process.[14] Such a performance measurement process begins with a concrete definition of success at all levels: the school, district, and the community. This definition enables leaders to recognize and reward progress in implementing new teaching practices, institutional designs, and central office systems that lay the groundwork for improved student outcomes, while avoiding faulting teachers and schools when they do not achieve instant success. A benchmarking process must also define clear stages of implementation with goals, guideposts, and appropriate performance indicators. This type of measurement system fosters an environment that nurtures innovation by holding off premature judgment even as it maintains the improvement of student outcomes as the ultimate measure of success.

This benchmarking process will require a complementary collection and analysis of more fine-grained measures of progress than many districts now have in place. One of the side effects of dismantling large, comprehensive high schools in Boston has been to put into stark relief the composition of the student body in nonselective schools, especially those with a reputation of poor performance and poor school climate. In Boston's choice-based system, these schools end up primarily serving students whose top choices could not be accommodated, or who did not make a choice at all. In such classrooms and schools, what constitutes acceptable progress towards the goal of proficiency for all? To answer this question, schools must be benchmarked against other schools in the state with similar populations—not just demographically, but in terms of age, credits, and skill levels upon high school entry. In addition, schools need valid measures for comparing similar schools and the degree to which they improve students' skills from year to year, even when their students still have not reached the goal of proficiency.

Ultimately, federal, state, and local policymakers will need to align efforts and investments to achieve the level of data that can be both reliable and meaningful to ongoing high school reform. Even in the short run, however, local reform leaders can make progress by starting to implement the benchmarking system described here and, in fact, use that process to inform their work with state leaders as they work to improve the quality of their data systems.

CONCLUSION

The longevity and the systemic nature of Boston's high school renewal work continues to draw attention from many parts of the country. At the same time, as this chapter documents, high school reform is an unfinished agenda in Boston. While the data indicate some positive trends, too many young people are still not on track to graduate from high school, and many of those who do graduate have not been fully prepared to succeed in college and careers. And while some of the smaller learning environments are well on their way toward creating an academic climate in which a sense of belonging, student-centered instruction, inquiry-based learning, and authentic community collaboration will thrive, others are still at the beginning stages. By learning lessons from the past decade of high school reform and building on the firm foundations that have been laid, Boston has the opportunity to demonstrate the best potential of an urban school district. The district must focus on going to scale with a full array of learning options that meet the diverse needs of its students and culminate in college readiness for all.

CHAPTER VIII

Escaping from Old Ideas

Educating Students with Disabilities in the Boston Public Schools

ELLEN C. GUINEY
MARY ANN COHEN
ERIKA MOLDOW

With assistance from staff members at the Boston Plan for Excellence

The real difficulty in changing the course of any enterprise is not in developing new ideas, but in escaping old ones.

JOHN MAYNARD KEYNES

KEYNES'S INSIGHT is as true in its application to education as it was to economics. Recently cited by researchers Howard Adelman and Linda Taylor to argue for changes in school improvement planning, it aptly fits the state of educating students with disabilities across the country.[1] In many cities, special education is stuck on the idea that it is a place to put students with special needs rather than an approach to educating them.[2] Further, special education is driven by a compliance model of accountability in which "effectiveness tends to be defined in terms of whether or not procedural regulations were satisfied, the proper steps taken, and the right paperwork processed correctly and on time."[3]

In 1997, the federal government recognized the need for major changes in the delivery of special education services with its reauthorization of the Individuals with Disabilities Education Act (IDEA). The new act incorporated important shifts in emphasis from a focus on regulations to academics and outcomes for students, and stressed that students with disabilities should have access to the same curriculum as their nondisabled peers. Implementing that shift, however, has proven difficult. Holding students with disabilities to the same academic standard as other students has too often simply meant holding those students to the same test required under No Child Left Behind (NCLB) or using the same curriculum without adjustments, rather than figuring out how to make sure they receive high-level instruction in the manner and at the pace they need in order to meet the standard.

Successfully educating all students, whatever their learning needs, will remain an unmet challenge in public education until districts "escape from old ideas," in particular, the idea that special education is the appropriate response for any student with learning or behavior problems, and that within special education an emphasis on following procedures is paramount.

This chapter focuses on ten years of special education in the Boston Public Schools (BPS), using the following three indicators as evidence of the imperative for change. These three areas, however, bear consideration in any district:

1. There are high percentages of students in special education, with an overrepresentation of black males.
2. There are high percentages of students in special education with learning or behavioral *difficulties*, not *disabilities.*
3. There are high costs for poor student outcomes.

DATA FROM BOSTON: EVIDENCE THAT CHANGE IS IMPERATIVE[4]

Boston has worked steadfastly in the last ten years to create a coherent framework for instructional improvement and increased student learning in all classrooms and has achieved strong results for many students. In 2003, Superintendent Thomas W. Payzant and his team of leaders began focusing greater attention on closing achievement gaps in the system, including the gap in the performance of students with disabilities (figure 1). Their central strategy for improving instruction for these students is based on lessons learned about improving performance for all students and includes extensive professional development specifically for teachers of students with disabilities in approximately one third of BPS schools. The effort began with determining the gaps in teachers' training and providing additional coaching and courses in reading and in special instruc-

Glossary of terms

Resource room: in-school services for students with disabilities who are in a regular education class but need specific additional support; students go to a resource room for varying amounts of time each week, depending on need.

Substantially separate: classes for students with disabilities who have a particular impairment; typically, they are with other students only for noninstructional activities, such as lunch.

Inclusion: classes with both regular education and students with disabilities who qualify for substantially separate classes, with additional staff to provide in-class support for the students with disabilities.

FIGURE 1

How Wide Is Boston's Special Education Achievement Gap?
MCAS 2005 Grade 10 English Language Arts & Math

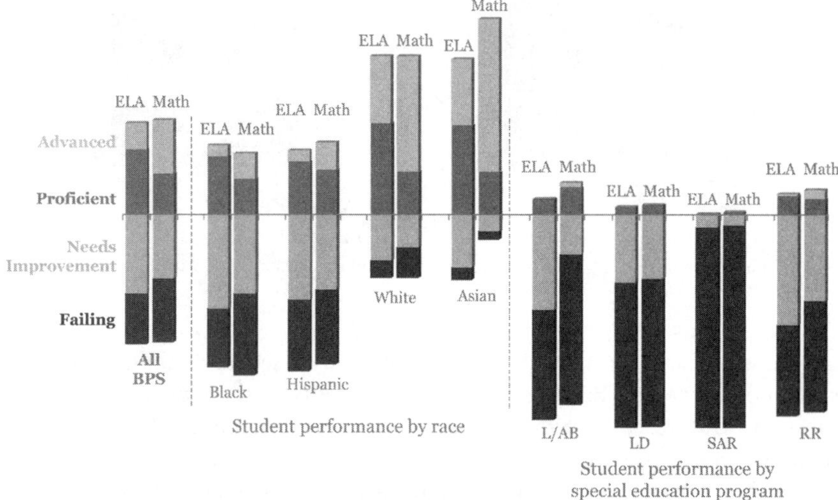

tional strategies. The BPS effort also includes a strong focus on leadership and on opportunities for leaders to work together to solve common problems in educating their students with disabilities. In 2006, the district's special education leadership began strategic planning to continue improving its work.

The evidence we present below indicates that despite these efforts and significant expenditures during Tom Payzant's tenure, Boston has not solved the fundamental problems many districts face: that special education is compliance driven and costly and has resulted in poor outcomes for students.

High Percentages of Students in Special Education

One in five Boston students is classified as having a disability (figures 2 and 3), a high percentage even for Massachusetts, whose numbers are also above the national average. Close to half of these students, 43 percent, are in "substantially separate" classes all or most of the day with students with similar disabilities.[5] That figure is abnormally high, more than double the national average and almost three times the state average—a signal that something is wrong (figures 4 and 5). Overrepresentation is also a problem: Black males are overrepresented in special education overall and greatly overrepresented in substantially separate classes for certain disability areas.

Of all students in special education in Boston, 1,549 (15%) have a readily identifiable severe disability such as blindness, autism, or cerebral palsy. BPS

FIGURE 2
Who's in Special Education in BPS?

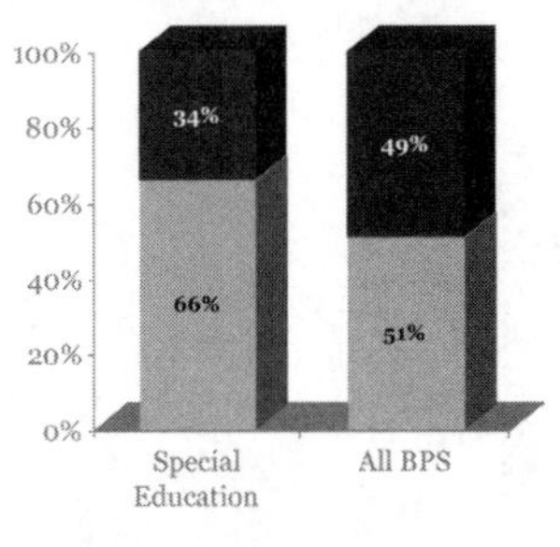

Source: Boston Public Schools, 4-1-05

FIGURE 3
Who's in Special Education in BPS?

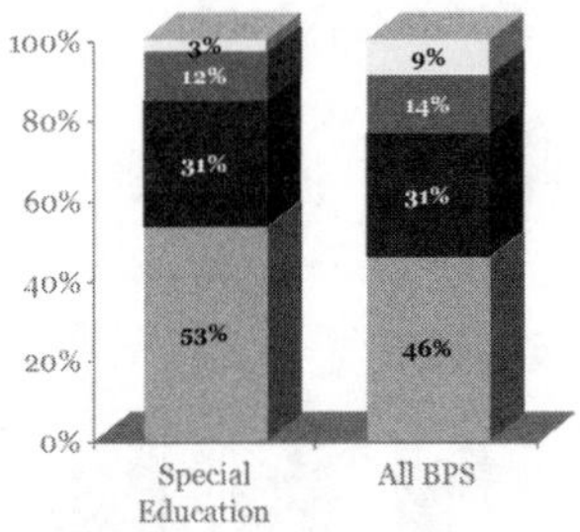

Source: Boston Public Schools, 4-1-05

not only educates virtually all students (99%) with severe disabilities who go to school in the city, but in addition, districts outside the city sometimes pay tuition to BPS to educate their students with severe disabilities because of the high quality of certain of Boston's services.[6]

For the purposes of this chapter, we focus on the remaining 8,999 students—85 percent of all BPS students in special education—whose disabilities are less clearly defined. Of these, half fall into one of the three broad disability categories (listed below) used by local, state, and federal agencies, and most are assigned to substantially separate classrooms. The other half are assigned to regular education classrooms but get special education services part of each week in a Resource Room.

FIGURE 4
What Percentage of Students Are in Special Education?

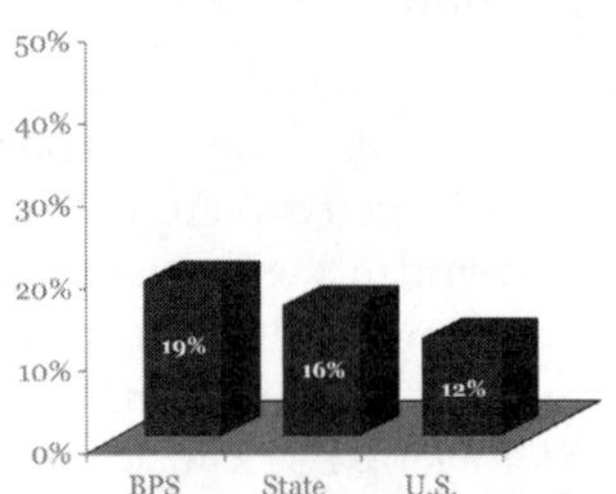

Source: Massachusetts Department of Education website, enrolled 10-1-05; 25th Annual Report to Congress on the Implementation of IDEA, 8-17-05 (data: SY2001–02)

FIGURE 5
What Percentage Are in Substantially Separate Programs?

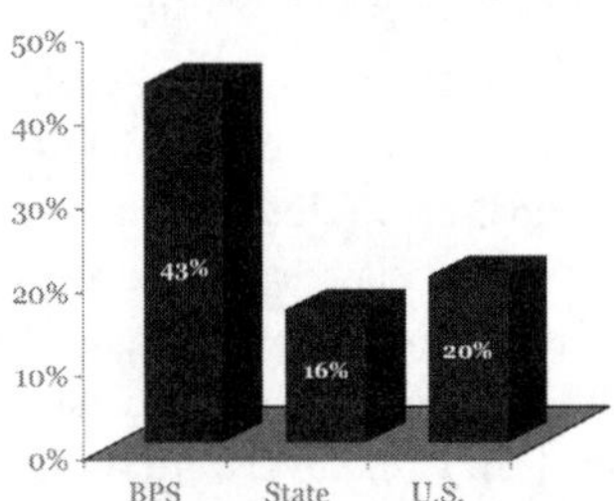

Source: Massachusetts Department of Education website, enrolled 10-1-05; 25th Annual Report to Congress on the Implementation of IDEA, 8-17-05 (data: 2000)

Of the 8,999 students:

- 1,198 students receive services for Emotional Impairment. In BPS this comprises Learning Adaptive Behavior (L/AB), L/AB Cluster, and McKinley Schools. Most are substantially separate programs. For this chapter, we use the term "L/AB" to mean students in these programs.
- 1,564 students receive services for Intellectual Impairment. In BPS this comprises Supportive Academic Remediation (SAR), SAR/Language, and Education and Social Development (ESD). Most are substantially separate programs. For this chapter, we use the term "SAR" to mean students in these programs.
- 1,657 students receive services for Specific Learning Disabilities. In BPS this comprises Learning Disability (LD) and LD/Language. Most are substantially separate programs. For this chapter, we use the term "LD" to mean students in these programs.
- 4,580 students receive services in Resource Rooms. The disabilities of these students vary and their designation is a location—Resource Room—not a disability area. Most of these students are in a regular education classroom. For this chapter, we use the term "RR" to mean students in Resource Rooms.

Blacks, especially males, are overrepresented in special education

In all programs, there is significant overrepresentation and underrepresentation (figure 6). In L/AB and SAR programs, black students are overrepresented by 23 and 13 percentage points, respectively. In all programs, whites are

FIGURE 6

Who's in Special Education in BPS?

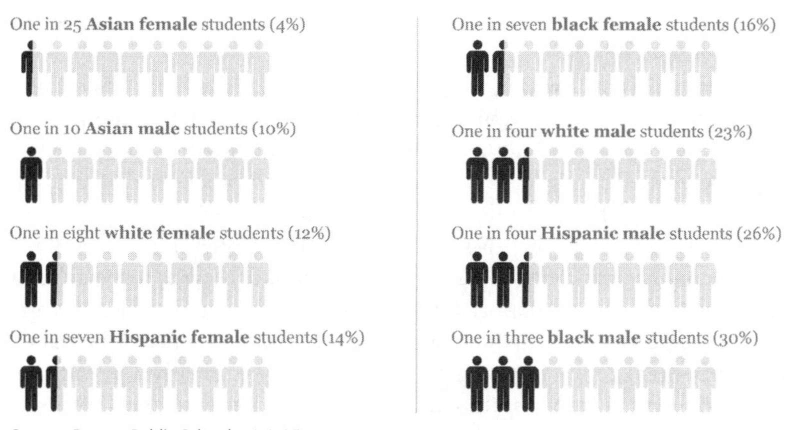

Source: Boston Public Schools, 4-1-05

underrepresented by 2 to 5 percentage points, and Asians by 6 to 9 percentage points. Hispanics are generally evenly represented except for L/AB, in which they are underrepresented by 10 percentage points.

Black males especially are overrepresented: They comprise 24 percent of all students in BPS but are 35 percent of students in special education. In L/AB programs, 80 percent of the students are male, and 69 percent of those males are black. This overrepresentation calls into question the referral and placement processes, which will have to be addressed if BPS is to rethink educating students with disabilities within the framework of regular education.

Why the Number of BPS Students with Disabilities Is Higher Than in Other Districts

Boston has a long history in special education. Massachusetts pioneered educating students with disabilities by passing in 1972 the nation's first special education law, Chapter 766, enabling thousands of children with special needs to attend school and changing their lives forever. From the beginning, BPS (and many other Massachusetts cities and towns) had trouble fulfilling its obligations, and the prolonged *Allen v. McDonough* court case, based on Boston's lack of compliance with Chapter 766, lasted twenty-four years and ended only after Tom Payzant successfully led a concerted effort to disengage. The court case had positive consequences for many previously poorly served students, but it also established a permanent emphasis on process and instituted a costly compliance structure and a climate of pressure to provide services regardless of benefit. Administrators admit that fear of court cases affects decisions to this day. Chapter 766's directive "to provide maximum feasible benefit" was intended to make sure that students with disabilities received every service that they needed. But Boston officials, who in 2002 supported eliminating this language and reverting to the less stringent federal language, believe it may have contributed to special education placements for regular education students who fared poorly in general education and to more substantially separate placements overall (figures 7 and 8).

The other reasons for BPS's high numbers of students with disabilities are less Boston-specific. Superintendent Payzant contends that the federal government also contributes to high numbers of students being placed in special education by prescribing special education services and processes that the district is required to undertake but not adequately funding them. The result of these federal mandates is that few districts have enough money for prevention services that might ameliorate students' difficulties and prevent a special education placement.[7] More support for students with learning difficulties in the regular classroom would reduce special education placements, he says, but Boston has not been able to fund this sufficiently. Similarly, the state reimbursement formula in Massachusetts is complicated and, in the view of officials in BPS (and other districts as well), inadequate.

FIGURE 7
Who's in High-Incidence Programs in BPS?

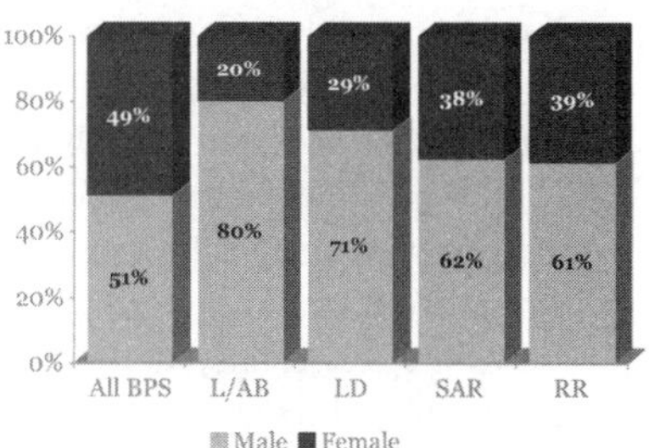

Source: Boston Public Schools, 4-1-05

FIGURE 8
Who's in High-Incidence Programs in BPS?

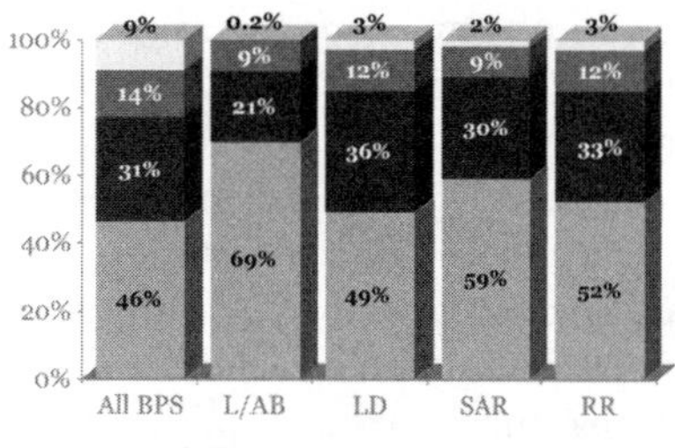

Source: Boston Public Schools, 4-1-05

Still another reason for Boston's large numbers is BPS's past use of the "discrepancy standard," which the federal government sanctioned until recently and was widely used nationwide. Under this model, when a young student, usually in the second or third grade, had not yet learned to read, the law allowed the child to be measured for general intelligence and other tests. If the intelligence tests were normal but the student was well behind in performance, he was assumed to have a disability and was issued an Individual Education Plan (IEP) for services in or out of the regular education classroom. If the child had average or above average intelligence, he would usually be labeled "LD" for Learning Disabled, and if his intelligence quotient was slightly below average, he would be labeled "SAR" for Supportive Academic Remediation. At one point, Boston routinely gave students special education services if the child failed one grade twice. In all cases, the problem was always assumed to be with the child, not with the child's educational experience. In 2002, the National Joint Commission on Learning Disabilities recommended abandoning the discrepancy standard because it generated nonspecific diagnoses about learning problems. Nevertheless, many Boston principals and teachers still expect special education to deal with almost any student who is either far behind or is disruptive.

A final explanation for Boston's having so many students receiving special education services is the entanglement of reading problems and behavior, and teachers' confusion about what to do to address these challenges. "I'm not sure if he has a behavior problem because he never learned to read or if he never learned to read because he had a behavior problem," was a comment we heard frequently. Research is increasingly finding that difficulty learning to read often produces behavior that teachers view as unusually aggressive and antisocial.[8]

High percentages of students in special education with learning or behavioral *difficulties*, not *disabilities*

The high numbers in special education in the BPS indicate that students are being placed in special education for learning or behavioral *difficulties* rather than learning *disabilities*. To prepare this chapter, staff at the Boston Plan for Excellence (BPE) visited schools and talked with over seventy students, teachers, administrators, parents, and knowledgeable BPS observers. These visits and discussions, coupled with Boston's high numbers, indicate that a special education designation remains the accepted remedy not just for students with clearly defined disabilities, but also for those whose problems are less clearly definable. Many students exhibit specific disabilities and must be in settings that help them learn and grow in specific ways. The case is less clear, however, for many other students. From our interviews and school visits, we determined four reasons why students who do not exhibit specific disabilities might receive a special education designation:

- The discrepancy standard and principals' and teachers' opinion that there is no recourse for students whom they do not think they can reach
- The absence of clear, schoolwide behavior management systems that students understand and follow
- Teachers' feeling that they are unprepared to deal with behavior issues, particularly in males, especially African American males
- A widely shared opinion that regular education teachers should not have to deal with students whom they think would be better served by specially certified teachers

Behavior issues bothered teachers particularly. As noted earlier, they aren't sure what comes first: a behavior disorder that is so disruptive the student loses significant instructional time and thus can't read, or a reading struggle that makes it less humiliating for a student to simply misbehave. Either way, once disorderly behavior becomes an issue, teachers turn to special education for help and advice. From her national research, Dr. Lisa Delpit suggests that cultural differences between students and teachers may explain some overidentification.[9] She stresses the importance of knowing the history of families and communities in order to recognize the strengths rather than just the deficits of children. Part of becoming a more effective teacher, she notes, is understanding students' out-of-school lives and learning how to relate to them. What to an untrained eye might look like unmanageable behavior, may in fact be manageable by a teacher who understands better what is going on with the student.

Tom Hehir, former director of the U.S. Department of Education's Office of Special Education Programs, raises another issue in overidentification and warns principals against tolerating too many separate placements:

FIGURE 9

Of 12,357 Black Males in BPS . . .

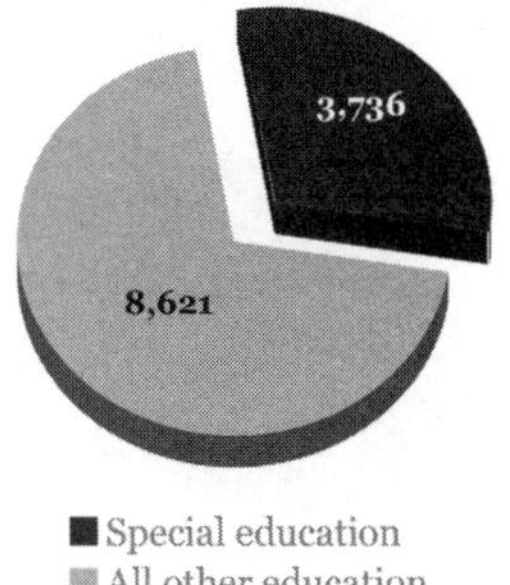

Source: Boston Public Schools, 4-1-05

FIGURE 10

Of 3,736 Black Males in Special Education . . .

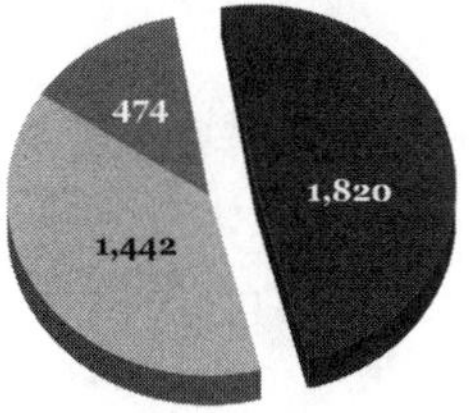

- SAR, LD, L/AB classes, which are substantially separate
- Resource Room
- Other* special education classes, most of which are substantially separate

*Comprises students with severe medical and other disabilities, such as autism

Source: Boston Public Schools, 4-1-05

Although the law is clear, I frequently hear from parents and teachers that children with disabilities are not allowed in general education classes because they cannot read on grade level or because they need support in meeting classroom behavioral requirements. The "tolerance level" for this discriminatory behavior is too high. Though it may be difficult for school principals to force integration on a recalcitrant teacher, failure to do so will keep the system in place and result in lost opportunities for students. From its inception, the IDEA has been about changing how schools serve students with disabilities. Difficult as they may be, we must continue to push for full access for all students.[10]

An especially troubling category of overidentification: Learning/Adaptive Behavior (L/AB)

The substantially separate L/AB designation used by BPS especially calls out for attention. While the district spends an average of over $28,000 per L/AB student annually, results point to a need to rethink the concept. Of 119 BPS students in ninth grade L/AB classes in 2001, for example, only thirty-two graduated five years later.[10] The disproportionate numbers of males, especially black males, in special education classes are a national problem (figures 9 and 10). In BPS, the concentration of black males in L/AB classes raises questions of discrimination and of segregation (figures 11 and 12). L/AB students are those who have been designated as Emotionally Impaired, which Massachusetts broadly defines as follows: exhibiting an inability to learn that cannot be explained by intellectual, sensory, or health factors; an inability to build or maintain satisfactory interpersonal relationships with peers and teachers; inappropriate types of

FIGURE 11
Of 1,198 Students in L/AB Programs in BPS . . .

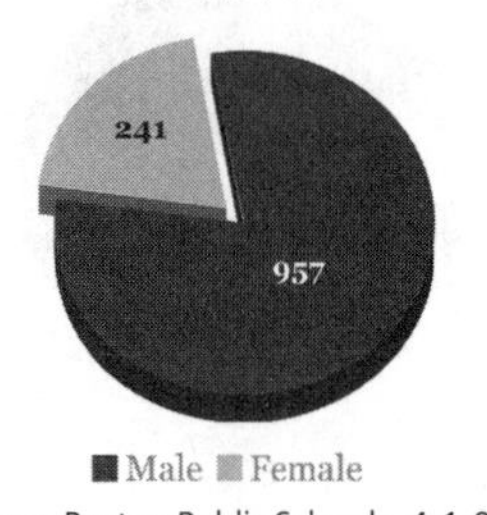

Source: Boston Public Schools, 4-1-05

FIGURE 12
Of 957 Males in L/AB Programs in BPS . . .

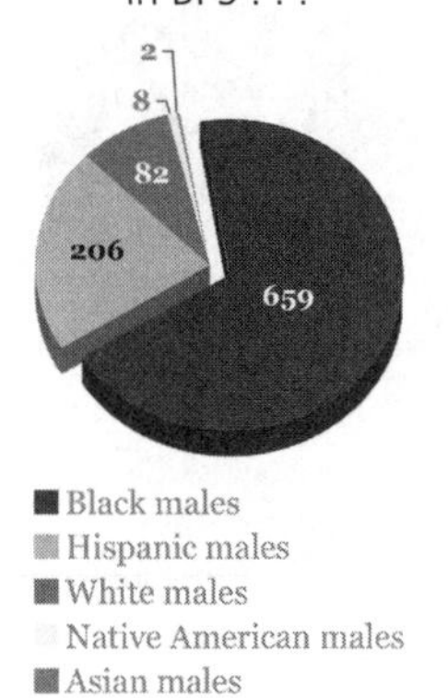

Source: Boston Public Schools, 4-1-05

behavior or feelings under normal circumstances; a generally pervasive mood of unhappiness or depression; a tendency to develop physical symptoms or fears associated with personal or school problems. The definition includes a caveat that students shall not be designated L/AB based on a violation of a discipline code or on involvement with a court or social service agency, or because the student is maladjusted.

Recognizing the great needs of students who have been designated Emotionally Impaired, BPS offers L/AB classes, L/AB clusters, and a set of three separate schools known as the McKinley schools that educate students with severe emotional problems and that provide one-on-one counseling on site. A L/AB cluster groups several L/AB classes in one school in order to provide more services than a stand-alone class can offer. Intended to function as a school within a school, L/AB clusters usually have four L/AB classes, each with eight students, a teacher, and a paraprofessional, and each with a counselor and a coordinator.

School staff offered several explanations for the high numbers of L/AB placements, attributing students' problems to deteriorating societal and home norms. As one teacher said, "These kids just don't belong in regular school. Period."[12] Others blamed what they perceived to be the system's push for inclusion and felt students are left too long in the wrong classes: "I had a Q4 [L/AB cluster student] that didn't belong in my class, and they only found out when he attacked me." Finally, it is the view of many teachers that students become difficult when they can't read, and that if every student could read on grade level, some behavior problems would diminish, at least at the elementary and middle school levels.

Few argue that BPS has arrived at the right solution to educate students with difficult and serious behavior problems. In interviews, the students themselves acknowledge how difficult they are—"we ain't no angels"—and several talk about their involvement with the juvenile justice system. Teachers are vocal in their views, describing L/AB students as the most challenging students in BPS, and expressing frustration that "the system" hasn't figured out yet how to educate them. The teachers union frequently raises the issue of difficult students, and it has made creating more seats in alternative schools for the most disruptive students part of the bargaining package in each of the last several contracts, reinforcing the idea that these students do not belong in "regular" school.

At the elementary level, promising results are occurring in L/AB clusters when the school gives each student individual attention and secure support. At one school we visited, the Manning Elementary, the L/AB cluster was not operated as a school within a school, and L/AB students were an important part of the school. Significantly, the children are not labeled L/AB students at all, but rather Room Three, just as regular students are labeled Room One, Room Two, and so on. They are mainstreamed for mathematics, a core subject, which is unusual, and they also mix throughout the day with the other students: lunch, recess, library, assembly, and all field trips. These students are succeeding academically: a relatively high percentage of Manning students—22 percent—scored at proficient or advanced in math on the state test in 2005.[13]

When interviewed, Principal Casel Walker noted two elements of the school's success. First, it is a small school of just 175 students, so all faculty and staff know each student and all have the same focus in mind. L/AB teachers are treated the same as other teachers and participate in the same professional development. The second reason for success may be that the Manning educates only one type of special education student. Manning's success should point the BPS toward further investigating the essential conditions for L/AB clusters to work.

The belief that students with emotional and social problems need both the security of a small, nurturing class and the opportunity to learn how to develop positive social relationships outside such a class appears to become far more complex to implement as students get older. Discussions with students and teachers in middle and high schools raised disturbing questions about whether L/AB clusters work for either students or teachers at these grade levels. While students we interviewed praised their teachers and appreciated the counseling they received, they still perceive the L/AB cluster's purpose as keeping them away from other students rather than providing a better educational environment. In their opinion, the "school within a school" model serves chiefly to prevent them from causing problems elsewhere in the building. Almost all found their treatment overly restrictive and infantilizing. They particularly singled out point systems and "time-out rooms," one student wistfully saying, "They needa take that room out, put in a book room, book shelves, library, something." Other students were more resentful: "Juvenile delinquency. That is what they treat us like. We're juveniles. And we're just a menace to society, so we have to be locked down here. Look where we're at. You know, we have no windows. We only have one door." (student) "They treat us like we're nine, ten years old . . . some of us are eighteen and nineteen years old. Who wants to get walked to the bathroom?" (student)

Some administrators and teachers we interviewed accept the way the clusters are run, feeling that the needs and behaviors of the students are so severe that this separation is necessary. A few, however, questioned whether this approach was the right one and were concerned with two issues: that so many L/AB students dropped out and that counseling services were too little, too late.

> We have one population that we don't serve at all as far as I am concerned . . . the L/AB students. . . . We don't service those kids, and they end up dropping out. Then what happens to them? Does anyone know? (teacher)

> There are nowhere near enough support services for kids who need immediate counseling, immediate, on-the spot-counseling. There's a waiting list, but the system is overwhelmed already . . . These kids need access to serious mental health services. (teacher)

No one we interviewed, however, raised the question of whether separating a group of students, all hostile to school and with emotional difficulties, might exacerbate their problems by removing social contacts with other students. Recently, the National Work Readiness Council took the view that, besides strong reading, verbal, and writing skills, employers value highly the "ability to work on a team" and the "ability to cooperate and resolve conflicts."[14] The extreme separation of L/AB students raises the issue of how school is helping them acquire skills needed to be productive, working members of society.

Whatever the reason, the data show that most high school students in L/AB are not succeeding or being prepared for life after school. The average graduation rate of 27 percent consigns thousands over time to virtually no opportunities later on[15] (figure 13). Further, the low numbers of L/AB students reading at proficient or advanced levels, even though the students are not cognitively impaired, points to the need for a review of whether the annual $28,000 spent per L/AB student could not be more effectively used. If a student starts in a L/AB class in third grade, as many do, and drops out when he is sixteen, as many do, at least $250,000 will have been spent to very little effect.

High Costs for Poor Student Outcomes

The strongest evidence for the need to change the current model of delivering special education services is the cost-to-outcomes ratio. The BPS dedicates significant resources to special education, but it only rarely makes changes for students because the results for students are poor. According to BPS calculations, there is an average difference of nearly $13,000 per student per year between the cost of educating a regular education student and a student who

FIGURE 13

What Happens to Students in L/AB Programs?

119 students in grade 9 were in L/AB programs in SY2000–2001.
By the end of SY2004–2005 . . .

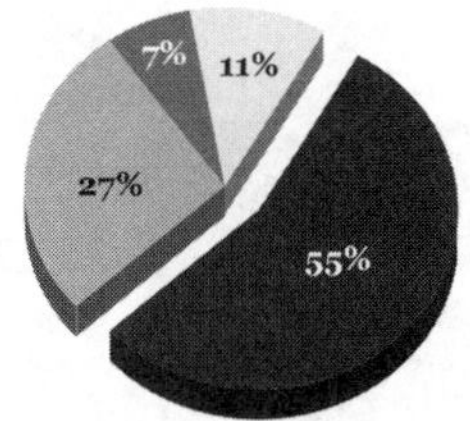

☐ were still enrolled
■ had dropped out
■ had graduated
■ were listed as "other loss"

* Expulsion, DYS, hospitalization, etc.
Source: Boston Public Schools Office of Research, Assessment & Evaluation, May 2006

spends all his or her time in a substantially separate classroom. The calculation method, however, averages the cost of students who need extremely expensive services, such as those with severe physical and mental impairments, with the much lower cost of less disabled students.

To illuminate some of the costs-outcomes issues in a more fine-grained way, we used the analysis recently done by Education Resource Strategies (ERS), an independent nonprofit organization led by Dr. Karen Hawley Miles.[16] Working closely with BPS and with its full support, ERS calculated cost by disability and distinguished among the costs of educating students in substantially separate classes: educating a deaf student, for example, costs $45,000 per year, while educating an LD student costs $19,000 per year. Their analysis enabled BPS to estimate how many resources might be available to be used in different, more effective ways for certain disabilities (figure 14).

If BPS set itself the goal, for example, of eliminating overrepresentation of students by race and program, that is, adjusting the percentages of students in special education to percentages of all BPS students, the district would have 959 fewer students in L/AB, LD, SAR, and Resource Room categories and more than $10 million per year to provide those 959 reassigned students additional support in regular education classrooms, perhaps in ways that would get better outcomes than the current system[17] (figure 15).

ERS also coded every BPS budget line so the costs of instruction could be separated from non-instructional costs.[18] BPS budgets almost $40 million in non-instructional costs annually in its $185 million total for educating about 10,000 students with disabilities (excluding early childhood programs and tuitions for

FIGURE 14

BPS Per-Pupil Expenditures by Special Education Program

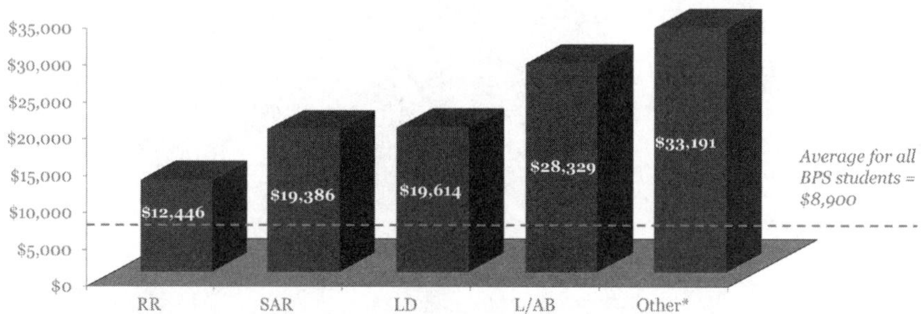

*Comprises students with severe medical and other disabilities, such as autism
Source: Education Resource Strategies & Boston Public Schools, SY2004–05

students in private special education placements).[19] Not all of the $40 million noninstructional cost is for compliance, but much is, certainly the $16.5 million annually for evaluation team clerks, facilitators, and overtime and stipends for teachers to attend team meetings. Time spent on paperwork, which teachers and administrators report as overwhelming, is an uncalculated cost.

ERS's analysis also makes possible the consideration of alternate decisions about how to spend funds to meet the needs of students with disabilities by identifying funds dedicated to certain services. A student's IEP, for instance, describes the disability, its effect on how the student can use the regular curriculum, and what modifications are needed to enable him to do so. But if the assessment finds no cognitive or physical impairment, only "failure to make progress," there could be many possible remedies. If BPS is to conceive of different ways to meet the needs of the students with less severe and less clear dis-

FIGURE 15

What if . . . BPS corrected the overrepresentation of students in special education?

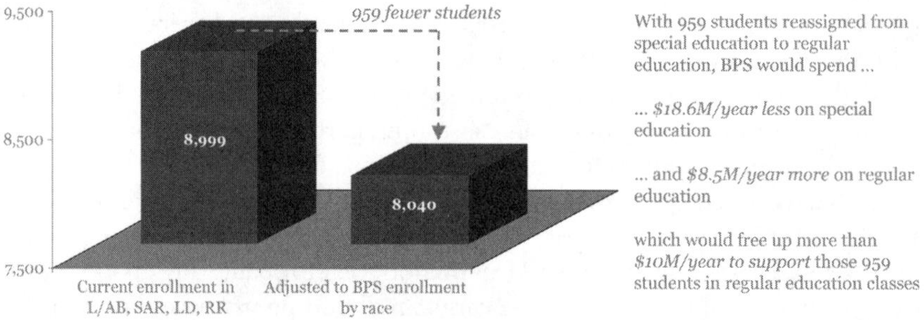

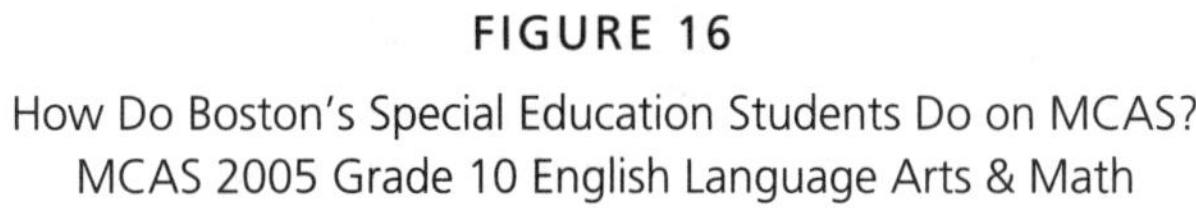

FIGURE 16

How Do Boston's Special Education Students Do on MCAS?
MCAS 2005 Grade 10 English Language Arts & Math

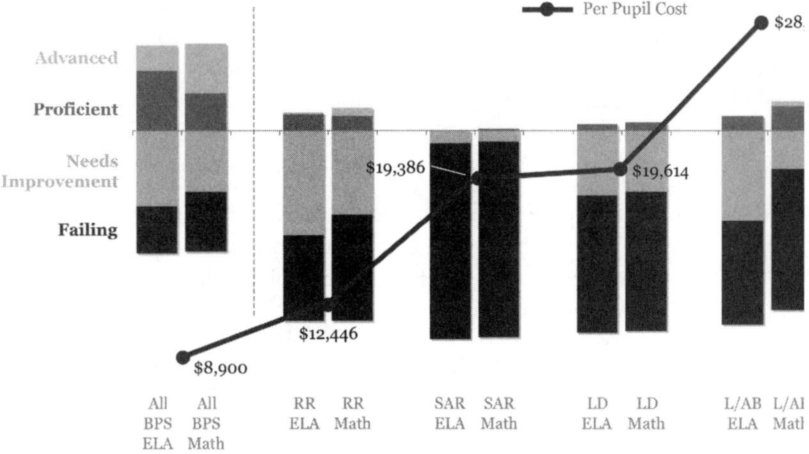

Source of per pupil costs: Education Resource Strategies & Boston Public Schools, SY2004–05

abilities, it must have resources to implement those ideas without adding new resources on top of old, ineffectual ones.

Finally, ERS data enabled BPE to tie results to costs; when this is done, the obvious question of whether there is a better way to allocate dollars to educate these students emerges. Only a few students are achieving the BPS goal of proficiency or better on MCAS (figure 16).

THE UNINTENDED NEGATIVE EFFECTS OF A SPECIAL EDUCATION DESIGNATION

Besides these discouraging outcomes for large annual expenditures, interviews with teachers and students give blunt evidence of the inescapable negative effects of having an extensive system with thousands of students in separate classes for more than 60 percent of the school day. This separate system is highly visible, with many classes held in windowless rooms that are too small, and often carved out of the basement or in a closed-off part of the building. Besides the physical separation, pervasive labeling is endemic to the culture of the system. Administrators, teachers, and students routinely refer to "sped" kids or more specifically, use terms such as "Q4s" for students with serious behavior problems:

> Everybody's thinkin' [about us] like, well, you know, they don't know anything. They're in L/AB cluster, they're slow, they don't know anything. (student)

> I think for kids [an inclusion classroom] is good. Having been here when they were resource—that was bad. Kids would call them "sped" and say they had to go to a little room. (inclusion teacher)

The separate system often depresses expectations for these students. When Dr. Payzant convened a subgroup of his leadership team to deal with special education issues in 2003, their thorough and honest report acknowledged that the "terms, labels, and codes we use to identify special education students and classrooms tend to perpetuate their status as separate . . . and can lead to different, often lower, expectations."[20] Other interviews corroborated these concerns:

> BPS's many labels predetermine teachers' views of what kids can do and who they are. Once prereferral starts, and there is a designation, this is what everyone expects kids are going to be able to do and how they are going to behave. (administrator)

> We been on this book forever, since the beginning of the year, no lie. The first day of school we started reading the first page. . . . It's the fourth quarter. Wanna know what chapter we're on? Chapter four. (freshman student)

We also found teachers and administrators who did not lower expectations:

> One of my other friends [in regular education] she got transferred to our class, and she was like, "We weren't even on this yet!" And she was like, "Now I see why you're in this class because they teach, like you understand it more." (student)

> I expect everybody to model the fact that all kids deserve our best shot, and we shouldn't be distinguishing between special education or regular education kids other than in ways to better improve teaching and learning. There shouldn't be labeling of kids. There shouldn't be a ceiling of expectations. (principal)

Raising expectations throughout the system, however, won't be easy. Lowered expectations for students with disabilities are the norm nationally. *Education Week's* "Quality Counts" report found that 80 percent of teachers think that students with disabilities should be held to different standards and that their performance masks the pretty good job most schools and teachers are doing.[20]

THE SEEDS OF A REMEDY: PROMISING PROGRAMS IN BOSTON

BPS is slowly moving toward the idea that there are other ways besides special education to support students with learning or behavior problems. In 2001, in a pilot effort in nine elementary schools in the city's Allston-Brighton and

Mission Hill neighborhoods, BPS and Boston College, in partnership with the YMCA of Greater Boston, launched Boston Connects, a privately funded university-school partnership offering the comprehensive services that students need to be academically successful. A student support team at each school screens children, sometimes every child in a class, for assets and risks, and identifies their needs; a school site coordinator finds services to solve students' difficulties by working within the school, as well as by partnering with agencies in the community, and monitors the results. The number of agencies with which these schools now work for provision of services has risen from twenty to sixty-five in the last five years.[22]

Although all Boston high, middle, and large elementary schools have student support teams, the emphasis in Boston Connects is less on students in crisis and more on prevention, school climate, and relationships. It includes efforts that help teachers think about the individual needs of each young person, and sometimes offers solutions as straightforward as placement in an after-school program. Boston Connects has broken the usual cycle that often led to special education services, and referrals to special education have declined from 35 percent of all students in those schools in SY2002–03 to 15 percent in SY2004–05.[23]

Boston Connects is a promising variation on the work recommended by UCLA's Center for Mental Health in Schools, which calls for "improvements that amount to much more than tinkering with existing roles, functions, and job descriptions."[24] The center's goal is to have schools set and meet standards for addressing barriers to learning. BPS plans to work with another university to expand to more schools.

Dr. Payzant and his team also initiated improvements in regular education that obviate the need for special education placements. Almost as soon as he assumed the superintendency, Payzant made literacy a focus, instituting extensive efforts to improve reading and writing instruction so students would read skillfully and not fall behind. He also introduced a mix of curricular interventions such as Lexia, Early Success, and Reading Recovery in the early grades, and Read 180 for older students. There are also individualized assessments for some students who are not in special education placements. In mathematics, besides adopting and supporting districtwide curricula and providing extensive professional development, Superintendent Payzant began an effort in some schools to tutor upper elementary students individually for fifteen weeks in basic math concepts.

There have been structural changes in recent years as well. Payzant moved special education under the deputy superintendent for teaching and learning and changed the process for initiating referrals to special education. While the decision for eligibility in a special education placement still rests with the school-based team, the teams are now chaired by a central evaluation team facilitator rather than someone based in the school, which brings a broader perspective to the process. After just two years, these measures brought about a 36 percent drop in special education referrals.[25] More recently, BPS has added twenty-one prekindergarten classes based on research about early intervention, and these should keep even more students in the mainstream.

SOLVING THE PROBLEMS: AREAS TO EXPLORE

While the district has made progress, there is a need for far deeper work. BPS allocates almost one third of its budget to educate the one fifth of its students labeled with disabilities.[26] This high percentage is common in many districts, but all districts, including BPS, need to look at their poor results and consider reallocation of resources. With the state as a partner, Boston could be well positioned to change the course of educating students with disabilities, escape the current ineffective structures, and create an entirely new system that better serves students. Doing so might change thousands of lives.

The work we described in Allston-Brighton points to one possible direction. Interventions in regular education point to another, and recent research on mediating bad behavior by using reading interventions suggests a third.[27] Research centers such as the Developmental Studies Center and First Things First have developed curricula that feature social skills development to help students deal with adjustments to school, a promising approach that should be more widespread.

The following recommendations are derived from the suggestions of parents, teachers, central office staff, and interested observers with whom we spoke in the course of our research. While these recommendations are tailored to Boston's needs, they may also be useful to other urban districts interested in revamping their approach to educating students with disabilities:

1. Refocus from referral to prevention and early intervention in reading.
2. Create a secondary reading course for middle and high school readers.
3. Expand inclusion classrooms.
4. Reconsider another "old idea": teacher certification.
5. Review the practice of placing many students with disabilities and many kinds of programs in a single school.
6. Revise Individual Education Plans (IEPs).

Refocus from referral to prevention and early intervention in reading.

After early childhood special education placements, most referrals to special education in the BPS and in most districts start once patterns of behavior and performance are clear, usually after second grade. Last year alone in BPS, there were 1,284 referrals in elementary grades.[28]

Because poverty is pervasive among students in the BPS (73%),[29] many students have preschool lives that have not prepared them to read and may have increased their likelihood for reading difficulties. To have one in five students labeled with disabilities that require extra help and accommodations throughout their school lives, however, suggests that special education placement has been accepted by school personnel as the best way to address these challenges. A better approach would be to divert some of the funds to assess each child, identify causes of reading or behavior problems, and provide solutions to the particular problems. Instead of investing heavily in evaluations that start with second grade, BPS might set up a uniform process to diagnose specific reading problems in kindergartners and first graders so that a reading problem does not become a behavior problem or a special education referral. Boston currently has no districtwide assessments in kindergarten or first grade. Both New York City (ECLAS) and Chicago (STEP) have adopted assessments BPS could consider.

The hidden costs of the referral system itself also could be reviewed so that BPS could fund proven strategies such as intensive support for early reading. In addition to the thousands of hours professionals spend reviewing referrals, the process also requires BPS to hire substitutes to free teachers to participate in the referral process and complete extensive paperwork. Boston does not calculate the cost of the estimated 15,000+ meetings required each year, but they must comprise a major part of the district's $40 million annual noninstructional costs for special education.[30]

If compliance and referral costs were reduced, BPS would have funds to reinstitute programs previously funded by the state to give struggling students extra help in reading and math. The district would also be able to start earlier and place extra reading specialists in every school to work individually with students in kindergarten and first grade.

Create a secondary reading course for middle and high school readers.

> I know I said this before, but I have to say it again. We need to seriously develop a formalized reading program in high schools. Not some reading strategies. A reading course in addition to their English course. (high school teacher)

On MCAS 2005, only 6 percent of tenth-grade BPS students with disabilities and only 38 percent of all students in tenth grade scored proficient or advanced in English language arts, reinforcing teachers' view that more reading instruction is needed for many high school students, especially nonreaders. A few BPS middle and high schools offer a separate reading course, but such a course is not standard for any student who needs it.[31] Two BPS programs have laid a foundation for increasing reading instruction in middle and high schools: Reading Across the Curriculum and in-school Collaborative Coaching and Learning (CCL) professional development. The district's poor MCAS results, however, signal that these efforts are not enough. The suggested approach for younger students could provide the systemic solution that is needed: assess each ninth grader and assign him or her to a course tailored to individual needs that combines the right mix of high interest, motivation, choice, use of technology, and social interaction about what is read. As noted earlier, two-thirds of Boston's students labeled with disabilities are male. There is growing research about improving reading skills, reading habits, motivation, and the value of technology for adolescent males that BPS could use to design its course.[32]

Expand well-designed inclusion classrooms so that permanent labels do not compound students' difficulties.

> If I had a child who had disabilities, I would ask, "Why can't he go to school with his nondisabled brother or sister?" (Dr. Tom Hehir)[33]

BPS seeks to provide many school options for students with disabilities, but the choices for 43 percent are limited if their IEP states they must go to schools where they can be in a class with similarly disabled students. One way to both expand choice and dispel the clear side-effects of extensive labeling (described earlier) would be to greatly expand the number of inclusion classes.

Currently BPS has 240 students in official "inclusion" classes that have a ratio of 1 teacher to 20 students, 6 of whom can have an IEP. If the class includes students with a "substantially separate" classroom designation, the class must have one regular education and one special education teacher. Only 15 of 145 schools in Boston have designated "I" classes: four Pilot Schools, five early education centers, and six regular schools.

There are, however, increasing numbers of unofficial inclusion classes as different schools seek to meet all students' needs more effectively. BPS encourages this informal inclusion as long as schools follow three guidelines: IEP matching, collaborative planning between regular education teachers and teachers of students with disabilities, and shared professional development. However, as BPS points out in its March 2002 paper, "Inclusion in the Boston Public Schools," a school should not practice inclusion without consideration of the specific plans of the students with disabilities. The most recent teachers' contract carefully circumscribes the conditions under which inclusion can be undertaken in a school, signaling teachers' wariness about too much hasty inclusion.

Increasing the number of inclusion classes should be possible because descriptions of effective inclusion classrooms sound much like the district's adopted approach to instruction in all classrooms, "workshop instruction." Strong inclusion classrooms:

- Group students flexibly; use formative assessments to gauge progress and move students to the next step in their learning
- Use peer support; learning is socially mediated
- Help students make their thinking clear to each other through talk or through visual representations
- Explicitly teach students skills and also give them a chance to solve problems independently
- Provide authentic tasks connected to their out-of-school worlds

Research confirms that when teachers work well together and students are carefully placed, inclusion can be powerfully effective for students. The same research also warns that poorly implemented inclusion can be as bad, or worse, than separate classrooms.[34] In an analysis of successful secondary inclusive classrooms, Mastropieri and Scruggs culled six characteristics that could provide guidance to BPS for overseeing the expansion of inclusion classes:[35]

- Inclusion classes have strong administrative support, including adequate resources.
- Inclusion teachers have support from special education personnel in the form of coplanning, the design of curriculum adaptations, coteaching, classroom assistance, and common planning time; the teachers work well together.
- There is an accepting, positive classroom atmosphere.
- Teachers have effective teaching skills with structure, clarity, enthusiasm, appropriate pace, and high student engagement.
- Classrooms build in peer assistance, and students have many different ways to respond; an added level of discourse is encouraged.
- Teachers have disability-specific skills for the individual students in their classrooms.

BPS teachers in successful inclusion classrooms confirmed the importance of these elements, and added one, "teachers expect students to meet standards."

The task of expanding inclusion, though, is daunting. The law is clear that students' needs, as defined in the IEP, must be met, and changing the way they've been addressed for decades will be opposed by many, but the effects of so many students being separated are irrefutable. If the results for separated classrooms were good, great caution might be justified, but they are not. BPS might make headway on its overly large percentages in separate classrooms if it proactively supported inclusion and fostered, documented, and spread well-conceived efforts put forward by schools.

In addition to inclusion classrooms, Boston leads the country in having several full inclusion schools. Boston Arts Academy, the Mary Lyon, the Mason, and the O'Hearn are frequently cited nationally as excellent schools that recognize that students with disabilities have special needs and meet them in careful and creative ways. Specialized supports at these schools include direct teaching about expectations for behavior for all students in the school. Each of these schools has outstanding student performance results.

Frequently observers ask, "Why can't we just replicate these schools?" and the answer is always, "It's too expensive." The costs laid out earlier make clear that tremendous resources, tens of millions of dollars annually, are being spent on compliance, administration, and separated classrooms—with poor results. If inclusive schools meet the needs of students, money should be redirected to create them by working with the state to dismantle the present system, improve it, and free resources to better educate the neediest students.

Reconsider another "old idea": teacher certification.

An assumption underlying separate rather than inclusive classrooms is that students with disabilities should be taught by specially certified teachers who know about cognitive difficulties, different multisensory approaches, or behavior and emotional problems, and that their certification provides a chance for their students to learn in all subjects. In 2002, NCLB challenged that idea, and by 2008 special education-certified teachers will need to become certified as well in the subject they teach. Although the problem identified by NCLB is correct, that is, that teachers of students with disabilities should know specific content as well as be expert in various disabilities, more certification requirements may not be the correct solution. As many researchers, notably Linda Darling-Hammond, have shown, *teachers* matter most in student achievement.[36] What is less clear, however, is whether *certification* matters most as well, and whether mandating hundreds more hours of coursework will solve the complex issue of providing each student with a disability the high-level content he needs as well as the specialized instruction.[37]

Meeting the new NCLB mandate for certification will be difficult, costly, and time-consuming for teachers and districts, and thousands of teachers are likely to fail to meet the mandate, just as thousands are failing to be "highly qualified" under NCLB. A conventional approach of relying on more certification is not only likely to fail, it is likely to exacerbate the current problem of too many resources going to process and procedures. It is a good example of a problem Jane David and Larry Cuban recently identified: policy made too far away from classrooms.[38]

Other approaches need to be considered. One suggested by Tom Hehir would combine teachers and classes so that students with disabilities get the content from knowledgeable content teachers and the specialized help they need to learn from special education teachers.[39] A second solution might be to consider a new dual certificate that strips the regular and special education certificate coursework to the essentials and requires more learning in practice after teachers begin teaching. BPS has recently developed and adopted the Dimensions of Effective Teaching, which give guidance about skills that are needed by every teacher. Three of the dimensions are particularly relevant:

- Demonstrate a commitment to excellence, equity, and high expectations for all students, with an emphasis on building on the strengths that students bring to the teaching and learning process and closing the achievement gap between subgroups within the school.
- Build and maintain safe, fair, and respectful learning environments that celebrate the diversity of the student population.
- Plan instruction and employ strategies that address the wide range of learning, behavioral, and communication styles of the student population.

Though the Dimensions do not yet include clear expectations for instructional practice nor an explicit picture of effective instruction, they put BPS in a strong position to determine concretely what teachers must know and do in a way that certification does not. The state should help Boston build on the work it has been doing with the Dimensions and target the development of a single, unified certificate that focuses on learning from practice and strengthening teachers' abilities rather than only increasing the number of required courses.

Review the practice of placing many students with disabilities and many kinds of programs in a single school.

While every school in the BPS educates some students with disabilities, many have no substantially separate classes, and others have a disproportionate share. Students labeled with severe disabilities sometimes comprise up to one third of a school's population. Because of the significant achievement gap between students with disabilities and regular education students, schools with high concentrations of students with disabilities frequently have the poorest MCAS scores and appear regularly on public lists of "schools in need of improvement." Fewer regular education students then choose them, and the spiral continues downward.

A related issue is the BPS practice of having many different programs in a single school. Principals who served on the superintendent's central policy group, REACT, discussed a "tipping point" that came with both the overassignment of students with disabilities to a particular school and the juggling of many different kinds of programs.[40] In a school where the number of students who have special needs approaches the number of those who do not, and where students with different disabilities all have to be considered in making decisions, the complexity and intensity of the demands rise—in scheduling, in cross-program professional development, in sharing materials, and in course creation. Everything becomes more difficult, yet no additional resources follow to manage the complexity.

Recognizing these issues, Superintendent Payzant created a study group in the spring of 2003 called the Special Education Equitable Distribution (SEED) workgroup to examine the distribution of substantially separate students across schools, starting with high schools, where the problem was most acute. The SEED group made a series of recommendations so that by the fall of 2006, substantially separate students would be more equitably distributed across all high schools, including Pilot Schools, but still excepting the examination schools. The most difficult-to-educate students, those in L/AB classes and clusters, however, were not redistributed and remain in the same buildings. The issue of a few schools having too many substantially separate classrooms remains unresolved.

Further, SEED did not fully discuss the question of whether it is better to increase choice for students by placing many different types of programs in a single school or letting schools concentrate on one disability, as the Manning

School has done successfully with a L/AB cluster. This important decision deserves greater discussion than it has had to date, and should include surveys of parents of students with disabilities to find out what their priorities are. Informal discussions with parents suggest that what parents of a student with a disability want above all else is development of their child. If that result cannot be achieved concomitantly with multiple school choices—and it appears that it cannot be—then the idea of as much choice as possible should be reviewed.

The SEED work is bearing fruit, and responsibility for educating substantially separate students is starting to spread across the district, but fundamental questions remain: How do we acknowledge the level of challenge of the students in a school and provide commensurate support? How do we stop comparing schools as if their level of challenge were the same? What do we do about a school's having too many substantially separate classrooms? What number of substantially separate programs in what combination allows a school to best serve students?

Revise Individual Education Plans.

Individual education plans (IEPs) are at the heart of the process and procedures governing educating students with disabilities, and, as noted earlier, they are labor intensive and costly. Though it was not possible to calculate precisely the overall cost of the IEP process, it consumes a substantial share of the nearly $40 million annual administration costs for special education.

An "ed plan" lists the student's disability, how it affects his or her learning, and what accommodations must be made to help him or her learn the regular curriculum. Teachers we interviewed praised some of the IEPs they received and found them helpful, but none thought IEPs regularly and consistently served their purposes well. The format for IEPs is closely defined by state and federal laws, and Boston cannot change it without their help and support. Teachers' and students' comments present compelling evidence, however, that IEPs are part of the problem, and they highlight areas for improvement:

- Language: "The information in IEPs is very generic to every kid. It seems like the objectives are the same for each student."
- Outdated: "There is no correlation between MCAS expectations and what the objectives are in the SEIMS (IEP management system). To me, that publication is so outdated in regards to identifying something that can be used."
- Usefulness: "I think that IEPs could be useful, and that they should be, but they are not. I don't think they are individualized. If it's not going to be a plan for individual instruction, then don't write an IEP."
- Access: "It's often hard to get access to a student's IEP. I don't see why we can't get them electronically. If we can access our students' MCAS scores, why can't we see their IEPs on MyBPS (intranet)?"

- Misuse: "They get on an IEP, then they get placed into a sped class regardless of what their IEP says because there is a seat free. It is often scheduling that determines where the kids go. I don't think some of the registrars even read IEPs."

With so many shortcomings, the IEP is overdue for review and revamping. Among the immediate steps the district could take, in partnership with the state, would be to improve the IEP process and quality by moving to an online system that enables it to do the following:

- Satisfy legal requirements
- Link to databases that contain information such as state and district curriculum standards, assessments, and results for students
- Reallocate savings from costs associated with printing and mailing to academic supports
- Reallocate time special education teachers spend on paperwork to time spent collaborating with and learning from colleagues
- Regularly monitor each student's academic progress and communicate with teachers and parents
- Give access to regular education teachers who teach special education students
- Let schools experiment with how to track services for students with mild disabilities and keep the money they might save for other services for these students

BPS has led the country in the creation of MyBPS Assessment for enabling Boston schools to access and use online data on its students, and it has plans to change its IEP tracking system, but it has not yet done so. A bold approach is called for as BPS continues its work.

FURTHER WORK

This chapter has focused on educating students with disabilities in the BPS in the last ten years, specifically, the issues that, if addressed, would do the students in Boston the most good and would affect the most students. For that reason, this analysis is only a beginning and does not tackle other issues that must be studied, for example, the interaction of student factors such as having a disability and also needing to learn English. It is also important to emphasize that the issues BPS faces in educating students with readily identifiable disabilities were not considered and are not part of this analysis. Nor was the crucial role of the state examined, although its role is almost as important as the district's in forging a new system for students with disabilities. Massachusetts led the country in creating Chapter 766. It is now time for it to lead again.

During his tenure, Dr. Payzant was forthright in his acknowledgement of the unsolved problems in educating students with disabilities. As we hope is clear throughout the chapter, despite the great tasks ahead, he and his team have attended to major problems: He ended a twenty-four-year-old court case that was draining energy, time, and resources from the system. He cut in half the number of students educated in costly private placements by creating new programs within the BPS. He reorganized departments to connect special education to teaching and learning. He dedicated additional resources to identified problems. Most significantly, perhaps, he and his team repeatedly said, "We have to do better than this. These students are ours, and we must show them every day that we are not going to give up on them," thereby providing the moral leadership the district needed in this challenging work—and will continue to need in a new superintendent.

CHAPTER IX

Family and Community Engagement in the Boston Public Schools: 1995–2006

ABBY R. WEISS
HELEN WESTMORELAND

FAMILY ENGAGEMENT at every stage of development matters for student success.[1] Decades of evidence suggest that high levels of family involvement increased children's educational achievement and social-emotional functioning.[2] The role of teachers, schools, and districts in increasing the involvement of families in their children's education is especially important for low-income, minority families who have historically been disenfranchised. For example, teacher outreach to parents has a particularly positive effect on the classroom involvement of less educated, poor, and single parents.[3]

Family engagement can be defined broadly to include the many ways that families may actively participate in their children's education.[4] From home visiting to parent leadership to community organizing, family engagement represents a wide variety of activities directed toward improving educational outcomes for children. Much research and program activity has focused on three particular processes of family engagement that promote healthy outcomes for children: (1) *parenting*, which includes the attitudes, values, and practices of parents in raising their children; (2) *home-school relationships*, which are the formal and informal connections between families and educational settings; and (3) *responsibility for learning*, which emphasizes activities in the home and community that promote learning skills in children.[5] There are many ways that schools can support families and increase their involvement in their children's education, including offering parenting classes; providing information about curriculum and specific strategies for talking with children about what they are learning; scheduling meetings at varying times to accommodate parents' work schedules; sending home information in multiple languages; connecting parents with community resources that meet their specific needs; and offering opportunities for families to participate in decision making. Initiatives may be systemwide or school specific—catering to an individual school's population and its particular needs. Some programs are initiated by the central office, some by individuals within schools. Others are prompted by the efforts of external community members or grassroots groups that might work in conjunction with districts and schools to develop programming, or exert pressure on the district or school to put programs in place.

Clearly, the landscape of family engagement activities is broad and complex, and depending upon the policy context, the population, and the politics, there are myriad ways families can become full partners in the education of their children. But in order for families to fulfill their responsibility—particularly families in lower income areas—supports must be in place at the school and district levels. Research shows that school districts in particular play a crucial role in sustaining family engagement programs in schools.[6] However, few districts are undertaking deliberate family and community engagement initiatives; to the limited extent that such efforts exist, they are largely undocumented.

In a few notable exceptions, districts are pioneering family engagement programs. New York City's parent liaison program, in which 1,200 liaisons serve all of the New York City public schools, provides a model that Boston and other districts have examined and attempted to replicate. In addition, the Chicago Public Schools have an interesting approach to family engagement, mostly focused on school governance, in which parents and community members hold seats on local school councils that make decisions about personnel, evaluations, and budgets. The Newark Public Schools also have a family and community policy that supports parent involvement programs and activities modeled after family involvement researcher Joyce Epstein's six types of family involvement.[7]

The bottom line, however, is that little is known about the work that districts are undertaking either through isolated initiatives or in implementing systemwide family engagement policies. Over the past year, the Harvard Family Research Project (HFRP) conducted interviews with nearly three dozen national experts in the family involvement field. In those conversations, some experts remarked that there is not much family involvement work taking place at the district level. In other words, there are few initiatives that originate from or are administered by school systems' central offices. Many districts talk about family engagement policies, but few actually implement them. This relative lack of district-level work is notable because the capacity and resources that a central office can offer are essential for scaling up school-level efforts.[8] In order for this work to take hold, district leaders need to hear what other districts are doing, what their successes and challenges are, and what strategies might work as they implement systems of their own. It is our hope that the story of Boston, with a particular focus on the district's family engagement policies, will be instructive for other urban school systems as they consider such work themselves.

This chapter explores family engagement in the context of the Boston Public Schools from 1995 until 2006.[9] The Boston story is one of family and community engagement.[10] We use a broad lens to define the ways in which the Boston Public Schools (BPS) has engaged the community and examine the role of community advocacy and organizing groups in the development of policies and programs that affect families in the BPS.

The chapter opens with some historical context from Boston. It follows with a discussion of the evolution of the district's policies over time, with particular emphasis on the final years of Superintendent Thomas Payzant's tenure. The chapter concludes with lessons learned and recommendations for other districts interested in implementing systemic family and community engagement policies.

For this chapter, we interviewed twelve key informants who have in-depth knowledge of the Boston Public School system. Many of these informants are also lifelong Boston residents with deep roots in the city. (The list of informants is in endnote 24.) In addition, we reviewed many documents, including memoranda written by the superintendent to the Boston School Committee and media reports.

BOSTON PUBLIC SCHOOLS: HISTORICAL CONTEXT

The evolution of family and community engagement in Boston has its roots in the aftermath of desegregation. Almost twenty years after the pivotal *Brown v. Board of Education* decision, a lawsuit was filed in Boston alleging a system of educational inequality. In 1974 Judge W. Arthur Garrity ruled in the *Morgan v. Hennigan* case that the Boston School Committee was guilty of running an unconstitutionally segregated school system. School officials and city leaders were reluctant to comply with the ruling, and it took over 415 separate orders and 8 years for BPS to implement a plan for racial balance among the schools. Various busing plans divided the city, largely along racial lines. Black students arriving at newly "integrated" schools were often greeted by swarms of white parents and students hurling rocks and shouting insults at them. Despite its reputation as a relatively progressive city, Boston received national attention for the violent and drawn-out desegregation of its schools.[11]

Part of Judge Garrity's order to desegregate BPS involved the creation of a three-tiered system of parent and community oversight. Begun in 1974 and 1975 and funded by BPS, this system was made up of parent councils at the school, district, and city levels. They were charged with monitoring the district's desegregation to "insure adequate and impartial investigation and responsible recommendations on racially and ethnically oriented problems arising at the school [and to] to create means of communication between parents, students, teachers, and administrators regarding the solution of such problems. . . ."[12] This three-tiered structure of parental and community oversight evolved over time into a school-based system of shared governance with citywide coordination. School Parent Councils (SPCs) are open to all parents and elect representatives to mandatory School Site Councils (SSCs).[13] For more than twenty years, the Citywide Parents' Council (CPC) acted as the umbrella organization for these school-based councils, providing parent training for participation in SPCs and conducting elections of parents to SSCs. The CPC worked to "foster parental involvement in the schools, provide positive input into educational policies and hold the Boston Public Schools accountable for providing a quality education to all students."[14]

In the wake of desegregation, new lawsuits prompted court orders for additional parent and community oversight at the city level to monitor BPS's commitment to work with historically marginalized students—those who were bilingual, had special needs, or attended Title I schools. This resulted in a complex dynamic of citywide parent representation in which three parent advisory councils and the CPC (hereafter collectively referred to as parent advisory councils [PACs]) received BPS funding but acted as autonomous units that held the district accountable for its legal and ethical responsibility to provide an adequate education to all students.

FAMILY AND COMMUNITY ENGAGEMENT IN BPS: 1995–2000

When Thomas Payzant became superintendent of the Boston Public Schools in 1995, he entered a school district that, like many other urban school districts, had suffered from low student achievement, unstable instructional leadership, and budgetary limitations. The historical and legal context in Boston presented a number of additional challenges for the superintendent. Arriving one year after the final court order banning segregation in BPS, Payzant took leadership of a district that had spent decades embroiled in various legal disputes. Several of these cases had pitted the BPS against community organizations, and the court battles created a perception that the district did not respect the families and community that it served.

Aware of this complex history of parent and community advocacy in Boston, one of Payzant's early goals was to bring voices and services together. During our interview with Payzant for this chapter, he acknowledged that he was viewed as unsympathetic to the need for parent advocacy, but he said that he believed "it was ridiculous to have so many silos of different groups of parents; what we needed to do was find a way to connect all of them to work together to support our kids." Payzant wanted to create a BPS team that could coordinate and respond to parent and community advocates and a plan that would affirm the importance of parents as partners in education.

Reorganization of the Administrative Structure

When he first arrived as superintendent, Payzant proposed an extensive reorganization of the Boston Public Schools central office, including consolidating a variety of family and community engagement activities under an administrative team, the Parent Support Services (PSS) team. The PSS team leader reported to the superintendent and was a member of his leadership team, alongside other top-level administrators within BPS. The PSS team included BPS parent representation and acted as an umbrella for school governance structures and a number of advocacy groups, including the four BPS-funded parent advisory councils (PACs).[15] Its other main function was to oversee Parent Information Centers (PICs), which aided parents in choosing and enrolling in schools. This new PSS infrastructure was designed to promote family and community engagement by improving home-school relationships. The goal was to facilitate better problem-solving for families through shared decision making in schools, and to improve interactions during the school registration process, which was typically a family's first encounter with BPS.

Despite a concerted effort to consolidate staff and support services for families, the resulting PSS team structure was not fully effective. A report written several years later described the PSS team as "incomprehensible, a piecemeal affiliation of BPS and non-BPS organizations, some of whom are accountable to and funded by BPS, some of whom are funded by BPS but accountable to their own boards, some of whom receive some funding from BPS for specific projects, and some of whom have no funding or accountability connection to BPS."[16]

Developing Family and Community Engagement Policies

In addition to reorganizing the administrative structure, Payzant began to integrate family and community engagement into his broader district goals. In particular, he recognized family and community engagement as a crucial component of student academic achievement. Payzant outlined his goals for BPS in a five-year school reform plan, *Focus on Children*, adopted in 1996. Among the policy goals provided in the reform plan was Goal 4, which stated that BPS was committed to "engag[ing] parents and community in school improvement through a unified, collaborative structure and effective communications."[17] A year later, Payzant articulated school and district expectations based on this vision statement in the BPS Plan for Whole-School Change, which required every school in BPS to report evidence of their progress toward six essential goals.[18] A set of priorities to guide school reform in Boston, these "Essentials" were defined by the district as "a framework" for its "ongoing effort to improve instruction in every classroom and to support every student to reach proficiency." The sixth Essential of this plan, "Partner with families and community to support student learning," emphasized the critical connection between student achievement and family and community engagement. For example, it listed specific expectations for schools and parents, including that teachers will communicate regularly with families in their native language about children's progress and ways families can support students at home; and families will demonstrate interest in their children's schoolwork and learning, including monitoring children's attendance, attending parent conferences, and participating in parent councils where possible. Expectations for central administrators included the superintendent and deputies holding principals accountable for measurable outreach to families and community, and district provision of technical assistance to schools as they develop and implement their family engagement plans.[19] (For the complete text of the sixth Essential, see Appendix on page 271.)

In September 1997, the school committee adopted an official Parent/Family Involvement Policy that brought together many of the priorities of the district regarding the way it worked with families and communities.[20] This policy required schools to incorporate their objectives into comprehensive school plans through parent/school compacts. It focused on building system-, school-, and classroom-level goals related to climate and culture, effective communication, avenues for engagement, linkages to resources and programs, training and support, and accountability.

Together, the BPS restructuring that created the PSS team and the policies supporting family and community engagement were meant to encourage and support schools' work with families and communities toward the goal of improved student achievement. While symbolically powerful, the restructuring and implementation of policies did not significantly affect the way BPS engaged with families. Although some schools clearly excelled at communicating with families and informing them about ways to be advocates for their children, many schools did not provide the basic services and supports required by the Parent/Family Involvement Policy and the BPS Plan for Whole-School Change. For example, many schools did not create parent/school compacts or have parent representation on school site councils, and those that did often did not engage parents in meaningful ways. Despite a number of written policies requiring schools to be welcoming places for families, parents felt disrespected and unheard by school staff and believed that schools did not view them as equal partners in their child's education.[21] BPS viewed parent involvement as school-directed *to* parents rather than cocreated *with* parents, and placed an emphasis on school-based engagement, such as volunteering in classrooms, attending meetings, and participating in school governance.[22] Rather than transforming the culture of how families could be partners in teaching and learning, these changes perpetuated a belief that family and community engagement was an "add-on" to regular class instruction. In practice, BPS remained disconnected from the needs of parents and community members and struggled to support a comprehensive plan to involve families.

REFRAMING FAMILY AND COMMUNITY ENGAGEMENT IN BPS: 2000–02

Community Organizing as a Force for Change

By the late 1990s, there was a growing sense of dissatisfaction in the community about the direction of family and community engagement at the district level. Many believed Payzant's stated commitment to this work needed to be challenged. Thus began a gradual but crucial shift from parent advocacy, which emphasized mobilizing and resolving the issues of *some* parents, to grassroots parent organizing, which prioritized the *collective* power and social capital of all parents.[23]

In 1999, representatives from three local foundations—the Boston Foundation, the Boston Globe Foundation, and the Hyams Foundation—as well as a member of the Boston School Committee and the director of the Citywide Educational Coalition began conversations about the status of family and community engagement within the BPS. As Henry Allen, then program officer for the Hyams Foundation, described it, there was a "belief that the stars were aligned for significant education reform in Boston" because of the partnership between Boston Mayor Thomas Menino and Superintendent Payzant. This group felt that despite the existence of many advocacy groups, there was an "absence of a strong parent and community *grassroots* organizing effort."[24] It was their goal to draw upon the experience and organizing power of existing community groups that may not have focused on school reform in the past, but had an established member base of BPS parents. Through the efforts of these individuals and foundations, the Boston Parent Organizing Network (BPON) was born. BPON was committed to building the power of parents so they could have a strong and meaningful voice at both the local school and district levels, including the ability to influence policy decisions.

Michele Brooks, BPON's first director (from 2000 until 2004), had extensive experience as a parent advocate and parent coordinator at a Boston high school. She said that her first order of business was to go and talk to the four parent advisory councils, in particular the CPC, which perceived BPON's existence as a threat, in order to "clarify that this was a network, not an organization." Brooks explained that the first year of BPON was focused on getting various community advocacy and organizing groups to work together effectively. Ultimately, the groups came to see the value of working together toward collective goals, but according to Brooks there continued to be some mistrust because BPON had greater access to the superintendent than did the PACs.

Payzant, who had worked with a less complex and more cohesive group of parent organizations in his prior superintendency in San Diego, grew frustrated with identifying the numerous advocacy groups in Boston and understanding and mediating their sometimes competing interests. By all accounts, Payzant accepted that the fact that he needed to give audience to parents in the community and BPON was the easiest, most efficient means for doing so. In a city with such a vibrant advocacy and organizing presence, working with BPON as a central source for information on parents' needs made good sense to Payzant. According to Henry Allen, Payzant was interested in "having a series of conversations that was more broadly representative of parents in BPS so that he and the mayor could be responsive to key concerns. . . .

Although he was looking at BPON to be an entity to talk to, I wouldn't say he embraced it."

A Task Force Assesses District Progress and Recommends Change

In addition to a feeling that the district needed to be more receptive to community input, community members and district officials acknowledged that the family and community engagement structure and district policies of the late 1990s were ineffective. The Boston School Committee was "aware of the generally low level of satisfaction with current services to families as evidenced by an internal survey and focus groups conducted over four years."[25] In response to this sentiment, in January 2000 the school committee convened the Boston School Committee's Family and Community Engagement Task Force (hereafter referred to as the task force), which was charged with making recommendations to the district about ways "BPS [could] fulfill its responsibility to increase the involvement of families in their children's education, systemwide and in each school and classroom." The task force sought to answer three questions: (1) What services should parents expect from the Boston Public Schools? (2) What is working well now in their school, in BPS, and in the community to help their children to succeed in school? (3) What services should BPS add, change, or eliminate to improve parent involvement and communication between home and school?[26]

The school committee, various advocacy and organizing groups, and BPS parents were represented on the nine-member task force. Together, they developed an inclusive methodology for collecting data about the district's family and community engagement policies that included mailing letters requesting responses to the three questions to more than one thousand individuals, including school site council members, school parent council members, BPS administrators, and community partners. The task force also held community forums, conducted interviews with BPS and community leaders, and reviewed relevant documents and other sources as part of their data collection efforts. The findings of the task force were mixed.[27] Many parents reported that their children's schools were welcoming and respected parents. Parents were pleased with a number of practices, including:

- Classes and workshops for parents
- Opportunities for parent leadership within the district
- School meetings and printed information distributed by schools
- Community partnerships and programs
- Parent liaisons and school/community organizers

However, most of those parents and students who attended the forums or who contacted the task force directly were dissatisfied. These parents felt that many schools lacked commitment to parent involvement. They said that schools failed to communicate ways in which they as parents could help their children at home and that some school staff neither welcomed nor respected parents. Other issues they cited included:

- A lack of communication in their home language between home and school, particularly regarding BPS policies and expectations
- Inconsistent services and information from Parent Information Centers
- A lack of information for parents about the PSS team and other parent advisory councils

In addition to these and other findings, the task force's final report included seven major recommendations (see appendix 9C) that suggested ways in which BPS, from district to school policies and practices, could improve family and community engagement. Over the course of the following year, Payzant met with the task force, reviewed their recommendations, made suggestions of his own in response, and appointed the Family and Community Engagement Work Group (hereafter referred to as the work group). This work group, composed mostly of district officials and some task force members, was charged with making implementation suggestions based on the task force's findings and recommendations. The work group's recommendations were influenced by many community-based organizations, which garnered media attention and provided testimony at school committee and city council hearings about issues of importance for parents of BPS students. The work group suggested that Payzant focus on the following goals:[28]

- Demonstrating that family engagement is a BPS priority and that schools will be held accountable for establishing strong partnerships with families
- Reexamining the role of the Parent Information Centers
- Examining the structure of the Parent Support Services Team
- Ensuring that principals and teachers develop a family engagement plan for their school/classroom with objectives that can be evaluated

Recommendations Yield New Objectives for Family and Community Engagement in BPS

After the task force and work group presented their findings and recommendations, community members as well as school committee members and other district officials began to pressure the district to focus on implementation. It was in this context that the superintendent developed a new plan for family and community engagement.

Payzant had received feedback from a variety of stakeholders, including community members and parents, regarding his ideas about how to create a comprehensive plan for family and community engagement. A series of memos from Payzant to the school committee from March 2001 through April 2002 reveal significant movement on his stance toward the recommendations, based largely on the influence of the work group and community groups. He believed that the findings and recommendations of the task force and work group required "a central BPS structure to provide district and school-based services that [would] improve the quality of family and community engagement and foster student academic achievement."[29] Of significance, Payzant was linking family and community engagement directly to student achievement in this goal. Considering Payzant's clear focus on instruction, this connection was a signal that he intended to integrate family and community engagement into the other work of the district so that it could have an impact on teaching and learning in schools.

In the end, Payzant's implementation objectives included:[30]

- Reallocating resources to better support implementation priorities
- Establishing a central organizational structure
- Transforming Parent Information Centers into three new Family Resource Centers
- Developing school-based strategies for increasing family engagement

IMPLEMENTING A REVISED FAMILY AND COMMUNITY ENGAGEMENT PLAN: 2002–06

Reallocating Resources to Support Implementation Objectives

Payzant's 2002 plan for family and community engagement included an increase in the staffing and service delivery for family and community engagement, requiring the district to reallocate funds. In a decision that caused widespread criticism from community activists, Payzant withdrew all of BPS's funding from the city's four parent advisory councils in order to free up monies to implement a new central organizational structure and revamp the Parent Information Centers (PICs). Payzant wrote:

> Limited resources and competing priorities for them require Boston Public Schools to allocate resources in ways that it can be responsible and accountable for their use. This can be done with support services for families. It cannot be done with funding for advocacy groups which must have the freedom to prod the BPS without the fear that if there is disagreement on some issues, funding will be withdrawn. However, BPS must collaborate with parent advocacy groups even though it will not provide direct funding to them.[31]

Payzant's decision to eliminate funding for the parent advisory councils (PACs) drew outrage from the community, largely because his actions suggested that he felt the PACs were not accountable, representative of parents, or providing designated services as they were mandated. Payzant felt that the number of PACs was overwhelming and that they also had no clear constituency to whom they were accountable. Moreover, the confrontational nature of the PACs and unclear representation did not sit well with Payzant, who remarked, "I didn't have a problem with the advocacy groups but it didn't seem right to me that we were spending our money on them to beat us up. What about a regular parent that was not a part of a [parent advisory council]?"

Creating a Central Organizational Structure

In memos to the school committee at the time, as well as in recent interviews, the superintendent explained that his intention was to create an administrative structure that provided both leadership and a departmental home for family and community engagement. But Payzant did not want to create a deputy superintendent for family and community engagement. He said, "I understood it symbolically, but I worried about this person carrying the burden for all of the schools." Payzant presented two different plans that created a team leader position that would report to one of the deputy superintendents for cluster and school leaders.[32] These proposals were widely criticized as burying family and community engagement under layers of bureaucracy within BPS instead of elevating it to the status that it deserved.

Parents and advocacy groups in Boston exerted a great deal of pressure on Payzant to instead establish an independent office for family and community engagement that would report directly to the superintendent. Payzant recognized that "the perception in Boston Public Schools is that those who report directly to the superintendent have functions that are more important and have greater status than those who report elsewhere."[33] For this reason, in the spring of 2002, Payzant announced that he would hire a team leader for an Office of Family and Community Engagement that would initially report to him.

Not satisfied with the idea of hiring a team leader, BPON and Voices for Children, a Boston-based advocacy group, actively campaigned to promote the new position to the deputy superintendent level. The work group that Payzant had appointed to help him implement the task force's recommendations also exerted pressure to elevate the position. In spite of Payzant's reservations about the position, community activists prevailed. As Kim Janey, the deputy director for the Boston School Reform Project at Massachusetts Advocates for Children, noted, "To his credit, Payzant was able to create this position and listened to the groups that wanted it." In April 2002, Payzant presented an updated plan for family and community engagement that included a deputy superintendent.

Community activists also provided input on the job description for the position, which had the following responsibilities:

> The new deputy will serve as the Superintendent's primary liaison with families, community organizations, and advocacy groups to collaborate with schools to support improved student achievement. Consistent with the Work Group recommendations, the deputy will lead all family and

> community engagement work in BPS. The deputy will implement this plan and oversee staff at the newly established Family Resource Centers, work with other district personnel supporting parent outreach and school-based family and community engagement efforts. The Deputy Superintendent will participate on the Leadership Team and as a part of the Superintendent's Deputy Team.[34]

Although the community successfully lobbied for the position of deputy superintendent in a separate Office of Family and Community Engagement, the district has struggled to support this position and maintain consistent staffing. Between 2002 and 2006, there have been three different deputy superintendents, and each has faced similar challenges in filling the new role. Primarily, the deputy superintendent has had to push for both the trust of community members and the support of district leadership, including the superintendent. Glenola Mitchell, the first Deputy Superintendent for Family and Community Engagement, described her priority as "mending fences" and leveraged her prior relationships with many of the players to build trust and ease hostility. Following her, Karen Mapp also worked to break down some of the barriers that existed between community groups and the district, and she actively engaged the community groups in setting common goals for her tenure.[35] Karen Richardson, the third and current deputy superintendent, felt that when she arrived, "people were on edge and wondered who I was [and] what was my management style like." These changes in leadership have been unsettling to community members and parents, who view the turnover in the position as a sign that it does not have the legitimacy originally intended nor the internal guidance and dedication to make it effective.

Transforming PICs into FRCs

Part of Payzant's 2002 plan for family and community engagement involved revamping district-level mechanisms to support families, particularly the function of Parent Information Centers (PICs), which primarily helped families with the school registration process. One of the first tasks was to transform the PICs into broader Family Resource Centers (FRCs), which would work with both schools and families to promote positive practices for family and community engagement. Although FRCs would still be sites for student registration, central office would provide the staff to carry out registration functions. This would allow FRC staff to devote time and resources to support family involvement in more meaningful ways. In particular, Payzant's new plan called for three district-wide FRCs and a Title I Training Center for Families and Educators (hereafter referred to as the Training Center) to provide "one-stop shopping" for services that were based on the needs of families and schools.[36] The services Payzant envisioned at these new district centers were ambitious and were meant to replace those that had previously been provided by the Citywide Parent Council (CPC) before it lost its BPS funding. It would be the responsibility of the FRCs and Training Center to:[37]

- Provide training to principals/headmasters and teachers to work with parents as partners
- Create guidance support areas for families to help with college enrollment and financial aid for their children
- Conduct workshops and distribute information to help families understand how to help their children improve academic skills, get help when needed, meet classroom expectations, and perform well on assessments
- Provide guidance to families on how to help assist student learning at home, at school, and in the community
- Provide workshops for school-based Parent Councils
- Help families access services (bilingual, special education, and regular education programs)
- Add programs to help families learn how to work with their children on math and literacy
- House student registration

In reality, student registration continued to take up an inordinate amount of time and prevented FRC staff from being able to carry out many of the school- and community-based support services intended. After the 2002 change from PICs to FRCs, center staff reported that student registration occupied a full twenty-six weeks of their time throughout the year.[38] Internally, the school committee, the deputy superintendent for family and community engagement, and the superintendent went back and forth about the appropriate institutional home for student registration. In 2005, a large restructuring separated student registration from the Office of Family and Community Engagement. With this separation, FRCs were also removed from the oversight of the Office of Family and Community Engagement, tacitly indicating that the majority of their time was spent on student registration, just as it had been years earlier when FRCs were called PICs.

The duties originally planned for the FRCs have recently been transferred to family outreach specialists and the Training Center. BPS now has four staff positions assigned to work in district triads and promote family and community engagement. Although the role of these outreach specialists is still evolving, they are charged with being on-call assistants for schools in helping to resolve disputes with families and to build school governance structures. Each triad also has two additional outreach specialists in order to meet the specific needs of families whose children are English-language learners or whose children have special needs. The Training Center, in conjunction with the work of school-based parent liaisons and district-level outreach specialists, continues to offer workshops for parents on topics such as understanding No Child Left Behind. More recently, the Training Center enhanced its professional development offerings for school staff to include topics such as building school-based parent centers and hosting family-friendly events such as math nights or open houses.

Payzant devoted much attention to grounding district-level resources for families in the practices of good customer service. This included major renovations at FRCs, which had lacked functional telephone service, automated data entry, and decent furnishings prior to 2002, as well as staff training on how to treat all parents respectfully. The district's focus on customer service signaled a commitment on the part of the district to improve its communication with families. However, the district-level services provided were difficult for an outsider to navigate and understand. The BPS website, for example, did not provide information about what these services were or how parents could access them.

Successes in School-Based Efforts to Increase Family Engagement

While the district-level mechanisms for engaging with families were not wholly effective, efforts to transform the relationships between schools and families proved more fruitful. Many schools within BPS had, for years, allocated funding to staff a position responsible for acting as a liaison between the school, its families, and community organizations. Often, however, these parent liaisons, as they were called, had multiple job responsibilities and, without the support of district middle management, sometimes found themselves performing functions based on specific principal interests and needs, ranging from secretarial duties to individual parent advocacy. In response to these concerns, in 2005 BPS initiated the Family and Community Outreach Coordinators (FCOCs) Pilot Initiative. The initiative was intended to address three main goals:[39]

- Creating a family-friendly environment in schools (for example, by greeting parents when they arrive at school and providing a family-designated space in the building)
- Helping families support their children's learning (for example, by offering classes for parents, making report cards user-friendly, and communicating with teachers on behalf of families)
- Improving relationships between schools and families by building trust and respect (for example, by creating opportunities for parents to talk to one another and increasing school-directed outreach into the community)

Part of what made the FCOC program unique was the collaborative process used in its foundation. Karen Mapp, in her role as deputy superintendent, seized the opportunity to be an "internal advocate" for the FCOC program. She recognized, however, that staffing schools with parent liaisons would be resource-consuming, particularly after recent, large state budget cuts. Mapp, therefore, brought a number of community-based organizations, including

BPON and a broad array of advocacy groups, together in a meeting and made the case for a synergistic effort to begin the FCOC Pilot Initiative. In the fall of 2004, BPON voted to make the FCOC program its main priority and began concerted organizing efforts to inform parents about the option of having school-based liaisons and how to advocate for this option. As part of this campaign, Boston parents testified at school committee and city council meetings, as well as voiced their opinion in the media and in direct meetings with the superintendent. This external pressure, coupled with Mapp's determination, resulted in the creation of the FCOC Pilot Initiative. Seventy-three schools applied to participate in the initiative, and seventeen schools ultimately received funding to hire an FCOC.[40] The job description of the FCOCs focused on building trusting relationships rather than on running programs or mediating school prerogatives.[41]

According to Katie Madrigal, the director of the FCOC program, family and community outreach coordinators occupy a unique role in schools as internal change agents and advocates for families. They make the case and set the tone for family involvement within schools, as well as offer training and workshop sessions for parents. FCOCs document how they are meeting their three program goals (family-friendly cultures, family involvement, and relationship-building) through work plans created with the school principals, a core group of teachers, and, sometimes, parents.[42] The FCOCs are assessed by the degree to which they are[43]

- cultivating relational trust between school staff and parents and among parents;
- helping to increase parental attendance at traditional school-based activities for family involvement, such as open houses and parent-teacher conferences;
- helping to increase parental participation in school governance;
- offering workshops in parent leadership and advocacy;
- implementing at least one parent-initiated and parent-led project at participating schools; and
- enhancing teacher and staff capacity to collaborate with parents to support children's learning.

Despite generally positive evaluations, some challenges remain. In part due to the fact that the FCOC Pilot Initiative is relatively new, clear expectations for participating schools are now beginning to take shape. A 2005–06 evaluation by Family Friendly Schools found that some parents have expressed concern that not all teachers in their school embraced the FCOC program.[44] While schools that are staffed by FCOCs all initially agreed to meet the program's goals, no formal agreement exists between the Office of Community Engagement and principals regarding their commitment to support FCOCs. Because FCOCs also report directly to school principals, their job duties and responsibilities are subject to interpretation by school principals and teachers.[45] Efforts are currently underway to establish more accountability through individual meetings with principals, better alignment between work plans and monthly reports, and voluntary professional development opportunities for school-based staff. Community members have also criticized BPS for not expanding the FCOC program districtwide. A tight budget and competing interests to hire more math and literacy coaches meant that the program expanded by only two half-time positions in 2006 despite evidence of its effectiveness in increasing family involvement.

REFLECTIONS ON A DECADE OF CHANGE

There is much to be learned from Boston's progress in implementing family and community engagement. Although the process has been imperfect, other districts can learn from its missteps as well as its successes. As we have noted, there is a dearth of information available about community and family engagement efforts, both because few districts have undertaken large scale initiatives and because these examples are not well-documented. With that in mind, we offer the following "lessons learned" based on Boston's experience—its progress and the challenges that remain.

Family and community engagement must be integral to any instructional improvement plan.

Research clearly indicates that family engagement has a positive effect on student outcomes. It follows, therefore, that involving families should be a deliberate and significant component of any district's school improvement plan. Over the past ten years, family and community engagement has been written into Boston's district policy. However, in practice, BPS still struggles with *fully* integrating its family and community engagement initiatives into its larger plan for improved teaching and learning. For example, some interviewees expressed frustration over a lack of alignment between the funding and evaluation procedures for family and community engagement and those for instructional improvement. From Boston's experience, it is clear that district leadership must reinforce the relationship between family involvement and student outcomes, in practice as well as in theory, at all levels—from the superintendent, to the deputies, to the principals, and into the classrooms.

Perhaps the most significant structural step toward meaningfully incorporating family and community engagement into the BPS improvement agenda was the establishment of a deputy superintendent position. This position gave a voice to parents at the senior leadership team level and sent a strong message to the community of the value of family and community engagement. But there have been some limitations to this position because of its separation from teaching and learning, the lack of direction it has received from the superintendent, and its frequent personnel turnover.

Successful community engagement requires continuity of leadership and district support for its leaders.

The Boston experience demonstrates that in order for a senior leadership position in community engagement to be successful, it must have the power and support necessary to execute its challenging mission. This requires the superintendent to be actively engaged in setting the agenda and direction for the district's family and community engagement policies as well as advocating for adequate funding to implement the agenda. Without a champion at the superintendent level, it is unlikely that family and community engagement will be taken seriously systemwide and have the impact that it might.

Success also requires continuity of personnel. Efforts should be made to identify the right person for the position and attempt to make the position a long-term hire. The success of this position depends largely on the relationships the deputy develops, and building these relationships takes time. If the position turns over every year or two, there is not adequate opportunity to build trust and for relationships to solidify. Moreover, the superintendent must choose an individual with a passion for family involvement and the ability both to broker relationships and competing interests between activists, families, schools, and district personnel.

Family engagement activities must be supported by district-level policies and be responsive to the specific needs of each school's community.

In order for families to take responsibility for supporting their children's academic success, programs and policies must be in place that are tailored to their specific circumstances. Activities that might serve one particular population well may not be relevant to another. Therefore, schools must identify their own families' strengths and needs—via surveys, informal conversations, and other means—and develop plans that capitalize on those strengths and address those needs specifically. In order for schools to take this responsibility seriously and undertake such information gathering, they need to be supported by district-level leadership and policies. Placing family and community engagement coordinators (or parent liaisons, as they are sometimes called) in individual buildings, for example, provides schools with the human resources to canvas families about their particular circumstances and needs, and to tap into the wealth of cultural information and resources that they represent. By engaging families in this kind of conversation, school-level personnel can foster ownership among families of the school's engagement activities and increase the likelihood of these programs' success.

District family and community engagement policies should include strong school-based elements such as schoolwide planning and professional development.

A significant challenge for districts is to create policies that reach down to support schools' capacity to build partnerships with families and to change the culture of schools to be welcoming to families. The BPS task force presented both district-level and school-based recommendations for family and community engagement in their final report to the superintendent. The task force suggested that principals and teachers develop schoolwide plans for family and community engagement, identify those people taking responsibility for outreach (e.g., parent liaisons), and offer professional development in how to communicate with and engage families.

Because BPS's initial family and community engagement structure was centralized, many of the school-based supports for families are only now beginning to take shape. For example, the FCOC Pilot Initiative has been successful at increasing family involvement through a focus on relationship-building. Other school-based efforts, however, such as parent, teacher, and principal training in family involvement, are only now beginning to be implemented. Any school districts seeking to create a cohesive plan for family and community engagement must build and evaluate school-level support systems, such as professional development, in order to affect change at the school level.

Putting family and community engagement plans into action in schools requires leadership at every level. The superintendent and his or her team must be united in their message—family and community involvement matters for children's success. Principals need to communicate and help their teachers and staff take ownership of the message that their school has open doors and will provide ample opportunities for families to engage, be heard, and support their children's learning. Teachers also must take leadership in developing relationships with the families of their students in order that families will both feel comfortable in the classroom and in participating in their children's learning. Families will be more likely to engage in their children's schooling if teachers treat parents with respect and acknowledge them as their children's first teachers.

School districts must evaluate their family and community engagement efforts and hold themselves accountable for meeting family and community engagement goals.

To achieve successful and sustainable family and community engagement, a district must be willing to critically appraise the current status of its family engagement work; define relevant, ambitious, and reasonable goals; and then determine the ways in which progress toward these goals will be measured. The process that Boston undertook for identifying the district's strengths and weaknesses and co-constructing strategies for family and community engagement provides a model for other school districts. The BPS took important first steps in committing to evaluation when it engaged the task force, endorsed its methods for gathering data in an inclusive way, and established a work group to suggest priorities and establish implementation suggestions. The missing piece for Boston, however, is a deep and critical look at how progress toward goals is measured and how it will hold itself accountable when it falls short of reaching them. Other districts might learn from Boston that this work takes consistent monitoring, reflection, and revision. Without such ongoing attention, the policies will not be sustained.

Districts must develop clear mechanisms to hold school-level staff members accountable for their work with families.

Principals and teachers need to be both supported in and held accountable for their work with families. Boston has promoted school-based family involvement by encouraging and motivating principals and educators to build meaningful partnerships with parents. There have been some successes with this approach, such as the FCOC program, but it has not been balanced by a parallel focus on accountability. Our informants suggested that there are few consequences for principals whose schools clearly do not meet the family engagement goals set by the district. Some informants suggested that family and community engagement needed to be a measure by which all educators are evaluated within the BPS.

Lines of responsibility and accountability need to be clear. If the district is going to hold schools—and principals in particular—responsible for carrying out their mandates, then all parties need to be clear about what the expectations are, who will be evaluating them, and how their success will be measured. One of the challenges in Boston, as Payzant predicted, is that principals may not have incentives to enhance their efforts to involve families in their schools because they do not report to the Deputy Superintendent for Family and Community Engagement. The effectiveness of the district's policies, then, has depended largely on the personal ability of the deputy superintendent to motivate cluster deputy superintendents, who evaluate principals, to make family and community engagement a point of evaluation. Similarly, the FCOC program is targeted to work with schools that have a stated commitment to family and community engagement, but few mechanisms exist to reach those schools that have not prioritized family involvement. Requiring professional development on family and community engagement for both principals and teachers is one way to address this issue.

The process for developing family and community engagement policies must include all voices, particularly the historically disenfranchised.

Much of the story of BPS's progress in family and community engagement can be traced to the outside forces that exerted enormous pressure on the district administration. The parent advisory councils (PACs), BPON, the Citywide Parent Coalition, Massachusetts Advocates for Children, Voices for Children, parents, and the many individual interests in the city all have helped to shape Boston's family and community engagement policies. Without these critical voices, it is likely that these policies would look very different or perhaps not exist.

Given the value of such voices, particularly those of the disenfranchised, it is important to ensure that they are given the opportunity to be heard. In Boston, when the task force gathered information about its family and community engagement policies, they modeled an inclusive process, ensuring that they had broad representation of Boston families and community members. The task force report was based on data from the district's families and community, and those data were gathered through facilitated focus groups, surveys, and community meetings at which members of the community could voice their concerns and ideas. According to one of our informants, this was a significant departure from prior practices. In the past, the district would seek input on policies after making decisions about them.

It should also be noted that resources to mobilize historically disenfranchised parents through grassroots organizing may be available outside a district's immediate community. The Working Group on Education Organizing, a national network of more than thirty funding organizations interested in communities organizing school improvement and reform, is working to establish a national Fund for Education Organizing. This fund will provide grants and technical assistance to local and regional education organizing groups.[46] This effort grows out of the Group's belief "that the voice of low-income parents, and especially parents of color, can be a powerful force in both creating and sustaining the public will necessary for school reform." Clearly, BPON is such a force, and funder-initiated endeavors such as the Fund for Education Organizing demonstrate a commitment to extending this type of work beyond Boston.

Districts that are taking leadership in family and community engagement should document their work and share best practices.

The interviews for this chapter revealed that district personnel, and others who are close to it, are largely unfamiliar with the family and community engagement work of their national peers. In recent years, however, BPS staff have begun discussions with New York City district officials and parent coordinators in order to learn from their practices, but these conversations are just a beginning.

Although there are not a great many districts that are taking such leadership roles, there are districts, both large and small, that are beginning to implement interesting family engagement policies. Without the knowledge of best practices, as well as the potential challenges and opportunities, districts that are interested in undertaking this work will be less likely to succeed. Just as there are often inadequate mechanisms for sharing best practices from classroom to classroom in a school, this lack of information sharing nationally is a significant missed opportunity. We would recommend that districts, like Boston, advocate putting family and community engagement on the agenda for national conferences, publications, and networking opportunities.

CONCLUSION

The dynamic between BPS and its community is complex; desegregation is relatively recent history and some of the wounds between the district and its communities of color have yet to heal. In part because of this history, Boston has an energetic and motivated activist community that maintains high expectations for the relationship between the school district and its families and community. Many community activists characterize the district's efforts at family and community engagement over the past ten years as a "back-burner" approach when contrasted to the superintendent's intense focus on instructional improvement. However, Boston's spirited and persistent community participation and organizing maintained pressure on the district to move family and community engagement to the center of its agenda. As a result, BPS laid the foundation for a larger system that will support schools' efforts to engage families, give families a voice at the district level, and hold district- and school-level personnel accountable for family and community engagement.

The accountability piece of this work should not be underestimated. Although it is difficult to directly quantify the effect of each successful "contact" with a parent or the community, we know that taken together such engagement makes a difference. So, while it may not be possible to hold schools or individual teachers held accountable for specific outcomes, it is nonetheless important that they be held accountable for delivery of services and development of a culture that supports meaningful interaction with families and the community. This means that districts must signal their expectations by establishing coherent engagement policies tied to transparent accountability mechanisms. Of equal importance, districts must put in place the supports and resources necessary for schools and families to fulfill these expectations.

Although not perfect, the policies and processes undertaken in Boston include many elements that other urban systems might consider incorporating into their own family and community engagement plans. Boston's experience over the past decade highlights the importance of a commitment to these partnerships at all levels. The superintendent, central office staff, school level leadership, and teachers must all demonstrate, through consistent policies and actions, that parents and the community play an indispensable role in improving student outcomes. Structures within the school system must be designed such that family and community engagement initiatives are supported, and there must be a place "at the decision making table" for grassroots organizations to represent their constituents' voices. With such a comprehensive approach and a systemwide culture that demonstrates both respect for families, as well as a belief that their participation is necessary, other school districts will be in a position to give their students the greatest chance for success.[47]

APPENDIX 9A

ACRONYMS

BPON	Boston Parent Organizing Network
BPS	Boston Public Schools
CPC	Citywide Parents' Council
CWEC	Citywide Education Coalition
FCOC	Family and Community Outreach Coordinator
FRC	Family Resource Center
PACs	The CPC and three parent advisory councils for students who are bilingual, have special needs, or attend Title I schools
PIC	Parent Information Center
PSS	Parent Support Services
SPC	School Parent Council
SSC	School Site Council

APPENDIX 9B

TIMELINE OF BPS FAMILY AND COMMUNITY ENGAGEMENT EVENTS AND POLICIES

This timeline represents some of the major events and policies related to family and community engagement in the BPS. It is based on information collected from individual interviews, written reports, and media coverage.

1996—*Focus on Children* is published.[1]

1996—BPS reorganization results in Parent Support Services Team.

September 1997—School committee adopts the *BPS Parent/Family Involvement Policy* to be incorporated into all Comprehensive School Plans.

November 1997—*BPS Plan for Whole-School Change* is published.[2]

1999–2000—Boston Parent Organizing Network is formed.

January 2000—The Family and Community Engagement Task Force is convened.

June 2000—The Family and Community Engagement Task Force releases its report.

2000–2002—An internal work group prioritizes the task force recommendations and suggests implementation plans to Payzant.

November 2001—Superintendent Payzant announces plans to eliminate funding for Parent Advisory Councils.

March 2002—Superintendent Payzant presents Family and Community Engagement Plan.

September 2002—Glenola Mitchell is appointed Deputy Superintendent of Family and Community Engagement.

August 2003—Karen Mapp is appointed Interim Deputy Superintendent of Family and Community Engagement.

September 2004—BPS Parent Manual is written and translated into seven languages.

April 2005—Karen Richardson is appointed as Deputy Superintendent for Family and Community Engagement.

August 2005—BPS begins the Family and Community Outreach Coordinator Pilot Initiative at seventeen schools.

Fall 2005—Student registration is moved from The Office of Family and Community Engagement to the Office of Enrollment Services.

---

1. Goal 4 states, "Engage parents, families, and the community in school improvement through a unified collaborative structure and effective communication."
2. Area 6 states, "Involve parents and the community in Citywide Learning Standards and assessments and introduce ways parents and the community can support students."

APPENDIC 9C

TASK FORCE RECOMMENDATIONS
Family and Community Engagement Task Force
June 23, 2000, pp. 9–13

1. The BPS must expand its understanding of "parent involvement."
2. The superintendent, principals, and headmasters must state strongly and publicly that family engagement is a BPS priority, and schools will be held accountable for establishing strong partnerships with families.
3. Principals and teachers must develop a family engagement plan for their school/classroom and set family engagement objectives against which they will be evaluated.
4. Schools must identify an individual who serves as the focal point for family engagement.
5. BPS family engagement efforts should focus on student learning.
6. Principals and teachers need ongoing training in how to communicate with and engage families.
7. The superintendent and leadership team must examine the structure of the parent support services team.

CHAPTER X

The Boston Story

Successes and Challenges in Systemic Education Reform

THOMAS W. PAYZANT
with
CHRISTOPHER M. HORAN

EACH OF US IN PUBLIC EDUCATION is in the business of teaching and learning. It is both a great honor and a great responsibility to be entrusted with the children of our community, to be charged with helping them grow intellectually, emotionally, and socially into the successful young men and women of tomorrow. As educators, we must be both *teachers* and *learners* ourselves. Although our goal is always for students to gain knowledge and skill, much of the Boston strategy for education reform, as noted throughout this book, has been just as much about adult learning: what we can learn from one another about how to improve our own performance in order to raise student performance and close the achievement gap.

This book and several other major studies of the Boston Public Schools (BPS) during the 2005–06 school year provide thoughtful examinations of our school district's past, its present, and most importantly, its future.[1] My retirement as superintendent in June 2006 and the resulting leadership transition have sparked numerous reflections and analyses. Scholars, reporters, and citizens alike have seized this moment to ask pointed questions and offer valuable insights about the successes and challenges of the past eleven years. As adult learners, we welcome these opportunities to hear from our colleagues. Their findings provide an historical record of our work together and help shape the next chapter in the story of the Boston Public Schools. I encouraged and supported these efforts because I believe that it is impossible to improve ninety thousand public schools in America one school at a time, and that systems of schools may be downsized but never eliminated altogether. In fact, there is very little research on systemic reform—what works and what does not—so the examination of Boston as a case study has benefits not only locally but nationally, too.

It is essential to tell Boston's story to increase the knowledge of parents, educators, students, and policymakers about what it takes to improve a whole system of schools. Particularly in America's cities, better systems of schools will continue to provide the best hope for those children now left behind to accelerate their achievement; narrow the gaps defined by race, income, and educational program; and graduate from high school ready to continue in one of many postsecondary education options.

On a personal note, the studies also have afforded me great opportunities to look back on my tenure in Boston—to take stock of where we came from and where we are today. Most of us who lead busy lives rarely have such occasions to reflect and assess our work. In doing so, I am once again awed by the tremendous privilege of leading a dynamic school system in one of the great American cities during such an exciting time in public education. The challenges are many, and at times can be overwhelming even to the most stalwart among us, but the rewards are great. Throughout these eleven years, during times of celebration and setback, I have been surrounded by people who care about children. In every school and central office, in every neighborhood of Boston, I have worked side by side with educators, parents, and partners who want nothing more or less than the very best for our young people. I am grateful to them for their support—and at times, their criticism—all of which has been in the spirit of our shared goal of a better life for kids.

BOSTON THEN AND NOW

A phrase often used to characterize the Boston Public Schools by the mid-1990s was "a district in crisis." While few may have agreed about *how* to start anew, there seemed to be consensus that the system was in need of dramatic improvement. Very few students were performing at high levels. Attendance and graduation rates continued to decline. Civic leaders and elected officials had little or no confidence in most schools. It had been years since a new school was built. Parents who wanted to opt out of BPS for private, parochial, and suburban schools now had yet another option as the charter school movement began to take hold in Massachusetts.

Those looking for a symbol of the system's decline found one in the Jeremiah E. Burke High School. Located in the Grove Hall section of Dorchester, a primarily low-income community of color, the Burke came to epitomize the crisis in the Boston Public Schools. By 1995, the Burke had fallen into such disrepair in terms of its physical facility and the quality of its programs that the New England Association of Schools and Colleges (NEASC) stripped the school of its accreditation. For many, this signaled the beginning of the end for Boston schools. For others, however, most notably Mayor Thomas M. Menino and his appointed school committee (the city's school board), the loss of accreditation at the Burke served as an opportunity to underscore the urgency of school reform and as the catalyst for a "wake-up call" to elected officials, civic leaders, unions, and the public that we could no longer afford to sit idly by while schools crumbled and Boston's young people were denied opportunities for a bright future.

Fast-forward to September 2006. Under the leadership of Interim Superintendent Michael Contompasis, the new school year has begun without a glitch. By now, the successful school opening has become so commonplace in Boston that one could easily forget that this was not always the case. Facilities are renovated and cleaned. Teachers have readied their classrooms and lesson plans. Nearly every educator has earned "highly qualified" status. Students arrive ready to learn, knowing that expectations are high. The conversations in hallways and faculty lounges are about teaching and learning: student work, instructional strategies, rigorous content. In the weeks that follow, the district earns one front-page headline after another. First, after being a finalist for four consecutive years, Boston wins the distinguished Broad Prize for Urban Education as the top city school district in the country. The following week, the governor announces the winners of the state's John and Abigail Adams Scholarships—free tuition to any public college or university in Massachusetts—at Boston's John D. O'Bryant School of Math and Science because of the dramatic increase in BPS students (nearly nine hundred seniors) earning the scholarships by performing at the highest levels on the state assessment. One week later, state officials hold a press conference at another Boston high school to release the state's Grade 10 MCAS exam results, which show record increases of BPS students scoring at the proficient and advanced levels. In a packed auditorium at the former Dorchester High School, which was closed in 2002 and reopened as three small schools, overjoyed students give themselves a standing ovation for making the most dramatic improvements in the entire Commonwealth. This is not the same old Boston Public Schools system.

Such accolades mean a lot to adults and students in urban public schools, which are too often maligned, dismissed, or overlooked altogether. To have their hard work, day after day, finally take hold and be acknowledged does wonders for morale. These moments in the spotlight, however fleeting, will sustain students and educators during the most trying times, when they need to remember that their efforts will pay off and that success, once unimaginable, truly is within their reach. The danger, of course, is to rest on one's laurels—to make the fatal mistake of simply coasting instead of pushing to the next level. The improvements in the Boston Public Schools are commendable and may provide some valuable lessons to other schools and districts, but they are only a promising start. This book examines the progress to date to uncover the keys to our success, and it reminds us that we have a long way to go before we can declare victory.

To what do we attribute the emerging success of the Boston Public Schools? There are some who would seek a simple answer to that question, as if the transformation of a public institution as large and complex as an urban school district could be explained with a single strategy. We know all too well that this is not the case. In part, that is the reason school districts cannot be reinvented overnight. To do so requires a well-orchestrated set of reforms, some simultaneous, others in succession, that must be cultivated and embedded before they will bear fruit. This study sheds light on some of the key factors that helped change the culture of the Boston Public Schools over the past decade. There are countless others that do not appear on these pages but also had a positive impact on the lives of our students and families.

GOVERNANCE AND POLITICAL LEADERSHIP

A critical element of the Boston story that cannot be overstated is the sustained, stable leadership provided by the mayor and the appointed Boston School Committee (see Portz, chapter 2 in this volume). Since his election in 1993, Mayor Tom Menino has made public education one of the top priorities of his administration. A very popular figure who has been reelected three times, Mayor Menino has devoted significant resources and political capital to improving the Boston Public Schools. Unlike many other large urban systems, Boston's school district is a department of city government, similar to police, fire, or public works. The superintendent serves on the mayor's cabinet, and the thirteen-member elected city council must approve the appropriations for the city's operating and capital budgets each year. (Today, at $735 million, the school department's annual budget represents about one-third of the total city operating expenditures.) Prior to this structure, it was not uncommon for past Boston mayors essentially to wash their hands of the public schools, particularly when the district was governed by a thirteen-member elected school committee with little accountability to city hall.

A referendum vote and legislative ordinance in 1991 gave greater control of the schools to the mayor by creating a seven-member appointed school committee. Along with Chicago and a few others, Boston was one of the first large cities in the country to grant greater authority and accountability to the mayor in school reform efforts. The Boston legislation has enabled Mayor Menino to assemble a diverse school committee composed of qualified professionals from business, higher education, human services, and other sectors—many of them BPS parents and alumni—whose interest is in the success of the schools rather than in their own political careers. In 1996, one year after my appointment, voters approved another referendum maintaining the appointed board. This was an important vote of confidence in the mayor, the committee, and the early stages of our reform work. Today, the appointed school committee remains a critical force in the district's reform efforts. Under the leadership of Dr. Elizabeth Reilinger, who has been a member since 1994 and its chair since 1998, the school committee is often lauded as a national model for highly effective urban school boards.

Several authors in this volume acknowledge the enormous impact of this governance structure, and I often have cited it as a major factor in my decision to come to Boston. This triumvirate approach has worked because each of us understands our unique role in moving the district forward, and we have consistently supported and challenged one another in order to get the work done. With more than a decade of consistent leadership, Boston presents a stark contrast to many other urban districts, where rapid turnover of school board members and a three-year average tenure for urban superintendents make long-term reform nearly impossible. The strong and sustained alliance among the mayor, school committee, and superintendent has set the tone for the district to move from fragmentation to coherence. Without this governance structure, I believe that the Boston schools could not have made the progress that they have made over the past decade. Together we have kept the focus on the overarching goals and the needs of families, and put an end to the infighting and political grandstanding that often characterized the district leadership in the past.

A NEW BEGINNING

The 1994 congressional reauthorization of the Elementary and Secondary Education Act was significantly influenced by the standards-based reform movement's philosophy that there should be clear expectations about what children should learn and how that learning would be measured. Moreover, these high standards should apply to *all* students, not just some. This was a radical idea. The new law expected states to set standards in the major curriculum areas and develop tests that assess students' progress in meeting them. The federal funds would continue to be targeted to schools and districts with high concentrations of low-income students. Many opponents feared the federal government would ultimately set the standards and infringe on the states' right to do so, but the new law was very clear about the states' responsibility for standards-setting. Others opposed the idea of setting the same standards for all students, predicting an increase in student dropouts and a decrease in the graduation rate because too many would not make the grade.

In Massachusetts, the Education Reform Act of 1993 was founded on similar standards-based principles and helped set the context and provide substantial funding increases for school improvement in Boston and the rest of the commonwealth. The legislation took dramatic steps to launch a new era of standards-based accountability for public education in Massachusetts, including new curriculum frameworks in all major subject areas, new state assessments aligned with the frameworks, ceding control of all personnel decisions from school committees to superintendents, and making principals part of superintendents' management teams by removing them from labor unions.

With federal and state governments making a renewed commitment to improving public schools, it was time for the capital city of Massachusetts to follow suit. During the 1994–95 school year, Boston began an aggressive search for a new superintendent who would lead the rebirth of the public schools. Mayor Menino and the Boston School Committee—with support from a somewhat skeptical business community who agreed to be part of a targeted reform effort one more time—launched a nationwide search for a superintendent who would make a long-term commitment to lead the district. There was a sense of hope and possibility that the stars finally were aligning and that Boston truly was ready to attract and support a leader willing to take standards-based education to scale throughout the city. After an extensive public review process, I was offered the position and a five-year contract, which was rare in large urban districts and unprecedented in Boston.

In August 1995, two months before I began as superintendent, I appointed a transition team to help me learn about Boston, advise me about key issues facing the Boston Public Schools, and recommend key areas of focus, as well as action steps for the first year. This was a common practice among elected officials but rarely used by educators in leadership positions. Bob Peterkin, a former BPS high school administrator, successful superintendent of schools in Cambridge (Mass.) and Milwaukee, and director of the Urban Superintendents Program at the Harvard Graduate School of Education, agreed to lead the transition team. I gave Bob and the teachers, administrators, parents, and community members who comprised the team a standards-based framework: clear expectations for what students should know and be able to do; a curriculum that provides teachers and students with access to strong, rigorous content; professional development for teachers and principals, focused on improving instruction; and assessments that would produce data useful for understanding what was and was not working as well as for accountability. I directed the team not to view each component as a separate initiative, but rather to make connections among them and ensure that the whole was greater than the sum of its parts. What motivated me as we began our work in Boston was to demonstrate that it is possible to improve a whole system of schools and make a positive difference in the lives of all students if—and *only if*—there is a laser-like focus on the improvement of teaching and learning and a commitment to setting key goals and staying the course to achieve them. In a short time, the transition team presented me with an excellent entry plan that served as a roadmap for the first crucial year of my tenure.

Within one year of my arrival in Boston, I visited every one of the 125 Boston Public Schools. I prioritized these visits in my schedule, usually setting aside two or three days each week to make my way around the city. These visits were essential (1) for me to understand what was happening in schools, and (2) for school leaders and staff to meet me and hear about my vision for reform. Some were surprised when my visits began to include more than a meeting with the principal, a tour of the building, and informal greetings in the hallway. Soon the main purpose of my visits became sitting beside students in classrooms to observe instruction. I wanted to see teachers in action—what and how they were teaching—and to hear from students about what and how they were learning.[2] Many teachers were unaccustomed to the principal observing their classroom, let alone the superintendent. (In fact, I was surprised at the number of teachers who told me they had never seen a superintendent in their school.) The unspoken rule in most schools at the time was that the classroom was the teacher's domain, and that the district's responsibility was to hire the very best, then trust them to do their jobs, usually behind closed doors.

What struck me most on these visits was the tremendous variation from school to school, not only in culture, climate, traditions and rituals, which will typically vary among schools, but in nearly all aspects of teaching and learning. Traveling from one school to the next, one felt little sense that this was a *system* of schools, given the apparent lack of consistency in goals, approach, or educational philosophy. Certainly there was no sense of a K–12 continuum, because elementary, middle, and high schools had little or no awareness about what was taking place at other levels or how they could support and learn from one another. Above all, there was no set of clear expectations about student learning. There were no citywide standards or district curricula in place. No two schools appeared to have shared benchmarks for student achievement, and many had no targets at all. One of the only measures of student performance in use was the Metropolitan Achievement Test, which was ten years old at the time and administered only once a year. It was unclear to me how—if at all—schools studied the results of this assessment to inform their teaching. There was very little evidence of teachers and principals using student attendance, achievement, dropout, and other data to help them understand the effectiveness of teaching and learning and how to improve them. The schools that engaged in some data analysis most often examined entire groups of students, without studying disparities by disaggregating among students of different races, genders, socioeconomic backgrounds, native languages, and educational programs.

Talking to principals, I quickly learned how isolated they often felt from one another, from the central office, and from the city as a whole. In many ways, each school was an island unto itself. Some principals stood out as visionary leaders who had galvanized their school communities into thriving centers of educational excellence. But too many saw themselves as mere administrators of operational tasks: working diligently on lunchroom supervision, bus arrival and dismissal, and student discipline, but with little sense of empowerment or responsibility as the instructional leaders of their buildings.

BUILDING THE FOUNDATION

I insisted at the outset that success could never be defined by improvement among a small group of schools. Rather, our agenda would be to transform *all* schools so that *every* child received a rigorous educational experience in *every* classroom. Our approach would be to identify strategies that worked and take them to scale throughout the district, so that high achievement was not an isolated phenomenon but rather an expectation citywide. We began by putting a plan in place that would foster consistency and collaboration among all schools. Adopted in 1996, the five-year reform plan *Focus on Children* brought standards-based education to Boston. The state's new curriculum framework provided the basis for our own Citywide Learning Standards in all the major subject areas. The school committee adopted new attendance and promotion policies. We introduced new assessments, including the more challenging Stanford 9 Achievement Test, which included open response questions in addition to multiple choice, and began teaching schools how to use the results to improve instruction.

Focus on Children challenged schools to take a "whole-school" approach to student achievement and led to the development of our "Six Essentials of Whole-School Improvement," built on the premise that every child should achieve high standards:

Boston's Six Essentials of Whole-School Improvement

1. Use effective instructional practices and create a collaborative school climate to improve student learning.
2. Examine student work and data to drive instruction and professional development.
3. Invest in professional development to improve instruction.
4. Share leadership to sustain instructional improvement.
5. Focus resources to support instructional improvement and improved student learning.
6. Partner with families and community to support student learning.

(A complete description of the Six Essentials can be found in the Appendix, page 271.)

We began to recast the role of the principal from that of building administrator to instructional leader, charged with galvanizing staff into a team of educators working together to advance the school's academic agenda. Instructional leaders are knowledgeable about teaching and learning, helping teachers improve instruction, and using data to determine what works. In short, they are teachers of teachers. They have to know the work in order to lead the work. Instructional Leadership Teams of teachers and other staff, appointed and led by the principal, began to emerge as the educational nucleus of each school, responsible for devising and monitoring the whole-school improvement plan, which set clear priorities and action steps for improving teaching and learning.

The cornerstone of Boston's reform strategy has been the belief that the key to higher student achievement is improved instruction. For students to perform at higher levels, teachers must engage them in rigorous learning through a challenging curriculum. Therefore the focus of our work has been on the classroom: fostering a culture in which every educator is engaged in ongoing examination of his or her pedagogy and its impact on student learning.

PROFESSIONAL DEVELOPMENT: INVESTING IN PEOPLE

I've often said and firmly believe that people are our most valuable asset. State-of-the-art facilities, thoughtful policies, and robust curricula do not mean a thing without the right people in place to make use of them. As described in several chapters of this book, many of the key reforms in Boston schools have centered on providing adults with ongoing training and support, both to improve the performance of current staff and to groom the next generation of top-notch educators.

Once the Citywide Learning Standards were approved by the school committee in 1996, the challenge was to determine where to begin adopting the curriculum and providing the professional development to support teachers who would teach it. Given that strong reading and writing skills are essential to high achievement in all subject areas, we began with a focus on literacy. New English language arts (ELA) programs required significant multi-year professional development for all elementary teachers and ELA teachers at the secondary level. The cost of districtwide implementation exceeded available dollars, but the Annenberg Foundation's five-year, $10 million grant awarded midway through the 1996–97 school year, and the additional $20 million in required public and private matching funds, provided support for a four-year rollout of our literacy work. We selected a first cohort of schools to pilot the work with our partner organization, the Boston Plan for Excellence, and enabled principals and school staff to select a literacy program from among a menu of six district-identified models. Not surprisingly, it was the most proactive schools that were most eager to get started, and they set a high standard for moving forward aggressively. They led well.

Hindsight is helpful, but the rollout of the literacy work in the remaining cohorts was too slow. Some of the schools most in need of improvement chose to wait until the last cohort and lacked the capacity to choose the program best suited to the needs of the children. In short, I should have accelerated the literacy work; narrowed the program choices, which would have more clearly focused the professional development at less cost; and provided help more quickly to schools that needed it most. Moreover, we could have accelerated the adoption of a citywide math curriculum, which elementary teachers were reluctant to take on when they were still immersed in professional development for literacy programs. We did settle on workshop as the approach to instruction, based on the experience with the first cohort of schools. The pedagogy was student-centered and relied on balance among teacher-directed instruction, small group learning, and independent learning. This pedagogy has been embedded in professional development to support improved instruction since the late 1990s across grade levels and in other content areas. Several years ago, we launched a more intense focus on science instruction, in part to prepare for the tenth grade science MCAS exam soon becoming an additional graduation requirement. New curricula in the sciences have begun to take hold at all levels, and with continued investment in materials and teacher training, Boston is poised to make gains in science comparable to those in the other major content areas.

It is important to listen to teachers reflect on what type of professional development enables them to improve their instruction in the classroom. Teachers are quite frank about where they need help with content, and they generally welcome professional development that meets those needs, but only if it connects to the work that they do in the classroom with the students. When the conversation shifts from the content to be taught to how to teach it, the dynamics become more complicated. For decades we have structured schools, schedules, and practices in ways that belie the work of professionals in other fields, who routinely observe, discuss, and critique the work of their colleagues as they reflect on their professional practice and learn from one another. Teachers spend most of their day left alone to do their work in classrooms behind closed doors with their students. Engagement with colleagues was often limited to a few minutes over lunch in the teachers' lounge and perhaps during a planning period. Professional development programs traditionally built in little time for interaction, group dialogue, or shared projects.

Boston's Collaborative Coaching and Learning (CCL) program is changing the way in which teachers are learning together, sharing best practices, reviewing student data, and reflecting on their instruction. They are doing so with coaches in collaborative groups of colleagues. They are learning from one another and validating their work as professionals. In many schools, teachers are creating leadership opportunities through instructional leadership teams, participation in writing the school plan, facilitating common planning time, supporting new teachers, and engaging families. This shift is changing the instructional culture from one of isolation and separation to one of collaboration and engagement.

With schools and central offices providing such an extensive array of professional development opportunities, it is essential to ensure coherence across the district. Boston's significant investment in professional development has not been accompanied by a districtwide set of standards for aligning content and evaluating effectiveness. Efforts to improve coordination and accountability have begun with the creation of the Institute for Professional Development (IPD), but the responsibility for oversight of *all* professional development has not yet been consolidated into this unit. Doing so would greatly improve the district's ability to measure the cost-effectiveness of its investments in various approaches to staff training and development.

DISTRICT REFORM

For Boston's school-based strategies to succeed, we also had to take a close look at the structure and function of the district itself, particularly the role of central offices in supporting schools. We had to build a sound infrastructure on both the operations and teaching and learning sides of the house, ensuring relevant, cost-effective, accountable services to schools and families. Just as schools have improved at different paces, some central offices have been quicker to reinvent themselves than others. Some required more urgent intervention and more significant investment in order to effect meaningful change. Of course, most important infrastructure improvements will require a cross-functional approach involving several central offices and, in some cases, labor unions, partner organizations, and the community.

Central Support

The organization I inherited in 1995 had several layers of administration between the superintendent and the schools. The transition team made clear to me then that the principals—who reported to assistant superintendents for elementary, middle, and high schools—felt disconnected from the superintendent. The assistant superintendents reported to a deputy superintendent, who was one of several members of a senior leadership group that reported to the superintendent. My reorganization plan eliminated the level offices (elementary, middle, and high) and had the principals report directly to the superintendent. This was an important symbolic step based on my belief that principals are one of the most important factors in our systemic plan to improve schools and raise student achievement, and that the district had to adopt a K–12 mentality to replace outdated division among elementary, middle, and high schools.

For the first eighteen months of my tenure, Janice Jackson (my first deputy superintendent) and I shared the responsibility of having 125 direct reports. Therefore, the bulk of our time was spent on supervising and supporting school leaders and on developing the *Focus on Children* reform plan, leaving little time and focus on the reorganization of the central offices. In retrospect, perhaps I should have made changing the culture of "Court Street" (as district headquarters is called) a higher priority in the early years. I did make some important personnel decisions by appointing a new chief financial officer at the end of my first year and by creating separate teaching and learning and operations divisions, each with strong new leadership, by the end of my third year. It took me too long to make the right leadership decisions to build much-needed capacity in Human Resources, but I was blessed to inherit a small but well-led and effective Research, Assessment, and Evaluation office.

The next superintendent of the Boston Public Schools will have a valuable opportunity to review and improve the organization of the central office and build on its much-improved record of serving the schools. Some of the chapters in this book, as well as other recent studies, recommend particular changes to the BPS organization chart, including the creation of a chief academic officer position to promote alignment and accountability in the teaching and learning supports for schools, and this proposal merits further exploration. In my experience, however, having the right organizational design is not sufficient. It takes talented, committed, effective, and accountable people for an organization to get the results intended. During my career, sometimes I have modified the organizational structure to align with the strengths of some exceptional staff members rather than embrace an organizational structure based on tested organizational theory that did not align well with the current political context and strengths of available staff. The challenge for any leader is to make sure that getting the right people in place is not stifled by the organizational structure, or that the potential of the organizational structure is not compromised by the leader's failure to make tough personnel decisions and remove those who stand in the way of improvement.

High School Renewal

As noted elsewhere, student performance at the high school level presented one of the greatest challenges for the district and resulted in one of our most targeted series of reform strategies. Earlier in this chapter, I described the loss of accreditation at the Burke High School, but this school was by no means alone with its low attendance rate, high dropout rate, and declining student performance. By the 1990s, it was clear that the large comprehensive district high schools in particular were in dire need of restructuring.

Since then, every district high school has been reconfigured, primarily into one of two models. Several former large schools were closed and reopened as autonomous small schools in a shared building, each serving fewer than four hundred students in grades 9 through 12, and each with its own staff, theme, budget, schedule, and course structure. In 1995, only six out of twenty-one Boston high schools (28%) enrolled fewer than four hundred students; ten years later, twenty-seven out of thirty-eight high schools (71%) enrolled four hundred or fewer students. Other large high schools have been reorganized into small learning communities with a more conventional administrative structure in which students spend nearly 85 percent of their day with a particular group of teachers and the balance of their school day in elective courses offered building-wide. The high school renewal work would not have been possible without strong support from Carnegie Corporation and the Bill & Melinda Gates Foundation, the local Barr and Boston foundations, and key local partners who helped shape and execute the restructuring.

We know that restructuring alone will not result in better relationships among adults and students unless the schools capitalize on what being "small" can provide—smaller classes, fewer students, proximity, and reduced chances that students or faculty will be merely a cipher who is ignored at best or soon forgotten. The early evidence is that these smaller, more personalized settings are helping to improve the climate for learning and the quality of instruction, creating schools where adults and students want to teach and learn, and where instruction is rigorous in every classroom and every subject area. Above all, this approach to reducing students' sense of anonymity or alienation is designed to curb the persistent dropout rate, which remains a major challenge in Boston and other urban school districts. Work has begun in the district to take a much more data-driven approach to this problem, with a focus on early indicators of students at risk of dropping out. These analyses will provide valuable data that the district and community must act on together to ensure that all students remain in school and earn a high school diploma.

As for the Burke High School, after a major investment in both the facility and academic programs, the school regained its accreditation in 1998. Four years later, the College Board awarded the school its distinguished Inspiration Award, in part because every member of the graduating class had been accepted to a two- or four-year college. The school that was once the symbol of the district's decline has now become a symbol of its rebirth.

Early Childhood Education

At the other end of the spectrum, Boston also has invested heavily in the youngest students—those just beginning their educational careers in the BPS. Research has validated the effectiveness of early childhood education in narrowing achievement gaps, and Boston has emerged as a leader in providing access to such programs. In 1998, the district began offering guaranteed full-day kindergarten to any five-year-old in the city. That same year, we opened three new state-of-the-art early education centers that provide developmentally appropriate education programs during an extended day to students ranging from ages three to six, including many students with disabilities. Mayor Menino also launched Countdown to Kindergarten, an innovative public-private partnership with local children's educational and health and human services providers to help families prepare for the academic and social transition to kindergarten, so that students would begin their formal schooling more ready to learn.

More recently, the district has expanded preschool offerings to four-year-old students. In 1994, fewer than seven hundred "Kindergarten 1" (or K1) seats were available for four-year-olds. By September 2007, the district will offer more than 1,700 seats, and the expansion will continue until Mayor Menino's commitment to provide a K1 seat for every child in Boston by 2010 is fulfilled. This expansion is coupled with a more coherent approach to early childhood education in which programs and staff members are consolidated into a new central office charged with examining capacity as well as standards, curriculum, and accreditation of preschool programs.

In addition to these targeted strategies for our youngest and oldest students, BPS must now be equally creative in meeting the needs of all the students in between. I remain particularly concerned about the middle schools, where achievement has not improved as dramatically as in the elementary and high schools. For these young adolescents, we must continue to create afterschool programs and other opportunities for learning and enrichment beyond the traditional school day. Three Boston middle schools are piloting a new extended day schedule this year, and it will be important to measure the effectiveness of that experiment. Similarly, at all levels, we must take a more comprehensive approach to supporting students and families, finding creative ways to work with community health and human service providers to address the broad range of needs prevalent among low-income urban families. The full-service schools movement is providing critical leadership in this area, challenging schools and communities to develop students who are academically proficient as well as physically, emotionally, and socially healthy.

Leadership Development

My understanding of leadership has been shaped by experience. Reflection about my own and others' mistakes and successes has required continuous learning, a willingness to give others permission to tell me what I may not want to hear but need to know, understanding that data are my friends, and being thick-skinned but not insensitive.

By the standards of the late 1960s and the 1970s, I was a nontraditional educational leader. My undergraduate major was American history and literature, and I did not take an education course until I entered the Master of Arts in Teaching program at the Harvard Graduate School of Education in 1962. (Even in that program, half of my classes were history courses offered by the faculty of Arts and Sciences.) My teaching experience totaled two and a half years when I returned to Harvard in the Administrative Career Program, which required two years of graduate study in residence at Harvard and a dissertation to qualify for an EdD. There were three of us in our cohort of thirteen doctoral students who were twenty-five years old. The others were ten or fifteen years older and had administrative experience.

My first position following my two years at Harvard was as administrative assistant to Carl Dolce, the superintendent of the New Orleans Public Schools. In many ways it was the best job I ever had. I got to see firsthand every aspect of a large urban school district. In short, the superintendent was a superb mentor who let me get involved in—or at least observe—just about everything. I was able to finish my dissertation the first year in New Orleans (1967–68) and take on more responsibility during my second year. When the superintendent announced that he was leaving at the end of the school year, I was faced with the challenge of finding a job and probably moving from New Orleans with my wife and three children, the youngest of whom was born there in the spring of 1969 during a teachers strike.

It was good luck, and the strong support of my mentor superintendent, several Harvard professors, and a nine-member elected school board that led me to Springfield, Pennsylvania, a suburb of Philadelphia that wanted a nontraditional superintendent to lead the way. I reported to my first superintendency in August of 1969, four months before my twenty-ninth birthday. It was a big risk for the board to hire me, and a big risk for me to take the job, but I believed I could do it if I were given the chance. I served as an "at will" employee and have had one-, two-, three-, and four-year contracts as a superintendent. My first five-year contract was in Boston, twenty-six years after I began my first superintendency. Ironically, most people today would consider me a superintendent with a traditional education background—and compared to the former private sector CEOs, governors, generals, and admirals who are being hired to lead big-city school districts, that is true. Whether searching for a superintendent, principal, or other leader, I believe there is no single career path or résumé that one must seek. Rather, the particular needs of the organization determine what sort of leader is needed, and what sort of skills and experience he or she must bring to the position.

I have often said that next to instruction, school leadership is the most important lever for improving student achievement, and of course these levers are inextricably linked. I believe that leaders have to know instruction to lead the work in schools and school districts. I also believe it is possible to learn how to be an instructional leader as a principal and superintendent if one is willing to do so. Aspiring leaders need mentors, challenging leadership development programs, and internships in which they can shadow successful leaders, as well as their own opportunities to lead. Most school and district leaders who were trained in the 1960s, '70s, and '80s were expected to be good managers, skilled at operations, and politically savvy.

Standards-based reform changed the expectations and requirements for leaders in schools and districts. The research became clearer that the most important school variable affecting student achievement is the quality of instruction. Therefore, good leaders have to understand how to help those they lead improve instruction. Increasingly, there is evidence that the best way to improve instruction is to support teachers as they learn in collaboration with one another.

The leadership development programs now offered through the BPS School Leadership Institute—most notably the Boston Principals Fellows program—prepare new cadres of graduates who will:

- be strong leaders of instruction;
- collect, analyze, understand, and use data for informed decision making, reflection on what works and what does not work, the improvement of instruction, the assessment of progress, and accountability;
- support and participate in professional development that engages teachers and coaches in collaborative learning about instruction and curriculum;

- model positive ways to communicate and develop healthy relationships among school staff and students;
- align financial and human resources to support the district and individual schools' improvement plans; and
- make engagement of families and community a priority for the entire staff.

Of course, leadership is not a role for central office and school principals alone. One of the positive outcomes of the instructional leadership teams that now exist in every Boston public school is the opportunity for teachers to take on roles as leaders of curriculum areas, coaches, teams of intern teachers, teacher developers, or other emerging roles. Boston has begun to find more opportunities for teachers to assume leadership while staying connected to students in the classroom and without necessarily aspiring to administrative roles. This trend to expand career ladder opportunities within the teaching profession must continue in order to retain skilled teachers.

In the Boston Public Schools, an aggressive effort is underway and must be accelerated to recruit, hire, induct, train, support, and retain more teachers and administrators of color. Dramatic improvements have been made to increase the diversity of BPS principals, who are now 65 percent leaders of color. Boston is holding its own in a very competitive market for teachers of color—now 41 percent in BPS—in a shrinking national market. Boston's senior leadership team is more diverse than those found in most urban school districts. Continuing and expanding these leadership development efforts will require determination and persistence.

It is advantageous for the field of public education to have leaders with traditional experience in schools and districts, as well as those with proven leadership skill from other professions. Organizations generally do not thrive with leaders who are all "insiders" or only those who come from outside the organization. In Boston, programs like the Broad Residents, Boston Teacher Residency, and Boston Principal Fellows are attracting and cultivating a healthy mix of both. These efforts, coupled with the reinvention of the district's Human Resources office, are helping the Boston Public Schools recruit and grow the next generation of educators and leaders with an impressive range of skills and experiences.

Family and Community Engagement

Two years ago, as we launched a sharper focus on closing the achievement gap, I used a visual representation adapted from the work of Dr. Ronald Ferguson at Harvard's Kennedy School of Government: an equilateral triangle, with each of its points representing a critical lever in improving student achievement—*curriculum*, *instruction*, and at the pinnacle, *relationships*. Our focus on curriculum and instruction had solid footing by this time, but we had not been as explicit about the importance of healthy relationships in closing the achievement gap. Several years ago, with the help of adults, a group of student researchers developed a school climate survey and administered it to their peers in thirteen Boston high schools. The data from the surveys provided powerful evidence that intentional efforts to focus on the quality of adult and student relationships were necessary to support improvement of curriculum and instruction. Periodic surveys that assess school climate should be administered regularly to generate data about the quality of relationships and the extent to which students and adults see their schools as safe, welcoming, supportive places to teach and learn. I challenged every school in the district to embrace this notion that these three areas deserved constant examination and attention: rigorous content, first-rate pedagogy, and a healthy school climate rooted in strong interpersonal connections among students and adults. A school staff that works to improve each of these priorities and understands the connections among them is poised to create a culture of high expectations and high achievement.

We also know, however, that educators and students alone cannot close the achievement gap. Research and our own experience tell us that students' parents and other family members have a critical role to play in supporting and reinforcing the learning that takes place in school, and therefore the relationships between schools and families are crucial. Most families and educators will agree that they need each other and must share the great responsibility of educating children. Generally, there is agreement that the parent is indeed the child's first teacher, and the schools alone cannot educate children to the fullest. And so the debate begins: Who has what responsibility? Where does accountability belong, and in what forms? These questions are particularly complex when the achievement gap comes up for discussion, with finger-pointing and defensiveness likely to arise. Parents send their children to the public schools with expectations that they will learn and succeed, but some educators believe they can get better results only if parents send children better prepared to meet the expectations of the schools. Issues of race and class often dominate the subtext, which can create feelings of alienation and disrespect on all sides. Moreover, the cultural norms shaped by white middle class values in most American public schools sometimes clash with those held by the families we serve—many of whom have emigrated to the United States and struggle to maintain their language and culture while aspiring to benefit from the opportunities that America has to offer.

In that context, Boston schools have been fostering a paradigm shift in the realm of family and community engagement. For too long, successful parent involvement was measured in terms of turnout at report card nights or representation on school parent councils. Surely both of those are strong indicators of healthy home-school ties, but the connections cannot end there. Rather, we must find creative ways to engage families in the very heart of the matter—teaching and learning—if we are to help children achieve at higher levels.

Boston's approach, then, has been to make parents true partners in their children's academic experience, to educate and engage families in the issues of standards, curriculum, assessments, and homework, all in language and content that are relevant and accessible. Often that is no small feat, particularly if the parent's own experience of school was not positive or affirming, or if the parent had little or no formal schooling at all.

To support schools in this essential endeavor, the district reinvented the Family and Community Engagement team. Once focused largely on conflict resolution and negotiation with paid advocates, its mission is now centered on helping schools make parents partners in their children's education. Boston was one of the first urban districts to create the position of deputy superintendent for Family and Community Engagement, overseeing a team that provides training to schools and parents, fosters parent participation in school-based management, and supports a growing network of parent engagement coordinators who work directly in schools. The model is proving successful in bridging the divide between home and school, with educators, parents, and students discovering the benefits of improved communication and cooperation. The continuing challenge is to take the best practices of family and community engagement to scale throughout the district.

These efforts go hand-in-hand with the district's more strategic approach to communications. Just as schools need families to be involved in their children's education, the school system needs the ongoing support and investment of the community in order to achieve its educational goals. Therefore it is essential that citizens, taxpayers, funders, partners, media, elected officials, opinion leaders, and countless others are aware of the state of the city schools, both their progress and their challenges moving forward. To strengthen the lines of communication between the district and the community, we launched in 2005 a multifaceted strategic communications initiative and appointed the district's first chief communications officer to lead the work. The initiative is rooted in the premise that improving communication is not separate from the teaching and learning agenda, but rather, essential to its success. Only when we do a better job of telling our story and identifying our gaps can we foster the confidence and investment needed to achieve our educational goals.

Evaluation of District Initiatives

With so many systemic reforms taking place at the same time throughout the district, one cannot easily isolate which efforts are having the most—or least—impact on improving student outcomes and closing the achievement gap. There is no easy answer to this challenge, but the school committee and others are right to push during the annual budget development process the question of effectiveness, or in private sector terms, "return on investment." School districts must become better equipped to answer such key questions by devising more credible means of evaluating district initiatives. Until then, superintendents will have to continue to rely on anecdotal evidence or informed speculation about which programs and services make a difference, and which do not. Boston's selection as the first school district in the nation to participate in the Strategic Education Research Partnership (SERP) project creates a valuable opportunity in this arena. The SERP Boston Field Site project will explore the relationships among educational research, policy, and practice using Boston as a case study, and its findings are likely to have implications both locally and nationally.

STUDENT ASSIGNMENT AND CHANGING DEMOGRAPHICS

No analysis of the Boston Public Schools is complete without reference to the volatile issue of student assignment. Ever since court-ordered desegregation busing began in 1974, issues of race, class, and equity have simmered beneath the surface of nearly every issue in the district. The evolution of school choice in Boston is far too complex to address with any depth in this volume. Coupled with ongoing debates about the admissions policy for the city's three public exam schools, the issue of student assignment remained one of the most politically charged matters throughout my tenure in Boston.

I believe the school choice process is better today than it was just a few years ago. Certainly there are those on all sides of the debate who continue to point to the shortcomings of the student assignment policy, not the least of which is the $68 million annual transportation budget. But as a city, we all can be proud of the more-than-year-long public engagement process, led by a community-based task force, to gather the viewpoints of parents and citizens in order to determine how the policy should be modified, if at all. After dozens of community forums, focus groups, surveys, and meetings, the task force recommended in 2004 a series of policy and procedural changes that would improve families' experiences of applying to the Boston Public Schools. Since then, the school committee has adopted many of the recommendations, designed to improve families' access to a wide variety of educational programs throughout the city. What the public engagement campaign affirmed, above all else, was the strong interest among all families of every race and income level, from every neighborhood of the city, in improving the quality of schools. They argued that if every school were to provide an equally outstanding education, the issue of where students are assigned might someday become almost irrelevant.

Boston's changing demographics and the district's gradually improving reputation present opportunities to attract families into the Boston Public Schools who might otherwise pursue other educational options. These prospective BPS parents include middle-class families who may be able to afford private or parochial schooling (or who might move out of Boston altogether in pursuit of suburban public education), as well as low-income families who have access to an increasing number of free public charter schools. In several neighborhoods of Boston, groups of middle-class families have chosen to "adopt" a lesser-known school, forming a coalition of sorts to send their children to the school and becoming active players in its reform. As a result, some of these schools have made tremendous gains and are now among the most sought after in the district. Every school in the city deserves that level of support to reach its full potential. A partnership between the district and the YMCA called Y/BPS—as in, "Why [choose] BPS?"—is encouraging middle-class Boston families of all races to take a closer look at what Boston Public Schools has to offer. The program takes a grassroots approach to engaging prospective families, encouraging current BPS parents to talk to their neighbors and peers in living rooms and other informal settings to answer questions and debunk myths about urban public schools. Preliminary studies show that these efforts are making a positive difference.

Every urban school district and increasingly more suburban districts must address the issues of race and class as diversity becomes more prevalent in major metropolitan areas. I confronted these issues in each of my superintendencies, and of course the context is different in each city. I was not a stranger to Boston's history because I was born there and spent most of the first twenty-five years of my life in the area. I left Boston in 1967 and did not return until 1995, although I followed from afar the evolving history of the city during the almost three decades I was away. Certainly the challenges the city faced with court-ordered desegregation beginning in the 1970s cannot be ignored, but I contend that it is not helpful to begin the conversation about race and class in Boston as if the context in 2006 were the same as it was in 1974. Yes, Boston was defined as a black/white city in the 1970s, but it is now a city defined by racial, ethnic, cultural, religious, and language diversity that presents many challenges and wonderful opportunities. The new Boston is an international city, and the important issues of race and class must be discussed in this context.

One needs only to look at the 2006 valedictorians of the thirty-eight Boston public high schools and learn that nearly half were born outside of the United States in twelve different countries to understand the importance of public education in America. We must recapture with a sense of urgency the belief in the purpose of public education first championed by Horace Mann here in Massachusetts in the nineteenth century. In a democratic society, public education exists to serve the common good. The public schools must serve all children and turn none away. Standards-based reform challenges the practice of sorting and sifting students. Instead, it recognizes that access to opportunity requires graduation from high school with a diploma that certifies readiness for continuing education. No longer is a high school diploma sufficient to qualify for anything other than a low-skill, low-paying job. Few safety nets exist for high school dropouts or even graduates unprepared to do post-secondary school work. That is why helping all students reach high standards and leaving no child behind are the right goals.

ASSESSMENT AND ACCOUNTABILITY

Boston Public Schools understands the importance of collecting data and making it accessible to teachers and administrators. Equipped with a variety of indicators of student performance, educators are better able to identify the strengths and weaknesses of curriculum and instruction and guide their decision making about necessary changes. Data are, of course, also key to accountability, to help students, families and the public understand how students, schools, and the district are performing. With the strong support of the mayor and school committee, BPS made significant upgrades in its technology beginning in the late 1990s. In fact, BPS became the first large urban school district to wire all schools to the Internet. MyBPS, the district's intranet portal, provides teachers and administrators with easy access to streams of student data from MCAS and other information of all kinds, including both raw data as well as customized reports to help analyze and illuminate trends in student performance.

Even before the enactment of the federal No Child Left Behind (NCLB) legislation, BPS had its own assessment and accountability system, with data disaggregated by race, gender, and other indicators. Schools and the superintendent had annual improvement targets for student achievement and closing the gap. The accountability systems also included a qualitative component, which required an in-depth review team to visit each school every four years, study the whole-school improvement plan, observe classrooms, and evaluate the school against a rubric of qualitative as well as quantitative indicators rooted in the Six Essentials of whole-school improvement. Attention to the qualitative indicators enhanced understanding of why student achievement was and was not improving.

Clearly there is much controversy about NCLB. Critics believe that the law requires too much testing and that pressure for results leads teachers to teach to the test. Massachusetts is one of the states that requires students to pass the tenth grade English language arts and mathematics assessment to graduate. Those opposed to the requirement have fought unsuccessfully to have it removed. The claim was that it was unfair, particularly to black and Hispanic students, English-language learners, and special education students who had not received the support necessary to prepare them for the MCAS challenge. In my view, it would have been a disaster to remove the requirement. Without it, the sense of urgency to provide extra support for those who failed, primarily urban students of color, would have disappeared and perpetuated the practice of awarding diplomas to those who were unprepared to continue their education beyond high school.

The story of the BPS class of 2003—the first to face the new graduation requirement—is remarkable. When these students were sophomores in 2001, only 40 percent passed both the ELA and math MCAS. By June of 2003, almost 80 percent had passed both and graduated. In December of 2003, BPS held its first citywide graduation, awarding diplomas to several hundred additional students who met the graduation requirement by passing retests in the summer and fall. Since then, each subsequent class has outperformed the one before it. The results of the Spring 2006 tenth grade MCAS reveal passing rates among Boston students at 78 percent in math and 86 percent in ELA. Even more encouraging are the improvements in students scoring at the two highest levels, proficient and advanced—53 percent in math and 51 percent in ELA. The gains in the two highest scoring levels are particularly telling, given that the MCAS standard of proficiency is among the most rigorous in the country and the most realistic based on what skills high school graduates should have to be ready for postsecondary education.

The most frustrating aspect of NCLB is the glib and inaccurate comparisons that result from the wide variation in state standards, the rigor of the assessments, and the scores required to reach proficiency. To provide more appropriate comparisons, several years ago Boston joined nine other urban school districts as part of a trial that released district-level National Assessment of Education Progress (NAEP) scores, not just state scores. The 2005 Boston results showed improvement rates in math greater than the other participating urban districts, and Massachusetts as a state led the country in performance in both reading and mathematics.

This is not the place to attempt a full review of NCLB. One of my greatest concerns is the calculation of adequate yearly progress (AYP), and the resulting improvement designations, that give a school or district the same label whether it has failed to make adequate yearly progress in one category or many among dozens against which improvement is measured. This one-size-fits-all label confuses parents and the public and more often than not spawns judgments that all schools not making AYP are "failing schools" with inadequate teachers and leaders. There must be changes that result in fair identification of truly failing schools and those that may have to make improvements in a few key areas.

The accountability aspects of NCLB also underscore the need for value-added assessments. A few states and school districts have adopted assessments that are used to measure the growth or improvement in student achievement from one year to the next. These assessments provide a better guide for schools to determine strengths and weaknesses in curriculum and instruction as well as acknowledge the impact of student mobility and stability in classrooms, schools and school districts. These assessments are more costly, but they will be worth the investment in terms of strengthening the information that educators, families, and communities have, and allowing more accurate and fair comparisons among schools and districts.

In this age of accountability, it must be made clear to students that they are being assessed on what they have been taught and have had the opportunity to learn. Adults, too, deserve to know how their performance will be judged.

Targets for improvement must be transparent and fair, and care must be taken to judge the quality of programs based on the fidelity of implementation as well as the results of student assessments. In political circles, rhetoric about accountability and its use as a hammer to improve adult and student performance must be accompanied by the financial resources needed to support improvement. Federal, state, and local policymakers must understand this dynamic and act accordingly.

LABOR-MANAGEMENT COOPERATION

In 1963, I began my first full-time teaching position as a junior high school Social Studies teacher in Tacoma, Washington. That teaching experience shaped my deep respect for teachers and teaching, which has been validated time and again during my thirty-five years as a superintendent. When I reported for my first official day of work at the auditorium of one of the large Tacoma high schools to hear the superintendent speak to all of the teachers, I was greeted first by a representative of the teachers association and invited to fill out my membership card. The association was affiliated with the National Education Association (NEA) and was eager to sign up new teachers. I became a member that day. It was a time when public employee collective bargaining was emerging, and some states were starting to formalize legislation granting collective bargaining rights to teachers. The American Federation of Teachers (AFT) was taking the lead in the early 1960s, and Al Shanker and the New York City teachers union set the early standard with its first teachers' contract. The NEA was slower to embrace collective bargaining because it was a professional association and not a union, a distinction that would disappear in time. I was quite skeptical about teachers unionizing, but I was impressed with the political savvy of the local teachers association. I was asked to travel to Olympia, the state capital, with a group of teachers to visit with my state representative and senator to discuss education issues a few weeks after I began teaching, and I was expected to stay in touch with them through the year. Political action was expected through involvement in campaigns and elections. When Lyndon Johnson defeated Barry Goldwater in the 1964 presidential race, my wife Ellen and I called in the results from our neighborhood precinct.

While I was a doctoral student at Harvard in 1966, I decided to write my qualifying paper on the public employee collective bargaining bill that the Massachusetts legislature had passed just one year earlier. At that time, I could not have imagined the extent to which public employee collective bargaining would affect my personal and professional life as a superintendent. It was all so new in the mid-1960s, but two of my doctoral student colleagues and I thought we knew enough to run workshops for teachers who were preparing to serve on teacher collective bargaining teams in local school districts. The Massachusetts Teachers Association (MTA) hired us to run the workshop, which helped pay some of our graduate student bills. For the remainder of my professional life, I would be on the other side of the bargaining table.

Forty years later, I've survived thousands of hours in contract negotiations in five different states, two teacher strikes, and several narrowly averted teacher strikes. My family and I have witnessed pickets at our house, seen teachers wearing "Payzant Buster" buttons in classrooms where my children were learning, and even having our own children cross picket lines to go to school during a strike. Through all of those storms, I still believe public school teachers should have a right to bargain the terms and conditions of their employment. However, I object to the broadening scope of bargaining that often results in contracts containing two hundred or more pages of work rules that limit the flexibility necessary to address the needs of students. Too often I have found myself at odds with union leaders determined to protect the working conditions of their members at the expense of legitimate reforms needed to transform schools for the benefit of children.

Teachers and other school system employees have been served well by their unions, but I believe that the time is fast approaching when public sector unions will face the same challenges the private sector unions have been experiencing in recent years. The costs of public sector employees' pensions and health insurance benefits continue to soar. These benefits are often viewed by the union as entitlements rather than as a piece of a total compensation package. Work rules that constrain the flexibility to create school schedules, assign staff, and provide professional development must be reformed. Just as principals are now nonunion employees in Massachusetts, other school administrators should be removed from collective bargaining as well. This will not happen if every school district is expected to negotiate these changes with its local unions. State legislatures must recognize the need to make these changes to restore more balance between the rights of school district employees and the obligation that school districts and schools have to meet the needs of their students.

In Boston, the teachers union and the district have collaborated on a number of important reforms that serve as models for labor-management innovation. Shortly before my arrival in Boston, the school committee and the Boston Teachers Union negotiated a groundbreaking contract that created, among other reforms, both school-based management and Pilot Schools. School-based management created in every building a school site council composed of teachers elected by the union and parents elected by the school parent council, co-chaired by the principal, and open to community members and (at the high school level) student members as well. This approach fostered more widespread involvement in decision making on matters left to the discretion of each school, such as hiring and some budget and policy issues.

The contract also created the district's first Pilot Schools, an innovation that would gain national attention for Boston in the years ahead. This model—a successful collaboration between the district and the teachers union—emerged in response to the growth of charter schools. In Massachusetts, charters are granted by the State Board of Education. The district has no control over the governance of these schools and must remit tuition to the state for every Boston student enrolled in them. Boston created the new Pilot Schools as "in-district charter schools," to be part of the system and funded by the city but free from many district and union regulations. The Pilot Schools have autonomy over many aspects of curriculum, hiring, budget, and schedule, with community-led governing boards that set school policy and hire school leaders. They were designed to be laboratories of innovation whose best practices would serve as models for other reform efforts in the district. In September 2006, Boston opened its twentieth Pilot School. Most Pilot Schools have performed as well or better than the district average on many indicators of student success, and the schools have proven to be very popular among parents. There is agreement with the union to expand the Pilot School network in the years ahead, and to share and replicate its best practices in non–Pilot Schools.

These and other agreements between the city and the teachers union—including a recent overhaul of the district's mentoring model for supporting new teachers—demonstrate what can be accomplished when both sides come together committed to improving student outcomes above all else. During negotiations for the next teachers' contract, this sense of shared purpose is particularly vital in devising a bold new approach to transforming underperforming schools, giving these schools the flexibility they need to make dramatic improvements in a short period of time. Perhaps more than any other area, it is in collective bargaining that I hope Boston can emerge as a true pioneer in public education, as one of the districts where district officials and union leadership come together as professionals with unprecedented collaboration and innovation to focus on the improvement of student achievement.

THE PROMISE OF SUSTAINABILITY

During this time of transition, there has been much talk about sustainability. Those who acknowledge the gains we have made in changing the culture of schools and the district appropriately ask whether these gains have traction, or whether they are likely to diminish with a change in administration. It is because of our significant investment in professional development and leadership that I have confidence these reforms will, in fact, be sustained. At both the school and classroom level, the principles of standards-based reform have become embedded. This is true in part because we have shifted the notion of professional development from an event—usually off-site and often disconnected to the school day—to an ongoing process that is school-based, highly interactive, and firmly rooted in the real-life context of the classroom. The district's School Leadership Institute, which includes both the Boston Teacher Residency and Boston Principal Fellows programs, is grooming the next generation of educators and school leaders trained in the Boston approach to teaching and learning. These programs successfully combine academic learning with practical experience in schools and classrooms. As noted above, the stability provided by a longstanding mayor and his appointed school committee also help ensure that reforms do not come and go with each new administration.

I am sure of at least one conclusion based on my own experience: Improving a whole system of schools cannot be done quickly with district and school leaders and governing bodies that are short-timers. I have made mistakes—and, I hope, have learned from them—but the improvements made for students are the result of countless teachers, administrators, central and support staff, students, families, the mayor, school committee, and community partners signing on for the long haul. With a mind open to continuous learning, continuity of executive and governance leadership, and shared goals, it is possible for urban school systems to be transformed. Here in Boston, there is compelling evidence that we have begun to do just that.

Despite these encouraging signs of progress, there is no time to rest. To ensure that this success is extended to all students in every school, Boston (and perhaps other cities around the country) must sustain several key elements and continue to make the connections among them:

1. Consistent goals: the focus on carrying out standards-based reform, acceleration of improved student achievement, and closing the achievement gap, particularly by improving the performance of black and Hispanic students, English-language learners, and students with disabilities; in short, a laser-like focus on teaching and learning
2. Stable political support from the mayor and appointed school committee
3. Ongoing support for whole-school improvement and the Six Essentials
4. Leadership development for teachers, administrators, and central office staff
5. Continued investment in high school renewal

Just as I cautioned my transition team eleven years ago, we must be careful not to view these as a laundry list of independent initiatives, but rather a series of interconnected levers that must be addressed in concert in order to attain the key goals of schools and the district.

CONCLUSION

At the time of my retirement, I received numerous letters and e-mails from friends and colleagues, and I am grateful for all of them. One in particular, however, meant a great to deal to me. It was a card from members of the Boston Student Advisory Council (BSAC), a citywide student leadership organization with members from every public high school in the city. In order to include student voices in the district's decision making process, the school committee and I had worked closely with this group on several policy issues, and I met with them periodically throughout the year. They are an impressive group of young leaders who approach complex educational issues with intelligence, maturity, and diplomacy. In their well wishes to me, the students reflected on our work together and commented on the value of being at the table to have a say in the decisions that affect their schools and their lives. Some of the seniors in the group, who were only in second grade when I arrived in Boston in 1995, wrote with great pride about being students in the Boston Public Schools. The students noted how much they value their education and how much they appreciate the improvements in their schools to prepare them for success after high school. The students' words provide compelling evidence that meaningful reform of large urban school districts can, in fact, be done. Test scores, graduation rates, and other indicators are important measures of our progress, but none is as powerful as the testimony of students themselves.

Each of these students—only a handful among the more than 100,000 enrolled during my tenure—has a unique story to tell. Each came to our schools with different strengths and challenges, different backgrounds and circumstances. This book describes many of our efforts to help build a better life for these young people and those who will follow, efforts to ensure that when they leave our schools, they are better prepared than when they arrived to reach all of their academic and personal aspirations. All of us in Boston can be very proud of the progress we have made for the sake of these students and their families. There is no question that much work remains to be done and that the road ahead will be long and winding, with formidable obstacles along the way. All of us can find comfort and strength, however, in knowing that the road the Boston Public Schools is on is the right road. The progress in Boston suggests that although we as a district don't have all the answers, we are better positioned than ever before to reach our full potential as a school district and as a world-class city.

Appendix

Boston Public Schools Whole-School Improvement

The Six Essentials

BOSTON'S PUBLIC SCHOOLS are engaged in an ongoing effort to improve instruction in every classroom and to support every student to reach proficiency. That effort, WHOLE-SCHOOL IMPROVEMENT, is organized around six ESSENTIALS, which provide a framework for the work.

THE CORE ESSENTIAL: EFFECTIVE INSTRUCTION

Use effective instructional practices and create a collaborative school climate to improve student learning

Expectations for Schools

- In every classroom, teachers use an inquiry-based approach — workshop instruction — that is organized in the following way:
  - Mini-lesson/Objective: The teacher presents and/or models the day's learning objective — a standards-based fact, concept, strategy, or skill (approximately 20% of class time, which includes a "Do Now" task, five-minute warm-up, or review of the previous day's work)
  - Independent Work: Individually or in small groups, students apply the learning objective to their reading, writing, or other work, while the teacher confers with some students about the learning objective (approximately 60% of class time)
  - Share/Summing Up: The teacher sums up the learning objective, and students discuss how they used it in their work (approximately 20% of class time)
- During class and in every subject, students read, write, and solve problems regularly, doing work of high cognitive demand to help them reach proficiency.
- The school uses a year-long curriculum in core subjects that delineates content and skills.
- The school develops positive relationships among staff and students that support a professional learning community for adults and an engaging, motivating learning environment for students. The school has a student behavior policy.

Evidence: What You Should See and Hear . . .

In Classrooms

- Students can explain what they are learning and why and how it connects to what they have already learned. They are able to talk about the quality of their own work and what they must do to improve it.
- The teacher and students engage in a high level of discourse that goes beyond right/wrong and yes/no answers to an emphasis on evidence.
- Teachers give prompt and specific feedback to students on their work, based on standards. In conferences, both the teacher and students talk about the work.
- Classroom walls display current student work and charts the teacher and students have created together about the content they are studying, standards for exemplary work, and class rules. Students refer to the charts frequently.
- Classroom space is organized so that students can get what they need — books, journals, other materials — on their own.

Around the School

- Every classroom has areas for students to read, write, and work on their own and in pairs and a common area for the whole class to meet and talk. Current, exemplary student work is posted throughout the school.
- Every teacher is able to explain what his/her students are learning and why and describe how his/her instruction will get students to proficiency in core academic subjects.
- The principal-headmaster and teachers — including teachers of special needs students and English language learners and teacher-specialists — meet regularly in teams to talk about instructional practice.
- The principal-headmaster spends time in classrooms every day, observing and discussing work with teachers and students.
- The principal-headmaster models learning by observing classroom practice, leading learning walks, and discussing his/her own learning with staff.

Expectations for Central Administrators

- The superintendent and his teams use expectations for schools when observing classrooms and evaluating principals-headmasters.
- Every employee is able to explain Whole-School Improvement (WSI) and his/her role in that effort.
- Central departments base their decisions on the question, "How will this decision help students become better readers, writers, and thinkers and reach proficiency?"

The Bottom Line: Closing the Achievement Gap

In every grade, every student will reach Proficiency on MCAS: regular education students, special education students, and English language learners.

Boston Public Schools Whole-School Improvement

The Six Essentials

BOSTON'S PUBLIC SCHOOLS are engaged in an ongoing effort to improve instruction in every classroom and to support every student to reach proficiency. That effort, WHOLE-SCHOOL IMPROVEMENT, is organized around six ESSENTIALS, which provide a framework for the work.

ESSENTIAL: STUDENT WORK & DATA
Examine student work and data to drive instruction and professional development

Expectations for Schools

- School staff analyze and use data — MCAS results, student work, formative assessments, classroom observations — for five purposes:
  - to track each student's progress toward proficiency
  - to plan instruction for each student
  - to check alignment among standards, curriculum, instruction, and assessments
  - to plan teachers' and the principal-headmaster's collective learning
  - to hold themselves accountable for students' achieving proficiency and for closing the achievement gap
- The principal-headmaster and Instructional Leadership Team (ILT) use data to develop the school's Whole-School Improvement Plan (WSIP), with ongoing performance measures.

Evidence: What You Should See and Hear . . .

In Classrooms

- Teachers keep track of each student's learning and share their progress with them regularly.
- Teachers use MyBPS Assessment to track patterns in their students' performance and modify their instruction in response.
- Teachers know the value and purpose of various kinds of assessments.
- Teachers use data to determine the specific content or pedagogical focus of their Collaborative Coaching & Learning (CCL) course of study.

Around the School

- A data management team, including the principal-headmaster, manages data and presents findings (disaggregated by ethnicity and program) to school staff twice each year to track each student's progress toward proficiency.
- School teams analyze data and student work to plan instruction and identify their own learning needs.
- The ILT uses data to identify schoolwide professional development needs in content or pedagogy, to select teams to participate in CCL, and to identify CCL courses of study.
- The school posts data publicly and in a timely manner.

Expectations for Central Administrators

- The superintendent, deputy superintendents, and central administrators use data to examine the effectiveness of major initiatives and to make decisions.
- The district makes available formative assessments in core content areas for each grade that are aligned with state standards; the formative assessments are for schools to use strategically to learn about their students in a timely manner.
- The district makes student performance data available to schools through MyBPS Assessment in a timely manner.
- The district provides training on data analysis and MyBPS Assessment to central and school staff.

The Bottom Line: Closing the Achievement Gap

In every grade, every student will reach Proficiency on MCAS: regular education students, special education students, and English language learners.

Boston Public Schools Whole-School Improvement

The Six Essentials

BOSTON'S PUBLIC SCHOOLS are engaged in an ongoing effort to improve instruction in every classroom and to support every student to reach proficiency. That effort, WHOLE-SCHOOL IMPROVEMENT, is organized around six ESSENTIALS, which provide a framework for the work.

ESSENTIAL: PROFESSIONAL DEVELOPMENT

Invest in professional development to improve instruction

Expectations for Schools

- The school's Whole-School Improvement Plan (WSIP) is based on data and includes a professional development plan that:
  - outlines the school's implementation of Collaborative Coaching & Learning (CCL)
  - explains the school's use of contractual time
  - addresses the school's content and pedagogical learning needs
  - reflects the staff's understanding of the cultural, economic, and family factors that affect student learning
- With its coaches, each CCL team outlines its course of study, reads inquiry texts, demonstrates, and analyzes practice together in classrooms. By engaging in CCL, teachers continue to learn to teach more effectively and get better student results.
- Choices about off-site courses and other professional development in which teachers participate are based on the school's goals and students' learning needs.
- The principal-headmaster makes his/her professional development public and reviews each teacher's professional development so that it is aligned with the school's goals.

Evidence: What You Should See and Hear . . .

In Classrooms

- Teachers adopt and refine instructional strategies they learn.
- Teachers use workshop instruction in reading, writing, math, science, social studies, and other subjects.
- Teachers make their practice public and visit each other's classrooms.
- Teachers know their content and their students well, and help each other improve their practice.

Around the School

- The principal-headmaster and other administrators participate in at least one CCL cycle each year.
- The principal-headmaster develops a schedule that allows all teachers to participate in CCL over time.
- The principal-headmaster meets weekly with the school's content coaches.
- The school's norm is one of continuous learning for everyone; staff discuss instructional problems and solutions in formal and informal settings, such as in hallways and teachers' lounges.
- The school's professional development plan and schedule are posted and shared with staff, families, school partners, and visitors.

Expectations for Central Administrators

- The superintendent and deputy superintendents are responsible for ensuring that professional development in schools and the central office has coherence, is aligned with the six Essentials, supports the improvement of practice, and enhances the sustainability of whole-school and whole-district improvement.
- The superintendent and the administrative team organize professional development for central staff so they understand Boston's reform framework and their role in it.
- The superintendent, deputy superintendents, and key central staff participate in CCL sessions when they visit schools.
- Deputy superintendents and assistant superintendents regularly review schools' professional development plans and schedules and look for evidence of implementation.

The Bottom Line: Closing the Achievement Gap

In every grade, every student will reach Proficiency on MCAS: regular education students, special education students, and English language learners.

Boston Public Schools Whole-School Improvement

The Six Essentials

BOSTON'S PUBLIC SCHOOLS are engaged in an ongoing effort to improve instruction in every classroom and to support every student to reach proficiency. That effort, WHOLE-SCHOOL IMPROVEMENT, is organized around six ESSENTIALS, which provide a framework for the work.

ESSENTIAL: SHARED LEADERSHIP

Share leadership to sustain instructional improvement

Expectations for Schools

- Principals-headmasters have concrete strategies to develop and share leadership with teachers and other staff.
- Teachers have opportunities to assume leadership roles outside of the classroom.
- Teachers share responsibility for the school's instructional decisions.
- The principal-headmaster and administrators make it "safe" for teachers to talk about their practice.

Evidence: What You Should See and Hear . . .

In Classrooms

- School administrators are in classrooms every day, talking with students about what they are learning and conferring with teachers about their informal observations and decisions on next steps.
- Teachers describe their colleagues and school leaders as resources for helping them improve instruction and meet their goals.
- Teachers teach each other, and some teach courses for colleagues.
- Teachers demonstrate lessons for CCL.

Around the School

- Teachers lead looking at student work sessions, data team meetings, inquiry groups, ILT meetings, and ad hoc committees.
- The agenda for ILT meetings is set by the principal-headmaster and ILT members.
- Teachers and other members of the ILT take part in learning walks in their own and other schools.
- Teachers help create school policies and practices, an indicator of an environment that is encouraging, inclusive, and "risk free."
- Staff refer to the school as "our" school, not "my" school.

Expectations for Central Administrators

- The superintendent, chief operating officer, deputy superintendents, and director of human resources align evaluation tools with expectations for instructional improvement and the goal of proficiency for all students.
- Mid-level managers visit schools and confer with school leaders in making decisions about their department's policies and practices.
- The superintendent convenes a teacher advisory committee to help him refine the district's work.
- Deputy superintendents work with principals-headmasters to increase teacher and student voice in each school.
- Cluster leaders are peer coaches for principals-headmasters, modeling best leadership practices in instruction.

The Bottom Line: Closing the Achievement Gap

In every grade, every student will reach Proficiency on MCAS: regular education students, special education students, and English language learners.

Boston Public Schools Whole-School Improvement

The Six Essentials

BOSTON'S PUBLIC SCHOOLS are engaged in an ongoing effort to improve instruction in every classroom and to support every student to reach proficiency. That effort, WHOLE-SCHOOL IMPROVEMENT, is organized around six ESSENTIALS, which provide a framework for the work.

ESSENTIAL: RESOURCES

Focus resources to support instructional improvement and improved student learning

Expectations for Schools

- The school's resources — people, time, funds, materials — are allocated to meet its student learning goals, and its budget is the financial plan for implementing the WSIP.
- Corporate, family, and community resources support specific student learning goals.
- School staff use student learning goals to decide whether to start, continue, or discontinue any initiative.

Evidence: What You Should See and Hear . . .

In Classrooms

- Teachers have help in the classroom from other professional staff and trained volunteers to give students more individualized attention.
- Each student has a daily (uninterrupted) block of at least 90 minutes for literacy and 60-90 minutes for math.
- Teachers start on time, get right to the lesson, and minimize "housekeeping" announcements.
- Teachers give individualized time to each student every week.
- Every classroom has a classroom library and instructional materials and equipment.

Around the School

- The schedule maximizes instructional time for core subjects and increases the number of professionals in each classroom.
- School staff use all contractual time for professional development. With few exceptions, teachers are not pulled from school for off-site professional development.
- School staff use MyBPS and other technology to minimize paperwork.
- Before- and after-school time is coordinated with in-school time so that students have extended coherent instruction.

Expectations for Central Administrators

- Deputy superintendents and the teaching and learning team support principals-headmasters to maximize instructional time and individualize support for each student.
- The superintendent, teaching and learning team, and budget office help schools align budgeted resources with WSIP priorities.
- Deputy superintendents share with schools examples of well-thought-out budgets, professional development plans, job descriptions, school schedules, and use of volunteers to maximize resource use.
- Deputy superintendents, with the high school renewal office, support schools to achieve personalized relationships for every student.

The Bottom Line: Closing the Achievement Gap

In every grade, every student will reach Proficiency on MCAS: regular education students, special education students, and English language learners.

Boston Public Schools Whole-School Improvement

The Six Essentials

BOSTON'S PUBLIC SCHOOLS are engaged in an ongoing effort to improve instruction in every classroom and to support every student to reach proficiency. That effort, WHOLE-SCHOOL IMPROVEMENT, is organized around six ESSENTIALS, which provide a framework for the work.

ESSENTIAL: FAMILIES & COMMUNITY

Partner with families and community to support student learning

Expectations for Schools & Families

- School staff reach out to show they value all children and welcome families and community members as their partners.
- Each school develops a plan to engage families in their children's school life. In middle and high schools, the plan details how staff will communicate with students to identify issues of importance to them. The plan is shared with families and community members and is posted in the school.
- Each teacher communicates regularly with families (in English and in the adult's first language) about their child's progress and ways families can support students at home.
- Families show interest in their children's schoolwork and learning, monitor their attendance, attend parent conferences, and participate in parent councils if they can.

Evidence: What You Should See and Hear . . .

In Classrooms

- Each teacher sends home an easy-to-understand "syllabus" based on the school's curriculum.
- Teachers call, write, e-mail, and/or meet with students' families regularly to share progress and suggestions about helping students learn.
- Teachers promote home reading and home math and reach out to those who don't participate.

Around the School

- Families and community members are present and active in the school, and the school organizes successful parent-teacher conferences each year.
- The school has a written Parent Involvement Policy and Home-School Compact.
- School staff follow a protocol for greeting visitors, take messages reliably, and respond promptly and respectfully to questions and concerns.

Expectations for Central Administrators

- The superintendent and deputy superintendents hold principals-headmasters accountable for strong and measurable outreach to families and community members.
- The deputy superintendent for family and community engagement shares examples of schools and practices that work effectively with families and community members.
- The high school renewal office highlights schools that are effectively soliciting students' concerns and acting in partnership with them on the solutions.
- Family resource centers provide technical assistance to schools to develop and implement their family engagement plans.

The Bottom Line: Closing the Achievement Gap

In every grade, every student will reach Proficiency on MCAS: regular education students, special education students, and English language learners.

Notes

INTRODUCTION

Setting the Stage

S. Paul Reville

1. Council of the Great City Schools, "Urban School Superintendents: Characteristics, Tenure, and Salary; Fifth Survey and Report," *Urban Indicator* 8, no. 1 (2006): 2–3.
2. Citizen Commission on Academic Success for Boston Children, *Transforming the Boston Public Schools: A Roadmap for the New Superintendent* (Boston: Citizen Commission on Academic Success for Boston Children, 2006).
3. Citizen Commission on Academic Success for Boston Children, *Transforming the Boston Public Schools.*
4. The Boston Education Funders Group met regularly to share information and strategy on their various initiatives in the BPS and to launch joint projects like the Fund for Non-Profit Partnerships in the BPS. Prominent among the local donors were the Barr Foundation, the Jessie B. Cox Charitable Trust, Nellie Mae Education Foundation, Strategic Grant Partners, the Trefler Foundation, the Balfour Foundation, EdVestors, several local corporations, and many others.
5. Richard Rothstein, *Class and Schools: Using Social, Economic and Educational Reform to Close the Black-White Achievement Gap* (New York: Teachers College Press, 2004).
6. S. Paul Reville, "Let's Get Back to the Blackboard," *Boston Globe,* June 20, 2006.
7. Thomas W. Payzant, "Adaptability and the Three A's of Educational Reform," in *Miles to Go . . .*, ed. S. Paul Reville (Bethesda, MD: Education Week Press, 2002).
8. Rennie Center for Education Research and Policy, *A Decade of Boston School Reform: Reflections and Aspirations; Executive Summary* (Cambridge, MA: Rennie Center for Education Research and Policy, 2006).
9. The author is grateful to the following individuals who consented to be interviewed and provide their perspective on the issues discussed in this chapter: Richard Stutman, Edward Doherty, Michael Contompasis, Jacqueline Rivers, Karen Mapp, Neil Sullivan, Ellen Guiney, and several others. Although this chapter may reflect some of their views, the perspectives expressed here are solely those of the author.

CHAPTER I

Strong Foundation, Evolving Challenges

The Aspen Institute Education and Society Program and Annenberg Institute for School Reform at Brown University

1. The article is available online at www.forbes.com/realestate/2004/02/13/cx_bs_0213home.html.
2. Paul C. Peterson and Frederick M. Hess, "Johnny Can Read . . . in Some States," *Education Next* 5, no. 3 (Summer 2005).
3. In comparison, 23 percent of New York City's budget was allocated to the public

schools in 2005–06. But Hartford, Connecticut, invested more than half of its budget in its public schools.

4. There is no one literacy program for all Boston Public Schools; schools can choose from a handful of literacy models approved by the district, including the Literacy Collaborative (grades 1–3), Developing Literacy First (K–3), Mondo Balanced Early Literacy (K–2), Supporting Literacy (4–8), Success for All (PK–5), and First Steps (K–3). In mathematics, the common curricula used are Investigations and Connected Math.
5. In 2005, BPS updated the audit, using the same framework, to measure progress on professional development spending since 1999.
6. An analysis done by the Boston Public Schools on 2005 MCAS data showed higher achievement levels for tenth graders in both English language arts and mathematics in Pilot schools than in non–Pilot Schools. In English language arts, 78 percent of tenth graders in Pilot Schools were passing, as opposed to 69 percent in non–Pilot Schools. In math, 70 percent in Pilot Schools were passing, as opposed to 63 percent in non–Pilot Schools. Thomas Payzant, "Ensuring Coherence in Transition and Sustainability" (BPS PowerPoint presentation, Boston Funders' Conference, November 14, 2005).
7. C. B. Swanson, *Who Graduates? Who Doesn't? A Statistical Portrait of Public High School Graduation, Class of 2001* (Washington, DC: Urban Institute, 2004).
8. In the 2005–06 school year, over five thousand students—who constituted 44.9 percent of special education students and 8.8 percent of the total BPS student body—were enrolled in separate special education classes ("The Boston Public Schools at a Glance," http://boston.k12.ma.us/bps/bpsglance.asp).

CHAPTER II

Governance and the Boston Public Schools

John H. Portz

1. Education Commission of the States, "Governing America's Schools: Changing the Rules" (Denver: Education Commission of the States, 1999).
2. Joseph Murphy, "Governing America's Schools: The Shifting Playing Field" (paper presented at the annual meeting of the American Education Research Association, Montreal, April 1999).
3. Donald R. McAdams, *What School Boards Can Do: Reform Governance for Urban Schools* (New York: Teachers College Press, 2006).
4. Jacqueline P. Danzberger, Michael W. Kirst, and Michael D. Usdan, *Governing Public Schools: New Times New Requirements* (Washington, DC: Institute for Educational Leadership, 1992); William G. Howell, ed., *Besieged: School Boards and the Future of Education Politics* (Washington, DC: Brookings Institution Press, 2005).
5. Larry Cuban and Michael Usdan, eds., *Powerful Reforms with Shallow Roots: Improving America's Urban Schools* (New York: Teachers College Press, 2003); Jeffrey R. Henig and Wilbur C. Rich, *Mayors in the Middle: Politics, Race, and Mayoral Control of Urban Schools* (Princeton, NJ: Princeton University Press, 2004); Kenneth K. Wong and Francis X. Shen, "When Mayors Lead Urban Schools: Assessing the Effects of Takeover," in Howell, *Besieged* (Washington, DC: Brookings Institution Press, 2005).
6. Wong and Shen, "When Mayors Lead Urban Schools."

7. John Portz, Lana Stein, and Robin Jones, *City Schools and City Politics: Institutions and Leadership in Pittsburgh, Boston, and St. Louis* (Lawrence: University Press of Kansas, 1999).
8. Mayor's Advisory Committee, "The Rebirth of America's Oldest Public School System: Redefining Responsibility" (Boston: Office of the Mayor, 1989).
9. Boston Municipal Research Bureau, "Bureau Supports Appointed School Committee" (special report, Boston Municipal Research Bureau, Boston, July 26, 1989).
10. "Shortchanging the School Children," editorial, *Boston Globe*, August 30, 1992; Mayor's Advisory Committee, "The Rebirth of America's Oldest Public School System: Redefining Responsibility" (Boston: Office of the Mayor, 1989).
11. Mayor's Advisory Committee, "The Rebirth of America's Oldest Public School System."
12. Raymond Flynn, "A Vision for Public Education Reform" (presentation to the Boston business community, mayor's office, January 29, 1993).
13. Boston Municipal Research Bureau, "Bureau Supports Appointed School Committee"; John Portz, "Problem Definitions and Policy Agendas: Shaping the Education Agenda in Boston," *Policy Studies Journal* 24 (1996): 371–86.
14. Michael Rezendes, "Council Votes to Back Appointed School Panel, Abolish Current Board," *Boston Globe*, April 11, 1991.
15. Richard Chaçon, "Menino: School Panel to Be 'More Accessible'," *Boston Globe*, November 7, 1996.
16. John Portz, "Boston: Agenda Setting and School Reform in a Mayor-centric System," in *Mayors in the Middle: Politics, Race, and Mayoral Control of Urban Schools*, ed. Jeffrey R. Henig and Wilbur C. Rich (Princeton, NJ: Princeton University Press, 2004), 96–119.
17. Raymond L. Flynn, "State of the City, January 9, 1991," *City Record* 183, no. 3 (January 21, 1991):1.
18. Thomas M. Menino, "State of the City Address," *City Record* 88, no. 5 (January 29, 1996):1.
19. Methodological note: Percentages were calculated by dividing the number of lines in the speech devoted to education by the total number of lines in the speech.
20. Calculated from data from Boston Municipal Research Bureau and City of Boston Financial Statements.
21. "Massachusetts Business Roundtable: Six Views from the Top," *Boston Globe*, December 1, 1996.
22. Karen Avenso and Patricia Wen, "Elected, Appointed Panels Show Differences in Style," *Boston Globe*, October 28, 1996.
23. Avenso and Wen, "Elected, Appointed Panels."
24. Tracy Jan, "Where NAY Is Rarely Heard: Is the Boston School Committee Working for You?" *Boston Globe*, October 9, 2005.
25. Barbara Neufeld and Ellen Guiney, "Transforming Events: A Local Education Fund's Efforts to Promote Large-Scale Urban School Reform," in *Research Perspectives on School Reform: Lessons from the Annenberg Challenge*, ed. Brenda Turnbull (Providence, RI: Annenberg Institute, 2003). This document can be viewed online at www.annenberginstitute.org/publications/acpubs.html#research.
26. "City's business, higher ed, non-profit leaders back Boston schools on MCAS, ed reform" (press release), *Focus on Children*, April 14, 2000. This document can be viewed at www.boston.k12.ma.us/bps/news/news_04_14_00.asp.

27. Steven Taylor, "Appointing or Electing the Boston School Committee: The Preferences of the African American Community," *Urban Education* 36, no. 1 (January 2001): 4–26.
28. Anand Vaishnav, "Are They Acting as Advocates or Appointed Rubber Stamps?" *Boston Globe*, January 28, 2001.
29. Critical Friends of the Boston Public Schools, *Status Report on Boston's Public Schools after Two Years of Reform* (Boston: Critical Friends of the Boston Public Schools, 1997).
30. Citizen Commission on Academic Success for Boston Children, "Transforming the Boston Public Schools: A Roadmap for the New Superintendent" (Boston, June 2006).
31. Frederick M. Hess, *Spinning Wheels: The Politics of Urban School Reform* (Washington, DC: Brookings Institution, 1999).
32. Boston School Department, "Focus on Children: A Comprehensive Reform Plan for the Boston Public Schools" (Boston: Boston School Department, June 1996).
33. Thomas Menino, "Mayors' Roles in School Change" (remarks by Mayor Menino to Education Writers Association, April 16, 1999).
34. Richard Wallace, *From Vision to Practice: The Art of Educational Leadership* (Thousand Oaks, CA: Corwin Press, 1996).
35. Citizen Commission on Academic Success for Boston Children, "Transforming the Boston Public Schools."
36. Larry Cuban and Michael Usdan, eds., *Powerful Reforms with Shallow Roots: Improving America's Urban Schools* (New York: Teachers College Press, 2003).
37. Richard Hunter, "The Mayor versus the School Superintendent: Political Incursions into Metropolitan School Politics," *Education and Urban Society* 29 (1997): 217–32.

CHAPTER III

Leadership Development at the Boston Public Schools

Karen L. Mapp and Jennifer M. Suesse

1. Richard F. Elmore, "Building a New Structure for School Leadership," in Richard F. Elmore, *School Reform from the Inside Out: Policy, Practice, and Performance* (Cambridge, MA: Harvard Education Press, 2004), 43.
2. Elmore, "Building a New Structure."
3. Linda A. Hill, *Becoming a Manager: How New Managers Master the Challenges of Leadership*, 2nd ed. (Boston: Harvard Business School Press, 2003).
4. In the BPS, some schools use the title "principal" and others use "headmaster." For the purposes of this chapter, we will use the title "principal" to refer to both principals and headmasters.
5. We wish to thank the following individuals who provided us with a wealth of information about the BPS leadership development process: Tom Payzant, Janet Williams, Muriel Leonard, Ingrid Carney, Chris Coxon, Barbara McGann, Rachel Curtis, Michael Fung, Michele Boyers, Ellen Guiney, Janice Jackson, Tim Knowles.
6. On page 376 of *Becoming a Manager*, Hill cites a classic definition of technical skills articulated by R. L. Katz in "Skills of an Effective Administrator," *Harvard Business Review* (1974): 90–103.
7. Hill, *Becoming a Manager*, 147.

8. Hill, *Becoming a Manager,* 310–12.
9. Between October 1995 and June 2006, Payzant oversaw the appointment of 121 principals and headmasters; 59 percent were people of color and 68 percent were female. As of June 2006, the Boston district consisted of 145 schools.
10. From 2003 to 2006, Payzant appointed 21 senior central office staff members; 57 percent were people of color and 71 percent were female.
11. "Boston Plan for Excellence Biennial Report: Transition, Transformation, 1997 and 1998" (Boston: Boston Plan for Excellence in the Boston Schools).
12. "Boston Plan for Excellence Biennial Report, 1997 and 1998," 11.
13. "Boston Plan for Excellence Biennial Report, 1997 and 1998," 14.
14. "Boston Plan for Excellence Biennial Report, 1997 and 1998," 25.
15. During his tenure at the BPS, Superintendent Payzant also hired two Urban Superintendents Program graduates for whom he did not serve as a mentor.
16. Barbara McGann, BPS director of human resources, is a fellow and graduate of the Broad Academy Program, a ten-month leadership development program for those aspiring to be urban superintendents. She was hired by the district in 2004 to head the Human Resources Department of BPS.
17. Levy B. Neufeld and S. Schwartz Chrismer, "The Boston School Leadership Institute: 2004–2005 Evaluation Report" (2005), www.edmatters.org.
18. J. Steele and R. Curtis, "Preparing Non-Principal Administrators to Foster Whole-School Improvement in Boston" (Boston: Boston School Leadership Institute, 2005), www.bostonsli.org.
19. The Boston School Leadership Institute is funded through a school leadership grant from the U.S. Department of Education Office of Innovation and Improvement.
20. In this discussion, we are guided by the Public Education Leadership Project (PELP) definition of strategy as "the broad set of actions a district deliberately takes to provide capacity and support to the instructional core with the objective of raising student performance" (teaching case PEL-023; see document at http://harvardbusinessonline.hbsp.harvard.edu/b01/en/common/item_detail.jhtml;jsessionid=SGR0CKD3LZKR0AKRGWDR5VQBKE0YIISW?id=PEL023).
21. We see examples of this in the Chicago Leadership Academies for Supporting Success (CLASS) at the Chicago Public Schools. For more information, see the CLASS website, http://www.classacademies.org/.
22. Some of these practices are described in James E. Austin, Robert B. Schwartz, and Jennifer M. Suesse, "Change Leading to Improvement: Long Beach Unified School District (A)" (teaching case PEL-006, Cambridge, MA: Harvard University Public Education Leadership Project, September 7, 2004).
23. Morgan McCall Jr., *High Flyers: Developing the Next Generation of Leaders* (Boston: Harvard Business School Press, 1998), 17.

CHAPTER IV

Building a Human Resource System in the Boston Public Schools

Susan Moore Johnson and Morgaen L. Donaldson

1. Daniel F. McCaffrey, J. R. Lockwood, Daniel M. Koretz, and Laura S. Hamilton, *Evaluating Value-Added Models for Teacher Accountability* (Santa Monica, CA: RAND, 2003).

2. John K. DiPaolo, "Towards an Open Teacher Hiring Process: How the Boston Public Schools and the Boston Teachers Union Can Empower Schools to Hire and Keep the Best Teams" (Boston: Boston Plan for Excellence in the Public Schools, 2000).
3. Richard M. Ingersoll, "The Teacher Shortage: A Case of Wrong Diagnosis and Wrong Prescription," *NASSP Bulletin* 86, no. 631 (2002): 16–31.
4. Boston Plan for Excellence in the Public Schools, "Building a Professional Teaching Corps in Boston: Survey of Teachers New to the Boston Public Schools in SY 2003–2004" (Boston: BPE, 2005).
5. "Boston Public Schools HR Reinvention" (internal report, Boston: Boston Public Schools, April 2006).
6. Jessica Levin and Meredith Quinn, *Missed Opportunities: How We Keep High Quality Teachers Out of Urban Classrooms* (Washington, DC: New Teacher Project, 2003).
7. Richard M. Ingersoll, "Teacher Turnover and Teacher Shortages: An Organizational Analysis," *American Educational Research Journal* 38, no. 3 (2001): 499–534.
8. "Boston Public Schools HR Reinvention" (internal report, Boston: Boston Public Schools, March 15, 2006).
9. Boston Higher Education Partnership to Morgaen L. Donaldson, personal communication, March 2006.
10. Boston Higher Education Partnership to Morgaen L. Donaldson, personal communication, March 2006.
11. Barbara McGann to Susan Moore Johnson, interview, March 2006.
12. Jesse Solomon to Morgaen L. Donaldson, interview, March 2006.
13. Edward Liu and Susan Moore Johnson, "New Teachers' Experiences of Hiring: Late, Rushed, and Information-Poor," *Educational Administration Quarterly* 42, no. 3 (2006): 324–60.
14. Edward Liu, "Hiring, Job Satisfaction, and the Fit between New Teachers and Their Schools" (paper presented at the annual meeting of the American Educational Research Association, Montreal, 2005).
15. Levin and Quinn, *Missed Opportunities.*
16. BPS Department of Human Resources to Morgaen L. Donaldson, personal communication, May 31, 2006.
17. Boston Municipal Research Bureau, in collaboration with the Massachusetts Advocacy Center, "Implementing the Boston Teachers' Contract: Progress Is Generally Successful, but Key Opportunities Missed" (Boston: Boston Municipal Research Bureau, 2002).
18. Boston Municipal Research Bureau, "Implementing the Boston Teachers' Contract," p. 1.
19. Eric A. Hanushek, John F. Kain, and S. G. Rivkin, "Why Public Schools Lose Teachers," *Journal of Human Resources* 39, no. 2 (2004): 326–54.
20. Sarah E. Birkeland and Rachel Curtis, "Ensuring the Support and Development of New Teachers in the Boston Public Schools: A Proposal to Improve Teacher Quality and Retention" (Boston: Boston Public Schools, 2006).
21. Birkeland and Curtis, "Ensuring the Support and Development," p. 8.
22. Texas Center for Educational Research, *The Cost of Teacher Turnover* (Austin: Texas State Board for Educator Certification, 2000).
23. Jennifer King Rice, "The Incidence and Impact of Teacher Professional Development: Implications for Education Productivity," in *School Finance and Teacher Qual-*

ity: Exploring the Connections; 2003 Yearbook of the American Education Finance Association, ed. M. Plecki and D. Monk (Larchmont, NY: Eye on Education, 2003).

24. Thomas Smith and Richard Ingersoll, "Reducing Teacher Turnover: What Are the Components of Effective Induction?" *American Educational Research Journal* 41, no. 2 (2004); Ingersoll, "Teacher Turnover and Teacher Shortages."
25. Heather Peske, Edward Liu, Susan Moore Johnson, David Kauffman, and Susan M. Kardos, "The Next Generation of Teachers: Changing Conceptions of a Career in Teaching," *Phi Delta Kappan* 83, no. 4 (2001): 304–11; Morgaen L. Donaldson, "On Barren Ground: How Urban High Schools Fail to Support and Retain Newly Tenured Teachers" (paper presented at the annual meeting of the American Educational Research Association, Montreal, 2005).
26. Maria McCarthy and Ellen Guiney, "Building a Professional Teaching Corps in Boston: Baseline Study of New Teachers in Boston's Public Schools" (Boston: Boston Plan for Excellence in the Public Schools, 2004).
27. Birkeland and Curtis, "Ensuring the Support and Development."
28. Ingersoll, "Teacher Turnover and Teacher Shortages."
29. Susan Moore Johnson and The Project on the Next Generation of Teachers, *Finders and Keepers: Helping New Teachers Survive and Thrive in Our Schools* (San Francisco: Jossey-Bass, 2004).
30. Richard Ingersoll and Jeffery M. Kralik, *The Impact of Mentoring on Teacher Retention: What the Research Says* (Denver: Education Commission of the States, 2004).
31. BPS Department of Human Resources to Morgaen L. Donaldson, personal communication, 2006.
32. Susan M. Kardos, "Supporting and Sustaining New Teachers in Schools: The Importance of Professional Culture and Mentoring" (PhD diss., Cambridge, MA: Harvard Graduate School of Education, Harvard University, 2004); Smith and Ingersoll, "Reducing Teacher Turnover."
33. Smith and Ingersoll, "Reducing Teacher Turnover."
34. Susan Kardos and Susan Moore Johnson, "On Their Own and Presumed Expert: New Teachers' Experiences with Their Colleagues," *Teachers College Record*, forthcoming, 2007.
35. Ingersoll and Kralik, *The Impact of Mentoring on Teacher Retention*; Anthony Villar and M. Strong, *Is Mentoring Worth the Money? A Benefit-Cost Analysis and Five-year Rate of Return of a Comprehensive Mentoring Program for Beginning Teachers* (Santa Cruz, CA: The New Teacher Center, 2005).
36. After launching a major marketing campaign, simplifying the application process, and offering targeted hiring incentives, Philadelphia increased the number of teacher applicants to its district by 44 percent. At the same time, the district instituted a system of support for new teachers, including new teacher coaches, induction, and special training for principals in how to support and retain new teachers. Retention of new teachers increased markedly; the number of teachers completing their first year in the district jumped from 73 percent in 2002–03 to 91 percent in 2003–04. Ruth Curran Neild, Elizabeth Useem, and E. Farley, *Quest for Quality: Recruiting and Retaining Teachers in Philadelphia* (Philadelphia: Research for Action, 2005).
37. Johnson et al., *Finders and Keepers.*
38. Birkeland and Curtis, "Ensuring the Support and Development," p. 13.
39. BPS Department of Human Resources to Morgaen L. Donaldson, personal communication, May 31, 2006.

CHAPTER V

Instructional Improvement in the Boston Public Schools

Barbara Neufeld

1. "Workshop" is a set of strategies that reflect the fact that students must actively create understanding and that instructional strategies should be designed to enable students to do this work. As a result, workshop (a) has a structure: minilesson, independent work, and sharing; (b) provides opportunities for teachers to work directly with every student in the class through conferencing and small-group, targeted instruction; (c) gives students the opportunity to read, write, talk, think, and construct their knowledge as part of the instructional process; and (d) gives students a "voice" in a community of learners.
2. Frederick M. Hess, *Spinning Wheels: The Politics of Urban School Reform* (Washington, DC: Brookings Institution, 1999); Larry Cuban and Michael Usdan, "Learning from the Past," in *Powerful Reforms with Shallow Roots: Improving America's Urban Schools*, ed. Larry Cuban and Michael Usdan (Cambridge, MA: Harvard Education Press, 2003); Michael Usdan and Larry Cuban, "Boston: The Stars Finally in Alignment," in Cuban and Usdan, *Powerful Reforms.*
3. "Where NAY Is Rarely Heard; Is the Boston School Committee Working for You?" *Boston Globe*, October 9, 2005.
4. Usdan and Cuban, "Boston: The Stars Finally in Alignment."
5. In the BPS, the heads of elementary and middle schools are called principals. Those who head the district's high schools are called headmasters.
6. Hubert E. Jones, "Preface," *Transforming the Boston Public Schools: A Roadmap for the New Superintendent*, ed. Susan Miller (Boston: The Citizen Commission on Academic Success for Boston Children, June 2006).
7. See, for example, David K. Cohen, "Educational Technology, Policy, and Practice," *Educational Evaluation and Policy Analysis* 9, no. 2 (Summer 1987): 153–70; David K. Cohen, "Teaching Practice: Plus Que Ça Change. . . " in *Contributing to Educational Change: Perspectives on Research and Practice*, ed. Phillip W. Jackson (Berkeley, CA: McCutchan, 1988); Larry Cuban, *How Teachers Taught: Constancy and Change in American Classrooms, 1890–1980* (New York: Longman, 1984).
8. Henry M. Levin, "Why Is Educational Entrepreneurship So Difficult?" (New York: Teachers College Press, 2006), 16. Levin notes that the word entrepreneurship "has been used commonly in recent years to describe strategies to improve education. Because the term has been associated generically with the development of new alternatives in the marketplace, its educational variant has typically referred to a system of school choice, and especially charter schools and vouchers" (p. 2).
9. See Cohen, "Educational Technology, Policy, and Practice," p. 168, for one analysis of the difficulty of changing teaching practice. See also Cohen, "Teaching Practice." There are numerous studies that document the challenges associated with implementing progressive/constructivist teaching practices.
10. See chapter 6, "Explaining How they Taught: An Exploratory Analysis," in Cuban, *How Teachers Taught*, pp. 237–69.
11. David K. Cohen and Heather C. Hill, *Learning Policy: When State Education Reform Works* (New Haven, CT: Yale University Press, 2001).
12. Nancy E. Jennings, *Interpreting Policy in Real Classrooms* (New York: Teachers College Press, 1996), p. 108.

13. The Effective Practice schools are twenty-six Boston Public Schools that have demonstrated (a) high levels of implementation of some of the essentials of whole-school improvement, and (b) strong principal leadership for instruction. These schools were recognized for their accomplishments in a public ceremony at the end of the 2000–01 school year. In subsequent years, a small number of schools lost this designation and a small number have gained the designation.
14. The Six Essentials are listed in full in the Appendix to this volume.
15. Funds from the Boston Annenberg Challenge provided the district with resources to support, among other things, a second cohort of reforming schools.
16. For a more complete description of the partnership see Barbara Neufeld and Ellen Guiney, "Transforming Events: A Local Education Fund's Efforts to Promote Large-Scale Urban School Reform," in *Research Perspectives on School Reform: Lessons from the Annenberg Challenge* (Providence, RI: Annenberg Institute for School Reform at Brown University, 2003), 51–68, www.annenberginstitute.org.
17. The definition of "Essential" in this quotation and the next comes from the February 1997 issue of *Focus*, produced by the Boston Plan for Excellence in collaboration with the Boston Public Schools, Summer 2001.
18. For a detailed discussion of standards-based education, see Barbara Neufeld, "Transforming Abbott Schools in New Jersey," in *Transforming Teaching and Learning in Special Needs Districts* (Newark, NJ: Education Law Center, 1997), 42–121, www.edmatters.org.
19. Whole-school change coaches were skilled in supporting organizational change. They worked closely with principals, supporting them as instructional leaders and leaders of whole-school change by assisting with implementing the Boston Plan for Excellence's focus for the school year and supporting the work of the Instructional Leadership Team.
20. Most of the schools selected literacy as their instructional focus. All of the schools in Education Matters's evaluation sample had chosen to focus on literacy.
21. A balanced literacy approach, one that relies on "a mix of specific strategies, assessments, and interventions," was recommended by the National Research Council's Committee on the Prevention of Reading Difficulties in Young Children in *Preventing Reading Difficulties in Young Children*, ed. Catherine E. Snow, M. Susan Burns, and Peg Griffin (Washington, DC: National Academy Press, 1998).
22. Teachers did not always agree that the programs provided a "balanced" approach to early reading development. Such teachers argued that the programs did not devote sufficient time to phonics instruction in the early grades. Over time, some programs responded to these concerns and included more phonics instruction.
23. Reading "to" students was conducted in what were called minilessons; reading "with" students occurred in guided reading groups formed to address students' identifiable needs; and reading "by" students occurred in independent reading time during which students practiced what they had learned in the minilessons and guided reading groups by applying those skills to books they had chosen to read.
24. The balanced literacy programs that were adopted included the Early Learning Literacy Initiative (ELLI), Success for All, and First Steps, for example. ELLI began as a primary grade-focused early literacy program. In short order, however, it expanded to include additional elementary grades and changed its name to the Literacy Collaborative (LC). Schools using ELLI and then LC referred to their program as the Literacy Collaborative.

25. These roll-out dates are important for the later consideration of the shift from literacy-focused instructional programs to the whole-district adoption of workshop as its instructional approach. Schools in later cohorts had barely begun their literacy-focused work when the shift occurred.
26. Programs selected by Cohort II included at least the following: Literacy Collaborative, Mondo Balanced Early Literacy, Success for All, Developing Literacy First, Supporting Literacy, and First Steps.
27. Schools that developed a home-grown model went through a different process. However, by autumn 1997, the BPS was encouraging all elementary schools to adopt a literacy model rather than develop a home-grown approach. By this time it was clear that it was too challenging for schools to develop their own high-quality programs.
28. Education Matters reported the same phenomena occurring during the 2004–05 school year, when the district's large high schools were planning restructuring designs and teachers' common planning time and other school-day meetings were devoted to the design process rather than to instructional improvement.
29. Looking at Student Work sessions involved teachers in assessing the quality of students' work in light of a scoring rubric that was tied to the expectations of the citywide learning standards. This was a dramatic shift from traditional assessment practices that considered a student's work in light of the work itself and in light of the teacher's expectations about the child who had produced the work.
30. Barbara Neufeld and Katrina Woodworth, "Evaluation Report on Year Two: The Boston Plan for Excellence's 21st Century Schools Program" (Cambridge, MA: Education Matters, July 1998); Barbara Neufeld and Katrina Woodworth, "The Boston Plan for Excellence's 21st Century Schools Program: Mid-Year Evaluation Report: 1998–1999" (report, Cambridge, MA: Education Matters, February 1999); Barbara Neufeld, Margaret McConchie, Jennifer Boothby, Bonnie Hausman, Gail Parson, and Neal Brown, "The Boston Annenberg Challenge: Baseline Evaluation Report" (Cambridge, MA: Education Matters, July 1999); all reports available at www.edmatters.org.
31. At the start of this school year, Cohort IV schools were beginning their first year of literacy program implementation.
32. See chapter 5, appendix 5A, in this volume, for the excerpted text of Superintendent Thomas Payzant's memo, "Workshop Instruction in Boston's Schools: Next Steps in Whole-School Improvement" (Boston: Boston Public Schools, August 2002).
33. Senior administrators in the curriculum and instruction unit had been lamenting the loss of attention to curriculum for a number of years, even when literacy programs were in place. They had raised concerns about the emphasis on the process of teaching without concurrent attention to what students are to learn, the content specified in the citywide learning standards. As reported by Cohen and Hill (2001), weak links between instruction and curriculum do not support the adoption of instructional innovations.
34. This discussion is taken from Barbara Neufeld and Annette Sassi, *Getting Our Feet Wet: Using Making Meaning™ for the First Time* (Cambridge, MA: Education Matters, August 2004), www.edmatters.org.
35. There are teachers who view the adoption of literacy programs as evidence that the district has, once again, changed its mind about supporting workshop instruction. District personnel reported that there are also some teachers who

were working diligently to use workshop strategies and now report feeling constrained by the programs. Although these views are held by small numbers of teachers, it is important to reflect them as well as the views of the majority of teachers.

36. Due to funding constraints, coaches were available to elementary schools, for example, between three and eight days per month, depending on school size and need. For most schools, this was less coaching time than had been provided by the one-day-per-week coaching allocation for literacy.
37. After the adoption of these standards-based materials, the Massachusetts Department of Education (DOE) released its Math Frameworks. Connected Mathematics materials were well-aligned to the DOE Math Frameworks. However, Math Connections, the high school program, was not well-aligned with the Frameworks and the MCAS. The superintendent authorized a new curriculum adoption for high school mathematics, and the Glencoe materials were selected.
38. There has been little evaluation of the math initiative in the district. Therefore, there is little to report about either teachers' and administrators' views of it or the quality of its implementation.
39. For a more detailed description of coaches' work, see Barbara Neufeld and Dana Roper, *Coaching: A Strategy for Developing Instructional Capacity; Promises and Practicalities* (Washington, DC: Aspen Institute Program on Education and the Annenberg Institute for School Reform, June 2003), 7–10, www.aspeninstitute.org and www.edmatters.org.
40. Helping teachers master mathematical content continues to be a great challenge to the senior program director for elementary mathematics and the math coaches who address these teacher needs through group professional development, grade-level team meetings, Looking at Student Work and Collaborative Coaching and Learning in Math sessions, and one-on-one coaching.
41. Boston Public Schools and Boston Plan for Excellence, "Coaching Resource Binder, 2001–2002," (Boston: Boston Public Schools, 2001).
42. Taken from Barbara Neufeld and Dana Roper, "Off to a Good Start: Year I of Collaborative Coaching and Learning in the Effective Practice Schools," (Cambridge, MA: Education Matters, July 2002), www.edmatters.org.
43. Boston Plan for Excellence's publication for the 2003–04 school year, *Straight Talk about CCL: A Guide for School Leaders*, is available at www.bpe.org.
44. Morgaen Donaldson and Barbara Neufeld, "Collaborative Coaching and Learning in Literacy: Implementation at Four Boston Public Schools" (report prepared for BPS administrators and BPE; not available for circulation), January 2006.
45. See Barbara Neufeld and Dana Roper, *Year II of Collaborative Coaching and Learning in the Effective Practice Schools: Expanding the Work* (Cambridge, MA: Education Matters, July 2003), www.edmatters.org; Barbara Neufeld, *Using What We Know: Implications for Scaling-Up Implementation of the CCL Model* (Cambridge, MA: Education Matters, January 2002), www.edmatters.org; Neufeld and Roper, "Off to a Good Start"; Donaldson and Neufeld, "Collaborative Coaching and Learning in Literacy."
46. This description is adapted from the April 2006 version of the Boston Public Schools Elementary Math Plan.
47. Principals and headmasters were to make their choices based on test results, faculty needs, and their whole-school improvement plans. Deputies were to be involved in the decisions.

48. This quote is taken from page 2 of a document called "Instructional Coaches: Summary of Policy Change on Allocation, Selection, and Assignment," March 2, 2006 (working document prepared for Boston Public Schools). A task force of relevant district stakeholders was meeting to address these issues during the latter part of the 2005–06 school year.
49. Barbara Neufeld and Katrina Woodworth, *Taking Stock: The Status of Implementation and the Need for Further Support in the BPE-BAC Cohort I and II Schools* (Cambridge, MA: Education Matters, July 2000), www.edmatters.org.
50. Nancy E. Jennings, *Interpreting Policy in Real Classrooms* (New York: Teachers College Press, 1996), 108.
51. See Amy M. Hightower, with Milbrey W. McLaughlin, "Building and Sustaining an Infrastructure for Learning," in *Urban School Reform: Lessons from San Diego*, ed. Frederick M. Hess (Cambridge, MA: Harvard Education Press, 2005) for a discussion of the ways in which administrators at all levels of the district in San Diego participated in professional development focused on instructional improvement. See also Barbara Neufeld and Judy Swanson, *San Diego City Schools: Update Report: August 1999* (Cambridge, MA: Education Matters, August 1999), www.edmatters.org.
52. In Neufeld and Woodworth, *Taking Stock*, Education Matters identified a range of explanations for why schools might exhibit what appeared to be the same lack of implementation. At that time, researchers suggested that the district learn why this was the case and target interventions in light of what it learned.
53. For a more detailed discussion of the conditions in the small high schools and small learning communities that pose challenges for instructional improvement in Boston, see Barbara Neufeld and Anne Levy, *High School Renewal in the Boston Public Schools: Focus on Organization and Leadership* (Cambridge, MA: Education Matters, 2005), www.edmatters.org.
54. While not all department chairs may have been experts in their areas, when the positions were in place, schools and the central office had the capacity to strengthen the individuals in those positions and use them more effectively.

CHAPTER VI

Using Data to Inform Decision Making in Urban School Districts

Richard J. Murnane, Elizabeth A. City, and Kristan Singleton

1. We would like to thank Maryellen Donahue and Ellen Guiney for helpful comments on an earlier draft of this chapter.
2. Memorandum to the Boston School Committee, January 12, 2001.
3. See John H. Bishop, Ferran Mane, Michael Bishop, and Joan Moriarty, "The Role of End-of-Course Exams and Minimum Competency Exams in Standards-Based Reforms," in *Brookings Papers on Education Policy*, ed. Diane Ravitch (Washington, DC: The Brookings Institution, 2001), 267–345.
4. In the 1996–97 school year, the document was known as a school improvement plan. It became the WSIP the following year. The WSIP is now completed on a two-year cycle, with schools reviewing the plan each year and making any relevant adjustments.

CHAPTER VII

On the Road to Reform

Adria Steinberg and Lili Allen

1. For statewide MCAS data, see Massachusetts Department of Education website at www.doe.mass.edu. For Boston MCAS data from 1998 to 2005, see http:// boston. k12.ma.us/teach/mcas.asp.
2. See, for example, American Institutes for Research, *Evaluation of the Bill & Melinda Gates Foundation's High School Grants, 2001–2004* (Washington, DC: American Institutes for Research, 2005); Robert Gladden, "The Small School Movement: A Review of the Literature" in *Small Schools, Big Imaginations: A Creative Look at Urban Public Schools*, ed. Michelle Fine and Janis I. Somerville (Chicago: Cross City Campaign for Urban School Reform, 1998); Valerie E. Lee, "School Size and the Organization of Secondary Schools," in *Handbook of the Sociology of Education*, ed. Maureen T. Hallinan (New York: Kluwer Academic/Plenum, 2000); Craig Howley, Marty Strange, and Robert Bickel, *"Research about School Size and School Performance in Impoverished Communities," ERIC Digest* (Charleston, WV: ERIC, 2000). Clearinghouse on Rural Education and Small Schools (ED 448 968).
3. "Progress and Promise: Results from the Pilot Schools" (report; Boston: Center for Collaborative Education, 2006), www.ccebos.org.
4. "Progress and Promise."
5. Karen Hawley Miles, "Rethinking School Resources," New American Schools District Issues Brief (no date).
6. "In Boston, Special Ed Students Find Barrier to Mainstream Classes," *Boston Globe*, March 6, 2006.
7. Boston Public Schools internal report on AP enrollment, school year 2005–06.
8. Adria Steinberg and Cheryl Almeida, with Cassius Johnson and Terry Grobe, "Improving Outcomes for Struggling Students and Out-of-School Youth: A Dual Agenda of High Standards and High Graduation Rates" (report, Boston: Jobs for the Future, 2006).
9. Youth Transitions Task Force, "Too Big To Be Seen" (Boston Private Industry Council, 2006).
10. See Robert Balfanz and Liza Herzog, "Keeping Middle Grades Students on Track to Graduation" (PowerPoint presentation, Johns Hopkins University and Philadelphia Education Fund, to the Youth Transitions Steering Committee, Philadelphia, March 18, 2005), on PEF website www.philaedfund.org; see also Melissa Roderick, "Closing the Aspirations-Attainment Gap: Implications for High School Reform" (New York: MDRC, 2006). The Johns Hopkins University and the Philadelphia Education Fund research reveals that close to half of the students who will drop out in Philadelphia can be identified in the sixth grade; the researchers are now collaborating on a comprehensive intervention model to keep students on track to graduation. Melissa Roderick of the Consortium on Chicago School Research indicates that a significant number of students who enter high school appearing to be on track then fall off track in their first semester of freshman year and never recover. However, her research demonstrates that high schools can build students' capacity to do high-level work by identifying those who are struggling academically as early as midway through the first semester of ninth grade and aggressively intervening through academic and developmental skill-building.

11. Constancia Warren and Mindy Hermandez, "Portfolios of Schools: An Idea Whose Time Has Come," *Voices in Urban Education*, no. 8, Summer 2005, 5–11.
12. The partner organizations that, with the Office of High School Renewal, comprise the High School Renewal Work Group are the Boston Plan for Excellence, the Boston Private Industry Council, the Center for Collaborative Education, Jobs for the Future, and, as of June 2006, Freedom House.
13. Lauren Allen, Eric Osthoff, Paula White, and Judy Swanson, "A Delicate Balance: District Policies and Classroom Practice" (report, Chicago: Cross City Campaign for Urban School Reform, 2005).
14. For more information regarding the benchmarking process, see Susan Goldberger, Robert Keough, and Cheryl A. Almeida, *Benchmarks for Success in High School Education: Putting Data to Work in School-to-Career Education Reform* (Boston: Jobs for the Future, 2001).

CHAPTER VIII

Escaping from Old Ideas

Ellen C. Guiney, Mary Ann Cohen, and Erika Moldow

1. Howard Adelman and Linda Taylor, "Addressing What's Missing in School Improvement Planning: Expanding Standards and Accountability to Encompass an Enabling or Learning Supports Component," (policy report, Los Angeles: UCLA Center for Mental Health in Schools, 2005).
2. Thomas Hehir, "Challenges/Obstacles in Public High Schools in Boston," (presentation, Boston Plan for Excellence meeting on special education, Boston, January 31, 2006).
3. Patrick J. Wolf and Bryan C. Hassel, quoted in Kalman R. Hettleman, "Still Getting It Wrong: The Continuing Failure of Special Education in the Baltimore City Public Schools" (report, Baltimore, MD: The Abell Foundation, 2002).
4. This chapter analyzes demographic, programmatic, and performance data from the Boston Public Schools of students who were enrolled in grades 1–12 on April 1, 2005. Unless otherwise noted, all data references in this paper are from that data set.
5. Massachusetts Department of Education, "Special Education Counts and Rates for Educational Environment," (special report for Boston Plan for Excellence on enrollment as of October 1, 2005), http://www.doe.mass.edu/infoservices/reports/enroll/default.html?yr=sped0506.
6. Massachusetts Department of Education, "Special Education Counts." According to state data, charter schools in the city enrolled a total of twenty-five substantially separate students.
7. Thomas W. Payzant [Boston school superintendent], interview with Boston Plan for Excellence, April 2006.
8. Sarah B. Miles and Deborah Stipek, "Contemporaneous and Longitudinal Associations between Social Behavior and Literacy Achievement in a Sample of Low-Income Elementary School Children," *Child Development* 77 (January–February 2006): 103–17.
9. Lisa Delpit, "Culturally Responsive Practice and the School Achievement of Students of Color" (lecture, Simmons College, Boston, April 26, 2006).
10. Thomas Hehir, "The Changing Role of Intervention for Children with Disabilities," *Principal* 85 (November/December 2005): 22–5.

11. Karen Hawley Miles, "Rethinking the Cost of Small High Schools Project" (PowerPoint presentation, Boston Public Education Leadership Project Group, Boston, March 23, 2006).
12. All of the individual quotations in this chapter are drawn from confidential interviews conducted by Ellen Guiney. From March to May 2006, the BPE staff held four focus groups with a total of twenty-five students from four Boston schools. The author also held three focus groups with teachers and administrators at three Boston schools in the same time period. Finally, in the fall of 2005, one meeting of the Teachers Advisory Committee of Boston's High School Renewal Group was dedicated to the issue of students with disabilities.
13. Massachusetts Department of Education, "Joseph P Manning—Test Results" (report, 2005), http://profiles.doe.mass.edu/home.asp?mode=so&view=tst&ot=5&o=164&so=214-6&mcasyear=2005.
14. Lynn Olsen, "Ambiguity about Preparation for Workforce Clouds Efforts to Equip Students for Future," *Education Week,* May 24, 2006, 18–20.
15. Boston Public Schools Office of Research, Assessment, & Evaluation (report, May 2006).
16. Miles, "Rethinking the Cost of Small High Schools Project."
17. Analysis by Boston Plan using enrollment data from April 1, 2005, and data on per-pupil costs from Education Resource Strategies.
18. Miles, "Rethinking the Cost of Small High Schools Project." While the allocation assumptions made by ERS and the BPS budget office provided valuable advice and technical support, decisions about how to allocate costs for this analysis were ultimately made by BPE.
19. Miles, "Rethinking the Cost of Small High Schools Project."
20. Boston Public Schools Superintendent's Leadership Team, "The Special Education Achievement Gap in the Boston Public Schools" (report, Boston: Boston Public Schools, April 2004).
21. Virginia Edwards, ed., "No Small Change: Targeting Money Toward Student Performance," *Education Week's Quality Counts* (special report, 2005), www.edweek.org/ew/toc/2005/01/06/index.html.
22. Lynch School of Education, "Boston Connects: A School-University-Community Partnership in the Boston Public Schools" (booklet, Boston College Lynch School of Education, 2005).
23. Lynch School of Education, "Boston Connects."
24. Adelman and Taylor, "Addressing What's Missing."
25. Boston Public Schools, "Least Restrictive Environment (LRE) Data, 2004–2005" (report, available through the Boston Public Schools Office of Unified Student Services).
26. Boston Public Schools budget, FY05 (available through the Boston Public Schools Office of Finance and Budget).
27. Kali H. Trzesniewski, Terrie E. Moffitt, Avshalom Caspi, Alan Taylor, and Barbara Maughan, "Revisiting the Association between Reading Achievement and Antisocial Behavior: New Evidence of an Environmental Explanation From a Twin Study," *Child Development* 77 (February 2006): 72–88.
28. Boston Public Schools, "Least Restrictive Environment."
29. Boston Public Schools Budget Book, FY06 (available through the Boston Public Schools Office of Finance and Budget).
30. Boston Connects estimates the cost of an evaluation at $2,000. If Boston Connects

is correct, then the cost last year for 2,121 referrals was over $4 million. "Boston Connects: A School-University-Community Partnership in the Boston Public Schools" (report, Boston: Boston College Lynch School of Education, 2005).

31. Massachusetts Department of Education, "2005 MCAS Results by Race, Gender, Special Education, Low Income and Migratory Status—Boston by Grade then Subject," http://profiles.doe.mass.edu/mcas/subgroups.asp?district=035&school=&mcasyear=2005; Massachusetts Department of Education, "Special Education Counts and Rates for Educational Environment," (MCAS report [district] for grade ten students, 2005), http://profiles.doe.mass.edu/mcas.aspx?year=2005.
32. Judy Duguid, ed., "Boys and Reading: Adolescent Literacy in Perspective" (report; Cincinnati: Ohio Resource Center for Mathematics, Science, and Reading, March 2006); Robert Rothman, "Adolescent Literacy: Are We Overlooking the Struggling Teenage Reader?" *Harvard Education Letter* 20 (September/October 2004): 1–3.
33. Thomas Hehir, "Accountable for Every Child: Thinking About Special Education in Boston" (presentation, Boston Plan for Excellence, Effective Practice Network Retreat, Boston, January 23, 2004).
34. Richard Jackson, Kelly Harper, and Janna Jackson, "Effective Teaching Practices and the Barriers Limiting Their Use in Accessing the Curriculum: A Review of Recent Literature" (report, Peabody, MA: National Center on Accessing the General Curriculum, 2002).
35. Margo A. Mastropieri and Thomas E. Scruggs, "Promoting Inclusion in Secondary Classrooms," *Learning Disability Quarterly* 24 (Fall 2001): 265–74.
36. Linda Darling-Hammond, "Research and Rhetoric on Teacher Certification: A Response to 'Teacher Certification Reconsidered,'" *Education Policy Analysis Archives* 10 (September 6, 2002): 36, http://epaa.asu.edu/epaa/v10n36.html.
37. Thomas J. Kane, Jonah E. Rockoff, and Douglas O. Staiger, "What Does Certification Tell Us about Teacher Effectiveness? Evidence from New York City" (National Bureau of Economic Research [NBER] Working Paper Series, March 2006).
38. Jane L. David and Larry Cuban, "Keeping Reforms on Track: Guidelines from Two 'Skeptical but Not Cynical' Veterans," *Education Week Commentary*, March 29, 2006, 38.
39. Hehir, "Challenges/Obstacles in Public High Schools in Boston."
40. In 1998, Payzant created REACT, the Resource Action Team composed of top administrators (COO, CFO, etc.) and staffed by BPE, to study systemic support issues.

CHAPTER IX

Family and Community Engagement in the Boston Public Schools

Abby R. Weiss and Helen Westmoreland

1. Heather Weiss, Margaret Caspe, and Elena Lopez, *Family Involvement in Early Childhood Education* (Cambridge, MA: Harvard Family Research Project, 2006).
2. For reviews, see Xitao Fan and Michael Chen, "Parental Involvement and Students' Academic Achievement: A Meta-Analysis," *Educational Psychology Review* 1 (2001): 1–22; Anne Henderson and Karen Mapp, *A New Wave of Evidence: The Impact of Family, School, Community Connections on Student Achievement* (Austin, TX:

Southwest Educational Development Laboratory, 2002); William Jeynes, "A Meta-Analysis: The Effects of Parental Involvement on Minority Children's Academic Achievement," *Education and Urban Society* 35 (2003): 202–18.

3. Henry Jay Becker and Joyce Epstein, "Teachers' Reported Practices of Parent Involvement: Problems and Possibilities," *Elementary School Journal* 83, no. 2 (1982): 103–13; Joyce Epstein, "Single Parents and the Schools: Effects of Marital Status on Parent and Teacher Interactions," in *Change in Societal Institutions*, ed. M.T. Hallinan, D. M. Klein, and J. Glass (New York: Plenum, 1990), 99–121.
4. For the purposes of this paper, we are using the term "family engagement" interchangeably with the term "family involvement."
5. Weiss, Caspe, and Lopez, *Family Involvement.*
6. Joyce Epstein, Laurel Clark, and Francis Van Voorhis, "Two-Year Patterns of State and District Leadership in Developing Programs of School, Family and Community Partnerships" (paper presented at the annual meeting of the American Educational Research Association, Montreal, Canada, April 1999).
7. Joyce Epstein, Mavis Sanders, Beth Simon, Karen C. Salinas, Natalie Jansorn, Frances van Voorhis, *School, Family, and Community Partnerships: Your Handbook for Action* (Thousand Oaks, CA: Corwin Press, 1997).
8. In the spring of 2006, Harvard Family Research Project (HFRP) also issued a call to the Family Involvement Network of Educators, HFRP's community of seven thousand educators who are committed to family involvement, requesting information about districts with innovative family involvement initiatives. We received few responses, and those we did receive were primarily examples of school or programmatic approaches nested within sympathetic districts.
9. See appendix 9B for a timeline of significant family and community engagement policies and practices within the BPS.
10. Despite a great deal of research about student outcomes associated with family involvement, evidence of community engagement work that results in transformed institutional practices and increased student achievement is scarce; see Robert L. Crowson and William L. Boyd, "Coordinated Services for Children: Designing Arks for Storms and Seas Unknown," *American Journal of Education* 101, no. 2 (1993): 140–79; U.S. Department of Education, Office of Educational Research and Improvement, "Parent and Community Involvement in Education," in *Studies of Education Reform* (Washington, DC: 1991–1995). The majority of studies examining community engagement have focused on the individual contributions of specific agencies involved with urban youth; see Mavis Sanders, "The Effects of School, Family, and Community Support on the Academic Achievement of African American Adolescents," in *Urban Education* 33, no. 3 (1998): 220–29; Shirley B. Heath and Milbrey W. McLaughlin, "The Best of Both Worlds: Connecting Schools and Community Youth Organizations for All-Day, All-Year Learning," in *Coordination Among Schools, Families, and Communities*, ed. James G. Cibulka, William J. Kritek, and Daniel L. Duke (Albany: State University of New York Press, 1996); Joy Dryfoos, *Full-Service Schools: A Revolution in Health and Social Services for Children, Youth, and Families* (Indianapolis: Jossey-Bass, 1998). Although there is a paucity of evidence regarding how community engagement impacts students, a growing body of research recognizes the benefits for communities. Using this framework, schools can provide health, education, and social services to community members; develop the democratic potential of communities; or act as agents of social change.

11. Ralph Edwards and Charles Willie, *Black Power/White Power in Public Education* (Westport, CT: Praeger, 1998).
12. Boston City Archives, Citywide Parents Council Records, http://www.cityofboston.gov/archivesandrecords/desegregation/findingaids/cpc.html (accessed August 15, 2006).
13. School site councils are governance boards composed of parents, teachers, and principals (and one student for high schools) that make decisions related to school policies, budgets, and personnel.
14. Boston City Archives, Citywide Parents Council Records. The Citywide Education Coalition (CWEC) and Massachusetts Advocates for Children (MAC), among others, also played an important role in ensuring a quality education for all students.
15. The PACs include the Citywide Parents Council (CPC), the Special Needs Parent Advisory Council, Bilingual Master Parent Advisory Council, and the Title I Parent Advisory Council.
16. The Family and Community Engagement Task Force Report to the Boston School Committee, June 23, 2000.
17. Boston Public Schools, *Focus on Children: A Comprehensive Reform Plan for the Boston Public Schools* (Boston: Boston School Department, June 1996).
18. Boston Public Schools, *BPS Plan for Whole-School Change*, November, 1997.
19. Boston Public Schools, *BPS Plan for Whole-School Change.*
20. Boston Public Schools, *Parent/Family Involvement Policy*, September, 1997.
21. The Family and Community Engagement Task Force Report.
22. The Family and Community Engagement Task Force Report.
23. For a discussion of organizing and advocacy, see Michael J. Brown, *Building Powerful Community Organizations: A Personal Guide to Creating Groups That Can Solve Problems and Change the World* (Arlington, MA: Long Haul Press, 2006). For examples of education organizing, see Kavitha Mediratta, *Constituents of Change: Community Organizations and Public Education Reform* (New York: New York University, Steinhardt School of Education, Institute of Education and Social Policy, 2004); Dennis Shirley, *Community Organizing for Urban School Reform* (Austin: University of Texas Press, 1997); and Mark Warren, *Dry Bones Rattling: Community Building to Revitalize American Democracy* (Princeton, NJ: Princeton University Press, 2001).
24. This and all following quotes, except where so noted, are derived from our interviews with the following people. (These interviews were carried out in Boston between June 26, 2006, and August 20, 2006): Henry Allen, Fund for Education Organizing; Michele Brooks, BPS School Committee; Dr. Deborah Dancy, Channing Elementary School; Kim Janey, Massachusetts Advocates for Children; Katie Madrigal, BPS Office of Family and Community Engagement; Dr. Karen Mapp, Harvard Graduate School of Education; Hattie McKinnis, Citywide Parents Council; Glenola Mitchell, formerly of the BPS Office of Family and Community Engagement; Dr. Thomas Payzant, Harvard Graduate School of Education; Marchelle Raynor, BPS School Committee; Karen Richardson, BPS Office of Family and Community Engagement; and Caprice Taylor-Mendez, Boston Parent Organizing Network.
25. The Family and Community Engagement Task Force Report, p. 4.
26. The Family and Community Engagement Task Force Report, p. 4.
27. The Family and Community Engagement Task Force Report to the Boston School Committee, June 23, 2000, p. 4.

28. Thomas Payzant, *Reinvention of BPS Central and School-Based Support Services for Families*, memorandum to chairperson and members of Boston School Committee, November 28, 2001.
29. Thomas Payzant, *Family and Community Engagement Plan*, memorandum to chairperson and members of Boston School Committee, March 13, 2002, p. 5.
30. Thomas Payzant, *Family and Community Engagement Plan Update*, memorandum to chairperson and members of Boston School Committee, April 2, 2002.
31. Thomas Payzant, *Reinvention of BPS Central and School-Based Support Services for Families*, memorandum to chairperson and members of Boston School Committee, November 28, 2001.
32. Thomas Payzant, *Summary of My Thoughts: February 21, 2001 Meeting*, memorandum to Marchelle Raynor and Karen Mapp, March 2, 2001.
33. Payzant, *Family and Community Engagement Plan Update.*
34. Payzant, *Family and Community Engagement Plan Update*, p. 9.
35. Mapp had initially accepted the deputy position on the condition that she could leave after twelve months. In the end, she stayed six months longer than originally planned and left early in 2005.
36. The Training Center complemented the work of Family Resource Centers (FRCs). Although it focused largely on providing workshops for families and school staff, its role was not distinguished from that of the FRCs by most district officials or in BPS documents.
37. Payzant, *Family and Community Engagement Plan Update.*
38. Family and Community Engagement and The Work Group, *Family and Community Engagement Implementation FY 2002–2003* (presentation to Thomas Payzant, Boston, May 27, 2003).
39. Steven Constantino, *Evaluation of the Family and Community Outreach Coordinators Pilot Initiative in the Boston Public Schools* (preliminary report to the Boston School Committee, Boston, March 15, 2006).
40. In the first year of implementation, fifteen Family and Community Outreach Coordinators (FCOC) were assigned to seventeen schools, resulting in four schools having half-time staffing. In 2006–07, in recognition of the difficulties for FCOCs at these four schools, the district hired two additional FCOCs so that all seventeen schools had full-time support.
41. Karen Mapp and Mark Warren, "Family and Community Outreach Coordinators Indicators/Outcomes," unpublished paper, September 29, 2005.
42. FCOCs report to the Office of Family and Community Engagement on a monthly basis about their progress toward meeting goals outlined in their work plans.
43. Mapp and Warren, "Family and Community Outreach."
44. Constantino, *Evaluation of the Family and Community Outreach.*
45. Constantino, *Evaluation of the Family and Community Outreach.*
46. Working Group on Education Organizing, "Fund for Education Organizing," from Henry Allen, unpublished concept paper, 2006.
47. The authors would like to thank all the individuals listed in note 24 for taking the time to share their perspectives on family and community engagement in the BPS. We would also like to thank Madeline Perez at the CUNY Graduate Center for speaking with us about New York City's parent outreach efforts. We also thank our colleagues at Harvard Family Research Project, particularly our director, Dr. Heather B. Weiss, for their invaluable guidance and review of this chapter.

CHAPTER X

The Boston Story

Thomas W. Payzant, with Christopher M. Horan

1. Recent studies include "Transforming the Boston Public Schools: A Roadmap for the New Superintendent," published by the Citizen Commission on Academic Success for Boston Children, June 2006; "Strong Foundation, Evolving Challenges: A Case Study to Support Leadership Transition in the Boston Public Schools," published by the Aspen Institute, March 2006 (chapter 1 in this volume); as well as numerous newspaper and magazine articles.
2. There was one pervasive tradition in the district, practiced in many classrooms, of the teacher asking students to rise and greet any classroom visitor. In subsequent years I discouraged this practice, as I quietly slipped into classrooms to observe teaching and learning without interrupting the lesson in progress.

About the Contributors

Lili Allen

Lili Allen is a program director at Jobs for the Future (JFF), where she manages several projects related to youth education and transitions to adulthood. She is a site liaison to Philadelphia and Las Vegas for the Strategic Assessment Grant initiative of the Youth Transition Funders Group, and she coleads JFF's work as a core partner in the Boston Public Schools' districtwide high school renewal effort. Allen has authored or coauthored several publications related to youth transitions and education. Before joining JFF, she worked extensively in the development, management, and replication of school- and community-based youth development programs. She holds a master's in education from Harvard University.

Annenberg Institute for School Reform

The Annenberg Institute for School Reform at Brown University is a national policy-research and reform-support organization that focuses on improving conditions and outcomes in urban schools, especially those serving disadvantaged children. The Institute works through partnerships with school districts and school reform networks, and in collaboration with national and local organizations skilled in educational research, policy, and effective practices to offer an array of tools and strategies to help districts strengthen their local capacity to provide and sustain high-quality education for all students. (Information at www.annenberginstitute.org)

Aspen Institute Education and Society Program

The Aspen Institute Education and Society Program provides an informed and neutral forum where education practitioners, researchers, and policy leaders can engage in focused discussions about their efforts to improve student achievement, and consider how public policy changes can affect progress. Through meetings, analysis, commissioned work, and structured networks of policymakers and practitioners over the past twenty-five years, the Program has developed intellectual frameworks on critical education issues that assist federal, state, and local policy makers who are working to improve American education. (Information at www.aspeninstitute.org/education)

Elizabeth A. City

Elizabeth City has served as a teacher, principal, and instructional coach, primarily in North Carolina and Massachusetts. She is a member of the senior faculty of Boston's School Leadership Institute, where she teaches courses in using data, learning and teaching, and leading instructional improvement to Boston Principal Fellows. As a doctoral student at the Harvard Graduate School of Education, City is currently working on her dissertation about how small high schools use their resources. She is coeditor of *Data Wise: A Step-by-Step Guide to Using Assessment Results to Improve Teaching and Learning* (Harvard Education Press, 2005) and coauthor of *The Teacher's Guide to Leading Student-Centered Discussions: Talking About Texts in the Classroom* (Corwin Press, 2006).

Mary Ann Cohen

Mary Ann Cohen is the communications director of the Boston Plan for Excellence (BPE). Most of BPE's publications and other communications are designed for the staff of the Boston Public Schools and are intended to support the district's instructional priorities. Before working at BPE, Cohen worked for an independent school advocacy group, the Citywide Educational Coalition, and later for the Boston Public Schools.

Morgaen L. Donaldson

Morgaen Donaldson is an advanced doctoral student at the Harvard Graduate School of Education and a Spencer Research Training Grant recipient. She is the author or coauthor of several books, articles, and book chapters. As a member of the *Harvard Educational Review* Editorial Board, she coedited *Education Past and Present: Reflections on Research, Policy, and Practice* (2005). A former high school teacher, Donaldson was a founding faculty member of the Boston Arts Academy, Boston's public high school for the arts. As a researcher, she studies teachers' career development and professional growth, teachers unions, and current changes in rural and urban schools.

Ellen C. Guiney

Ellen Guiney is the executive director of the Boston Plan for Excellence (BPE), the city's local education foundation. BPE is the primary partner with the Boston Public Schools in the district's multiyear effort to improve instruction in every school. Under her leadership, BPE's priorities now comprise collaborative work with school staff on instructional practice, management of the district's teacher preparation program, and a partnership with district leaders to correct policies and practices that impede schools' instructional improvement efforts. Prior to her work at BPE, Guiney was chief education advisor to the U.S. Senate Committee on Labor and Human Resources and one of the Democratic staff leaders on the reauthorization of the Elementary and Secondary Education Act in 1994. A former high school English teacher, she also served as education advisor to Boston mayor Raymond Flynn during his successful effort to improve school governance for the city's public schools.

Christopher M. Horan

Christopher Horan is the Boston Public Schools' first chief communications officer. He previously served as chief of staff for Boston school superintendent Thomas W. Payzant and as executive secretary for the Boston School Committee. Horan began his career with the City of Boston in 1995 as a speechwriter for Mayor Thomas M. Menino. A resident of Dorchester, Massachusetts, Horan is a graduate of Princeton University and earned a master of fine arts degree from Emerson College in Boston.

Susan Moore Johnson

Susan Moore Johnson is the Carl H. Pforzheimer, Jr. Professor of Education in Learning and Teaching at the Harvard Graduate School of Education. Johnson studies and teaches about teacher policy, organizational change, and administrative practice. A former high school teacher and administrator, she has a continuing research interest in the work of teachers and the reform of schools. She has studied the leadership of superintendents, the effects of collective bargaining on schools, the use of incentive pay plans for teachers, and the school as a context for adult work. Currently, Johnson and a group of advanced doctoral students are engaged in a multiyear research study, The Project on the Next Generation of Teachers, that is examining how best to recruit, support, and retain a strong teaching force in the next decade.

Karen L. Mapp

Karen Mapp is a lecturer on education at the Harvard Graduate School of Education (HGSE). Her research and practice expertise is in the areas of educational leadership and educational partnerships among schools, families, and community members. Mapp joined HGSE in January 2005 after serving for eighteen months as the interim deputy superintendent of family and community engagement for the Boston Public Schools (BPS). While working with the BPS, she continued to fulfill her duties as president of the Institute for Responsive Education, a research, policy, and advocacy organization that conducts research on and advocates for effective school, family, and community partnerships that support the educational development of children.

Erika Moldow

Erika Moldow is a research associate at the Boston Plan for Excellence (BPE). At BPE, she contributes research support to projects based in the Boston Public Schools, including a formative assessment for teachers, a high school course on student action research, and an ongoing survey of the experiences of new teachers. She is also completing her doctoral work in social policy at the Heller School at Brandeis.

Richard J. Murnane

Richard Murnane is an economist whose research focuses on the relationships between education and the economy, teacher labor markets, the determinants of children's achievement, and strategies for making schools more effective. He is the author of several books and more than one hundred articles. In 2005, Murnane and two Harvard colleagues edited *Data Wise: A Step-by-Step Guide to Using Assessment Results to Improve Teaching and Learning* (Harvard Education Press). This book stems from work Murnane started in 2001 to help the central office of the Boston Public Schools more effectively support the schools' efforts to learn from student assessment results. Murnane is currently working with Harvard Graduate School of Education professor John B. Willett on a book describing how improvements in research design and analysis strategies can help educational researchers make valid causal inferences in educational policy research.

Barbara Neufeld

Barbara Neufeld is the president and founder of Education Matters, Inc. Neufeld began her career in education as an elementary schoolteacher in the South Bronx and also taught in New Haven, Connecticut. She was a part-time lecturer at the Harvard Graduate School of Education from 1985 to 1997, teaching courses about qualitative methods for research in schools and school districts and the links between research, policy, and practice in urban schools. Neufeld has served as principal investigator over the last twenty-two years for numerous evaluations in urban districts, including Hartford, San Diego, Corpus Christi, and Louisville. Her work in Boston over the last ten years includes evaluating the Boston Annenberg Challenge, Collaborative Coaching and Learning, the School Leadership Institute, and high school reform.

Thomas W. Payzant

Thomas Payzant is currently a senior lecturer at the Harvard Graduate School of Education. He previously served as superintendent of the Boston Public Schools, from October 1995 until his retirement in June 2006. Before coming to Boston he was appointed by President Clinton to serve as assistant secretary for elementary and secondary education at the U.S. Department of Education. Over the past decade he has led a number of significant systemic reform efforts that have helped narrow the achievement gap and increase student performance on both state and national assessment exams. In addition to his tenure in Boston, Payzant has served as superintendent of schools in San Diego, Oklahoma City, Eugene, Oregon, and Springfield, Pennsylvania. His work has been recognized by educators at the regional and national level. In 1998, Payzant was named Massachusetts Superintendent of the Year. In 2004, he received the Richard R. Green Award for Excellence in Urban Education from the Council on Great City Schools. And *Governing Magazine* named Payzant one of eight "Public Officials of the Year" in 2005. Payzant also received the McGraw Prize for his leadership of the San Diego school system from 1982 to 1993. A prolific writer and researcher throughout his career, Payzant's many essays, book chapters, and book reviews have provided valuable insights for both professional educators and policymakers.

John H. Portz

John Portz is a professor in political science and education at Northeastern University and currently serves as the chair of the Political Science Department. He teaches and conducts research in the general areas of state and local politics, public administration, and public education. His research interests include school politics and governance, as well as leadership. Publications include a coauthored book, *City Schools and City Politics: Institutions and Leadership in Pittsburgh, Boston and St. Louis* (University Press of Kansas). In his home community of Watertown, Massachusetts, Portz has served as an elected member of the town council for the past eight years and was recently elected to the school committee.

S. Paul Reville

Paul Reville, a lecturer on educational policy and politics and director of the Education Policy and Management Program at the Harvard Graduate School of Education, is president of the Rennie Center for Education Research and Policy, an independent, policy organization dedicated to the improvement of preK–12 public education. The Rennie Center conducts research, convenes policy leaders, and advocates for solutions to significant educational challenges. Reville is the former executive director of the Pew Forum on Standards-Based Reform, a Harvard-based national education policy think tank that convened the United States' leading researchers, practitioners, and policymakers to shape the national "standards" agenda. He was founding executive director of the Massachusetts Business Alliance for Education, an organization that provided key conceptual and political leadership for the Education Reform Act of 1993. From 1991 to 1996 he served on the Massachusetts State Board of Education, where he chaired the Massachusetts Commission on Time and Learning. From 1996 to 2003, Reville chaired the Massachusetts Education Reform Review Commission, a mandated public commission charged with providing research and oversight of the state's role in implementing education reform. In 1985, Reville was founding executive director of the Alliance for Education, a multi-service educational improvement organization serving Worcester and central Massachusetts. He is a former teacher and principal and a frequent writer and speaker on school reform and educational policy issues.

Kristan Singleton

Kristan Singleton, tools and technologies manager at Education Resource Strategies, has thirteen years' experience helping private and public sector organizations make effective use of technology. In his current position, Singleton is responsible for working with the ERS leadership team to develop and implement the organization's technology strategy. Prior to working at ERS, Singleton was director of technologies for the Boston Plan for Excellence, where he was a member of the team responsible for the design and implementation of the Boston Public Schools' MyBPS Assessment portal, which provides schoolteachers and principals with access to formative and summative assessment data and supports them in their use of data as a lever for improving instructional practice.

Adria Steinberg

Adria Steinberg leads a Jobs for the Future (JFF) initiative, Connected by 25: Improving Options and Outcomes for Underserved and Out-of-School Youth. Steinberg has almost four decades of experience in the field of education—as a teacher, administrator, researcher, and writer. She leads JFF's work with the City of Boston's High School Renewal initiative and with a collaboration of three foundations to address the nation's dropout crisis. JFF serves as fiscal agent for a grant from the Bill & Melinda Gates Foundation for the creation and development of small, effective high schools. Steinberg has authored many publications, including a five-year stint as primary writer/editor of *The Harvard Education Letter.* She was also the academic coordinator of the Rindge School of Technical Arts in Cambridge, Massachusetts, where she codirected the federally funded Vocational Integration with Academics project.

Jennifer M. Suesse

Jennifer Suesse is a research associate with the Harvard Public Education Leadership Project, a Harvard Business School/Harvard Graduate School of Education collaboration of researchers working with urban public school leaders. Before joining the project, Suesse helped direct the activities of the Harvard Business School Leadership Initiative, including research projects, executive education programs, multimedia production, course development, and publications. She has also researched and written several case studies focusing on leaders and cross-cultural teamwork for Harvard's MBA curriculum.

Abby R. Weiss

Abby Weiss is a project manager at the Harvard Family Research Project (HFRP), where she manages HFRP's family involvement research and activities, which focus on shaping strategies for improving learning and development outcomes for all children. Weiss leads a team that informs practitioners, researchers, and policymakers about proven family involvement practices and the link between family involvement and student achievement. Her work also focuses on strategy evaluation for HFRP. Weiss previously worked for eight years at the Institute for Responsive Education in Boston, where she served as associate director and led the organization's research efforts on charter schools. She later worked as an independent consultant, conducting evaluations of family/school/community partnership programs, out-of-school time initiatives, individual charter schools, and a federally funded charter school accountability program.

Helen Westmoreland

Helen Westmoreland is a research analyst with the family involvement team at the Harvard Family Research Project (HFRP). In this capacity, she supports HFRP's efforts to build an expanded and improved understanding of family engagement in school and nonschool contexts by connecting research, practice, and policy. Westmoreland's work also includes conducting a cluster evaluation of the Atlantic Philanthropies' Disadvantaged Children and Youth strategy and contributing to the Evaluation Exchange. Before coming to HFRP, Westmoreland coordinated student partnerships and program evaluations for community-based afterschool programs in the Duke-Durham Neighborhood Partnership. Westmoreland received her master's degree in education policy and management from the Harvard Graduate School of Education and her BA in Spanish from Duke University.

Mission

The Rennie Center, which sponsored the conference from which this book emerged, aims to develop a public agenda that promotes significant improvement of public education in Massachusetts. It envisions an education system that educates every child to be successful in life, citizenship, employment, and life-long learning. The Rennie Center offers educators and policymakers a "safe place" to consider evidence and perspectives, discuss issues, and develop new approaches to their work. It seeks to foster thoughtful public discourse and informed policymaking through nonpartisan, independent research, civic engagement, and effective action.

The Center is committed to a set of strategies that involve collaborating with diverse organizations in the education reform field to pursue the following activities:

Independent Research

The Rennie Center produces independent research initiatives to promote public discourse on educational improvement and to inform policy discussions of key decision makers and opinion leaders. Our research reports and policy briefs are broadly disseminated to policy stakeholders in the public, private, nonprofit, and media sectors.

Civic Engagement

The Rennie Center is committed to engaging diverse perspectives and voices in a constructive policy discussion. By convening conferences, forums, meetings, policy briefings, panel discussions, town meetings and other events, we promote constructive dialogue on school improvement and student achievement.

Shaping an Effective Public Agenda

An effective policy agenda can be best shaped by applying independent research, creating opportunities for civil discourse and making a concerted effort to inform and engage policymakers, the public, and the field in the process. The Rennie Center is dedicated to widely disseminating its independent research to enrich the policy conversation.

Constructive Activism

The Rennie Center identifies timely opportunities for change in which it can lead policy discussion and development process to a new level. This type of activity includes follow-up research on issues raised during events, formation of representative working groups to draft policy proposals or meet outstanding policy challenges, extensive field work on major challenges, and concerted media outreach efforts to highlight critical, but neglected issues.

The Rennie Center focuses on policy areas that require independent research and civil discourse to inform policy decisions. It provides the attention needed to push issues to the forefront of the decision-making process. The Center's work focuses on K–12 public education reform topics such as building state capacity, high school reform, labor-management relations, and charters and school choice.

Index

Note: Figures are denoted by *f* following the page number.